American Schools, American Teachers

Issues and Perspectives

DAVID SCHUMAN

University of Massachusetts

PEARSON

Boston   New York   San Francisco
Mexico City   Montreal   Toronto   London   Madrid   Munich   Paris
Hong Kong   Singapore   Tokyo   Cape Town   Sydney

For Mom and Dad

Executive Editor: *Stephen D. Dragin*
Senior Editorial Assistant: *Barbara Strickland*
Marketing Manager: *Tara Whorf*
Composition and Prepress Buyer: *Linda Cox*
Manufacturing Manager: *Andrew Turso*
Editorial-Production Coordinator: *Mary Beth Finch*
Editorial-Production Service: *Shepherd, Inc.*
Electronic Composition: *Shepherd, Inc.*

For related titles and support materials, visit our on-line catalog at www.ablongman.com.

Between the time Web site information is gathered and then published, it is not unusual for some sites to have closed. Also, the transcription of URLs can result in unintended typographical errors. The publisher would appreciate notification where these errors occur so that they may be corrected in subsequent editions.

Library of Congress Cataloging-in-Publication Data

Schuman, David
    American schools, American teachers : issues and perspectives / David Schuman.
        p. cm.
    Includes index.
    ISBN: 0-321-05399-0
    1. Teachers—United States. 2. Education—Social aspects—United States. I. Title.

LB1775.S3456 2003
371.1'00973—dc21   2003054146

Printed in the United States of America.

10 9 8 7 6 5 4 3 2 1   08 07 06 05 04 03

TABLE OF CONTENTS

Preface   v

CHAPTER ONE

There Is Nothing (really) New Under the Sun:
A Background of Educational/Political Issues   1

CHAPTER TWO

Shaping the United States:
An Early History of Our Schooling   21

CHAPTER THREE

Common Schools to Conservative Reaction:
The Nineteenth Century to 1983   56

CHAPTER FOUR

In Search of an Identity: Teachers   88

CHAPTER FIVE

Sugar/Spice/Snakes/Snails and Testosterone:
On the Matter of Girls and Boys   122

CHAPTER SIX

Race   150

CHAPTER SEVEN

Training Americans: Urban, Multicultural,
and Bilingual Education   186

CHAPTER EIGHT

Dealing with Differences in the Land of Equality:
Special Education   210

CHAPTER NINE

Bureaucrats and Politicians: Who Controls
the Classroom?   238

CHAPTER TEN

The Tyranny of Number Two Pencils: Testing   260

CHAPTER ELEVEN

The Sky Is Falling: Who Are These Kids?   297

CHAPTER TWELVE

Restructuring Schooling: Looking for Answers
in All the Wrong Places   325

Index   349

I've made some studies, and reality is the leading cause of stress amongst those in touch with it.

—*Lily Tomlin*

All the interests of my reason, speculative as well as practical, combine in the three following questions:

1) What can I know?
2) What ought I to do?
3) What may I hope?

—*Immanuel Kant*

The journey itself is delight.

—*J. J. Rousseau*

This book is meant to be discussed. It is often written as a conversation between you and me, but the real discussions should be between you and those around you. I assume you will not agree with some (or even much) of what I believe. My feelings won't be hurt. Hopefully, you will talk with others and be able, in careful and thoughtful ways, to explain why your opinion is better than mine. This is a book about ideas that need to be considered, thought and talked about.

An issues book in education is a book about the world. When you open the door to a classroom, it is hard to keep anything out. Everything, it seems, is either part of the problem or part of the solution.

Schooling in the United States has, as we will see, been one of the main ways we try to solve our most serious social problems. Schooling hasn't been only about reading, writing, and arithmetic for a very long time. It has been about teaching children how to become workers in factories, or immigrants how to become "Americans," or integrating our public spaces, or producing scientists to fight the Cold War, or making sure students were computer-literate for industry—and stuff like that.

Not only does society demand that schools solve problems, it demands that schools teach everyone. A hundred years ago only a small percentage of children went to high school; now, everyone has to be schooled and, in some states, pass a standardized test before they can graduate.

There is a huge amount of pressure on schools to perform; on administrators to produce results; on teachers to make certain that their classes hit certain achievement targets.

Even as we ask so much of our educational system, we know that this is an underlying reality: schools are often poorly funded and teachers are not well paid. To the terrible old phrase, "Those who can't, teach," we can add this: Those who teach often burn out. When it comes to education, there are always more issues than answers.

This is a book about some of the things to think about as a teacher. After a short history, many chapters begin with this: You walk into your classroom and see . . . This book is about what you will see. You will see boys and girls and colors and different kinds of cultural backgrounds and different learning styles and intelligences and a flood of problems.

THE BOOK

The book is divided into three sections. The first four chapters are the context. The first chapter covers some of the background issues. We begin with a discussion of Plato and Rousseau. They help us see, in part, how the intellectual history of the West has dominated our thinking about education. One of the most basic lessons is that education has always been a political issue. Schools are set up to produce the kind of citizens wanted by the state.

In chapters 2 and 3 we will see a history of schooling in the United States. The history will contain some of our major educational thinkers. Finally, chapter 4 will review what we know about teachers. Again, it will be a historical view. In this chapter, we will also take up the ideas of professionalism and unionism.

The next four chapters focus on what a teacher directly encounters when he or she enters a classroom. The topics are: girls and boys; race; urban, multicultural, and multilingual education; and special education. The chapters are full of questions and data, with many different and conflicting answers.

The final four chapters are about issues that affect each classroom but are "invisible." By invisible I mean, for example, that it is not as tangible as a kid who does not speak English, but is just as real. In chapter 9 we discuss who controls the classroom. We look at the structure of education, and who pays for what. Testing is the topic of the next chapter. It is a contentious topic these days, and we will go into the pros and cons of testing.

In chapter 11 we look into the idea of popular culture. From drugs, sex, and music to the role of advertising, television, and computers, we explore the pressures of culture on our children. In the final chapter, we look at school choice.

SCHOOLS AND TEACHERS

I believe that schooling has always been the handmaiden of politics. There is no reason that shouldn't be the case: every society wants to make certain that the next generation will learn those things it holds dear.

Saying that implies certain things. First, it implies that while many of the discussions we have in education are important, they often miss the main point. For example, the question might not be "Do students in charter schools test better than those in public schools?" but this: "Does the structure of choice help further a politi-cal agenda?" In other words, what are the political purposes of charter schools and voucher programs?

Second, I want to argue that, at another level, some kinds of structure may have less of an impact on teaching than we believe. I think that, in the end, issues in education—current or ancient—in important ways revolve around teachers. As we will see, there have been remarkable changes in the reasons for our schools, how they are organized, and the ways we teach. But the bottom line is that education is personal: It is about teachers and students, about a teacher and a student.

What I propose is that all the schemes and techniques and technologies might help in incremental ways, but they will not make a bad teacher a good one. The things that made teachers good a thousand years ago are the same qualities that make teachers good today. I am not saying that there is one model of a good teacher. As students, it is always surprising that some of our friends like (and learn) from teachers we can't stand.

What I am saying is, there is a fundamental caring that seems to be a trait of those teachers we admire. What's interesting is that it does not matter a great deal exactly what the caring is for: it might be for students, for the environment, for his-tory or for two-year-olds. The good teacher somehow is able to convey that care to his or her students. Being articulate and good-looking and well-organized and really smart are all helpful, but none is really necessary.

There is a love of the task, a great caring for a subject that can overcome a sloppy lesson plan or a bad hair day. I will say all of this again, at the end of the book. Hope-fully, it will make more sense then.

The book is written for those of you who might someday teach. It asks you to consider a remarkable number of issues that have more than one right answer. You will confront them on a daily basis when you begin to teach, and it is best to begin to sort them out now. They are issues you will revisit and rethink often during your career.

But remember this: Whatever answers you choose, they should be in the con-text of what each student needs in order to learn what you are teaching. They are important issues, but none is as important as how well you will do your job.

THANK YOUS

Most acknowledgements say nice things about those who have read the manuscript, friends, family and that one special person. That is both understandable and the right thing to do. I will certainly do that . . . but not just yet.

Books are written in context and from a particular history. I'm not a young guy; I've been writing books for thirty years and each one somehow reflects a lot of stuff that doesn't seem to be part of the topic of the book. It's proper to acknowledge at least some of that stuff.

We now live in the country—in a particularly Eastern United States kind of way. Henry David Thoreau lived in the "wilds" of Massachusetts. He loved the loneliness and isolation of Walden Pond. He also walked to his mom's house every Friday night for din-ner. In other words, the "country" of the East isn't like the "country" of, say, Montana.

The country we live in is a ten-minute drive to downtown Northampton. An interesting little town, it's the county seat so there are a lot of lawyers; there is Smith College; there are a remarkable number of restaurants, psychologists, and middle-aged bikers who park their bikes in the middle of downtown. *Newsweek* magazine called Northampton Lesbianville, for whatever that's worth. So, the little town that is full of artists and writers is an interesting place.

But we don't live there anymore. We live at the end of a dead-end road. Not even a street—a road. Big news for us has to do with the flocks of turkey, the occasional deer, and the even more-occasional bear. Living with that level of excitement must have had something to do with what went into this book. Whether it somehow added perspective, or simply separated me from reality is a judgment I cannot make.

And we all have our own history of schooling. Mine stunk. I just sat in class for the first twelve years. I loved my classmates and hated my classes. No college track for me. I just sat. I never read a book. It wasn't until college that some dim light was turned on . . . and it wasn't until graduate school at Berkeley in political science that someone turned on the screaming bright light of the life of the mind. Who knew?

The kids are grown. Ben is a successful dj and music director. Pierced and painted and playing music I don't like by people I have never heard of. Music he loves. He's doing well. And Tama and Amy are raising the grandsons. Avoiding the mistakes we made by making their own mistakes. Worrying about what the best school will be for their sons. Worrying about giving them the best chance of getting ahead. All of that is context for thinking about what to write about schooling.

And even my sports have changed. Instead of more surgery on my shoulder, I decided to stop tennis and start golf. The move was from straight aggression to four nice hours of walking and talking and trying to hit one shot at a time. When you play golf, you play yourself. And the conversations with good friends are always helpful. Who knows, maybe this book will have fewer edges than some of the other things I've written.

And I have new colleagues. There was a wave of retirements, and new people came. My workplace is absolutely different. That means something. And I now work more closely with TAs who I enjoy and respect, and I even lecture to a big hall full of people. Those things mean something. They affect how I understand and act in the world, and they have to influence my attitude when I write.

I just don't know how.

Finally, the book would not have been written without help. The following people talked with me and read stuff and were just plain helpful. Thank you Andy Effrat, Sid Olufs, Steve Sirici, Eloise Pelton, Bob Waterman, Katie McDermant, Michael Gilbert, Barbara Roach, Marilyn Herring, Brian McCoy, Carolyn Pillow, and Hal Soloff. I would also like to thank Jackie M. Blount of Iowa State University and Susan Talburt of Georgia State University, who reviewed the manuscript. It is true that many of the good ideas in the book came from them, and many of the others were of my own doing. Give them credit.

And Sweetie, with her good heart and clear sense of right and wrong, was sympathetic and a careful reader and never backed off of making judgments about good and bad. Her moral compass is certainly a big part of what underpins the book. I bow to the beauty of her self; of her soul.

CHAPTER ONE

THERE IS NOTHING (REALLY) NEW UNDER THE SUN
A Background of Educational/ Political Issues

The beginning is not merely half of the whole but reaches out toward the end.
—Polybius

Although the past does not always repeat itself, it does rhyme.
—Mark Twain

Education is the influence exercised by adult generations on those that are not yet ready for social life. Its object is to arouse and to develop in the child a certain number of physical, intellectual and moral states which are demanded of him by both the political society as a whole and the special milieu for which he is specifically destined. It follows . . . that education consists of a methodical socialization of the young generation.
—Emile Durkheim

In this chapter we will explore basic philosophic questions. These will serve as a basis for the issues in the book. The chapter will center on what we think education is about, why we do it, and just how important we think it is.

The relationship between the state and schooling is one of the central themes of the chapter. We will introduce the basic tension between societal and individual needs. The discussion begins with the *Republic* and *Emile* in order to get a sense of how our current thinking began to develop.

Answers make sense only in context. For example, if someone called you long-distance and asked what he or she should wear the next day, you would have no idea what to say. Where did the person live? What was the weather going to be like? Was it day or night? Where was this person going—a grand event, a ski party, and a lecture on the nature of time? Without knowing those things, there would be no sensible answer to the question.

1

In order to begin thinking about the current problems of our educational system it is necessary to understand their context. To judge what the best education is, you need to know where the students live, what they believe, and what they want from that education. In this chapter we will begin to understand the context of education in the United States. The context, as we shall see, is a seemingly constant struggle over this question: What do we want from our schooling?

There is tension that underlies much of our educational debate. It revolves around public demands and private needs. One of the primary goals of education—anywhere—is to promote the values of the society in which it exists. In the United States, government pays for most schooling and naturally wants those who go through that system to become good citizens. That means they will not only support the central values of the country, but will become hard-working, productive people.

It is easy to see (and we will in chapter 2) that at every stage of history the public schools have been focused on helping the United States become a stronger nation. The schools educated people to become farmers when we were an agrarian nation; they helped make people good factory workers when we became industrialized; they helped children of immigrants understand how to be "American" after the second world war; they produced engineers in order to compete with Russia in space, and they are now educating people to work in service professions for our new, international economy.

Education has done more than prepare people for jobs. It has provided moral education at different stages of our development. As we have evolved as a society, what we think of as moral education has also changed. The bottom line is this: We expect our educational system to produce good people and productive citizens.

Paradoxically, in the United States we have a deep faith in individualism. Each of us would like our educational system to take our specialness into account. Our liberal ideology (liberal here is used in the broadest sense; it is a reference to John Locke and the liberal English philosophers the Founding Fathers read and respected) teaches that each of us is unique. We seem to have a great need for that uniqueness to be acknowledged and understood. As we will see later, the basic tenants of liberalism are shared by Republicans and Democrats alike, and include, among other things, a belief in individual freedoms, some form of capitalism, and a sense that there are limits on what the state can and should do.

At the root of our educational system is a conflict between our intense individualism and the overriding interests of the state. When we argue about how much money should be spent for special needs students, or fight about English as a second language, or discuss the idea of tracking in schools, it makes sense only when put in a broader context.

AN IDEAL ANSWER

Let me outline a short, ideal solution to the problem. It is a simple attempt to pay attention to the needs of both the state and the individual.

■ Everyone in the United States should have equal access to quality schooling. Nothing—money, color, sex, religion, cultural background—will interfere with this goal.

- School will be free, teachers will be well paid, and education will be first-rate.

- The students will be taught positive lessons that have been agreed upon by parents, teachers, and administrators. The underlying prejudices of the culture about race, sex, cultural differences, and the like will be portrayed as harmful and wrong. The material taught will focus on enabling students to take their studies seriously so they can contribute positive things to society.

- At different levels of education students will take tests to judge their achievements, interests, and potentials. As a result of these tests, students will continue an education most suited to their talents.

- At each level studies will become more specialized. Some students will go into vocational training; others will go into the arts, business, or the professions. The driving principle will be to make certain each person gets the best education in the area in which he or she is most well-suited. Certainly there will be tests that are sophisticated enough and educators sensitive enough to make sure the correct decisions are made.

The results: If this is done properly, education will be able to bring together the needs of the individual and the country. As part of their education students will learn that by doing what they are best suited to do, they can be both personally happy and fulfill the needs of the state. The terrible hierarchy of jobs that now exists in the United States will fade away when individuals learn to take pride in doing well that which they can do best.

A system like this might initially take more money than is currently being spent, but it can be argued that, in the long run, it would be worth the cost. With this kind of schooling it is possible that other kinds of social problems will be eliminated. By providing appropriate education to each person, we might assume more people would stay in school and become productive members of society. Merging public and personal needs would help us know how to answer the current problems we have with schooling.

While you might see the logic in this solution, it is entirely possible that there is something about it you just do not like. Something seems wrong. There are underlying assumptions that make you uncomfortable. If that is the case, welcome to a debate that is thousands of years old.

Two philosophers, Plato and Jean-Jacques Rousseau, stake out important philosophical and pedagogic points. Be aware that theirs are not the only voices nor the only positions. I chose them because they represent ideas that are fundamental to Western thought, and they remind us that our "current issues" rest on tensions that go back at least as far as the Ancient Greeks.

THE REPUBLIC

> . . . *[P]romiscuity is impious in a city of happy people, and the rulers won't allow it.*
> —Socrates

In Western culture the earliest and probably strongest political/educational statement was written by Plato about 380 B.C. It is a dialogue between Socrates and people he meets while returning from a religious festival. The discussion begins with a search for the meaning of justice and evolves into a description of the ideal city. At the base of his belief, Plato was certain that the soul of each individual and the soul of the state needed to be in harmony. The way to ensure harmony between the two was through proper education. While we in the United States generally put "soul" in the realm of religion, the spirit of the argument needs to be considered. To put Plato's idea in a way we are more familiar with: The well-being of the state depends upon the well-being of each individual. Education needs to be concerned with that relationship.

The argument of the *Republic* is complex and wide-ranging. Plato lays the groundwork for what we know and how we know it. Many of the foundations of Western thought can be found in the *Republic*. It is a window into the strengths and weaknesses of Western culture. In his dialogues, if you agree with his first premise, it is remarkably difficult to dismiss his ideas. While we will concentrate on his ideas about education, it is important to remember that the *Republic* is concerned with much more then that.

The Soul and the State

Plato proposed that there are three parts of the soul: wisdom, moderation, and courage.[1] While there needs to be some balance of these in all souls, in each of us one of those parts is dominant; some are brighter, some are stronger, and so on. In the state, different professions reflect these traits. The military depends on a certain kind of courage, judges should have a certain kind of wisdom, and the like. An ideal school will identify the strengths of each person and make certain that person receives the right education. The point he makes is that an individual with the proper education not only fulfills him or herself, but also makes an important contribution to the society.

Here is how Plato describes education:

> Education isn't what some people declare it to be, namely, putting knowledge into souls that lack it, like putting sight into blind eyes . . . the power to learn is present in everyone's soul and that the instrument with which each learns is like an eye that cannot be turned around from darkness to light without turning the whole body . . .
>
> Then education is the craft concerned with doing this very thing, this turning around, and with how the soul can most easily and effectively be made to do it. It isn't the craft of putting sight into the soul. Education takes for granted that sight is there but that it isn't turned the right way or looking where it ought to look, and it tries to redirect it appropriately.[2]

Each of us, he argues, is capable of doing something well. It is a task of education to help us discover what that is and teach us how best to do it. Put in Platonic terms, when we fulfill our souls we live a just life. What educator would disagree with this description of an ideal citizen: "He puts himself in order?"[3] The person who ful-

---

[1] The first descriptions are found in Book VI. I am using the G. M. A. Grube translation, *Plato's Republic* (Indianapolis: Hackett Publishing Company, 1974).

[2] Ibid., p. 190.

[3] Ibid., p. 119.

fills his or her talents and who lives a life of moderation will, according to Plato, lead a good and just life. In his city, just individuals produce a just society.

Plato makes certain that the ties between education, the state, and the individual are clear. The just life is a moral one—and each member of society is capable of living such a life. It is the job of education to help the individual fulfill his or her potential. For educators, this certainly makes sense. Many of the best teachers want to make a difference in a student's life. Plato teaches us that education can have a powerful effect on the life of society as well as on the life of each citizen. He plays to some of the best instincts of teachers.

To help make certain this can happen, Plato believed that the young should learn only certain stories, hear only certain music, and so on. He writes: "Then we must first of all, it seems, supervise the storytellers. We'll select their stories whenever they are beautiful and reject them when they aren't."[4] He believed that there should be harmony in a young person's life, so the music should be of only a certain kind and the myths of childhood should not portray the gods in a bad way. Put simply, for the sake of a good education Plato thought that censorship was necessary. He also believed that only the best educated should be leaders—philosopher-kings—and that they should live communally. Further, he believed that women should have the same educational opportunities as men: ". . . women of the same sort must be chosen along with men of the same sort to live with them and share their guardianship."[5]

Critics and the *Republic*

From the time he wrote the *Republic*, it has been criticized.[6] The easy targets have been the censorship and the clearly undemocratic (guardians—philosopher-kings— were not elected, but because they were the "best" people, would naturally govern) system of government. People have disagreed with his notion of a soul, with what he would have taught, and with the idea that others can make a choice about the kind of education a student should be given. Plato has been dismissed for hundreds and hundreds of years, but that should alert you to something important: His ideas are central to the way so many people in the West think that no matter how much people do not like the details of his arguments, the *Republic* is still a work with which we need to deal.

Censorship makes us very uncomfortable. Ours is a country where people want to feel secure in their freedoms. The reality, of course, is that we care very much about what is taught and what our young people learn. We have invented chips that go into our television sets so that our children do not have access to certain things. There are those who assume naked people and nasty language will corrupt our youth. Our religions are nothing if not careful about the stories children hear in Sunday school. Each

---

[4] Ibid., p. 53.

[5] Ibid., p. 130.

[6] There have been defenders of Plato. The idea of virtue being the underpinning of education can find defenders in such people as Allan Bloom and William Bennett. See *The Closing of the American Mind* and *To Reclaim a Legacy*, respectively.

religion makes certain that its god is powerful, good, loving, and just. There are even scientific studies that tell us what a fetus should hear while in the womb. Classical music, we are told, is good for the yet-to-be-born child. No rap music for them. We are advised to censor it out. While the ancient Greeks thought relationships between powerful men and younger boys were acceptable, we send men to jail for that.

Although we strongly defend our freedom, we do our best to provide our youth with what we believe to be the right things. That Plato actually outlines what is acceptable and unacceptable might be understood as merely acknowledging what most cultures practice. Too often we limit speech and music and control the very myths of childhood while hiding behind the notion of freedom.

This chapter is about the context of education. We are in search of the purpose of education so that we will be able to make some sensible judgments about current problems we are having. The first point is this: There seems to be a tension between the needs of each individual and the needs of the state. It is easy to agree that any system of education should support the society in which it exists. Yet, as individuals we want what is best for us—or for our children. While the society might be best served by educating only those who are the brightest, what is to be done about those who don't "fit," who do not test well, or who are bright in a different way?

The answer given by Plato is reasonable: Each person should do what he or she can do best. He argues for what he believes would be a moral and just education. He believes that education is the path to virtue. Why, then, do we have such a difficult time accepting what he wrote? What is it about our beliefs that makes it so difficult for us to accept a moral argument about education?

Have we gotten to the point of believing that all education is about helping the person get the best (most highly paid) job?[7] If that is the case, then when we turn to particular issues in education we will be able to answer them easily. Of course, education has always been more than mere economics in the United States. If money were the major concern of education many of us would never have considered being teachers.

The relationship between the state, the individual, and education was given a very different turn by a man born in Geneva in 1712.

JEAN-JACQUES ROUSSEAU AND EMILE

> . . . [L]et him learn in detail, not from books but from things, all that a man in such a situation is bound to know. Let him think he is Crusoe himself.
> —J.-J. Rousseau

If the state controls education in the Republic, nothing could be further from that than the education proposed by Jean-Jacques Rousseau. His ideas seem remarkably

---

[7] Interestingly, Plato's guardians lived communally and owned no material things. Money was clearly not the aim of education. Nor was power. Plato writes that those who were qualified to be guardians did not want the job. They were more interested in the life of the mind. When they completed their duty as ruler, they were retired to an island so they could live in peace with their ideas.

modern, wonderfully romantic, and surprisingly acceptable to a certain segment in the United States. In the book *Emile*, which he finished in 1760, Rousseau describes the ideal education for a young student of that name.

While you will see that *Emile* appeals to our most individualistic instincts, it is important to know that the education Rousseau designs for Emile has nothing in common with what he wants for young women. He believes that the basic nature of the sexes differ, and devises a special education for each. We will deal with these ideas later in this chapter. In chapter 5 we will return to the topic, and discuss how we understand girls and boys in our classrooms.

Nature and Society

Rousseau was a powerful opponent of the society in which he lived. He thought it was corrupt and, when it came to education, corrupting to the next generation. The sins of the adults were passed to the children. To counter the culture in which he lived, Rousseau called for a return to and belief in nature. "It is thus," he writes, "that Nature always acts for the best, constitutes us at birth."[8] He believed that the greatest blessing was liberty—and it was a blessing that could not be found in society. Indeed, we read: "Civilized man is born and dies a slave. The infant is bound in swaddling clothes, the corpse is nailed down in his coffin. All his life long man is imprisoned by our institutions."[9]

But in order for education to work we know that there must be some relationship between an individual and society. Rousseau's solution was much different than Plato's. Rousseau believed that each man (and he did mean man) should be educated alone in order to understand himself and his relationship to nature. But he knew that we could not return to a state of nature, so he wrote about the *general will* of a state. This general will was like nature in that it was an impersonal set of laws in which all men would be treated the same. If each properly educated man did what he believed was right, and concerned himself only with public issues when dealing with the state, then the general will of the society would be strong.

His society is one in which there is not a great deal of interaction between citizens. The strong individual of Rousseau's state lives a "natural" life, well outside the corruption of society. It is a notion with which we can relate. Thomas Jefferson mistrusted the morals of city-dwellers, and many of our myths continue to center on a cowboy culture. As part of our liberal heritage we seem to have an almost instinctual mistrust of government and the secular sins of metropolitan life. In chapter 3, we will see this in greater detail. What we need to acknowledge is that the individualism Rousseau writes about seems closer to our national beliefs than the ideal city of Plato.

[8] Archer, R. L. (ed.), J. J. Rousseau, *His Educational Theories Selected From Emile, Julie & Other Writings* (Woodbury, NY: Barron's, 1964), p. 90.

[9] Sheldon Wolin, *Politics and Vision: Continuity and Innovation in Western Political Thought*, (Boston: Little, Brown and Company, 1960), p. 369.

The Importance of Experience

Rousseau proposed that Emile be given a tutor who would be responsible for all of his education. He believed that the best education comes from the student learning from experience, so things like reading were put off to a boy's teenage years. Two educational examples should help give us an idea of what Rousseau constructed.

Each of these lessons gives us a good sense of Rousseau's "hands-on" methods. The first example might not be what we are accustomed to when we read educational theory, but Rousseau is convinced that it will bring no harm to the student. The young man breaks the window in his bedroom. You say nothing, but you do not repair the window. The young man is uncomfortable ("Do not mind his catching a cold. It is better that he should catch a cold than that he do such silly things.")[10] and, after a few days, you have the window fixed. Regrettably, he breaks the window a second time.

This time you tell him, "very coldly," that the windows are yours. You then lock him in a room without windows. Rousseau writes that the young man will "cry and storm." No one pays attention. Finally, with help from sympathetic servants, he proposes that you let him out if he promises to never break another window. The lesson is learned, the boy is released, and the principle is taught: Never punish for the sake of punishment—only punish as a natural consequence of misdeeds.

There is a way this is very understandable. While it seems harsh that the student might catch a cold, or that he is locked up in a dark room, Rousseau is convinced that two important points be understood. First, that the student can expect consequences from his actions and, second, the best way to teach that lesson is to do it in a real-life situation. Things taught in principle are simply not as effective as things taught in practice.

The second example from Rousseau seems more clever and, possibly, more acceptable to our modern sensibilities. In this lesson, the tutor wants to teach Emile the course the sun travels during the day, and how to use it for directions. The tutor takes his student out in the woods and explains about the sun and why that knowledge might be useful. The student does not care. A few days later, before breakfast, the tutor suggests that the two of them go for a walk. Emile is delighted.

They go into that very same forest and get lost. They cannot find their way out. They wander aimlessly, get tired, and get hungry. They sit and try to think about their situation. Cleverly, the tutor begins a discussion about where they were earlier when they had talked about the sun and its position in the sky. Finally, Emile figures it out; he remembers the lesson about the sun and is able to lead them to the town. The tutor buys them a good meal.

Rousseau tells us that this is the kind of lesson that will never be forgotten. He argues that a good tutor can teach a student to figure out how to use and be comfortable in nature if the lesson is presented in the right way. His ideal student becomes an ideal citizen: independent, self-sufficient, and thoughtful. Certainly that has much in common with what we believe a citizen should be.

There is something very appealing about this vision of education. Of course there are problems when we think about any modern day application of the theory.

---

[10] Rousseau, op. cit., p. 103.

Few of us, for example, can afford a tutor, along with bright and caring servants who could help coach our children along the way. And we would have to ask if there could be someone capable enough to know what should be taught and be clever enough to mold those lessons into a form in which learning them would seem practical and natural. The tutor must have mastery over both the student and the environment in order for Rousseau's educational schemes to work. Still, it may be the wish of many who teach to be able to know enough, and have enough power, to make education work in just this way. In the last chapter we will see that there are parents who decide to educate their own children. One might assume they have decided they know enough and have enough power to provide the best education possible.

But there is much about Rousseau that is appealing. He is able to give voice to many of our concerns. When Rousseau says that he hates reading for young people, he both irritates us and somehow brings back bad memories of grade school. If he were alive today he would remind us that even with the latest beepers, most sophisticated computers and do-everything-palms, we are still a part of nature. Rousseau would argue that the further we get from our natural essence the more likely we are to live corrupt lives.

The role of education, then, should be to redirect our attention to our natural selves. We need to be more independent and to more fully understand our role in the world. Education should stop teaching the artifacts of society and turn to the lessons of nature. As teachers, we must shape programs so that we talk less and have the students do more. That does not mean more reading and writing, but more doing—actually doing things that will, in a practical way, teach life lessons. We must be clever and patient while letting our students learn by making mistakes and understanding the consequences.

A nation of natural, self-sufficient people seems like an almost ideal America.

Women

As is so often the case in Western thought, this independent, self-sufficient citizen of Rousseau's was a male. Plato, as we saw, was an exception when he argued men and women should have the opportunity for the same education and role as philosopher-king. But Rousseau's ideas were merely a reflection of his social and political context in which women and men were thought of as being different, and as needing different kinds of education. For almost the entire history of the United States, we have treated men and women differently. In order to understand why that is so, we need to know our intellectual heritage.

Rousseau is clear: "Woman was made specially to please man . . . her strength lies in her charms."[11] The education for women, then, would be nothing like that for men. Rousseau's female student, Sophie, did not get the kind of vigorous activity that his male student got. He believed that girls were much more docile than boys. Women would first learn "needlework" because "little girls, almost from their cradle, love

---

[11] Ibid., p. 218.

dress." We read that boys like "movement and noise" and girls "prefer decorations that please the eye . . . particularly dolls." And he goes on and on. Girls are different and they should not be educated like boys.

We know that Rousseau is, in too many important ways, simply wrong about the sexes. While there may be differences, we will see that the way he has divided the world has been systematically discredited. But to stop here would be foolish. We can learn from Rousseau's mistakes.

Emile, without Sophie, is incomplete. Remember that the ruggedly individual Emile was often alone. He kept his own counsel and was constantly skeptical of society. That meant women were responsible for much. We read that women are responsible for "our manners, our passions, our tastes, our pleasures, and even our happiness . . . [women] bring them [men] up when young, tend them when grown, advise and console them and make life sweet and pleasant . . ."[12] In short, much of those things that make up the texture of life are the responsibility of women.

At one point, Rousseau describes a dinner party of a married couple—we can assume it is Emile and Sophie. After the party, Emile repeats the gossip at his table and what people said and did. He is merely a reporter. Sophie, on the other hand, "noticed what was whispered quite softly at the other end of the room; she knows what So-and-so was thinking . . . in short, there has scarcely been a significant movement which she is not ready to explain, and nearly always to explain rightly . . ."[13]

As one reads Rousseau, the case is easily made that women are more interesting than men are, and certainly more subtle. Emile would not do well in the world without Sophie, and yet Rousseau fails to give her much of an education. It is possible that when individualism becomes too strong in an educational system those getting the education will be as ill-prepared for a life in a viable society as Emile. The balance between the power of the state and the power of the individual is not easy to find. It is difficult to believe that either Plato or Rousseau has the answer.

Before leaving the interesting but poorly educated Sophie, it is only fair to give Rousseau his due. Sophie has a certain amount of power: "She must only marry one whom she loves . . ." One has no clear reason to believe she would love Emile.

EDUCATIONAL PRIORITIES: WHAT WOULD YOU DO?

Many of our current issues continue to revolve around the tensions we have seen in Plato and Rousseau. Let me tell you a story.

A good friend of mine, a doctor, is very interested in all kinds of political and educational issues. Because those areas are my business, he frequently asks my opinion about things he is reading or ideas he has come across. (In turn, I ask him about my current aches and pains.) My friend had heard a speaker discuss his book about a

---

[12] Ibid., p. 221.

[13] Ibid., p. 231.

plan to change current educational policy. He had enjoyed the speaker and was attracted to the idea.

Basically, the speaker had written a book that advocated putting more money in schools with the best students. He made the argument that the poorer students should get vocational training in high school, while the brightest would be given accelerated classes. The best students from the worst schools would be bused to the good schools.

For example, our local schools (in a middle/upper-middle-class neighborhood) would be given additional funding while the public schools in a nearby lower/lower-middle-class town would be turned into vocational high schools. The good students from that town would be bused to our town.

My friend was attracted to the idea that our best and brightest would be given a first-rate education. He argued, in the end, that is how civilization advances. He thought it was foolish that everyone should be given an identical education when individual abilities and interests are so different. He said that we needed to be realistic about it, and in a world of finite resources it is wasteful and destructive to deny the best possible education to those who would clearly contribute the most to our society.

My friend, taken by the talk he had attended, wanted me to understand the wisdom and power of the ideas.

There were things that did not come up that need to be acknowledged. While what he was saying, in principle, had a certain logic, there were things that were left out. Nothing was said about color, culture, or class. The speaker—and I honestly do not know the truth—was either uninterested in these issues, or simply assumed that those in the audience understood that the white school would be given funds for advanced academic work, and the racially diverse school would become a training school. By merely assuming the context of his talk was the United States, we know that what he had to say had implications beyond educational policy.

Back to the conversation. Yes, I said, it might be a good idea to redistribute funding for public schools. Why not make some schools much stronger academically and make other schools simply places to train workers? It would be wonderful to know that our schools were fully funded for their particular missions. The idea, it seemed to me, was Platonic to the core.

Of course, I continued, those buses that bring bright kids here will turn around and take our less-gifted students down to those vocational schools. You know that Eveyn (a son of his) and Gretchen (a daughter of mine) will have to leave our local school and be bused to the other one. Both of them are bad students. Neither is interested in academic things, and they both cause trouble in class. I know we love them, but to really make your plan work they would be on the bus to the vocational school. If we make some schools better than others, then it only makes sense that the best students go to the best schools. Eveyn and Gretchen will never be outstanding students, so others should take their places.

Not surprisingly, my friend did not like the idea of his son not being part of the upper-middle-class. He was torn between the fact that he could provide a good education for Eveyn, and the clarity and appeal of an interesting idea. In the end, the reality of what he wanted for his son was stronger than what he could see might be a very good idea.

What would you have said? What do you believe? Would you have a daughter or son bused to a vocational high school out of your neighborhood for solid, academic reasons? Would you have that same child be bused to another school to get a "better" education?

Maybe a more basic question is this: What do you do when the best public policy does not seem to be in the best interest of your child? What is the right, "moral" thing to do? The conflict is real. Certainly it is easy to believe we should provide good schools for our best students. But, emotionally, how would it feel to see your child get on a bus to go to a vocational school outside of your upper-middle-class neighborhood? Yes, you can reasonably admit that poor neighborhoods generally have subaverage schools, and they might be better served with good vocational schools. But can you follow the logic to the end and have your child sent to what seems to be a less desirable school? Could you love your country more than you love your child?

While that last sentence may seem a little over-dramatic, the question remains: What would you do?

WHY SCHOOLING?

Let us return to the issue of what schools are about. We are neither ancient Greeks nor eighteenth century European philosophers. While we may be their intellectual or spiritual descendents, we certainly need to consider the conditions in which we find ourselves. We need to know our context. One way to do that is to look at what our current texts tell us about schools. What follows is a list of questions from a well-respected book. We are told that the questions reflect concerns "individuals and mass media often express about the overall quality of our society's public school system."[14] These questions are at the heart of what the authors believe are at the reasons for public education.

> Is public education equipping our young to support themselves in a changing economy?
>
> Is it promoting an equitable society by educating all our students?
>
> Is it equipping them with the skills and attitudes needed to live in a society that is increasingly diverse and pluralistic?
>
> Is it teaching them to respect and protect an increasingly endangered environment?
>
> In short, how well does our nation's public school system serve the major needs of our society?

The questions are straightforward and important. They represent a set of values that reflect—one would guess—a huge segment of the literate population. The underlying vision of these questions is of a country in which we live together in a civ-

---

[14] Tozer, Violas, Sense, School and Society: Historical and Contemporary Perspectives, 3d ed.(Boston: McGraw-Hill, 1998), p. 1.

ilized way, with good jobs and good neighbors, in a natural environment that is not being destroyed.

Why would one want to disagree with these basic tenets? The questions can be turned around. Would we support a system that taught its students to be bigots, or to dislike or resent anyone who is different, or were unprepared to be employed? Do we want those who go to public school to learn how to destroy the environment? These are the tenets of a centrist political agenda. It seems clear that the authors are correct in assuming there are a great many people who support the basic assumptions of their questions.

What is also obvious is that these are serious political statements that are in question form. There is nothing wrong with that. It is clear from our discussion of Plato and Rousseau that there has always been an important relationship between the state and schooling. What could be more basic than a society that prepares its young to become good citizens? Political ideals have always been close to the surface of education. Teachers should be very clear about why they are teaching, and how (or if) that relates to politics. If we believe that schooling helps shape lives, then the shape those lives take may certainly have political meaning.

Let us take a closer look at those questions as political aims. Do you believe, for example, that one of the primary tasks of education is to train people to support themselves in a changing economy? Can we assume, because it was the first question on the list, that preparing people for work is the most important role of education? If that is the case, what will we make of the argument that education might play a deeper and more significant role in an individual's life? Is it possible that education is first and foremost about preparing people to make money?

Schooling, Training, and Education

Educators are careful to note the difference between *schooling, training,* and *education.* **Schooling,** basically, means anything that happens in school.[15] While everything that happens in school might teach the student something, not everything is "educational." Playing football, for example, is not considered education—nor is cheerleading, planning the senior prom, getting to class on time, and the like. Education is one of the things that takes place in schools, and much may be learned doing those activities associated with schools, but schooling and education are not identical.

Part of what goes on in schools is **training.** Students are trained to do specific skills or fulfill certain roles. This training takes place on different levels. We can be trained to write papers using accepted academic form; we can be trained to learn how to use a computer or to become electricians, plumbers, or dentists. Training consumes a substantial part of our lives as we grow up. One of the important parts of schooling is to train students. As we better understand how to teach, our methods of training have become more sophisticated and effective.

---

[15] School comes from Greek and meant "a halt, hence a rest, leisure, hence employment for leisure, esp such employment for children, hence training or instruction, hence, schooling." Eric Partridge, *Origins: A Short Etymological Dictionary of Modern English* (USA: Greenwich House, 1983), p. 594.

There is a second level of training.[16] For example, how schools are organized helps train students in various ways. When the United States was changing from an agricultural to an industrial country, schools helped train students to become workers. Schools became highly regimented, with bells that told people when to go from place to place, and classes in which students had to sit still, be quiet, and do what the teacher said. Those were the skills they needed if they wanted to move from the country to the city and do industrial work.

But neither schooling nor training is education.

Education has to do with more intellectual and creative processes.[17] While there is no single, agreed-upon definition there is enough agreement to make sense of the word. Education involves the use of reason and creativity. It is the process of an individual understanding not only the world, but himself or herself. Education helps the individual become his or her best self. Education helps the person make sense of the world, and helps that person experience all those things he or she could never imagine.

There is a genuine danger of giving education an almost mystical sense. Because we do not fully understand how education works (we know a great deal, but the number of variables are so great in any individual case that we can predict very little), the language we use to describe the moment that something "clicks" tends towards the mystical. And the more one tries to define an educated person, the more one is likely to fall into a self-involved, self-revealing funk. While we measure certain aspects of learning, the idea of being truly educated varies from one person to the next.

Schooling and training are much easier to understand than education. There are those who define being educated by knowing certain categories of things. For example, John Searle believes an educated person should: 1) know about his or her cultural tradition, 2) be literate about the physical world, 3) know how society works, 4) be sufficiently literate in a foreign language to know its best literature and be able to carry on a conversation, 5) know the methods and content of philosophy well enough to follow and construct a logical argument, and 6) be able to write and speak well.[18]

It would seem that a person who knew and could do all of those things would be well educated. However, there is no agreement that knowing certain things makes a person well educated. There might be an underlying sense of the world that a well-educated person develops. Knowledge needs to be shaped by each individual. It is possible that one's aesthetic sense—a sense of what is beautiful in the world—might be the key to education.

We just read that education was more than intellectual and creative activity. While education involves both of these, there is no agreed upon definition. Let me suggest a way to think about education.

---

[16] Training comes from the word *track*. It makes sense that one stays tracked when one is trained. Ibid., p. 731.

[17] Education comes from the Latin *to lead*. Its roots are "to rear (a child), hence, to educate . . ." Ibid., p. 170. Barry Sanders writes that education "was first used in English in the early seventeenth century to refer to rearing children by paying attention to their physical needs—in the earliest years of the child's life this meant attention to nursing." See *A Is for Ox*, (New York: Vintage Books, 1994), p. 190.

[18] John Searle, "The Storm Over the University," *New York Review of Books* (Dec. 6, 1990), p. 42.

Consider this: "'What is good is light, everything divine runs on delicate feet'—this is the first proposition of my aesthetics."[19] What is important is that the author's aesthetics informs everything else. His life—physical, intellectual and psychological—rests on his aesthetic sense. I believe that education is so difficult to define because it is not merely what we know—Searles' list, for example—but how we shape it and form it and use it. Education has to do, in no small part, with what we do with what we know. This definition involves the intensity of one's aesthetic sense. The essence of education informs our self. That self is often beyond the reach of our political and cultural institutions.

Education, to put it a little differently, takes place in the context of society. What we learn and how we learn it conforms, in many ways, to what we need to know in order to live a good and productive life in that society. But the suggestion is that there are times when education can take an individual beyond the boundaries set by society. Genuine education has no cultural limitations.

What we have, then, is a genuine dilemma. It is widely agreed that the close relationship between the state and schooling is the normal and accepted state of affairs. While there have always been a minority of citizens who object to that, it is still widely accepted by most Americans. Yet, the essence of being educated is beyond the scope of the state. Education may well be a subversive activity. Friedrich Nietzsche, the author of the above quote about everything divine running on delicate feet, was both well educated and subversive. His education, with his aesthetic sense, drove him to rage against what he believed to be the corrupt culture of Western Europe. Possibly the seeds of such rage lie in every act of education.

We need to be more clear about how to understand education before we turn to the issues we currently face.

RESEARCH APPROACHES AND BIASES

Earlier we discussed the importance of context. Questions and answers make sense only when we understand their context. It is equally necessary to understand how one approaches problems. Answers, after all, depend on how questions are asked. Different theories and frameworks are used in educational research. What follows is a quick sketch of a few of these approaches. They are offered only to suggest that answers are dependent on how questions are framed—and each of those frames carries a certain bias. The following examples are not intended to be full explanations, but are offered only as a way to make the broader point.

Theories are systematic ways of organizing the world. They help guide us through our everyday lives, and are so central to our thinking that we rarely pay attention to them. We have theories about all kinds of things: why some people can never get dates, why some teachers are so good, why former President Clinton had so much trouble with monogamy. Our actions are generally not random. We do things based

---

[19] Lesley Chamberlain, Nietzsche in Turin: An Intimate Biography (New York: Picador, 1998), p. 59.

on our theory of how we believe things will turn out, and why. Beyond our personal theories, there are broad, social theories that people use to organize information. Sigmund Freud had elaborate theories about why we act the way we do, and Karl Marx thought he had figured out how societies work. Each of these theories carries a point of view that maximizes some and minimizes other kinds of information.

For example, we can begin with Karl Marx. He (and there have been many, including Max Weber and Lewis Coser) developed what we know as conflict theory. These theorists focus on the conflicts in society, and tell us that those groups that can control the conflicts become powerful. They argue that society is then structured so that the powerful groups can maintain their positions.

Conflict theorists explain our educational system in a straightforward way. Those with wealth, those groups who are in control of most resources, are able to afford the best schooling for their children. They are able to keep high quality schools in their neighborhoods while paying little attention to schools in the lower-income areas. The purpose of schooling, as seen by these theorists, is to prepare the majority of students to become conforming, well-behaved citizens. Through the legitimate means of power (legislatures and the like), the highest socioeconomic classes are able to stay in control.

A short description cannot begin to do justice to conflict theory, but it reminds us that theories are not neutral. Conflict theory has a point of view. While it makes sense to be aware of the tensions in a culture, and to understand that there are winners and losers and consequent outcomes, there are often other things at work.

Interpretive theories have a different point of view. These theories, generally, are qualitative. They focus more on individual actions than on the macro-focus of conflict theorists. These theorists attempt to pay attention to the actions of everyday life, and to understand the levels of meaning of what we do. Interpretive theorists are phenomenologists who, in various ways, help us discover the underlying messages of our everyday acts.

Finally, a third approach is critical theory. It has become a popular and powerful way to study our institutions and culture. Critical theory combines conflict and interpretive theory by looking at both micro and macro levels. Also, and importantly, critical theorists have an agenda of change, so they make no claims that what they are doing is "neutral" science.

Critical theorists believe that schools are the result of what the dominant classes want, but these theorists will also study students and the ways in which students might resist oppressive education. Critical theorists use the critiques developed by the conflict theorists, the insights developed by the interpretive theorists and search for ways in which schooling might improve.

There are variations in all of these theories as well as many approaches that play important roles in how we think about education. For example, there are those who organize schooling around religious beliefs and those who are bitterly opposed to that approach. A Catholic curriculum, for example, was the inspiration for Paulo Freire's curriculum of liberation. In colleges we have seen that the traditional courses about Western civilization have been challenged by feminist theories—among others.

How we approach a problem—the things we look at and the questions we ask— is an important part of the context. The person doing the study brings along his or her biases. In addition to approach, the words one chooses to use, the facts one decides to include (or exclude), and the order in which things are presented all serve as clues to what a person thinks and believes. For example, because this is a textbook I should do my best to be as fair-minded as possible. My goal is to introduce you to the genuine educational issues of our time, and to do so in an unbiased way.

What we know from research is that being unbiased is impossible. The topics I choose, the information I decide to include, and the way I order materials all betray my view of things. Interestingly, you may see these biases more clearly than I can. However, those times I want to argue a point, I will tell you.

One person who reviewed this manuscript wrote: "If the author is going to write using 'I' and 'you,' . . . I strongly encourage him to lay bare a bit of who he is. That only seems fair . . ." While I suppose the point is a good one, he failed to suggest what might be interesting or important. What follows are two paragraphs of what I guess he might want to know.

I am married and we have children and grandchildren. We always have a dog. I was born in Tulsa, Oklahoma, got my Ph.D. in political science from the University of California, Berkeley, and teach in the School of Education at The University of Massachusetts, Amherst. I write about American politics and American political thought, organization theory, methodology and, of course, education.

Maybe the reviewer would find this "important" information for the book: From K through 12, the very years this book is about, I just sat. I never read a book. I was not in the college track. I hated being in any classroom. What kept me going was that I had wonderful friends. I still don't know what kept me quiet. My sense is that my experience with schooling played a part in why I wrote this book, and what I chose to write about. How could it not?

Finally, as we begin to discuss important educational issues it is necessary to understand as fully as possible not only the biases of what you are reading, but also your own biases. Your beliefs and biases form an important part of how you read this, or any, book.

EDUCATION AND THE INDIVIDUAL

The more we try to define our terms and understand the nature of what we are discussing the more complicated things become. We have seen that the state and education have an important relationship and that schooling, training and education are not the same things. Also, how we study these things have an effect on what we find.

There is one last topic that is important to introduce before we go to a history of schooling in the United States. In this section we will deal with the nature of education and why people teach.

In the beginning of this chapter we dealt with broad themes. In our history, schooling has always been an important aspect of culture. Schooling has helped carry the burden of preparing the next generation of citizens. We noted that the state/school relationship was not without its tensions.

As we looked a little closer, we saw that schooling and training were much easier to understand than education. With that in mind, let us return to the discussion of education.

I would like to propose that all education is personal. No matter where it is, or what method we are using, I would like for you think about the idea that education depends on one individual at a time. Reading is learned a person at a time. While learning is often discussed in terms of statistics—what percentage of your class is at grade level, what percentage in your school needs special help—learning does not take place statistically but on an individual level. Each of us learned to read. Each of us learned math. Each of us is on track to learn some or all those things that John Searle believes we need to know to be well educated.

We can see the point in a negative way: No one can learn for us. No one can know something for us. We can either speak French or not, understand the natural world or not, behave appropriately or not. If education is more than simply knowing things, if it is also knowing in the context of one's aesthetic sense, then education is surely personal.

The ideas that have been presented will come into play when we discuss the problems of schooling in the United States. As we will see in chapter 3, ours is a nation built on individualism. The liberalism of John Locke and Thomas Hobbes is deeply ingrained in our character. Broadly speaking, the United States is not a culture built on the traditional idea of community. The first settlers, the Puritans, arrived full of self-righteousness and a strong sense of community. As soon as their children realized all they had to do was move West and build their own towns, they left what they felt was the repressiveness of their parents.

Community became individualism, and our central myths revolve around pioneers who founded a new nation. We are cowboys and entrepreneurs. We believe each of us is responsible for our own well-being, even when this is not the case. (For example, during times of economic recession people are fired not because they are poor workers but because there is no work. Regrettably, they feel a sense of guilt as if the recession was somehow their fault.) We hang on to our individualism.

While it is simply a truism that each person must learn to read and spell by himself or herself, in the United States that takes on added meaning. School is the first genuinely competitive situation in which the individual begins to practice for the competitive environment of capitalism.

There are levels to the tensions of the state and the individual. The state, with its claims, and the individual, with his or her claims, are at the heart of many tensions. What, for example, is at stake when we think about funding for English-as-a-second-language programs? What is the role of English in the life of our nation? Certainly speaking the same language is an enormously useful tool in uniting us. It is easy to see how different languages have helped divide other countries.

We also know that the language in which we think and speak, in part shapes our sense of the world. If you were raised thinking and speaking in Spanish your world would be a little different than if you had grown up thinking and speaking German or Chinese. If you happened to live in the United States, a strong case could be made that all students should be tested in English. It makes perfect sense to many people.

But "making perfect sense" hides many problems. What of the individual who must change his or her language? Should we force a person to lose that central part of his or her self in order to live in the United States? If the state pays for education, then is it safe to assume that there is a price to pay by each individual in that educational system? Later, we will see in greater detail how this issue is played out.

The idea here is that if education is personal then what the state requires might not benefit any particular individual. Plato and Rousseau pointed out, in different but equally compelling ways, the underlying tensions of the state and the individual. While we in the United States have added our own variations to the themes, what we are dealing with is not new. As we begin to investigate education in America, and think about what good education and public policy might be, we need to think about this tension. It will give us needed perspective on what might be done.

Finally, why do people go into education? People love to teach, they love kids, they love different subjects, they believe it is a good way to earn a living. Some have the agendas we mentioned earlier. They want to help people be better citizens, to get good jobs, to respect others, to take care of the environment and so on. Theirs is often a wonderful combination of personal empathy and political action that makes teaching, or school administration, a natural vocation.

It is not as easy to understand or explain those people who go into education for more personal and aesthetic reasons. Those are the teachers and administrators who seem more like artists. Their jobs are an expression of more than a political end or even a carefully crafted skill. There seems to be satisfaction not only from what the students learn, but also from the work itself.

Later, we will explore teaching more carefully. We will try, in part, to understand why so many different kinds of teachers can be so effective. But if education is personal, it is also possible that some teaching is personal. In the debate about teaching being a science or an art, it will make sense for us to fully understand why people decide to teach.

SUMMARY

Before we are able to discuss serious educational issues it is necessary to begin to see the context in which those issues appear. In this chapter we asked about the purpose of education, and the relationship between the state and schooling. We found no easy answers. While Plato compelled us to acknowledge the good of the state, there were many questions about the freedom of the individual. Rousseau makes the individual (male, to be sure) the center of his education, but his methods were economically unrealistic and his well-educated Emile seemed socially incomplete.

Schooling continues to serve political ends. We found that popular and understandable school agendas have clear social and political aims. Schooling and training naturally help the student become an active and productive citizen.

However, education may not necessarily be in the best interests of the state. We saw that education is sometimes highly personal and may be very subversive. The argument was made that all education, in the end, was personal.

There was a discussion about why people entered the field of education, and speculated that the reasons often paralleled schooling, training, and education. In later chapters, we will return to these ideas.

In this chapter we have started to understand the context of schooling and education in the United States. The tensions of the state and the individual underlie many of the particular issues that face our educational system. In the next chapter, a history of schooling in the United States, we will see how those tensions were resolved during different time periods. We will see how various themes have been played out.

THINK ABOUT

1. Why do we educate?

2. Do you feel more strongly about the needs of the state or the individual?

3. What is a "good" education?

4. What do we need to know before we can begin to answer the above questions?

CHAPTER TWO

SHAPING THE UNITED STATES
An Early History of Our Schooling

Our changing society . . . has produced a sense of historical dislocation, a loss of older American modes of temporal relatedness, and 'alienation' from all sense of historical position.

—Kenneth Keniston

If everyone has the right to express his will . . . what does this right mean if their will is merely an echo of the chorus around them?

—John Schaar

. . . you think this is too horrible to have really happened, this is too awful to be the truth? But, please. It's still hard for me to have a clear mind thinking on it. But it's the truth even if it didn't happen.

—Ken Kesey

In many ways there has been no Golden Age in American education. Indeed, there may never have been a Golden Age in education anywhere. Certainly there have been periods of extraordinary achievement in different areas of the world. China, Florence, Athens, the Middle East, and Japan, to name a few, have produced remarkable works of art and science and philosophy. One can only imagine the sheer energy and excitement that existed in those times of invention and innovation.

But education doesn't necessarily have much to do with those productive periods. Until very recently, when people thought about education they thought about an activity for the sons of the elite. Formal education was for the few. Most people who have lived on this planet have not been educated. (Currently, about 70% of the people in the world cannot read.) Certainly adults made certain that each new generation knew enough to keep their culture alive. Families, elders, tutors, religious leaders—or some combination—helped children understand what was needed to have a place in their society.

When we talk about education we do not generally think about that kind of activity. In our daily life, we understand that education revolves around schooling. In

21

this country we have come to believe that it is an important and necessary condition for everyone to have equal access to a good education.

This chapter is centered on how that idea came about in the United States. We will see how perceptions changed from the early American colonies to today. We will study how the meaning, structure, and influence of schooling has developed and changed over the last 300-plus years.

As we review our history, it is easy to be critical of schooling. It is easy, and natural, to judge our past with our current sensitivities. For example, I can't imagine what it would have been like to be a student in Puritan Massachusetts. My sense is that I would not have liked one minute of it. But what does it mean to say something like that? Is it fair to make that kind of statement? Does writing that I do not believe I would have liked to be a student in Puritan times say more about me than it does about schooling in those days?

In the first chapter the point was made that context is important. The argument was that to fully understand something, it was necessary to know the setting in which it occurs. Of course, that is true, but it is much more complicated than that. To pretend that I could take my twenty-first-century self and put it into a seventeenth-century school makes little sense. Can you imagine walking three miles to school, can you imagine learning by rote, can you imagine getting beaten by the teacher? I honestly cannot. In truth, I can't even imagine being a Puritan.

The problem of context is more difficult than that. For example, we will see that most women and minorities were denied education. How do we handle that? Or, if we argue relative context, what if owning slaves happened to be an accepted part of the times we are studying? Do we merely accept slavery as a given and make no judgment? Do we simply acknowledge that, depending on your color, two hundred years ago you would have accepted being a slave or a slave owner? Or, do we say that owning slaves is wrong now and it was wrong then? Is it legitimate to make moral judgments about earlier times? Is it possible to merely report what was going on and be neutral and uninvolved about it?

There is no easy way out of the dilemma. We know that it is foolish to apply all of our current standards to the past, and we also know that it is foolish and dangerous to accept morally repugnant things such as slavery. Most agree that everything a person believes is important influences how he or she understands something; that what a person chooses to write about betrays his or her judgments. Every text is a record of the bias of the author; every interpretation is a record of the bias of the reader.

This chapter, then, is about how our schools came about, what they were like, and the meaning they carried. We will follow the trail from then to now and see how more than three hundred years of fighting over schools has gotten us to the twenty-first century. As you read about our schools, make as many judgments as you like. But as you do, please try to use as much historical imagination as you can. Try to get a sense of what it was like to be in those schools as either a student or a teacher. What it was like sitting on those hard desks, or trying to teach a boy from the country the skills needed to live in the city, or explaining the United States to immigrants? Make an effort to understand how strongly people felt about controlling their local schools, and how much they feared the federal government.

In this chapter we will see the underpinnings of education in the United States, how that education began, and how it developed into the mid-1800s. It is necessary to study how liberalism grew out of feudalism in Europe, and how it developed in the American colonies. We will see how it influenced both our politics and our education. There will be a review of why different sections of the country developed different kinds of schools, and we will follow those developments to the Civil War.

By the end of the chapter, you may well come to a different conclusion than I have. Possibly you will believe that we have had a Golden Age of education in the United States. You may be right.

COLONIAL EDUCATION

While our early American education was divided into three geographic regions, each third was not equally influential. Education in the South and the Middle Atlantic States has always been overshadowed by education in New England. We will see that religion, economics, and Old-World ties combined to create different kinds of schooling in these different regions, and in the following sections we will see how other differences have become important. In this section we will see that New England, and especially Puritan Massachusetts, was central to how education has developed.

There are several things to keep in mind during this discussion of schooling in the New World. Education was simply not open to everyone. Blacks were excluded, girls were often excluded, and people of different religions were often excluded. In some regions, money was an important factor. In almost every region, many people never went to school. While many came to America to escape religious bigotry, that did not necessarily mean they were not religious bigots themselves. While they did not want to be persecuted, some were certainly willing to persecute others when they had the chance. Public schools, called common schools then, were frequently not common at all.

It is also important to know that schooling was generally what we call grammar school. Secondary schools, high schools, did not exist in most places, and if they did it was for a very small percentage of the population. What we think of when we think about schools has almost nothing to do with what went on three hundred years ago. Certainly people learned things, read and wrote things, and even a small percentage of young men went to colleges. But do not confuse that with our current experience with schooling.

The last thing to remember is this: What went on in some of the colonies was pretty advanced for the times. There was a serious effort to make certain that people could read. That effort is a good place to begin this history.

New England

The quality of the land, the Puritan religion, and the emerging economy each had an effect on schooling in New England. They folded together in a way that encouraged a particular kind of schooling. The colony of Massachusetts led the way.

Massachusetts, like most of New England, is a harsh land. The winters are long and cold, the summers are sometimes painfully hot, and the land is full of rocks. Unlike the South, where there were huge plantations and profitable crops, in New England it was difficult to clear land for farming, and the growing season was short. Importantly, there were few slaves in New England. While farming was not easy in the South, it was profitable because of slavery.

There were some natural resources in the East. There was the sea, with fishing, whaling, and trading. There was timber for building ships. As early as 1624 ship carpenters in Plymouth, Massachusetts, built two boats that men "used in fishing and in trading with Indians as far away as the Kennebec River in Maine."[1] While there was some manufacturing in New England, fishing was the main industry. Cod was the most profitable fish as it could be cut, salted, and shipped to Europe. By 1631 they began to build big ships, and for the next two hundred years shipbuilding in New England was an important American industry.

The economy in New England encouraged people to live in towns. Building and trading and fishing are activities that call for social interaction.

As we know, a central reason that Puritans came to America was to worship without being persecuted. The Puritans believed that in order to be saved it was necessary to know God. To know God one had to be able to read the Bible. They took the Bible literally, and believed nothing else. So, for example, Puritans did not celebrate Christmas because it was not in the Bible. The belief that reading the Bible could help save your soul was the key to education in Puritan America.

While certainly more complex than this, we can see the important variables: In the Northeast the land supported an economy in which people needed to congregate in towns, and the religion insisted that everyone learn to read the bible.

In 1642, the colony of Massachusetts required that parents and guardians (generally apprentices' masters) make certain that their children could read. While this did not mean that children had to attend school, it was important because education was legally recognized as being the business of the state. If the child could not "read and understand religion and the capital laws of the country" then the parents or guardians were fined.[2] What had been deeply rooted English tradition was taken up in the New World.

Five years later, in 1647, there was legislation that ordered every town with fifty families or more to hire someone to teach reading and writing.[3] The legislation was known as the "Old Deluder Satan Law" because with education one could read and understand the Bible and thus be protected from Satan. Education was an important first step in saving souls. Religious and political leaders agreed that schooling was central to the development of the right kind of citizen. The colony of Massachusetts took

---

[1] Louis B. Wright, *Life in Colonial America* (New York: Capricorn Books, 1965), p. 82.

[2] S. Alexander Rippa, *Education in a Free Society: An American History*, 8th ed. (New York: Longman, 1997), p. 36.

[3] See Lawrence A. Cremin, *American Education: The Colonial Experience, 1607–1783* (New York: Harper & Row, 1970).

the responsibility of education out of the hands of the parents and guardians and gave it to the community.

The idea of school districts came from New England. On the average, each township was about six miles square. As the population grew, villages and small towns generally gained control over the schools. These small villages acted as school districts.[4]

Since the beginning, then, our schools have been decentralized. Each village paid for its schools through local taxes, and hired the teachers and ran the schools through their elected officials. They decided what was to be taught and even how long the school year should last. As we shall see, that tradition of local power has continued to this day. While the federal government certainly contributes to schooling, state and local governments generally finance and run public schools.

These early schools were far from elegant. Girls and boys aged five to fifteen shared a one-room school. The teacher was often thought of as an assistant minister because most of the lessons were religious. Attendance varied depending on work that needed to be done at home, the weather, the distance a student had to walk from home, and so on. The rhythm of school depended on the rhythm of nature, the growing season, and the needs of the family.

The purpose of schooling was to conserve the Puritan way of life. It was a way to control the future of the village, town, religion, and Commonwealth. To develop scholars or critical thinkers or social activists was not part of the program. Community leaders wanted students to become adults who automatically accepted the existing religious and political arrangements. In many ways, the aim of education—both what was taught and how it was taught—was to break the spirit of the student. Puritan adults wanted to raise a generation of Puritan children.

Most learning was done by rote memorization. It was not much more complicated than that. Students sat and were quiet until it was their turn to recite the lesson. Teachers were strict. Students were beaten. Not only were students hit for misbehaving, but there were teachers who believed in "beating some learning into them."[5] In a twist that seems appalling, it was not unusual for students who had been whipped at school to go home and get a second whipping from their parents. It was a way for the parents to show support for the teachers.

Beginning students learned from a *hornbook*. It was simply a wooden handle and a piece of paper mounted on a carved board. A transparent piece of cow's horn covered the paper to protect it. A student progressed from the hornbook to the *New England Primer*. The first *Primer* was printed in 1690, and over the next 150 years it is estimated that over three million copies were printed and distributed. It was textbook of choice, by a huge margin, during colonial times.

The *New England Primer* was Puritan to the core. It dwelt on religion with a strict and dark moralistic tone. The old stereotype of Puritans—that they were afraid

[4] For a short discussion of this, see Joseph W. Newman, *America's Teachers*, 3d ed. (New York: Longman 1998), pgs. 166–167.

[5] Wright, op. cit., p. 138.

someone, somewhere, might be having fun—has more than a little basis in truth. The tone of the *Primer* was the tone of Puritanism. Probably the most famous part of the *Primer* were the rhymed couplets used to teach the alphabet. It was the alphabet plus religion. For the letter A we find:

> In Adam's fall
> We sinned all.

The *Primer*, then, was not Big Bird presenting the alphabet; it was a lesson with a religious warning about sin and sinners. In 1662 Harvard-educated Michael Wigglesworth wrote and published a long poem titled *The Day of Doom*. The first printing, eighteen hundred copies, sold out immediately. For the next hundred years it was one of the best known poems in America. School children were forced to memorize long passages of it, passages with a message.

What Wigglesworth wrote was a detailed description of Puritan belief. It was full of warnings about the depravity of human beings since Adam's original sin, and the prediction that hell is where most of us are going. Gloom and doom; the Puritan version of life. For decades public schools in New England focused on exactly that. Students memorized it and stood up in class and repeated it, and were whipped if they didn't get it right.

It is easy to make fun of those public schools in colonial New England. Few of us walk miles to school; few of us get whipped in class; none of us, at least in our public schools, memorize religious poems with the message that we are all sinners who will probably go to hell. Even living in the Commonwealth of Massachusetts, it is impossible for me to imagine myself in Puritan Massachusetts. Trying to grow a garden might give me some insight into how hard it was to farm, and trying to walk to my mailbox in weather below zero reminds me how terrible the conditions were, but nothing comes close to giving me a sense of what school was like. I simply cannot put myself into that situation.

But the Puritans' view of life was not their lasting contribution to our schooling. In spite of their very gloomy vision of the world, they left us the structure of a democratic, decentralized school system. They rejected centralized governing power in favor of local school districts. It is a genuinely important gift. At the turn of the last century it was said that the French Minister of Education could look at his watch at any time of day and tell you what each student was studying at that moment. The Puritans made certain that kind of centralized, lock-step education would never happen in America.

Beyond Grade School

The first secondary school in the colonies was the Boston Public Latin School. It was opened in 1635 for the few boys who would go beyond the common schools. Harvard College was established in 1642 to educate clergy and political leaders for the New World. The few secondary schools (Latin grammar schools) were founded in order to prepare boys to go to college. The boys enrolled in these schools as young as seven or eight, and stayed until their mid-teens. They were taught Latin and Greek, some math and geography, and occasionally astronomy. It was not unusual for students to go to school six days a week, winter and summer, from six to eleven in the morning and one to four or five in the afternoon, for as long as seven years.

Again, the method of teaching was by rote. They were drilled in their lessons, and repeated things over and over. They were taught to answer specific questions with specific answers. Classroom discussions were not allowed. After Latin grammar school graduation, they went to college.

Later in the chapter we will see that people in other parts of the country did schooling differently. But for better or worse, the main traditions of American education began in New England.

There are two additional aspects about New England education that need to be mentioned. One is not much more than a historical footnote, while the other is important. The footnote has to do with what existed before the common schools came into being. At the very beginning, schooling was private and for boys. They were called "dame" schools and were generally taught by a spinster or a widow in her own home. Parents paid a small fee for their son to attend. These schools provided the simplest instruction in reading and writing. As we know, neither political nor religious leaders believed these schools provided adequate education.

While "dame" schools were relatively unimportant, that was not the case of apprenticeships. It was typical for young people in colonial America to learn a trade by becoming an apprentice. Apprenticing was serious business. Generally, a contract (indenture) was signed between the two parties. The apprentice agreed to serve his or her master faithfully, to keep trade secrets of the master, and to generally be a moral and trustworthy person. The apprentice lived in the master's house and in many cases was treated like an adopted member of the family. It was not unusual for an apprentice to marry one of his master's daughters at the end of his apprenticeship.[6]

An apprentice worked hard. Not only did he or she work from dawn to dusk, but was then expected to do jobs around the house. Leisure was virtually unknown in colonial days, and was certainly unknown to apprentices. There was no time off, and if the master's family happened to be religious, then the apprentice would go to church on Sunday. But there were tasks to perform, even on Sundays.

Some children began their apprenticeships as young as six. Boys generally served their masters until they were twenty-one, while girls served until their late teens or until they were married. Boys learned a trade or a craft while girls (and we are talking mostly about girls from poor families) were generally servants who learned a trade such as needlework, sewing, weaving, or the like. The lucky girls might learn how to become professional cooks or bakers while the unlucky ones simply did the hard work of a domestic servant.

The master was to provide a place to live for the apprentice, with food and clothing. The master contracted to teach the apprentice his trade, as well as to read and write. It should be no surprise that some masters were very good while some were not. Masters had the authority of parents and stern punishment was not unusual.

[6] See chapter 5 in Wright, ibid.

Court records show that masters were charged with cruelty to their apprentices. Because beatings were considered normal, the court cases indicate that worse things than that went on. In Maine, in 1666 a servant died when the mistress of the house cut off his toes.

Being an apprentice in colonial America was a way many young people learned their trade, and we are not simply talking about becoming a carpenter or baker or silversmith. Physicians and surgeons learned their profession by watching their master work; lawyers learned their profession the same way. Learning by apprenticing is a time-honored tradition; it was a way for many children from poor families to learn a trade and become successful. That was the normal way of things for centuries.

Benjamin Franklin learned his trade by being an apprentice. His father had wanted young Ben to learn the cutler's trade. In some fields, as a way to keep competition down, masters required a fee from the apprentice. Father Franklin, not a wealthy man, could not pay the fee, so Ben became an apprentice in a print shop. Who knows how American culture would have developed without Franklin the Printer teaching us that "A penny saved is a penny earned," or that "An idle brain is the devil's workshop"?

As we will see, the economy of the South was much different than that of the other colonies. Apprenticing in the South was not as important as elsewhere. The reason, of course, is that slaves did almost all of the work. There was little need for an owner to hire workers with skills because slaves could learn and practice those skills on the plantation. But in New England and the Middle Atlantic colonies, more learning took place in apprenticeships than in schools.

The South

The land in the South, as well as the religion, was different than that of New England. Southerners were Anglicans, not Puritans. The Anglican Church did not tie redemption to the ability to read the Bible. While they did believe in education, they thought it should be the responsibility of the parents. The Anglican Church did establish some schools in the South. These schools were generally for families too poor to educate their children at home.

Possibly the economy of the South was more important to education than was religion. The plantation economy meant, among other things, that people were isolated. It often took days to travel from one plantation home to another. The villages and towns that were characteristic of New England simply did not exist in the South. It was physically impossible for a school to serve the population.

It is important to note that population, here, means the small, free white population. Slaves, who were the majority in the South, were not allowed to go to school. Generally, the white population tried to keep the slave population illiterate. As we will see later in the chapter, and again in chapter 6, there have always been those who believe in universal education.

Rich white families hired tutors for their children (sometimes they shared tutors with other families) or sent them to England to be educated. While school in England was the fancy thing to do, the long ocean trip was full of dangers, including childhood diseases such as smallpox. Mostly, the children of the elite stayed home and were tutored. Those who went to college had their choice of staying in the South or going to New England or the Middle Atlantic colonies, or England.

The young women learned social graces while the young men were taught Renaissance culture.[7] Boys studied translations of Latin and Greek classics, as well as histories, government, science, medicine, and the like. Girls, in addition to the graces, studied grammar, arithmetic, and sometimes a language such as French. They were taught to dance and play a musical instrument. Put a little differently, the sinfulness of human beings was not beaten into Southern children.

Children of poor parents were rarely educated. While occasionally there were "free" schools for orphans and the poor, these were certainly the exception. Rich plantation owners sometimes set aside money in their wills to establish these schools, but discussions about education in the South are almost always about the children of the rich.

While good craftsmen and artisans were needed in the South, they were rarely needed for long. A carpenter, for example, could come over from England and find work teaching carpentry to slaves. Once the skills were learned, the carpenter was out of a job. As mentioned earlier, because of slavery apprenticeships made little sense. The world of the South was a world of big farms, small farms, and slaves. While there were cities of some size, and port cities that supported commerce, the economy generally ran on the backs of black labor.

We know that the first college to be established was Harvard, but the first proposed college was to be in the South. In 1619 King James told his bishops to raise money so that a college could be built in Henrico, Virginia. It was close to Jamestown. It was to be a "college for the conversion of infidels." A college, in other words, for American Indians.

The University of Henrico was never built. On Good Friday, 1622, the "infidels" attacked and killed hundreds of Virginia colonists. This massacre, to quote Wright, "not only dimmed the enthusiasm for educating the heathen but it also destroyed the undertaking completely."[8] In 1693 the College of William and Mary opened in Williamsburg. It became an influential school, educating such men as Thomas Jefferson, James Monroe, and John Marshall. It was one of the colleges of choice for the Southern elite.

Burdened by slavery, and the physical limitations imposed by travel from plantation to plantation, the South had little positive influence on education as it has developed in the United States. Education was primarily for those who were well off economically. It was intended entirely for those who were white. As we know, and as we will see in detail later, schooling and racism are closely tied in our history.

The Middle Atlantic Colonies

When we talk about education in the Middle Atlantic colonies we are mostly talking about Philadelphia. The population of these colonies was sparse and scattered. It was, after all, the frontier. There were few settlements and almost no organized schools.

[7] Newman, op. cit., pgs. 25–6.

[8] Wright, op. cit., p. 135.

The people in these colonies immigrated from different countries and brought with them different religions. The diversity of the population had an effect on education in the area.

The Quakers and the Germans were powerful forces in Pennsylvania. Both groups believed in education, but the government instituted no formal schooling system. The Quakers did have parochial elementary schools in which reading and writing were taught. The students learned to read the Bible, but were not subjected to the oppressive Puritan version. The Quakers were most interested in teaching their children a trade or practical skills.

The Mennonites, another sect, also established schools for their children. Christopher Dock wrote *Schul-Ordnung* (1770), the first book on pedagogy printed in America, for the Mennonite schools. The book, which literally means school-management, advised teachers that there were differences between individuals, as well as differences in ability. He suggested how to treat, and teach, different types of students.

Schools, especially in Philadelphia, were more secular than those in either the South or New England. Many foreign languages were taught, as well as different commercial skills. By the first half of the eighteenth century many private schools were opened to cater to the variety of needs in the developing commercial economy of a great port city. Teachers and schools advertised their particular specialty in papers, and always seemed to find students.

There was as much diversity in the other Middle Atlantic colonies—New York, Delaware, and New Jersey. There were Roman Catholics, Jews, and Dutch Reformed. Schools were established by different groups and for different reasons. While some attempts were made to organize education in some logical way, there was not enough agreement among the various groups for any kind of legislative action. The bottom line was that "absolutely nothing was done by the general assembly with intent to influence the schools of the Province. The laissez-faire policy, so far as elementary education was concerned, reigned supreme."[9]

We can see the roots of much of our schooling in colonial America. At one level it is difficult to imagine. Schooling, like life itself, was harsh; it was harsh both physically and psychologically. While there was a genuine effort to teach children to read and write in New England, that was certainly the exception. The South depended on tutors, and education was for only a tiny portion of the population. The Middle Atlantic colonies pursued schooling very unevenly. Yet, there is much to be learned from our educational beginnings.

The power over schools was decentralized. Local populations had the last word. The legacy of school districts is as strong as any element of our culture. As we will see, the tradition of local power has been a mixed blessing to education.

The idea that the state can mandate education is important. The rest of the nation followed the New England example. As we expanded west, new states made provisions for public schools and gave power to local districts. The looser arrangements in the Middle Atlantic colonies and home education in the South made sense

[9] William Heard Kilpatrick, *The Dutch Schools of New Netherland and Colonial New York* (Washington, D.C.: Government Prining Office, 1912), quoted in Rippa, op.cit. p. 30.

given the culture of those regions. However, as Americans settled in villages and towns, the idea that each state could mandate education for every child was the model that was used.

Many of the issues that have been brought up are still with us. Home schooling, which is how schooling began in the colonies, is with us again. Parents with a good educational plan may now take their children out of public schools and teach them at home. Just as there were schools that fit different segments of the population in the Middle Atlantic colonies, we are now in the middle of trying to figure out how our schools might change. Charter schools, for example, are being established to offer a variety of special kinds of education. And we are still dealing with the issue of exclusion. How can we make schools inclusive? How can we provide good education to those districts that have little money?

It is impressive and important that New England decided education was essential to all children. It is equally impressive that they let local districts have power over that education. Those decisions have done much to shape the present. The emphasis on apprenticeships underlines the notion that there were opportunities to learn skills and earn a living. It was the way children could assure themselves a viable future. It was a path of upward mobility that was later taken over by schooling.

THE TRANSFORMATION

By the middle of the eighteenth century there was a decline in the power of religion. Although the Puritans began to disappear, "their educational tradition survived, a legacy to their commitment to intelligence and to humane values."[10] As we know, there are still remnants of Puritanism in our cultural—as well as our school—systems. But the changes that had begun generations earlier came to a head by the time of the Revolutionary War. By the end of the eighteenth century the influence of many parts of Puritan education was about over.

During the 1700s it was difficult to maintain public schools in New England. There were financial issues: Many towns could not afford to maintain public schools. Even when the courts of Massachusetts would fine towns for not having public schools, it was cheaper for the towns to pay the fines than to maintain the schools. Towns simply paid the fines. Also, as we have seen, the classical learning demanded by the Puritans did not seem to be "practical" enough for the colonists. Writing schools and private–vocational schools were established to provide the kind of instruction needed for young people to enter into the commercial world.

By the time of the Revolution the grammar schools that had been so important to Puritan/colonial America had just about disappeared. The Commonwealth of Massachusetts no longer penalized towns for not supporting these schools. As

---

[10] Robert Middlekauff, *Ancients and Axioms: Secondary Education in Eighteenth-Century New England* (New Haven, 1963), pgs. 8–9; quoted by Jon Teaford, "The Transformation of Massachusetts Education, 1670–1780" in B. Edward McClellan and William Reese, *The Social History of American Education* (Urbana and Chicago: University of Illinois Press, 1988), p. 23.

commercialization slowly began to form an increasingly important part of society, grammar schools became increasingly unimportant. And finally, the Indian wars and the Revolution took energy and money—both of which came, in no small part, from the funding and support of the remaining classical schools.

By the time of the Revolution there were critical shifts in our ideology as well as our schooling. The changes were so central to what we have become that it is important to understand them in some depth. The liberal revolution, which began in Europe, played an important part in colonial politics. The Revolutionary War was fought, in part, so that we could become our own liberal nation. The easy way to understand the changes that took place is to simply acknowledge the remarkable set of institutions that were developed, and the number of freedoms that are guaranteed by the Constitution. The more accurate way to understand what was going on, and what it has meant, is to think about the biases that were built into the founding of the United States.

Feudalism and Eighteenth-Century America

The starting point to change was feudalism. While there was never feudalism in America, it was the way of life that liberal thinkers revolted against in Europe. America had a feudal tradition, once removed.

Feudalism was a fixed society. Land-owning nobles and the clergy were powerful. They controlled society. The third group, serfs, worked the land for the nobles and listened to what the clergy told them. Property was passed down to the eldest son (primogenitor), and other nobles became part of the clergy, while the life of serfs remained much the same. There were Kings, who were the most powerful of the nobles, and who believed that they had a divine right to rule. They served at the pleasure of God.

The sons of the nobility were educated. They learned Latin and Greek and the best of them became men of culture.

What is important to understand is that the dynamic of feudalism was so different than our liberal state, that the absence of education was not important. Serfs were going to be serfs. They were to work as hard as possible so that the life of their masters would be comfortable. There was not the kind of economic activity that we understand. There was no sense that science or progress or equality or rights could add anything positive to society. As we will see, those are liberal additions to our thinking.

In feudalism, life was fixed. A person knew his or her place. Life was extraordinarily hard for serfs, and in reality was not all that easy for nobility simply because things were primitive. Even the biggest, most elaborate and fanciest castles were cold, damp, stone places that were heated by fireplaces. While it seems clear that being a noble was much better than being a serf, it is wrong to imagine their lives were like ours.

The morality of feudalism centered on religion. The structure of society, the sureness of what to expect and why, came from the power of owning land and the sense that it was God's will. The right order of the world had been discovered. Feudalism lasted for hundreds of years as generation after generation of nobles, serfs, and clergy gathered strength from their community and their religion.

From our twenty-first century perspective it is not easy to imagine the centuries of sameness of feudal life. We have no experience in the kind of community that existed, or in living a religious life that everyone shared. It is much easier for us to feel the instincts of early liberal writers who placed their faith in more secular activities.

Before a discussion of liberalism, we need to know something about America of the late eighteenth, early nineteenth century. In a practical way, it is important to fit the ideas of liberalism into the reality of the place.

Agrarian America

In 1800 there were fewer than six million *free* people in the United States. More than 90 percent of the population worked on farms. (All of these figures are, at best, approximations. The biggest obvious problem was that slaves did not count as people.) There were few cities. New York was the largest, with more than 50,000 people. About 6 percent of the people lived in cities.

Not only was the population dispersed, but travel and communications were very slow. Travel speed depended on animals, people, or rivers. For a population that gets angry when an airplane is twenty minutes late, the slowness of the times seems difficult to imagine. In 1791, it took Thomas Jefferson nineteen days to go from New York to his home in Virginia.[11] It is a trip of 920 miles. Put differently, college-aged students in a relatively fast car could make the same trip in a hard day.

Communications were equally slow. Letters, newspapers, pamphlets, and gossip were the ways news traveled. Not to belabor the point, but to a society that frets over the few seconds a "slow" computer takes to get E-mail, communications at the time of the Revolution seem just plain primitive.

Those who lived in communities were isolated from other communities, and those who lived on farms were frequently isolated from almost everyone. As we saw, it took people in the South days to travel from one plantation to another.

The society was patriarchal. Men ruled the family and women took care of the home. As people moved west, women became more equal partners with their husbands. The first co-ed public universities were in the West, an acknowledgment of the work that women did. That gets us a little ahead of the story. Thomas Jefferson gives us a sense of how women were thought of during his time:[12]

> Female education should concentrate, he said, on 'ornaments too, and the amusements of life. . . . These, for a female, are dancing, drawing, and music.'

As we shall see, in a society that prized reason what could be more meaningless than learning dancing and drawing and music? To be educated in those things was to be educated to have no role in public life. It was, as we know, the education Rousseau wanted for his Sophie.

[11] Steven Tozier, Paul Violas, and Guy Senese, *School and Society: Historical and Contemporary Perspectives,* Third Edition (Boston: McGraw-Hill, 1998), p. 19.

[12] Howard Zinn, *A People's History of the United States* (New York: Happer & Row, 1980), p. 116.

The average American wife gave birth to eight children.[13] One child in ten died before the age of six months and one in four died before the age of twenty-two. One in five adult women died from childbirth-related causes, and one of every thirty births resulted in the death of the mother. For men who reached the age of twenty-one, the average life expectancy was about seventy years old. For women it was sixty-three.

The family was the primary element of social life. What schooling does these days, the family generally did in those. Culture, and the virtues of society, were taught at home. The almost virgin American location for liberalism was a seemingly endless land with an agrarian and isolated population. The New World could not have been more antifeudal. It was an almost ideal setting for the new liberal philosophy that was being developed in Europe. There was a huge amount of land, rich in resources, to be explored and exploited. One could be free in an environment that was antifeudal and that had no feudal institutions to overcome.[14] The United States was to become liberal, with a vengeance.

Liberalism and Adam Smith

By the early 1700s feudalism was beginning to break down in Europe. The stable class system could survive neither the change in commerce nor ideas. Trade with the Middle East required the development of a different kind of activity. There needed to be the stuff of commerce: money, things to sell, people to make those things, banks, and an attitude that reached beyond the beliefs of the fixed feudal arrangements.

Towns grew around ports of trade. (*Bourg* was the term for the fortress around which cities developed—from that we get *bourgeoisie*, the name for those people engaged in trade; a name for what many in the United States were to become.[15]) A new middle class was developed that did not depend on owning land or luck of birth. Some of these merchants become very wealthy, and with the wealth came power.

Power changed in another way. Merchants imported explosives from China. With explosives came the invention of guns and cannons. A serf with a gun was more than the equal of a feudal soldier who had spent years of hard training in heavy armor to be able to defend the social order. Along with the development of guns and money was the invention of new ideas.

Scientific ideas came first. The notion that the earth traveled around the sun was enough to get Nicolaus Copernicus, a Polish astronomer, in serious trouble with the Catholic Church. In 1530 he completed *De Revolutionibus Orbium Coelestium* and published it in 1543. The idea that the sun was stationary and the earth revolved around it threw everything out of balance. That we were not the center of the universe (and the vast majority of humans believed the earth had been the center of the universe until that moment) was literally heresy. In 1600 Giordano Bruno was excommuni-

---

[13] This material comes from Tozer, op. cit., p. 20.

[14] For a remarkable discussion of this point, see Louis Hartz, *The Liberal Tradition in America* (New York: Harcourt, Brace & World, Inc., 1955).

[15] Henri Pierenne, *A History of Europe* (Garden City, NY: Doubleday) in Tozier, op. cit., p. 22.

cated from the Church and burned at the stake for trying to popularized the Copernican conception of the universe.

Sir Isaac Newton discovered gravity (and published *Philosophiae Naturalis Principia Mathematica* in 1687), and slowly religion lost its control to explain the physical world. Part of the fall of feudalism was because scientific reason provided more powerful and accurate descriptions of the world than religion. The idea that the universe was a huge machine that acted according to physical laws that humans could discover became a powerful force. Faith faltered before science.

Adam Smith was central to the emerging liberal/capitalist thought. He was born in Scotland in 1723. He was a sickly lad who was kidnapped by a band of marauders (known as tinkers in Scotland) who wandered the country and did things like that. Smith's uncle rescued him. It is reported that his mother totally indulged him.

This young man was an excellent student. He won a scholarship to Oxford, where he studied philosophy. It took him five years to find a place to teach. He taught logic for a year and then moral philosophy. In 1759 he published *Theory of Moral Sentiments*, which was a discussion of the ethical standards that bind society together. The book was unpopular with his colleagues. He resigned his position and moved to London.

The reason for the details is to make the point that our base in liberal economics was a moral one. Smith was probably the greatest theorist of capitalism, and his first book was about societal morals. While it was clear that an era of manufacturing, commerce, and social mobility would take the place of feudalism, there needed to be some kind of acceptable way of understanding why the change was good. A major problem, of course, was to somehow replace the God who had been the center of the static, feudal society with something just as powerful for a society that had few rules.

If we can get a clear image of who this early liberal person was, it is possible to understand some of the deepest biases of our society. To know our ideological base is to better know the people we are dealing with in our classroom. While it would be foolish to assume everyone in the United States is a classical liberal, it would be more foolish to ignore what drives this society. A huge majority of our immigrants swim in the ocean of liberalism. Even if people do not accept liberalism, it remains the most powerful thing they must fight.

As we will soon see, reason and rationality are commonly said to be at the heart of our liberal thought. It is argued that they are the soul of our liberalism. That might not be entirely accurate.

Adam Smith published *An Inquiry into the Nature and Causes of the Wealth of Nations* in 1776. It was the first strong statement of economic freedom and the implications of things like a division of labor and self-interest. He discussed markets and international trade and generally gave us a picture of the dynamics of capitalism.

At the most simple level, Smith wrote that in order to make money people had to produce things that others would buy. In a free marketplace, the most popular things, the products that people were willing to spend their money on, would continue to be produced. The other things would disappear. Smith believes this buying and selling, this pattern of production and purchasing, results in social harmony. All of this happens best in an environment of freedom. A good economy was not the result of any conscious control, but the result of free people producing and buying what they wanted. The entire process was given direction "as if by an invisible hand."

Smith also argued that the source of value was neither land nor money but labor. Individuals, and what and how much they could produce, now stood at the center of society. Nothing could be further from feudalism. His vision was of a society in which there was no governmental intervention, and the invisible hand was able to guide an ever more prosperous economy. With people acting in a free market and making the choices of what to produce, and with profits being put back into manufacturing to increase production, there would be an ever increasing prosperity. So, capitalism was a cycle of producing, selling, profits, more producing, more jobs, more selling—and on and on.

What drove all of this was not rationality but—to use the terms of those times—passions or appetites. People wanted things. Smith argued that nature endowed men "with the necessary . . . 'appetites' for the ends of self-preservation and the propagation of the species. Moreover, she implants in man an 'instinctive' sense of what to approve and disapprove and thereby creates the moral norms of society."[16] The key for economic liberalism, then, is not reason. The passions and appetites of free-acting citizens decide the good of society. Economic well-being is the product of each citizen acting in his or her own self-interest.

Reason was important, but in a technical sense and not in a moral sense. For Smith, and early liberal economists, reason was used to understand the most efficient way of getting to the goal set up by passions. Reason, to put it differently, was put to the service of practical ends. Morality was left to individual wants and an invisible hand.

Religion played an important role in the liberal/capitalist mix. Protestantism and capitalism relied on the same traits (discipline, self-reliance, hard work, and the like). The accumulation of wealth was a visual sign on God's elect. The spirit of capitalism and the spirit of Protestantism folded into one another. To quote John Calvin: "Christians are not only a body politic, but they are a mystical and spiritual body of Christ."[17] Religion, at least in the colonies, helped give capitalism a moral base.

Economics has become much more complex than in Smith's day, as our culture is much more complicated than it was in 1776. But we and our teachers and our students are all descendants of Adam Smith. Our public schools and colleges and graduate schools mirror the capitalism Smith projected. Our emphasis on technique is powerful testimony to our belief that larger moral issues will take care of themselves while we try our best to feed our passions and appetites. I understand that this sweeping generalization is not true for everyone. But check enrollments in business schools and law schools against the enrollments in, say, religion departments or moral philosophy. What do engineers believe? Or people in computer science? More importantly, is there an effort being made to teach much more than sophisticated technique to those students?

I would argue that because there is a strongly held belief in some kind of modified invisible hand, we are a nation of people who would like to understand every-

---

[16] Sheldon Wolin, *Politics and Vision* (Boston: Little, Brown, 1960), p. 333.

[17] Quoted in ibid., p. 182.

thing as a technical problem that reason can solve. A surprising amount of our common life depends on our personal need to consume. Much of that is deeply ingrained in our being, and drives much of what our students are about.

Liberalism, Locke, and the Constitution

The spiritual father of the Constitution is John Locke. In 1689 his *Second Treatise on Government*, a strong liberal vision of what he believed politics should become, was published in England. It was written during the time of general rebellion against the tyranny of the monarchy and a move towards parliamentary government. His is the one we have chosen as our liberal voice. There were others who might have been equally important to how we developed ideologically, such as Thomas Hobbes, but we claim Locke as our own.

As a little background, John Locke was a wealthy man.[18] He had investments in both the silk and slave trades, and was heavily invested in the first issue of stocks of the Bank of England. Before the Revolution in America he served as an advisor to the Carolinas. His advice was that they set up a government run by forty wealthy land barons and slave owners. His head might have been in an ideal world of political freedom and equality, but his feet were firmly planted in the realities of his time.

The liberal Locke believed that government should be strong enough to protect people from oppressive institutions (he was talking about who had power and how it was used in feudalism), but not strong enough to interfere in the life of an individual. Government was to promote the general welfare of society and protect the freedom of its citizens. He argued that in the state of nature people were free and equal, but a government was needed to act as a kind of judge and arbiter to make certain those conditions continued to exist.

Education is key to his central ideas. He believed that when a baby enters the world its mind is a *tabula rasa*, a blank slate, a piece of white paper. Locke writes that the baby's mind is "void of all characters, without any ideas." What the baby learned was "through sensation and reflection, ideas come to be scribbled upon the 'white paper' of the mind, forming a circumscribed world from which there was no escape, at least by natural means . . . [the child] could never break out of a world bounded by 'sounds, tastes, smells, visible and tangible qualities.'"[19] The theory cuts in two directions: first, it seriously questions the idea of hereditary social position. If we are all the same at birth it is wholly unreasonable to assume, for example, that the oldest son of the landowning noble would be the obvious, best choice of all the children to inherit all of the property. Second, the assumption made is that since we all begin the same, then those who learn the most and work the hardest should gain the most.

Locke, at least in principle, tells us that if we all begin the same, then we are each responsible for what we make of ourselves. Far from feudalism, in which everyone knew his or her place, Locke and his liberal citizens were now on their own. Instead

---

[18] Zinn, op. cit., pgs. 72–4.

[19] Wolin, op. cit., p. 296.

of a preoccupation with the moral issues of an afterlife, people now focused on economic and social concerns in an immediate way. The liberal citizen turned from an inner life focused on a heavenly reward to one of exploring, and ultimately exploiting, the natural world. We traded salvation for an earthly itch.

The world of Locke looked much like the world of Adam Smith. Sheldon Wolin writes:[20]

> Hence what was truly radical in liberalism was its conception of society as a network of activities carried on by actors who knew no principle of authority. Society represented not only a spontaneous and self-adjusting order, but a condition untroubled by the presence of authority . . . As Bastiat declared, "the end of law is not, rigorously speaking, to cause justice to prevail," but "to prevent injustice from reigning. In fact, it is not justice which has a real existence, but injustice."

The question becomes, in part, what do these new people . . . these liberals . . . believe, and what can education do to help them?

One way to see how we have come to understand liberalism is to review how it is described in a popular education textbook.[21] The authors tell us the following six tenants of liberalism played an important role in shaping our politics and culture.

Faith in Reason. The argument is that to counter the feudal faith in religion and tradition, the classical liberals thought human reason was the "best and most reliable guide in this world." Given the remarkable scientific discoveries of the times, and the political agenda of the liberals, we shouldn't be too surprised at their faith in reason.

The phrase "faith in reason" is an interesting one. By the late 1700s there was, indeed, a religion based on reason. Deism was an attempt to continue to believe in God while acknowledging what science was doing. To put it most simply, God created the universe as a huge, rational machine. Science, then, was a systematic effort to understand God's work. In 1796 Thomas Paine wrote: "The Creator of man is the Creator of science, and it is through that medium that man can see God, as it were, face to face."[22]

There is little doubt that faith in reason is still with us. The promises and gifts of science have been overwhelming, but it is not so clear that they have been satisfying at a deeper level. Stephen Hawking is possibly the most brilliant scientist of our generation. His search has been to find one unified theory that explains the physical workings of the universe. If successful, he would have concluded Paine's quest to "see God, as it were, face to face." But Hawking writes that even if the unified theory is discovered we would still need "to take part in the discussion of the question of why it is that we and the universe exist. If we find the answer to that, it would be the ultimate triumph of human reason—for then we would know the mind of God."[23]

---

[20] Ibid., p. 301.

[21] This comes from Tozer, op.cit. Quotes come from pages 23–26.

[22] Quote in Rippa, op. cit., p. 50.

[23] Stephen Hawking, *A Brief History of Time: From the Big Bang to Black Holes* (New York: Bantam Books, 1988), p. 175.

We need to remember that the liberals' faith in reason was less concerned with the "why" questions than with those questions that dealt with "how to." And, as we saw with Adam Smith, not all liberals believed we could trust our reason to be good and powerful enough to serve as our only guide.

Natural Law. This also stems from the fundamental belief that the universe is a rational machine. If it is true that the universe is like some giant, perfect clock just ticking away, then it follows that there are laws that govern the workings of the clock/universe. These are natural laws. The classical liberals believed in the possibility of discovering the natural laws that govern society.

It was the job of philosophers to find those natural laws that governed humans and would allow our societies to work perfectly. The right system of government was the goal of a civil society.

John Locke believed there was a body of political truths that could be discovered by reason. The problem Locke had was that he thought that for the vast majority, human reason had been corrupted.[24] That, possibly, was one of the reasons he advised the Carolinas to set up a government made up of the slaveholding elite.

To anticipate later discussions, earlier liberals did not believe everyone was capable of being rational. Women, blacks, and American Indians, for example, were counted as less than white males because it was believed they could not be rational. They were given no Constitutional guarantees because of this perceived shortcoming.

Republican Virtue. Classical liberals, according to our popular textbook, "had great faith in the perfectibility of the individual." The belief was that each person, through reason and virtue, had the ability to live a good and moral life. There are a couple of things we need to note.

The emphasis, again, was on the individual. In feudal religion, for example, the primary religious relationship was between the person and the church. With the Protestant Reformation there were no institutions between the individual and God. Morality and virtue were centered on each person. Liberals were at the mercy of their own consciences. Souls adrift in a sea of commerce. A study of the history of religion in the United States is the study of how different denominations and sects played out the theme of each person finding his or her own salvation.

Also implied is a work ethic that would help make individual success possible and a commercial economy viable. In the idea of republican virtue are notions of the "dignity of labor" and the "virtue of diligent application to one's job" that could lead not only to personal success but could also help establish a society in which the liberal/capitalist spirit could thrive.

Finally, there was the accepted belief that the virtues of women and of men were different. What was clear to Rousseau was clear to our liberal founders. Women cultivated those virtues that were appropriate in the private sphere. Women did not need reason to be good in their roles as mothers and wives. Men were simply to run the

---

[24] See Wolin, op. cit., p. 335, for the argument.

world. They not only engaged in the public sphere, but because society was a patriarchy they also had the final say at home. Classical liberals thought men were capable of reason and women were not.

Progress.   Liberals believed in progress. Instead of putting all their faith in the idea that there would be a better life after death, liberals believed that there could be a never-ending improvement of life here on earth. It is important to note that this liberal belief was not taught to the slaves on Southern Plantations. An effort was made to convert slaves to Christianity and preach that eternal salvation would be their greatest reward.

We know and live the progress that has been the result, in part, of our liberal heritage. Human reason could discover both the natural laws and natural rights for individuals. The right social arrangements would be the perfect stage for the science and commerce that would provide endless progress. Citizens needed to be free so that reason—and the personal appetites that prove market forces—could continue unimpeded.

Thomas Jefferson had a deep belief that progress was inevitable if the central government was not strong enough to interfere with the free workings of society, and if the educational system was strong enough to develop reason and virtue in its citizens. Education was necessary to make classical liberalism work. Lockes' liberal children, born knowing nothing, needed education to imprint the tools of the emerging culture on those blank minds. As we shall see, there was a great deal of debate among the founders about just what to do with education in the new United States.

Nationalism.   The monarchy during feudal times was not always a strong, unifying force. Feudal lords were masters of their own domains and resisted the idea of national governments being too powerful. In Europe the liberals believed that a central government must be stronger than the individual domains within the country. Put differently, the new national government had to be more powerful than the remnants of feudalism. The end of feudalism marked the rise of the nation-state. Nationalism would become the driving force in Europe.

As we have seen, people in the colonies were strong believers in local power. After the revolution and before the Constitution there was a short experiment with the Articles of Confederation. In the Articles there was a very weak central government that had virtually no control over matters of importance. The constitutional convention was the result of problems that stemmed, essentially, from there being no final source of authority or power to deal with conflicts between the colonies.

Even with a genuine fear of a strong national government there was a strong feeling of nationalism. Patrick Henry believed, even before we fought the Revolution, that "the distinction between Virginians . . . and New Englanders are no more. All America is thrown into one mass. I am not a Virginian, but an American." Certainly nationalism is part of our liberal tradition, but so too is a certain distrust of a strong central power as well as an attraction to regionalism and localism. This tension has been played out in our educational system since the beginning of our country.

Freedom.   The final tenant of classical liberalism is freedom. This is, in many ways, the tenant that ties the important parts of liberalism together. There are four basic freedoms: intellectual, political, civil, and economic. Without these, liberalism couldn't work. Reason, progress, and the others rest on the assumption that people will be able to have the freedom to do these things. (Much of the history of the United States can be viewed as the struggle to make certain that more than just white males have these rights. Schools have played a key role in the struggle.)

An interesting element of these freedoms is that they are what the philosopher Isaiah Berlin calls "negative freedom." The main idea is that individuals must not be kept from doing things, they should not be restrained or interfered with by the government. The economy can take care of itself, and individuals should be able to pursue the ideas they want. As citizens, we are free to participate in making laws that we must live by (political freedom) and live as we please (civic freedom).

It is easy to relate to these freedoms. Most of us, most of the time, do not like to be told what to do. When threatened we retreat to the Bill of Rights that offers protection not only from the government but also from our neighbors. It is those liberal sensitivities we grew up in that makes us, almost instinctively, reject the censorship of "The Republic" . . . even though we routinely censor "socially unacceptable" practices.

It is equally easy to sense that it would be a disaster if, indeed, we really did live in a totally unregulated environment. We know that without governmental intervention our economy would be dominated (even more than it is) by huge, monopolistic companies. We know that there would be no such thing as minimum wage, child labor laws, and the like. Without some kind of "interference," who knows what would be available in terms of everything from guns to selling human beings? We continually find reasons, and they are generally good ones, for governmental regulation and action.

This, then, is the mainstream view of our liberal heritage. Most would agree that these are freedoms worth fighting for. But there is more to liberalism than these six tenants . . . and even these tenants are not unmixed virtues.

A Closer Look at Liberalism

There are tensions that run through our liberalism that we need to explore in order to get a better understanding of education in the United States. To take the work of John Locke as gospel seems, at first glance, like a good idea. His liberalism appears to be reasonable, nonthreatening and well suited for a country that, in 1776, had few people, a seemingly limitless amount of land, and remarkable natural resources. It can be argued that the six tenants of classic liberalism—faith in reason, natural law, republican virtue, progress, nationalism, and freedom—form the very dynamic that drove the development of the United States.

It is easy to realize that something is wrong. If Locke's ideas were so ideal and his liberalism was without flaws, then why do things seem out of control? Too many of our children are unhappy; indeed, are suicidal—or homicidal. The economy, even when very good, favors those who already have money; when the economy is bad, it seems those in the lower socioeconomic class are hardest hit. The distribution of wealth is, in its way, as uneven now as it was in feudal Europe. Our healthcare system is the best in the world, but it is available to only a small percentage of our population. We are forever changing what we do in school, while the bottom line remains the same: children of parents with money are generally better educated than children of parents without money. (To put a sharper edge to that point, we read that more affluent school districts are generally able to attract teachers with better qualifications because they offer higher salaries. Better teachers, we have learned, mean better education.)[25]

It sounds foolish to argue that somehow reason or progress or freedom is bad. I don't want to do that . . . exactly. What I would like to do is take a closer look at what we are asked to accept. All of us—students and teachers alike—swim in the ideological waters of liberalism, and if there are flaws, we need to know what they are. It would seem impossible to have an intelligent discussion of possible educational changes without having some sense of underlying ideological weaknesses.

For our purposes, a full critique of liberalism is both inappropriate and unnecessary. But, by looking more closely at the underlying biases of John Locke, and possible problems with a belief in reason, we should have a more clear idea of our liberalism.

We need to reacquaint ourselves with how Locke understood humans. He, like many liberal thinkers such as Thomas Hobbes and Adam Smith, believed people were driven by strong passions. Locke wrote of "the lawless exorbitancy of unconfined man" and remarked that "passion' and 'interest' had, in the state of nature, caused man to misapply the laws of nature; civil society, from this point of view, formed the remedy to man's passions."[26] While Thomas Hobbes had written that, in the state of nature, life was nasty, brutish, and short, Locke's approach was milder. His state of nature was full of passion-filled, self-interested people who needed some kind of governmental structure that would judge disputes when they arose. Hobbes thought of the state of nature as a state of constant war, and there needed to be a government strong enough to protect us from each other. That vision was not accepted in the United States.

And what of these citizens of the new liberal state? They were, we read, "impelled towards civil society because they are anxiety-ridden, 'uncertain' about their rights, 'full of fears.'"[27] If John Locke is our spiritual ideological father, then it is no surprise that to this day we are never quite certain of our rights, and full of fears about what might happen. Ours is not a pacific state of nature in which we go about our business in a carefree way; ours is a society in which insecurity is second nature. As we shall soon see, that insecurity is a defining feature of our liberalism.

Earlier, we read how the liberal economist Adam Smith glorified both our passion and self-interest. He wrote that capitalism worked best when all of us acted on our appetites.[28] The invisible hand would coordinate our activity and the result would

---

[25] See Ronald Ferguson, "Paying for Public Education: New Evidence on How and Why Money Matters," (*Harvard Journal of Legislation*, 28, 1991), pgs. 465–497.

[26] Wolin, op. cit., p. 332.

[27] Ibid., p. 307.

[28] Ricka Schwartz believes capitalism demands we act on our worst instincts in order to work.

be a continually growing prosperity. What is missing from this calculation is one of the basic building blocks of liberalism—reason.

The classic liberal economists did believe in reason, but thought it was useful only to find the most efficient ways to do things. In the realm of liberal politics, Locke too believed in reason but was not at all certain many people were capable of it. Our liberalism, then, is basically motivated by passions and appetites and all the while worshiping reason. We need to find the best way to live together in order to insure the freedom of each individual to act.

Calvinism, and Protestantism in general, provide a spiritual link between society, capitalism, and the individual. Success in the public realm was seen as a reflection of God's will. Wealth was a visual sign of being one of the elect. The traits of religious and secular life were much the same: being a hard-working, conservative, moral, individual. Success in the one was mirrored by success in the other.

According to Locke, we come into the world knowing nothing. We are wholly dependent on what we sense and what we are told. One obvious lesson is that schooling is important in order to allow each of us to learn the skills it takes to live in a liberal society. That seems difficult to deny. But there is a more basic question: What does it mean to be born with a mind that most closely resembles a white piece of paper? What does it mean that all we will ever know comes from sensation and reflection? What does it mean that we can never break out of a world "bounded by 'sounds, tastes, smells, visible and tangible qualities.'"?[29]

What this means, in part, is that our liberal citizen is thrown out into the world and is hopelessly dependent upon it. Material reality defines liberal reality. We become the sum of our external acts. Classical liberalism failed to replace the internal life of feudalism, and our current life is certainly no different. The person who has the most toys when he or she dies is not a joke but is literally the moral equation of liberalism.

As a nation we are the huge combination of individual agents who are at the mercy of a powerful and impersonal force. Each citizen is simply the sum of his or her interests. It is no mistake that interest groups form the core of our understanding of politics in the United States.[30] Much of what we have in common, as our liberalism has evolved, are our interests. Our morals have so folded into our interests that it is impossible to tell one from the other. Any inner life has either been factored out of the human being, or has been taken over exclusively by religion.

The roles of will and reason are put to the service of interests. Reason allows us to be more efficient in our personal quests, even if it means putting off the question in order to defer gratification for a more satisfying prize.

With no moral compass other than personal interest, each of us is at the will of the many. As liberals, we have agreed that there should be limits on what the government can do, and we know the power of religion is wholly dependent upon personal choice. In place of those two institutions there is the common will, the will of society.

[29] Ibid., p. 296.

[30] For a clear statement on pluralism, see almost any work by Robert Dahl.

This power of society is remarkable in at least two ways. First, it is an impersonal power; it is directed towards everyone indifferently. We all feel its sting. While it affects us all, it is also the sum of the power of all of us. No one is in charge.

Second, this power can be overwhelming. It is always stronger than any single individual, and is generally stronger than most groups. While it is possible to oust a government, or a whole governmental system, and certainly it is possible to simply stop believing in a religion, there is no obvious target when power lies in each of us. You can't vote everyone out of office, or simply stop attending meetings, or find even a million people to shoot in order to make things different. If everyone is a target, then no one is a target. We are at the mercy of an indifferent and impersonal mass.

The role of education in a liberal society then becomes much clearer. These three things need to be taught to the children of a liberal state. First, the individual needs to "adjust his tastes, actions, and style of life to a social denominator." More simply, the citizen must learn to conform to the social will. Second, the individual needs to understand that "a happy and successful life . . . can be attained only by observing society's standards . . ." The values of society have to be the values of the individual. Third, the citizen needs to do more than simply accept social norms. These norms "should be internalized and, as such, operate as the individual's conscience."[31] With this, the dynamic is complete. Each individual conscience is, in reality, social rather than personal.

There are no more moral questions in this kind of society, only technical ones. If we accept the social will as our own then all we need to do is use our reason to work out what is best for us. If we are agreed that the sum of our passions and interests results in an unerring public good, then the only remaining job is to make certain we are efficient in how we look after, promote, and protect those interests.

The role of education, given the liberal dynamic, is to teach each child to internalize social norms and employ reason to pursue his or her interests. We teach the techniques of living a liberal life because there is not much more to teach. The framers of the Constitution, taking their cues from the classic liberals, provided us with our secular faith. A major role of education has been to make certain we keep that faith and help refine it for each new generation.

While the above can easily be read as a dismissal of capitalism and liberalism, that is not what it is intended to be. I do not believe that every person simply acts on his or her passions and appetites, nor do I think that every schoolteacher is a blind ideological slave to liberalism. There are parts of our liberal society that, personally, I think are wonderful. Many of our beliefs, and this is certainly only my opinion, represent a kind of world in which I am most comfortable.

The point of critiquing liberalism is to help us better understand what we have done, are doing, and what might be done with education. Liberalism is the ideological water in which we swim. We need to know how our students will react, and why. Equally important, we need to know our own biases. We need to understand those cultural norms we accept and those with which we are uncomfortable. If we do not

---

[31] The points are made in Wolin, op. cit., p. 342, in a little different context.

know our students, we make the difficult job of teaching much more difficult; without knowing ourselves, we make the job impossible.

It is silly to accept, in an uncritical way, our liberal/capitalist/constitutional foundation. If education is more than simply swallowing the norms of society so that things work well, if we accept a more traditional goal of knowing ourselves then it is necessary to know not only the strengths of our liberal society, but its built-in biases.

Reason

Our faith in reason and rationality is not nearly as strong as the optimism of the enlightenment. Even science is skeptical about what we are able to know and predict. Far from expecting to find the "truth," modern science now searches for those things that are statistically most likely to happen. Natural laws have given way to statistical probabilities.

This section is not a contemporary critique of reason, but an example of the power of reason during the decades surrounding the writing of the Constitution. It is about Mary Wollstonecraft, her faith in the Enlightenment version of reason ("The being cannot be termed rational, or virtuous, who obeys any authority but that of reason"), and her belief that women should be understood and treated as human beings.[32]

In 1792 Wollstonecraft published *A Vindication of the Rights of Women*, just thirty years after Rousseau published *Emile*. Wollstonecraft's world was dominated by the idea that women were to be given an education that would allow them to be good wives, mothers, and keepers of the house. As we have seen, that idea was good enough for Rousseau's Sophie and Jefferson's daughters. For Wollstonecraft, the character of Sophie "appears to me grossly unnatural." This is how she understood the role of women in her time:[33]

> Confined then in cages like the feathered race, they have nothing to do but to plume themselves, and stalk with mock majesty from perch to perch. It is true they are provided with food and raiment, for which they neither toil nor spin; but health, liberty, and virtue are given in exchange.

Wollstonecraft wanted more and better for women. In *A Vindication*, Wollstonecraft argues three things: 1) that women can be rational and are not slaves to their passions, 2) if women were given the same rights as men, they would be able to do their domestic duties more efficiently and better, and 3) if women were brought up and educated to develop their ability to reason independently, then they would clearly deserve the same political rights as men.

One wonders how many women would want what Wollstonecraft wishes. Do women—does anyone?—want to be rational more than anything? And, if rationality anchors our actions, would women argue that by being rational they would be better

[32] This discussion is taken from Jane Roland Martin, *Reclaiming a Conversation: The Ideal of the Educated Woman* (New Haven: Yale University Press, 1985), p. 73.

[33] Ibid., p. 72.

at their household chores? While it was certainly not radical for Wollstonecraft to agree with Rousseau about the traditional role for women, what was radical was her belief that women were capable of reason and should have political rights.

Wollstonecraft argues that women are either human beings or brutes. If they are human beings, then they are capable of rational thought. By posing the question like this, she puts her opponents in the awkward position of arguing that women were not human. As a person, an intellectual, of her time she believed that rationality was the defining characteristic of being human, so if women are human then they are capable of being rational. She goes on to argue that because of socialization and training women are not allowed to develop their abilities to reason.

Formal education needs to be developed so that women can escape the pressures that confine them "in cages like the feathered race." Her argument that women are human and therefore capable of reason, and that socialization has held that development back, makes her first point in a logical and interesting way.

Her second point is that rationality will make women better at their job, which is being a wife and mother. In doing so Wollstonecraft redefines the wife-mother role. She argues that in order to be a good mother, a woman must be an intelligent, thoughtful, strong and independent person. Martin writes:[34]

> Good mothers, Wollstonecraft insists, will often be obliged 'to act contrary to the present impulse of tenderness or compassion,' . . . because they must exemplify order, 'the soul of virtue,' and . . . because to be useful they must have a plan of conduct to be resolute enough to persevere in carrying it out.

This is a description, if you will, of a rational person who has thought out what it means to raise children and is emotionally strong enough to never get off-task. It is the faith that rationality is the highest good and will somehow provide the greatest emotional reward. Wollstonecraft carries that rationality into the marriage itself. Again, Martin:[35]

> Love, which she [Wollstonecraft] associates with instability, disappears quickly in a marriage. . . . "To seek for a secret that would render it constant, would be as wild a search as for the philosopher's stone, or the grand panacea." The master and mistress of a family "ought not to continue to love each other with passion," for if love does not subside into friendship it will be succeeded by indifference.

How much more clear can a person be about the power of rationality? The point she wants to make is that a rational woman will do much better at her domestic tasks than a woman driven by emotions and appetites. She will be able to conceptualize and implement a plan to raise the children and form a solid friendship with her husband. Wollstonecraft has taken the traits of citizenship for a republic—rationality and personal autonomy—and made them the attributes of good mothers and wives.

One hardly knows what to say.

[34] Ibid., p. 78.

[35] Ibid., p. 79.

Finally, there is the issue of education. Wollstonecraft needs her new woman to be able to use her reason in order to understand natural law and be able to distinguish right from wrong. She wrote that the best education "is such an exercise of the understanding as is best calculated to strengthen the body and form the heart. Or, in other words, to enable the individual to attain such habits of virtue as will render it independent. In fact, it is a farce to call any being virtuous whose virtues do not result from the exercise of reason. This was Rousseau's opinion respecting men; I extend it to women."[36]

Wollstonecraft believed that boys and girls should be educated together, and in public schools. Both of these are major departures from norms of her eighteenth-century English context. Private schools were more deeply ingrained in English tradition than they were in the United States.

In the early years, the children were to learn reading, writing, arithmetic, natural history and philosophy, history, politics, and the like. Elementary education would provide a firm, liberal knowledge base. (A liberal education should not be confused with our discussion of liberalism. In the preceding chapter, the idea of what a well-educated person should know is, roughly, the idea of a liberal education. The idea of individualism, for example, would be one of the lessons of liberalism.)

Wollstonecraft also believed that during those years there should be exercise and play for the kids. Girls and boys needed physical activity, and physical activity was an important part of education. She believed in a healthy body for a well-educated person in the Age of Enlightenment.

Wollstonecraft understood that the role of education was to help people carry out their functions in society. She accepted the traditional role for women, that of wife/mother, but she also argued that the second role should be that of citizen. By arguing that women were capable of rational thought, she made the case for an education in which women would be both better mother/wives and good citizens.

While Wollstonecraft helps us see how seriously the Enlightenment liberals believed in rationality, she unwittingly exposes some of the genuine problems with that belief. While her use of rationality allows her to argue for a kind of equality for women, it also takes away the emotion and affection that certainly makes life worth living. Rousseau took emotion away from Emile, and thirty years later Wollstonecraft took it away from women. Each is a genuine measure of how strong the Enlightenment belief in reason really was.

Of course the belief never quite disappeared. B. F. Skinner invented a twentieth-century, rational way to raise children. He believed that because all behavior was conditioned, the best way to raise children was in a completely controlled environment. His invention of the Skinner Box allowed the child to develop in a safe, controlled, and loveless environment. It was a rational approach that was perfectly senseless.

[36] Found in *A Vindication*, p. 21; quoted by Martin, ibid., p. 81.

Wollstonecraft was as original and enlightened a thinker as Thomas Jefferson.[37] They each believed natural laws could be found that would make the world a much better place in which to live. They were optimistic about the potential of any society that was free and open. Importantly, education played a central role in the changes that needed to take place. It was clear to Wollstonecraft that if women were given a chance, educationally, they would become much better in their social roles. It is with irony that we can both admire her ideas while discounting—in important ways—the rationality that was at the center of her beliefs.

Founding Debates

In this section we will return to the debates about education at the time of the Constitution. The short history is this: Neither the writers of the Articles of Confederation nor the Constitution believed that education was a task that should be undertaken by the central government. Education was considered a state and local matter then, as it is now.

Education slowed down during the Revolution. During the British occupation of New York they shut down the schools, and, as we saw, the schools in Massachusetts had financial problems. Many rural schools simply closed during that time. Illiteracy increased.

There were intellectual tensions. Because so many of the schools were tied to British thought, it became important for the former colonies to somehow stake out their own intellectual territory. The issues that emerged were distinctly political and revolved around the freedoms that were to characterize the newly independent colonies.

There was debate at the Constitutional Convention about the role the federal government should take in education. Two delegates to the convention, James Madison and Charles Pinkney, wanted the Constitution to establish a national university. Even after the idea was rejected, many powerful people supported it. Thomas Jefferson, John Jay, and John Quincy Adams all thought there should be a national university. George Washington failed in his efforts to get Congress to make a law mandating a national university. Indeed, in his farewell address, Washington argued that a strong educational system was needed for the welfare of the nation. When he died he left part of his estate for the national university that was never established.

In 1795 the American Philosophical Society offered a prize for the best essay on the subject of a national system of education.[38] The essays were rooted in the idea that a public system of education was necessary for a free republic. A liberal society needed an educated citizenry.

Many colonial heavyweights submitted essays to the Philosophical Society (Noah Webster, Samuel Smith, Benjamin Rush, Samuel Knox), which split the prize

---

[37] To understate, Wollstonecraft was not well accepted. In 1946 the writers of a psychoanalytical text wrote: ". . . Mary Wollstonecraft was an extreme neurotic of a compulsive type there can be no doubt. Out of her illness arose the ideology of feminism, which was to express the feeling of so many women in years to come." See Martin, ibid., p. 70.

[38] This discussion is taken from John Pulliam, *History of Education in America*, 5th ed. (New York: Merrill, 1991), p. 48.

between Rush and Knox. The essays represent the collective feelings of the elite that some kind of national system of education might be useful as the United States began to invent itself. The Congress did not agree, and our education remained in the hands of states and local communities.

That does not mean nothing was done to encourage education. Even before the Constitution was drafted in 1787, there was an effort to help education under the Articles of Confederation. The Ordinance of 1785 (the Northwest Ordinance) was legislation concerning the territory west of the Alleghenies. It called for townships to be divided into sections, and the sixteenth section (one square mile) was to be used to support schools in that township. Two years later a second ordinance allowed each state to set aside two sections for the support of a university. The second ordinance also stated that education should always be used for the benefit of human happiness and good government.

With the precedent set, most new states that were added to the union were given federal land for educational purposes. And, while there was never to be a national university, in 1802 West Point was created as the first American educational institution to train engineers.

Each state was free to do as it liked with education. In Pennsylvania, which would serve as a model for many states, the Constitution required the state to take care of the salaries of the public school teachers. New York set aside public land for schools, and added other funding, while Massachusetts legalized its traditional local school districts. In 1789 it admitted girls to its district schools.

The most well-known advocate, and activist, of education was Thomas Jefferson. Jefferson simply dominates much of who we were and what we have become as a nation. Bright and well-educated and seemingly always interested in learning more and different things, Jefferson was a classical liberal who was able to make certain those ideals were incorporated into the Constitution and the Bill of Rights.

He believed deeply in reason and a republican form of government as well as science and self-government. Like so many of the intellectual elite of his time, he believed that science and reason would, eventually, solve both physical and human problems. His was a deist view. Jefferson thought that city life was corrupt and always favored villages and rural life. He believed in the freedom of the press and religion. Religion, though, had no place in government. The separation of church and state was necessary.

He wrote remarkable prose. While the language of the Bill of Rights and the Constitution seems to be inclusive (all men are created equal), when written they were not meant to include everyone. Jefferson had clear ideas about just how equal people were. Even white males, the group he trusted and admired most, were not equal. He thought there was a natural aristocracy who would naturally govern. The most that could be hoped for with the common man was that he would be able to choose the right leaders. We should be grateful that Jefferson's words did not match his actions. As a nation we have been able to grow into his words—words we can assume he did not believe.

Jefferson believed, for example, that whites and American Indians could intermarry—but only after the later had become more civilized. They needed to learn the white culture. Whites, he believed, were simply culturally superior. He believed that women were incapable of reason. They were suited to be wives and mothers and run the household. A woman was to please her husband. As we saw earlier, that also meant women and men should be educated differently. Girls could go to elementary school, but no further. Learning to dance was not the classical training for citizenship.

Blacks were at the bottom of Jefferson's hierarchy. He believed they were incapable of reason, so whites and blacks could never intermarry. For Jefferson, blacks were too ruled by their passions and appetites. While he proposed legislation that would allow slave owners to free their slaves, he had slaves all his life. Is irony too tame a word for the family gathering held in the mid-1990s for his descendents? From all accounts it was a wonderful get-together; a gathering of people who were the result of the union between a truly great president and a particular black slave with whom he had a long relationship.

Do with that what you like. Certainly given the context, Jefferson was very much ahead of his times. His ideas were radical and provided a framework within which a great deal of freedom could develop. For our purposes, what is important is that Jefferson was concerned with education. We know the basic dynamic: For self-rule, the population needed to be educated well enough to make reasonable choices. We also know that the demands of the emerging economy required certain skills that needed to be learned. Capitalism required schooling. What Jefferson did was work on the details in order to actualize the dynamic.

In 1779 Jefferson proposed his Bill for the More General Diffusion of Knowledge to the legislature of Virginia. The bill called for state-supported elementary education that would be free for the first three years. It was for white boys and girls. They would be taught reading, writing, and arithmetic. There would be twenty grammar schools for a few, talented, poor students. (He would later write: "twenty of the best geniuses will be *raked from the rubbish* annually, and be instructed, at public expense, so far as the grammar schools go."[39]) It would be free for these students, these white boys, for up to six years.

The plan was elaborate. It called for dividing the states into districts. These districts would be both a unit of local government as well as the body that established the elementary schools. There was to be a supervisor over approximately ten schools, who would be appointed by the district. This supervisor would have control over these schools in areas that included hiring and firing of teachers, examinations, and curriculum.

Looked at with the standards of today, it is easy to be horrified. Blacks were ignored, girls were not given the same opportunities as boys, and attendance was not mandatory. There was the added theme that it was aristocratic: "The ultimate result of the whole scheme of education would be the teaching of all children [a good example of language hiding what he meant] of the state reading, writing, and common arithmetic; turning out ten annually of superior genius . . ."[40] Given our standards, the plan

---

[39] Thomas Jefferson, *Notes from the State of Virginia*, in Rippa, op. cit., p. 55. Emphasis added.

[40] Ibid., p. 56.

looks racist, sexist, and elitist. Those ten of "superior genius" would be the people who ran the government or who would be the scientists looking for natural laws.

In Jefferson's context it is a forward thinking, liberal plan for education. The actual citizens of the state were to be given enough education to be both involved with the economy and make reasonable voting choices. The very bright, even if they are poor, were "raked from the rubbish" and given a good education in order to make significant contributions to society. It was very progressive for its time.

It was also defeated by the state legislature of Virginia. They were simply not ready to accept anything that even approached universal education.

Later, Jefferson proposed and established the University of Virginia. In addition to being physically beautiful, it was an accurate reflection of much of his beliefs. During that time the ideal college education was the traditional Harvard model that emphasized study of Latin, Greek, and the classics. A student had little choice of what to take. It was a liberal arts education, rigorously enforced.

Jefferson not only believed that the student should have choices, he believed that the purpose of a college education was much more practical. In the Rockfish Gap Report he wrote in 1818, Jefferson summarized the goals of a college education.[41] Higher education should develop:

> Understanding of science and math to promote the general health, security, and comfort Political leaders
> Knowledge leading to political freedom
> Understandings to improve the economy
> Reason, morals, virtue and order
> Habits of reflection and correct actions in students that render them examples of virtue to others and bring happiness to themselves.

The list makes perfect sense. Harvard was established to educate an elite clergy for the British colonies in the New World. The liberal Jefferson was far more interested in educating a citizen who understood political and economic freedom and the basics of self-rule. In Jefferson's estimation, the University of Virginia would produce an elite just as Harvard did, but his graduates would be different. They would further freedom, ensure a kind of democracy, offer opportunities for the brightest to advance, and create a world in which it was possible to discover its natural laws.

The purpose of the University of Virginia was to produce a liberal citizen. It was a practical exercise in helping the natural aristocracy to emerge.

If you look carefully, an interesting pattern emerges.[42] Jefferson had a deep understanding of the relationship of education and the state. In order for his natural aristocracy to rise, there needed to be public education that was free to even the poor children. For a republican form of government to work, those who would run it

---

[41] The following list is from Roy Honeywell, *The Educational Work Of Thomas Jefferson* (Cambridge, MA.: Harvard University Press, 1931), found in Tozier, op. cit., p. 33.

[42] Ibid., p. 35.

needed to be well-grounded in the importance of freedom and self-rule. For Jefferson, education was the only way in which the right people could get to the right places.

The most obvious other example of someone who understood the ties between education and the state was Plato. His was a more thorough statement of the process of having the natural aristocracy rule, and he certainly was not interested in a republican form of government, but the *Republic* is the model of how education feeds the needs of the state. While Jefferson professed to dislike the *Republic*, in the end it was the actual form of the *Republic* that dominated his ideas.

Other Schools

Not all schools were public, and not all states and local communities supported education.

Monitorial schools developed in some areas.[43] The idea for these schools originated in England through the work of Andrew Bell and Joseph Lancaster. The appeal was that they provided inexpensive education.

The brightest students in these schools were selected as monitors. They were instructed by the Master and in turn taught the lessons they had learned to small groups of students. The monitors generally taught simple lessons that the students memorized. It was inexpensive, as one Master could "teach" hundreds of students.

Monitorial schools first appeared in New York City in 1806. The idea spread fairly rapidly; indeed, Joseph Lancaster came to the United States in 1818 and spent the next twelve years promoting this kind of education.

Sunday Schools were another educational plan that was originated in England and used in the United States. Robert Raikes of Gloucester was its most powerful and well-known advocate. The purpose of the schools, for Raikes, was to rescue the children of English factory workers from terrible poverty and living conditions.

These children worked in factories all week, and Sunday was their only free day. If there was no schooling on Sundays, then there would be no schooling for these children. Several religious groups supported the plan, and provided both money and teachers for Sunday Schools. These schools provided a kind of rudimentary education to the working-class children of England.

A Sunday School Society was formed in Philadelphia in 1791. The concept spread to most of the major cities in a relatively short time. These Sunday Schools were for the poor, but unlike England not merely for the factory or mill workers. The students were in school from six to ten in the morning, and from two to six in the afternoon. The time between ten and two was for worship.

Sunday Schools present us with a familiar dilemma: while it was important to provide something for poor children, not much could be learned in eight hours of instruction one day a week. Generally, these kids were taught to read and were given the most minimal education. Should one think that some education is better than none, or simply be outraged at the unfairness of it all?

Free School Societies were organized in various states to promote and develop Sunday schools, monitorial schools, and free public schools. These societies tried to

---

[43] This discussion comes from Pulliam, op. cit., p. 52.

provide schooling for girls and/or poor children. But the assumption of the times was that if the parents could afford it they would send their children to private schools. Public schools and free schools were considered charity institutions and carried the stigma of poverty. They were not intended to educate the next generation of the natural aristocracy.

In early America, efforts were made to educate blacks. The clergy, abolitionist societies, and some Northern towns provided educational opportunities for blacks. By the end of the first quarter of the nineteenth century, things changed. Slave owners in the south believed that education was the cause of the increasing number of insurrections. As a result, the slave states passed laws restricting travel by blacks; there were also laws that prohibited all education of blacks. The laws even denied parents the right to educate their children.

Education of blacks did take place during those times. There were secret schools and informal instruction was carried on in families and in communities. The efforts of the slave owners and their state government to deny literacy to blacks was undermined by untold numbers of individuals who believed in the power of education.

There were two major trends in schooling by the end of the eighteenth century. The first was the idea that religion should be taken out of the school. That was the result of the decline of the Puritan influence, the rise of liberalism in which belief rested more in a rational universe than an institutional god, and the development of capitalism for which people needed practical skills.

The second trend was that education should reflect the political values of liberalism: individualism, self-reliance, self-government, and capitalism. There was an underlying optimism in freedom and economic opportunity that was transmitted to students. The idea was that with a combination of basic educational skills, hard work, and the right attitude an individual could be successful. Although the development of public schools was sometimes slow, most states were anxious to build universities in order to make certain the children of the elite would be prepared to take over power when it was their turn.

One of the great educational figures of those times was Noah Webster. He was born in 1758 and died in 1843. He was a strong advocate of free schools, the separation of church and state, and education for girls. Like most of the powerful people of the times, his were Enlightenment ideas. Noah Webster was a liberal who believed that schools should be the centers of patriotic thinking. He had great faith in the virtues of working hard and being thrifty. His books were about the value of honest work and avoidance of poverty. He believed that the first word a baby should learn was "Washington."

Webster was known as the "Schoolmaster to America" because of his *Elementary Spelling Book* textbook, which was published in 1783. Two books followed, one on grammar and the other a reader. The "blue-backed speller" (called that because of the color of its binding) was by far the most successful text in the history of the United States. Over a sixty-year period it sold almost 20 million copies. While other texts sold more (the McGuffy *Reader*, for example, sold 122 million copies) it was Webster's book that set the direction of our early education.

Along with the push for an educational system that accepted more people, there were also changes in what was being taught. We have seen that liberal values were emphasized, as well as those skills that were necessary for the emerging capitalist economy. There were also new texts in geography, history, mathematics, and geography that helped bring a more current sense of the world to the students.

But we should not forget that school was much the same as it had been in the colonies. Teaching was about memorizing and helping to discipline the mind of the student. The teaching methods were "traditional" and the punishment was corporal. It would be many generations before education would become more enlightened.

SUMMARY

From the Puritans' insistence that their children be able to read, education in America has been important. By the time of the American Revolution we saw that the reasons for education had changed. Reading was taught less so that each child could read the Bible and eventually have a personal relationship with God, and more in order for the future citizen to become a good liberal/capitalist adult.

The optimism of the Enlightenment, the belief in progress and self-rule, and the emphasis on individualism rested on the notion that people needed to be educated. Jefferson's natural aristocracy had to be well-educated to discover natural laws and, equally important, everyday citizens had to be well-educated enough to not only select the right leaders but be able to carry out the duties required by commerce.

There was the coincidence of the Puritan belief that schooling should be controlled locally, and the liberal distrust of too much central control. From the beginning, the power to create (and finance) education would belong to local and state governments. While the arrangements were different in the slave-owning South, there was never much doubt about how our education would develop.

It is clear that the freedom offered in a liberal state is remarkable. Our liberalism offers a combination of progress and freedom that has produced unimaginable wealth. Ours is a history of having increasing freedom for more people, and education has helped do that. It was also clear that there is an underlying insecurity and vulnerability in liberalism. There is an ongoing danger of the immense power of the will of the majority. Individualism can too easily turn into isolation and helplessness. There is no ready cure for that in our liberal society.

From colonial America to 1800, education was imprinted on our culture. From "dame" schools to apprenticeships to Harvard, there was a never-ending need for more and different kinds of education. And we know that when we discuss those times, we do so with the understanding that education did not include black, women, or the poor. While there were some exceptions, the rule was that education was only for white boys—and not even all of them. Yet, there were ways in which we were in the forefront of education, and the words of the Founding Fathers provided room for us to change.

Much of our history is playing out the themes that were in place by 1800. Certainly there have been huge changes, but many of them rest firmly on old issues.

There is one last underlying tension that has formed an important strand of this chapter. The tension revolves around historical imagination and how we can get perspective on what took place. We are children of the speed, change, and chaos of our time. What seemed unimaginable to a Jefferson or Locke has been the norm for all of our lives. Our reality is different than the reality of our parents, and each generation views events in its own, particular way.

When it was clear that the automobile was here to stay, the president of Mercedes predicted that, because of the possible number of chauffeurs, there would never be more than a million cars in all of Europe. It was nothing more than a common-sense estimate rooted firmly in the social reality of the time. The question is this: What do you believe is the single biggest blind spot of your generation? What do you think everyone takes for granted that will change and make life different for everyone? For example, would you have ever guessed what would happen to the World Trade Center? Before 9/11, would you have imagined that terrorists would make war on United States soil?

What, to put it a little differently, would you bet money on about the future that—in your wildest dreams—you believe will never change?

If you can honestly do this exercise, then you will begin to have a sense of how surprised people in 1700 or 1800 would be if they were alive today. It will also allow you to understand in a more sensitive way what it might have been like to live during those times.

THINK ABOUT

1. One of the tensions of liberalism revolves around individualism. We are taught that we can define ourselves and are responsible for our successes and failures. Yet, we can also feel isolated in our mass society. Do we, in the end, define ourselves— or are we defined by those around us?

2. Can you imagine losing electrical power for five years?

3. If you decide to become a teacher, will you be comfortable with knowing that your most lasting lessons might be those of liberalism, and not the subjects you teach?

CHAPTER THREE

COMMON SCHOOLS TO CONSERVATIVE REACTION

The Nineteenth Century to 1983

I had learned many English words and could recite part of the Ten Commandments. I knew how to sleep on a bed, pray to Jesus, comb my hair, eat with a knife and fork, and use a toilet . . . I had also learned that a person thinks with his head instead of his heart.

—Sun Chief

It's awful being a child, always at the mercy of other people.

—Donna Tartt

Society in the United States changed a great deal during the nineteenth century. Public education began to evolve in many ways in order to help people cope in a rapidly changing society. The Puritan and Enlightenment phases of American education gave way to helping young people adjust and be integrated into the emerging urban, industrial society. Education, in no small way, helped teach people to live in what was to develop into our modern life.

In this chapter we will see the growth of common schools through the nineteenth century, and the spread of high schools by the beginning of the twentieth century. As schooling became more serious, many states made school attendance mandatory as much for social and economic, as intellectual reasons. As the nation became more urbanized and industrialized, as the structure of the family changed and as immigrant populations became more numerous, what was taught—and how it was taught—began to change.

Schools became more centralized and bureaucratized, vocational schools became more popular, and by the end of the nineteenth century there was a serious clash over the role schools should play in society.

We are still fighting over many of the problems that began during those times. In this chapter, we will see how education continued to evolve during much of the twentieth century. The survey will end with a discussion of *A Nation at Risk*, a report published in 1983 by the National Commission on Excellence in Education. That report has, in many ways, shaped our debates about education for almost a quarter of a century. As we begin the twenty-first century, for example, there still seem to be as many people in favor of a fixed curriculum as those who favor a more progressive approach to public education. To understand the forces at work during the last two centuries is to understand the underpinnings of many of the issues that continue to trouble us.

THE NINETEENTH CENTURY SETTING

We need some kind of background in order to get a good sense of the dislocations and public issues during the last two hundred years.

As we know, the population during the 1900s was mostly rural. At the beginning of the century schools were not only predominately rural, but were very much under the control of the locals. Professional educators had little or no say over rural schools. Indeed, professionalism was not really a part of education at that time. Selectmen from each district would generally consult the local clergy and then hire whomever they pleased. In each classroom there might be a large number of students who ranged in age from two to twenty-five. We read that "usually young, inexperienced, and poorly trained, teachers were sometimes no match for the older pupils."[1] Not surprisingly, teachers were not well paid.

The schools themselves were poorly constructed and neither well-lighted nor well-ventilated. There were hard chairs and desks that were anything but comfortable. These schools had no standard curriculum, and the teachers simply used those textbooks that were readily available. Compared to today, schools and schooling were primitive.

These small agrarian communities were homogeneous. People in the villages shared similar backgrounds, beliefs, and color.[2] It was easy and natural for them to make certain that their children were schooled in the "right" moral lessons. There was a belief in the Bible and a fear of "outsiders." There was local uniformity, but no fixed curriculum from district to district. Education meant something different from place to place. These rural communities were also antagonistic towards the cities and what they saw as a corruption of American values.[3] Certainly Thomas Jefferson would have approved of this prejudice.

Probably the best way to think about these schools is to remember that they originated within the community and their influence did not go past its boundaries. It was the very definition of local education, the natural outcome of our

[1] David Tyack, *The One Best System: A History of American Urban Education* Cambridge, Steton Mass.: Harvard University Press, 1074), p. 19.

[2] See Joseph Newman, *America's Teachers: An Introduction to Education*, 3d. ed. (New York: Addison Wesley Longman, Inc., 1998), p. 169.

[3] For a history of these schools, see Carl Kaestle, *Pillars of the Republic: Common Schools and American Society, 1780–1860* (New York: Hill and Wang, 1983).

New England Puritan tradition, our belief in federalism, and mistrust of a highly centralized government.

One reaction to this environment of "rampant decentralization" was the call for more national cohesion. A group of educators believed that public education— common schools—would be able to help unify the growing nation.[4] The person most closely associated with these common schools is Horace Mann, who was the secretary of the Massachusetts Board of Education from 1837 to 1848. If there is a Father of American Education, it is Horace Mann.

Horace Mann was born in Franklin, Massachusetts, in 1796. He attended a one-room district school and his family tutored him at home. To give you a sense of the times, with only a few years of elementary schooling, some home tutoring, and a winter of college preparatory work, Mann applied to Brown College. He was interviewed by the president and two faculty members, and was accepted with sophomore standing. After graduating from Brown, Mann studied law.

He was raised a strict Calvinist, the religion of his father. When he was young, Mann's brother died. Stephen Mann had decided to go swimming instead of going to church one Sunday, and on that very day he drowned. Not only did the death of his brother affect Mann, so too did the lesson drawn from the tragedy by the minister, a Reverend Emmons. At the funeral, Emmons said that because Stephen had disobeyed God's commandments he would surely go to hell. Emmons had said the same thing about his own son's death. This Calvinist reaction was so harsh that Mann eventually became a Unitarian. All of his life he rejected the strict and moralistic teaching of religion.

Mann was in politics before he became interested in education.[5] He was a member of the Massachusetts legislature and was an advocate for commerce and manufacturing. He was, we read, ". . . in favor of industrial development, improved transportation, and the growth of towns and cities."[6] He was also in favor of a more active public response to what had always been private problems. He believed, for example, that the state should build and maintain a hospital for the mentally ill.

As we shall see, Mann's interests and concerns help highlight the changes that were taking place at the time. In the following section we will concentrate on how these changes helped shape nineteenth century schooling in the United States. While Mann was not an original educational thinker, the sheer number of changes he helped bring about played an important role in shaping the common school movement in America. Not surprisingly, he opposed the dogma and orthodoxy of religion and made certain that they were kept out of common schools. While there was certainly a religious overtone to schooling in those times, common schools were never religious schools.

---

[4] Elizabeth Steiner, Robert Arnove, and B.Edward McClellan, *American Educational and American Culture* (New York: Macmillan Publishing Company, 1980), p. 19.

[5] This practice continues. The president of the University of Oklahoma and the head of higher education in Massachusetts, to name just two, came to their position from political office.

[6] Jonathan Messerli, *Horace Mann: A Biography* (New York: Alfred Knopf, 1972), p. 107, quoted in Steven Tozer, Paul Violas, and Guy Sense, *School and Society: Historical and Contemporary Perspectives*, 3d. ed. (Boston: McGraw Hill, 1995), p. 55.

There were strong protests to Mann's nonsectarian view of education. He was, in the spirit of those religious times, called godless. The fight about the role of religion in Massachusetts's schools lasted well past his resignation as secretary of the board of education.

One of the interesting things Mann did was begin to gather facts about the schools in Massachusetts and then campaign publicly for educational reform. He told wealthy, conservative groups that schools were "the cheapest means of self-protection and insurance" from the lower classes that were beginning to develop in urban areas.[7] He argued that there should be more systematic teacher preparation, and to that end helped establish normal schools to train teachers.

In a similar vein, he helped popularize schools by talking about their economic impact. He told his audiences that their children could become rich by going to school. While he did not believe that the most important end of schooling was for economic advantage, it is certainly one of the most enduring of his educational contributions. It has become commonplace to judge the worth of years in school by just how much more money a person will earn in his or her lifetime. A college degree is worth more than a high school degree; professional school is worth more than college, and so on. That kind of argument, which was being made more than 150 years ago, still fills our educational literature.

Before it was popular, Mann believed that women should teach the early grades. He argued that a "vast amount of female talent" was being wasted, as there were few opportunities for women in that social environment. He believed "that woman, by her livelier sensibility and her quicker sympathies, is the forechosen guide and guardian of children of a tender age."[8] By the end of the century teaching would be feminized.

In 1843 Mann toured Europe studying different educational systems. He did not think much of either the British or the French systems, but he was very impressed with the Prussian system, and in particular their *volkschule*. The *volkschule* was a state-financed and supported compulsory free school. Mann thought that this kind of system would work remarkably well in the United States. He simply ignored the fact that the Prussian system also had *vorschules*, which were much better schools for the aristocrats. Mann constantly campaigned against private schools in Massachusetts, and always lost. (As I write, Massachusetts remains the home of a remarkable number of prep schools.)

The Prussian system seemed to work, in no small part because of the training given to the teachers. It was here that he got the idea for the normal schools that he helped establish. He was also very impressed with the positive relationship between students and teachers. These well-trained teachers had the ability to make school a good experience for their students. Prussian teachers, unlike most of those in the United States, did not use corporal punishment and Mann "never saw one child in tears."[9] In one of his annual reports, he was able to offend the teachers of Boston with his Prussian insights.

[7] Quoted in S. Alexander Rippa, *Education and Free Society: An American History*, 8th ed. (New York: Addison Wesley Longman, 1997), p. 95.

[8] Tozier, op. cit., p. 66.

[9] Ibid., p. 61.

In his report, Mann wrote: "I heard no child ridiculed, sneered at, or scolded, for making a mistake. I wonder whether a visitor could spend six weeks in our own schools without ever hearing an angry word spoken, or seeing a blow struck, or witnessing the flow of tears?"[10] Thirty-one Boston principals took offense at what Mann was insinuating and wrote their own 144-page reply. There were several intense exchanges, and what we need to see is that at the heart of the matter was how educators understood the nature of students. Mann insisted on a more humane view of children and resented the "stern virtue, and inflexible justice, and scorn-despising firmness of the Puritan founders of our free schools."[11] The principal's vision reflected the Puritan/Calvinist sense of humanity. As the world changed, Mann's view finally became the popular one. By the time of John Dewey, there would be an effort to make schooling more student-centered.

Mann was very successful in reinventing the missions and even the attitude of common schools. He took many of the decisions about schooling away from local districts and gave those powers to the state. He created normal schools that taught would-be teachers different ideas about how they should act. Schools took on the job of preparing students for life in a rapidly changing environment.

At the heart of his work was the idea that "In a social and political sense, it is a *Free* school system."[12] He was dedicated to the idea that education should be free and equal for (almost) everyone. It is a powerful notion that has produced remarkable results.

UNDERLYING CHANGES

The success of the common schools took place in a time of great change. The social changes during the nineteenth century were to eventually change the life on our planet. We would urbanize, industrialize, mass-produce, automate, shrink the world, and support an ever-increasing human population. For example, three times as many people were alive in the year 2000 as the year 1900. The twentieth century was, in many ways, the working out of changes that started in the nineteenth century.

There were four developments in the United States that we need to understand to best see the roots of change.[13] These developments were 1) industrialization and urbanization; 2) the assumption by the state of direct responsibility of various social services; 3) the invention of institutionalization as a way to solve social problems; and 4) the redefinition of the family. While the problems are intertwined and it is foolish

---

[10] Rippa, op. cit., p. 96.

[11] Ibid., p. 97.

[12] Ibid., p. 98.

[13] This discussion comes from Michael Katz. *The Origins of Public Education: A Reassessment*, found in B. Edward McClellan and William Reese, eds., *The Social History of American Education* (Urbana: University of Ill. Press, 1988).

to pretend to know the difference between which were causes and which were effects, it does make some sense to take each development by itself.

During the nineteenth century the United States became more industrialized and urbanized. That, along with increased immigration, reshaped the economic and social order. The economy shifted from a mercantile–peasant economy to a mercantile–capitalist to an industrial–capitalist society during the 1800s. The key change was that under capitalism, labor became the central commodity. Without that idea of labor, industrialism as we know it would not have been possible.

In order to produce a labor force fit for industry, there needed to be a change in the way people were schooled. Children had to learn the habits that the new institutions of production would require. They had to be trained to become part of a mobile, free workforce that understood the requirements of becoming a laborer.

Society was faced with a dual problem. Not only was the older schooling ineffective, but apprenticeships, which had been a traditional way to enter the work force, could not produce the kind of laborer that the new industry needed. The emerging economy needed workers with a particular set of skills, and there needed to be a place to train them. Carl Kaestle writes that the number of men who described themselves as laborers rose from 5.5 percent to 27.4 percent from 1796 to 1855.[14] Put differently, a new kind of schooling was needed to educate the "wandering poor" of the 1800s.

These newly displaced people needed to learn the skills required by industry: punctuality, regularity, docility and the postponement of gratification. In preindustrial society, workdays were generally governed more by the sun than by a clock and seasons and festivals guided production more than the arbitrary schedule of the factory. Coming industrialization was changing the world from a natural rhythm to an artificial schedule. It seems no mistake that the mass production of clocks and watches began at about the same time as the mass production of public schools.[15]

Possibly the biggest change was the separation of the workplace and home. People had to go to factories for work. In earlier times, farming or doing piecemeal work was done at home. The actual fact of having to *go* to work changed the focus of the family. With jobs out of the house, there was a heightened attention on the family. In earlier times children would often leave home by the time they were fourteen. They would be servants or apprentices or, if they stayed at home, they would help with whatever work the family did.

As families moved to urban areas for work there was little for young men to do. Between 1820 and 1860 urbanization grew at a faster rate than in any other period in our history. During that time the number of people who lived in urban areas increased from 693,255 to 6,216,518.[16] The number of cities over 100,000 grew from one to nine, and towns of five-to-ten thousand increased from 22 to 136. Between 1870 and 1910, 8.8 million people moved to the cities. With that came a huge

[14] Found in Katz, ibid., p. 102.

[15] Leo Marx, *The Machine in the Garden: Technology and the Pastoral Ideal in America* (New York: 1984), p. 248, cited in Katz, ibid., p. 105.

[16] These figures come from Tyack, op. cit., pgs. 30–1.

increase in railroad mileage and a shift in wealth to nonhousehold manufacturing. One of the casualties of these changes was young people.

Urban youth did not have schools, jobs, or apprenticeships. There were fewer opportunities to become an artisan as well as fewer family businesses to enter. The children of lower-class parents were left to wander the streets. These children had become a genuine problem in urban areas.

We can see this from a different point of view. During this time the notion of adolescence was being invented. We have seen it was difficult for those who had expectations redefined by the needs of the culture as they were growing up. It was equally difficult for their parents, who had little idea about how to best raise these future citizens. Parents not only needed to change what they did, they also looked more towards the institutions of society for help. They especially looked to schooling to help raise their children to help cope with the new demands of a changing social context.

An additional problem, as understood by the middle and upper classes, was the immigrants. During that period Irish and German immigrants were the new "diversity" and were treated with scorn. The Irish were Catholic "foreigners" who were thought to be lawless paupers, and Germans did not speak English. There were, for example, 37,000 Irish immigrants who came to Boston in 1847. The Irish were said to enjoy the "lower pleasures" too much. They were mistrusted and mistreated. The attitudes about the Irish were remarkably like the bigoted attitudes towards urban minorities today. (Research shows us that the Irish immigrants were "a select, especially highly motivated, and unusually literate portion of Irish society."[17])

The nature of prejudice precludes the importance of facts. The anxiety about foreigners was to be taken care of with systems of public education that became agents of cultural standardization.

Urbanization and immigration resulted, in part, in an emerging lower class that seemed lost. Bored youth roamed the streets and got into trouble. Urban areas were the new home of crime and poverty. Thomas Jefferson seemed to have been right in his great dislike for cities. Families grew more concerned about their children. For the first time, large families did not make economic sense, but simply meant more mouths to feed. Families began to turn in and become more important. Children were a focus, and it was during this time a new stage in growing up was invented: adolescence came into being, and something needed to be done for this phase of growing up.

Again, to fast forward, we shall see that adolescence became more than just a phase of growing up. It became an important economic entity that needed not only educating, but also clothes, entertainment, and an identity for marketers. By the 1960s adolescence became a central group in cultural and economic America. Capitalism was given a huge boost with the merging of the baby-boomer rebellion and economic good times. It is estimated that in 1999 teenagers spent $140 billion on themselves.[18] A staggering amount.

---

[17] Katz, op. cit., p. 104.

[18] "Shop and Save?," *Newsweek*, August 9, 1999, p. 14.

To go back, crime and poverty were understood as moral problems. They were thought to be the fault of lower-class parents who failed to implant the proper values in their children. Neglected children were simply unprepared to do honest work. The simple myth was that lower-class families produced paupers and criminals. Urban areas were centers for drunks and prostitutes. It seemed natural for those who were more successful to want something to be done to protect their interests. The obvious and most inexpensive solution was the common school.

There were, of course, other solutions. David Tyack writes: "The creation of efficient and uniformed police paralleled the movement to standardize schooling. Both were in part responses to the influx of the immigrant poor."[19]

This was also the time that women were being more actively recruited to become teachers. Because the school was now understood as taking care of some of the functions that had once been done at home, school became the work of women. In the stereotypical version of men and women it made sense for women to teach. Women were seen as being emotionally better able to deal with children than were men. Men were stern and unforgiving while women were more affectionate and caring. If schools were to help instill the qualities traditionally taught at home then it made sense for women to teach.[20]

The other very good reason for women teaching was there were surprisingly few other ways for them to earn a living. There were some domestic jobs, there was prostitution, and little else. So the woman/mother became a teacher—at a very low wage. In 1840 about 30 percent of the teachers were women. By 1900 the percentage had risen to 70 percent. Women in teaching reached its height in the 1920s when almost 85 percent were women; the percentage of women teaching was in the 60s in the year 2000.[21]

As these changes were taking place, there were equally important institutional changes. The liberal fear of government action began to break down, and the state slowly took over tasks that had traditionally been private. Welfare became a public problem and it was beginning to be taken care of institutionally. Bureaucracies were seen as the most efficient way to deal with social problems. W. T. Harris argued that bureaucratized schooling was a social and economic necessity. He wrote: "[T]he modern industrial community cannot exist without free popular education carried out in a system of schools ascending from the primary grade to the university."[22] The former solutions of private and community actions no longer seemed to be able to deal with large social issues.

Institutionalization took place before industrialization. This shift in social organization paved the way for changes not only in manufacturing, but also in schooling.

[19] Tyack, op. cit., p. 33.

[20] Much of the literature in the psychology of women during the past twenty-five years has been about these very differences between men and women.

[21] See the chart in Joseph Newman, *America's Teachers: An Introduction to Education*, 3d. ed. (New York: Longman, 1998), p. 171.

[22] Quoted in Tyack, p. 29.

People became more and more accustomed to dealing with formal organizations. While it countered the kind of liberal/individualism that so characterized much of our ideological thinking, there was a sense that radical decentralization and individualism would too easily lead to anarchy. We began to fold our ideas about individualism into the practical solutions of institutionalization.

As a kind of safety valve, there was still the West. Those who were emotionally unable to deal with formal organizations or cities could always move west. There was a huge continent to inhabit.

It needs to be noted that the institutions of the nineteenth century hardly resemble the institutions of today. They were just developing, and only the most basic of habits needed to be learned. But that mindset was critical to how we were to develop. Schools were reorganized in order to solve a variety of social concerns.

Schools became a miniature version of society. They became agents for the spread of a common culture, places to learn the skills needed for factory life, and a substitute for the family that took care of adolescents. Schools were not only an economic necessity, but were said to be a cheap and efficient way to keep down urban crime. It was, after all, much less expensive to keep a young person in school than in jail.

Schools, then, became less about the mind and more about character. Cognitive skills were not as important as socialization. And the secret, the thing that made common schools so important, was that they were for everyone—at least everyone who was white.

STANDARDIZATION AND HIGH SCHOOLS

Clearly, the future of the United States seemed to be in the cities, and the future of the economy was manufacturing. By the last quarter of the nineteenth century the traditional family and community structures in the United States had begun to collapse. Schools took their place. School picnics, group singing, and athletic events became community affairs, and domestic and manual skills such as cooking, woodworking, and sewing were now learned at school instead of at home. Robert Wiebe writes "citizens increasingly attributed mystical powers to it, for education alone seemed to have that knowledge prerequisite to entering the broader society."[23] This reflects, in part, the idea that parents were unsure how to best raise their children.

By 1874 the goals of schooling were clear. In a pamphlet written by William Harris and Duane Doty, it was argued that "military precision is required in the maneuvering of classes. Great stress is laid upon (1) punctuality, (2) regularity, (3) attention and (4) silence, as habits necessary through life for successful combination with one's fellow-men in an industrial and commercial civilization."[24]

There was a need for high schools. Although the first high school began in Boston in 1821, by 1875 there were fewer than 25,000 high school students in the

---

[23] Robert Wiebe, *The Social Functions of Public Education*, in Steiner, op. cit., p. 25.

[24] Quoted in Tyack, op. cit., p. 50.

country, and in 1890 the number of students had grown to about 202,000. At the turn of the century there were more than 6,000 high schools and more than 500,000 students, and by 1920 there were 2,206,000 students in grades 9–12.[25]

At first, high schools were not as well accepted as common schools. There was opposition to the use of tax money to support public high schools. In some areas of the country, "public" high schools charged tuition. The issue was settled in the most American of ways—with a lawsuit.

In 1858 the town of Kalamazoo, Michigan, created a tax-supported secondary school system. Three citizens who argued that it was illegal for taxes to go to high schools sued the town. The case was decided by the Supreme Court of Michigan. The Court held that secondary schools were a vital link between common schools and the state university. In the opinion of the court, the absence of a free secondary school would be a form of discrimination against those who could not afford to pay tuition.

While there were other cases in other states, the Kalamazoo case became the precedent. It had become legal for tax money to be spent on public high schools. From the time of the ruling until World War I, there was a huge growth in the number of high schools in the United States. (At the time of the Kalamazoo ruling, fewer than 6 percent of high school aged students were in school; by 1920 the percentage was up to 31 percent.)

It is important to remember that this was just the beginning of our current system. High schools had traditionally served the higher classes. The 600,000 high school students did not represent much of the adolescent population (children could still be employed as full-time workers), and it was certainly not a ticket to college. In 1890 only 6 percent of the eligible population was in high school—4 percent in public schools and 2 percent in private. In 1900, about one tenth of the students in high school went on to college. It was not the primary role of high schools to prepare students for further education.

While schools did offer a "classical" course that many students took, the real education was to train students to become good citizens. It was a more sophisticated version of elementary school. Students learned how to adapt to changing situations, what their responsibilities were to their community and government, as well as practical skills like business math and "manual training."

Money certainly played a role in schooling. Before 1900, wealthy families rarely sent their children to public schools. The time between 1880 and 1930 was one of great activity for private schools. The rich, and friends of the rich, were busy founding schools that promoted their visions of society. Founders of schools relied on their friends, and friends of friends for their first students.[26] These schools were not always about superior education. Often the goal was social; that the students would make

---

[25] For numbers, see *Historical Statistics of the United States* (Washington, D.C.: U.S. Bureau of the Cenusus, 1960), p. 207.

[26] This discussion comes from Authur Powell, *Lessons from Privilge: The American Prep School Tradition* (Cambridge, Mass.: Harvard University Press, 1996), pgs. 43–4.

friendships that would last a lifetime and would help them throughout their lives. It was, incidentally, a place to find the right person to marry.

During this period, a phase of life called adolescence was solidified by the studies of G. Stanley Hall. Hall was Harvard's first student to earn a degree in psychology. In 1883 he founded the first psychology laboratory in the United States at Johns Hopkins University. Four years later he founded the *American Journal of Psychology*, and in 1889 became the president of Clark University. He made Clark the center for research and study of child development.

Hall was influenced by the work of Charles Darwin, and his study of child development had an evolutionary sense to it. He believed that there were stages of development that parents and teachers needed to understand and pay attention to. Hall argued that schooling should be child-centered and that the curriculum was to be evaluated against the students need at his or her stage of development. As we will see, Hall was one of several psychologists who helped change our sense of education.

High schools became places to help ease transitions from home to society and from childhood to adulthood. Attention was paid to psychological growth, and to help socialize students in a world that was increasingly dominated by group activities.

Most high schools admitted girls and gave them a roughly equal chance to compete with boys. The girls, who outnumbered the boys, often outperformed them. Because there were so few jobs for women, those in high school often took more academic classes. The exceptions were those who went into teaching. Boys understood that high school was for job preparation. Most public schools were not open to blacks. Mostly, they were places that actively kept blacks from entering mainstream society. It would be decades before that changed.

During this period of the growth of high schools, there was an equally dramatic growth in immigration. From 1870 through 1920 approximately 28 million people came to the United States. By the twenties more than one-third of the population was either foreign-born or the child of a foreign-born. More than half of those came from Central, Eastern or Southern Europe. They came with different languages, customs, food, and culture. In all, they seemed even more "foreign" than the earlier immigrants from Germany and Ireland.[27]

Much can be learned about high schools by reviewing the debates during that time. We begin with the fight over what should be taught.

THE STRUGGLES AT THE TURN OF THE CENTURY

As we have seen, the rate of change that began during the nineteenth century simply kept increasing. By the turn of the century conditions in the United States were much more complicated than they were a hundred years earlier. The immigrant population, urbanization, industrialization, and institutionalization were all more powerful forces than ever.

[27] Found in Newman, op. cit., p. 180.

Before we look at the educational debates of the time it is necessary to know a little more about the context. In an effort to absorb the number of new citizens, there was an increased focus on patriotism. By the 1890s schools began to develop patriotic exercises. In part because of the increased immigration, public schools engaged in "Americanization" programs.[28] These programs taught immigrants the customs, laws, and language of the United States. By World War I, it was common for students to say the pledge of allegiance, to sing patriotic songs, and to participate in school government.

Business became an active force in education.[29] Business, and it had a forum in the National Association of Manufacturers (NAM), became highly critical of public education. In 1898 the second president of the NAM said, "it is well to hold fast to the classical and literary studies. They have their place in all educational systems, but it is unfair to the great material interests of the land to leave out of account the obvious demands of industry and commerce." A few years later *Nation's Business* argued that the "aim of Education must be to prepare each child for self-support and thus make every school of the nation a place for life preparation." By 1916 the National Chamber's Committee on Education believed that unless vocational training was firmly established in the public schools, "the industrial and commercial position of the United States as a nation will be progressively impaired."

Public education was simply not satisfying the interests and concerns of business. (One needs to add the significant reminder that business, at that time, was heavily involved in sweatshops that employed young children and was at war with labor unions because of low wages and unsafe working conditions.) In 1914 the NAM argued that "the United States [was] spending a half billion dollars a year teaching nobody anything in particular." That same year they concluded that the almost 65 percent of students in common schools dropped out by the end of the fifth or sixth grade, "having learned nothing but a little reading, writing and arithmetic, which most of them quickly forget."

One suspects that business was more than a little right. While public schools probably were not very good, it seems fair to wonder about the goals of the NAM. Certainly schools need to be more than merely places to train people for work. Classical studies did have a place in schools. On the other hand, schools listened to the critique offered by business. Efforts were made to operate schools more efficiently, and somehow have at least some of the skills needed in industry taught in common schools. What is important for us to remember is that by the turn of the century, business had begun to make a systematic effort to use schools for its own purposes.

We need to note that the purposes of the South were not those of the rest of the country. The history of schooling, especially the influences of urbanism, immigration, institutionalization, and industrialization is mostly the story of the Northeast. Western expansion was laced with its own issues, while the northern tier of states had its own set of unique issues. Schooling in the East is what we generally think of as the development of schooling in the United States.

---

[28] Joel Spring, *American Education*, 8th ed. (Boston, Mass.: McGraw-Hill, 1994), p. II.

[29] This discussion comes from Rippa, op. cit., pgs. 127–31.

The issues of the South revolved around race. After the Civil War, public education in the South was in total disarray. Most schools were closed during the fighting, and many never reopened. There were no schools for black children at the end of the war. The South was still mostly rural; it was fully segregated and very poor. Together these added up to almost no public education.

I do not mean to imply that the issue of race was limited to the South. There was no section of the United States in which the school system was well integrated. Segregated schools were legal until *Brown v the Board of Education* of Topeka in 1954. As we will see, the issues of race and socio-economic class continue to be major concerns in schooling—as well as in other segments of our society.

The federal government and private foundations tried to establish schools for black students. The states were less willing. Indeed, education was a very low priority for most southern states. For example, in 1890 the national average of state expenditures was $17.22 per student. That year South Carolina spent $3.38 per student. That meant poor or no schooling for all of the population. In 1872 a private charity found "that while the white population had increased only 13 percent during the preceding ten years, white illiteracy had increased 50%."[30]

There were, of course, remarkable exceptions. Mary McLeod Bethune was born in South Carolina in 1875.[31] She was the seventeenth child in her family and the first who was not born a slave. At nine she attended a free school opened by missionaries near her home. After school, she would teach her family what she had learned.

A white Quaker seamstress from Colorado provided a scholarship so Bethune could attend a seminary in North Carolina. After her graduation in 1893 she attended the Moody Bible Institute in Chicago. After her request to be a missionary in Africa was denied, Mary Bethune decided to concentrate on providing educational opportunities for poor black girls. In 1904 she started her own school—The Daytona Beach Normal and Industrial School for Negro Girls—in a run-down building in Daytona, Florida. The first class enrolled six girls.

By 1912 she had powerful benefactors (one was a Gamble, the son of a founder of Proctor & Gamble), and eventually she became president of the coeducational Bethune-Cookman College. Mary Bethune was politically active all of her life, and served in many powerful positions. She was a spokesperson for human rights and education. She was a special advisor to President Franklin Roosevelt, she was awarded seven honorary degrees, she was the vice president of the NAACP, and she was a consultant for the drafting of the United Nations charter.

Mary Bethune was a remarkable woman who lived a remarkable life. That she was born poor and black in the South in 1875 makes it almost impossible to imagine just how special she was.

While the rest of the country was trying to come to terms with a stunning set of changes, much of the South seemed set on reclaiming a pre-civil-war past. If that

---

[30] Quoted in ibid., p. 118.

[31] The following comes from Arthur Ellis, John Cogan, and Kenneth Howey, *Introduction to the Foundations of Education*, 2d. ed. (Englewood Cliffs, N.J.:Prentice-Hall, 1986), p. 105.

meant ignoring or denying education to the next generation, then that is exactly what would happen.

Later in this chapter, and again in chapter 6, we will study the history of segregation and education in some depth.

Two other parts of the context of schooling need to be at least mentioned. Both will be taken up in greater detail later. It was the Progressive Era, a time during which there were calls for changes in many places. At the heart of the Progressive program was a great optimism that things could change and change for the better. Educational progressives believed that science, and the scientific method, could provide the answers needed to improve schools. (Does this sound familiar? Is it no mistake that these great-grandchildren of the Enlightenment would turn to science for answers?) By the 1920s and '30s these "scientists" were looking for the scientifically best way to teach subjects like reading and math. Their faith in the experimental method would have made our Enlightenment founders proud.

Experimental psychology turned its attention to education. We will study science and its place in schooling later, but now it is enough to repeat the judgment of Richard Hofstadter. He has written that these progressive educators' "misuse of experimental evidence . . . constitutes a major scandal in the history of educational thought."[32]

It is part of our mind-set to believe that science will solve our problems. It is an effort to turn every problem into a technical problem—and a belief that these technical problems can be solved by science. While that mind-set can certainly produce wonderful things, we know that it will not solve the problems of how best to teach each child. However, at that time, there was a great deal of optimism that there were genuine answers to problems of pedagogy, and those answers could be found using the methods of science.

That is, briefly, a sense of what was going on at the turn of the century. The changes that had started during the nineteenth century had developed into clear and strong trends. Industrialization was now finding its institutional voice, immigrants and their children made up almost a third of the population, and the movement to reform schools (and almost everything else) was gaining strength. Science was, again, a force with which to deal. Between the mid-1890s and 1918 there were three reports that dealt with education. What those reports suggested have shaped many of our current issues.

Committee of Ten. In 1894 the Committee of Ten published a report with their suggestions about what an academic curriculum should be for all high school students. The committee was established in 1892 by the National Educational Association and its suggestions have served as a standard for a hundred years. Five of the members of the committee were college presidents, and the chair was Charles Eliot, the president of Harvard. Their report was an outline for all students, whether or not they were going to college.

First, the committee gave high school a structure. All high schools were to consist of grades seven through twelve, courses were to be arranged in sequential order, very few

---

[32] Ravitch, op. cit., p. 49.

electives were to be offered for students, and a unit of credit was to be given for a course that met four or five times a week for the entire school year. We know much of that has changed, but the committee was attempting to standardize what high school should be.

They recommended a core curriculum in which every student take four years of foreign language, English and literature, three to four years of math and science, and two to four years of history. While we can easily recognize that as normal for college prep, the Committee of Ten believed it doubly important for "school children who have no expectation of going to college" to take these courses. To be good citizens, this kind of education would have "a salutary influence" on the affairs of the country.[33]

The committee went further and critiqued education of that time. They were against the lifeless education provided by textbooks, and argued that schooling was intended to develop "the invaluable mental power which we call judgment." Their report called for students to study original documents, to study topics in-depth, and to do individual and group projects as well as take field trips and visit museums.

They believed that there were many subjects that should be taught together. For example, they urged that history, civil government, and geography would be more interesting and meaningful if taught as one. The committee believed that foreign languages should begin to be taught in elementary school. Finally, they wrote that the continuing education of teachers should be more rigorous. Continuing education was needed so that teachers could break out of the limited and confining educational methods used up to that time, and make education exciting and interesting.

Within twenty years the report by the Committee of Ten was doomed.

Committee of Nine.   In 1911 the Committee of Nine on the Articulation of High School and College issued its own report. It was a group made up primarily of high school administrators. The core of their thought was that school should focus on the interest that "each boy and girl has at the time." They argued the curriculum suggested by the Ten would enslave high school to the needs of college. The Nine thought each student should do what he or she was best adapted to do, and that meant more industrial arts, agriculture and "household science." The Nine undercut the Ten in every important way.

Cardinal Principles.   Another report was issued in 1918. It was the *Cardinal Principles of Secondary Education,* the most influential of the three. It was produced by the Commission on Reorganization of Secondary Education and was distributed by the U.S. Office of Education. The commission was made up mostly of school administrators and can be thought of as the formal launching of progressive education in this country.

The cardinal principles by which a high school education should be judged were: "1. Health; 2. Command of fundamental processes; 3. Worthy home-membership; 4. Vocation; 5. Citizenship; 6. Worthy use of leisure; 7. Ethical character."[34] The report

---

[33] See Paul Gagnon, "What Should Children Learn?," *The Atlantic Monthly,* vol. 276. no. 6, December, 1995, p. 70.

[34] See Diane Ravitch, *The Troubled Crusade: American Education 1945–1980* (New York: Basic Books, 1983), p. 48.

did not include a single academic subject that should be taught. The "objectives of secondary education should be determined by the needs of the society to be served, the character of the individuals to be educated, and the knowledge of educational theory and practice available." The cardinal principles stressed that their goals should be taken from the life activities of the adults in society.

For a progressive statement, that kind of thinking led to very unprogressive suggestions. For example, because few women went to college then, college-preparatory studies were "particularly incongruous with the actual needs and future responsibilities of girls." Girls in high school were urged to take homemaking.

Many of our current issues were fully engaged with these three reports. The idea of high school as a place for genuine academic learning to take place was countered by the idea that we should shape education to the needs of each student. Moreover, because so few students went to college, high school was the last best place to make certain that people learned citizenship skills. We will see educational theorists such as John Dewey explore progressive education, and see how his ideas were systematically misunderstood and misused.

What is important to remember is that this was taking place in a time of great change and experimentation. People made honest attempts to solve serious political and pedagogical problems. Some, like the business community, were all about self-interest. That is certainly not an uncommon part of our liberal tradition. Others, like the professionals in psychology and education, turned to the scientific method for answers. Again, it is in line with our liberal/Enlightenment beliefs. There were those with a political agenda who argued that education should be used for the purpose of "Americanizing" the population. This is a common theme in most discussions about education.

Liberalism was often the unarticulated basis of what was being suggested. Pragmatism, the contribution to philosophy by the United States, was developed during this period. Charles Peirce and William James, Harvard professors at the time, invented and helped popularize pragmatism by the end of the nineteenth century. At the heart of their thinking was the idea that instead of worrying about metaphysical questions, it is more important to ask practical questions. We should be asking how things should be rearranged so that they will work better, instead of asking deeper questions about why things worked as they did.

Only in a country where most of the important principles are agreed upon could there be a philosophy that focuses on practical questions. Pragmatism needed the comforting consensus of liberalism to be considered a viable choice. It is precisely because of the overwhelming agreement on the basic questions that fundamental change is so difficult in the United States. While there have always been groups who were not liberal—American Indians and various religious groups are obvious examples—liberalism has been so overwhelmingly accepted that other ways of dealing with fundamental questions have had little chance. Given our faith in liberalism and our invention of pragmatism, the questions of schooling are often about what will work best and not about the basis of what is going on.

We can get some perspective on this by thinking about our current situation. The attack on the World Trade Center was, in many ways, an attack on our liberal/individual sense of the world, and on our sense of progress and modernity. We were reminded, in the most horrifying way, that there are people who do not share, nor like, our liberal values, and who believe these very values have created an immoral culture.

Before turning to the intellectual context of the times, we need to remember that schools at the turn of the century were not very good and that only the well-off went to high school. Of those who actually graduated from high school, fewer still went to college. During these times, education was under increasing pressure to serve more practical purposes. Education, to put it a little differently, was beginning to move closer to the center of American culture.

INTELLECTUAL UNDERPINNINGS

As children became a problem and a focus for the developing culture in the United States, and schooling was becoming the way to prepare people for adult life, an effort was made to understand the age group. We will begin with how the developing field of psychology helped shape our idea of children and how they learn.

Until the late 1800s the human mind was thought to consist of three separate sets of faculties: 1) the will; 2) the emotions; 3) the intellect. Taken together that would account for an individual being able to act, to feel, and to think and reason. Schooling was the place to discipline and train the intellect. Given the prejudice that the intellect (thought to be a masculine faculty at the time) was the most important faculty, schooling was aimed at intensive drill and practice and development of the memory. The goal was to train the mind and that would be, it was thought, enough to enable the student to do anything.

The idea that mental discipline was the heart of schooling was the driving principle of schooling at the turn of the century.

The challenge of the faculty theory of the mind was based on the evolutionary work done by Charles Darwin. The underlying idea was that survival depended on how an organism reacted to its environment. It did not take long for the psychologists to argue that the mental activity of human beings was a key function in adapting to changing contexts. The mind—mental activity—was reconceptualized from being divided into three separate areas to being understood as part of a dynamic whole. There were not discrete faculties of the mind that worked in their own separate areas, but the human mind was part of everything that went on.

William James was the first American-born psychologist. He studied chemistry, physiology, anatomy, biology, and medicine. In 1872 he accepted an offer to teach physiology at Harvard. He read philosophy and physiology and believed they converged in psychology. In 1875 he began teaching a course in psychology (saying that the first lecture he ever heard on the subject was his very own) and began writing a text, *The Principles of Psychology*. It was published in 1890.

In his text, James argued that there were not faculties in the mind, but there was a stream of thought that flowed like a river. Mental activity was, according to James, a total experience. Our minds were constantly making and remaking associations, redoing experiences and going back and forth in time. We might dip into this stream and examine what we see, but James reminds us that these thoughts do not come from different faculties of the mind. Essentially, perceptions and associations, and sensations and emotions cannot be separated. Humans are connected to their environment with this constant flow of consciousness, and have the choice of either adjusting to, or changing, what they find.

By focusing on everyday life, it seemed natural that James would study habit. He believed that much of what we do was automatic and it was his sense that we develop these "habit systems" in order to make life simpler. As we develop habits, our nervous systems are changed so that each time we do this thing it is easier than the last time. Habits allow us to do routine things without having to rethink them each time. This is, for James, the heart of adaptation.

But the key contribution of James, for our purposes, was his argument about mental activity being a stream of consciousness. Given that image, the world—and certainly teaching—became much more complicated. The great American tradition of having children do endless drills in order to memorize material in order to sharpen their "mental discipline" was being challenged in the most basic and significant way. A static way of learning was inadequate in an ever-changing world. In essence, the lesson from James was that what was taught, as well as how it was taught, needed to be different.

One of James's students, Edward Thorndike, did experiments that supported the evolutionary concept of the brain. Using data from his experiments on animals, Thorndike argued that the mind develops as the organism responds to its environment. Like James, he believed that the human brain was capable of changing the environment. The human mind, in this view, was becoming increasingly powerful. How that mind was trained had potential effects on everything around it. As we changed our ideas about the mind, it became clear that schooling needed to be rethought.

Thorndike did not believe that human nature was either good or bad. He was attracted to neither the Puritan nor Rousseauean view. He thought that human nature was neutral and would become what we made of it. That put added pressure on schooling. He wrote: "It is a first principle of education to utilize any individual's original nature as a means of changing him for the better—to produce in him the information, habits, powers, interests and ideas which are desirable."[35]

This view of human nature and the mind begins to change the whole sense of schooling. We have seen the political, social, and economic context of education and the kinds of pressures each put on education. Part of the environment for education was intellectual, and the movement in psychology was to make the child both more special and complex than before. Students were to be seen as having much greater potential than at any time in our history, and teaching methods needed to be invented if that potential was to be reached.

It was in this environment that progressive education developed. In particular, it was the time of John Dewey.

[35] Quoted in Rippa, op. cit., pgs. 181–2.

JOHN DEWEY AND PROGRESSIVE EDUCATION

John Dewey looms over education not only in the United States but the whole world. He traveled the world lecturing and consulting. His ideas, for example, had a huge impact on China, where they dominated for thirty years until the Communists took control of the government. Dewey is not only pivotal in how we think about education and schooling, but he is also a remarkable representative of the age in which he lived. His ideas and actions were at the forefront of his times. It is necessary to understand in some depth what he did and what he thought.

Dewey was born in Burlington, Vermont, in 1859. He attended public school, the University of Vermont, and did his graduate work at Johns Hopkins University. He studied philosophy under Professor George Morris, and heard lectures by G. Stanley Hall and Charles Peirce. He was also influenced by the work of William James and Charles Darwin.

In 1884 he followed his mentor, Morris, to the University of Michigan, where he taught philosophy for ten years. During that time he did not teach courses in educational theory nor did he publish anything significant. In 1886 he married Alice Chipman. At the age of 35 he became the chair of the department of philosophy, psychology, and education at the University of Chicago. At that time—1894—the University of Chicago was one of the main centers of the reform movement in education. Deweys' new position allowed him to expand his philosophical ideas to include work in educational theory, and to build a department that would reflect his ideas.

In 1896 Dewey, Alice, and his associates created an experimental elementary school—the Dewey School—that still exists as the laboratory school at the University of Chicago. (It has a Web site, if you are interested in learning more about it.) In 1904 he became a professor at Columbia University, where he continued his work in education and pragmatism. With Dewey and his followers, Teachers College at Columbia University was one of the leaders of educational thought in the United States. During that time, Edward Throndike was also at Columbia and was the director of its Institute of Educational Research.

Dewey not only published a great deal (thirty-six books and over eight hundred articles), conducted research, consulted around the world, and taught, he was also active in progressive political causes. He was the founder and president of the American Association of University Professors; he marched for women's right to vote, he headed a commission to investigate the assassination of Trotsky, and lectured around the world. His wife Alice died in 1927 and he married Roberta Grant in 1946. They adopted two Belgian children who had been orphaned during World War II. Dewey died in 1952.

He lived in extraordinary intellectual times. In addition to Darwin, James, Peirce, and Hall, during his life Tolstoi, Kierkegaard, Bergson, Whitehead, Einstein, Montessori, Buber, Piaget, Skinner, and Sartre made their most significant contributions. He also lived through two world wars, the rise of communism in the Soviet Union, and the depression that changed how we were to think about government activity in the United States. John Dewey, who is considered at the forefront of progressive thought—and who embodied the politics of those times—is considered by many as the single most influential person in the history of American educational thought.

When Dewey started the lab school at Chicago in 1896 there were twelve students and two teachers. He "envisioned a school where children would grow mentally, physically, and socially, where they would be challenged to think independently and investigate the world around them, and where school subjects would expand on children's natural curiosity and their desire to communicate with others."[36] Over the years, Dewey worked out exactly what he meant. During the time in Chicago, he and Jane Addams were friends. They shared ideas, and their progressive visions changed both education and social work.

Dewey believed that education was an inclusive activity. For example, in *My Pedagogic Creed*[37] he wrote that there were two sides to the educational process—one psychological and one sociological. One is no more important that the other—indeed, they are "organically related and . . . education cannot be regarded as a compromise between the two. . . . In sum, I believe that the individual who is to be educated is a social individual and that society is an organic union of individuals."

That same spirit was at work when he discussed traditional education and progressive education. In *Experience and Education* he wrote that traditional schools relied upon a subject or cultural heritage for content, while the "new" schools were more concerned with a student's interests or current social problems.[38] He believed that, alone, neither of these sets of values was sufficient. Dewey argued that a student must discover the connection that exists within experience between the achievements of the past and the issues of the present. Good education, in other words, must be inclusive.

At the heart of his beliefs John Dewey believed that it was scientific study that leads to and enlarges experience. The key is that the experience must be educative in that it must begin with an appropriate problem, lead to significant knowledge, and then somehow modify or modulate the student's outlook, attitude, or skill. Education needs to be experiential; it must be tied to what is already known and be powerful enough to cause the learner to change.

Schools, according to Dewey, are different from all other social institutions. The purpose of schooling is to prepare the young for a successful and responsible life. The student needs to acquire both information and skills for that to be possible. Schoolbooks represented the wisdom of the past, and it had been the job of teachers to communicate that wisdom, help connect it to the students, and enforce its importance. In his time, Dewey believed that the "wisdom" being taught was often static, was out of touch with the world in which the children lived, and was simply imposed on them. He believed that schooling needed to change, and change dramatically.

---

[36] Taken from their Web site, http://www.ucls.uchicago.edu.

[37] John Dewey, "My Pedagogic Creed," in *The Second Journal*, vol. LIV, Number 3, January 16, 1897, pgs. 77–80.

[38] Much of the following comes from John Dewey, *Experience and education* (New York: Macmillan Publishing Company, 1963).

His new education called for the expression and cultivation of individuality, free activity, learning through experiences, making the most of a present life, and understanding the changing world. He rejected, in full, the traditional ways in which schooling was carried out. The roles of both the students and teachers needed to be rethought.

While experience was to be the key to a new theory of education, Dewey did not believe that all experiences were educational. Experiences might result in anything from a lack of sensitivity to a disconnection from other experiences. To be educative, an experience had to be important to the student, and be fruitfully and creatively linked to subsequent experiences. It was the job of the teacher to see that the experience (the problem the student was interested in) grew out of what was present, was within the capacity of the student to solve, and that it was interesting enough to make the student look for information that could lead to new ideas.

It was the job of the teacher to make certain that the students understood the scientific method and could apply it to everyday situations. Life in the classroom was to become a model for all of life: continual scientific experimentation that results in linking the present with the past. Dewey describes the process like this: first there is a "felt difficulty" (a problem); second there is an analysis of the problem; then a hypothesis of possible solutions; followed by experimentation, and finally corroboration of an idea. It is simply inductive reasoning that was part of the scientific revolution of the enlightenment.

The approach is to focus on everyday life in a particular way. It is a scientific sense of the world that leads to a kind of systematic way of making decisions that is heavily empirical. We have seen that faith in science from the Enlightenment writers of the Constitution to the pragmatism of Peirce and James. Dewey brought these tools and biases about the world into the classroom and has shown us how they can be the foundation of both education and life. His ideas are powerful, in no small part, because science is powerful. That inquisitive way of literally attacking the world seems to be in the very air we breathe in the United States.

Dewey tells us that possibly the greatest pedagogical fallacy is the idea that a person learns only the particular thing he or she is learning at the time. He writes that collateral learning always takes place. For example, an enduring attitude of likes or dislikes may often be more important than a spelling lesson that is being learned. He argues that those who believe education is an end-product are wrong; education, rightly understood, is a never-ending process.

Dewey hated the traditional classroom "with its rows of ugly desks placed in geometrical order, crowded together so that there shall be as little moving room as possible, desks almost all of the same size."[39] The military regime of the students could no longer continue to exist. The classroom had to become a very active place in which students selected things to study, interacted with each other and the teacher, and where the scientific method and experience formed the heart of learning. Dewey wrote that school should be like a game, and the teacher was the referee or umpire.

---

[39] John Dewey, *The School and Society* (Chicago: University of Chicago Press, 1927), p. 32.

The school was to be child-centered, and each student needed the freedom to explore individually interesting problems. The idea that education was a constant reorganizing or reconstructing of experience seemed to be a perfect example of the philosophical pragmatism that so defined American intellectual thought.

As an aside, it is interesting to note that as a college professor Dewey took almost none of his own advice. He would be at the front of the room and lecture to his students. He would stare out of the window and, periodically, speak. His ideas (and no one since Rousseau had put so much importance on direct experience) and his pedagogical methods could not have been more different. In this way, it was a familiar old lesson: Do as I say, not as I do.

Dewey believed that if the child was free to explore his or her interests (with appropriate guidance from the teacher) learning could be fun and interesting and very meaningful. He believed his method would eliminate the divisions of thought and method and result in an adult who was an individual able to live in an emerging culture that relied on group activity. He consciously constructed his method so that students would be able to actively participate in a democratic system. Like himself, Dewey wanted others to be productive and politically active citizens.

Underlying his ideas was a deep sense of optimism. He believed that we could constantly evolve and that life and society could continue to get better. His was the optimism that was so important to the progressive spirit and which had been a by-product of the scientific method for a very long time. The underlying feeling was that if people would just explore life in the right way, the obvious result would be never-ending social and personal improvement for everyone. It translated into a faith in students, their teachers, and the method that John Dewey had devised.

What he suggested was extraordinary. Consider how difficult and interesting it must be to try and implement a child-centered classroom in which students worked on appropriate problems that interested them. The teacher had to make certain that each student understood scientific inquiry, chose a problem that would lead to increased knowledge and personal change, and would be able to handle the tensions between individual work and the interests of the groups.

Could you be flexible and inventive enough to take an interest of a student and make it a project that would teach necessary lessons? If students genuinely wanted to know about snakes, or how to produce a video, or snow in the Arctic, could you construct the exercises that would teach the use of the scientific method, reading, spelling, and math? To make that even more difficult, could you do that and teach them how to take and pass a standardized test?

On the other hand, imagine how wonderful it would be to have a child-centered education that was built around personal interests and freedom. In our era that seems to favor standardized exams for whole states of students, the idea of in-depth learning about interesting subjects sounds more like a fantasy than an academic program. The confidence that might come from the Dewey-inspired progressive education would have a profoundly positive effect on each child.

Nothing Dewey suggested was easy to operationalize. For all of the respect given Dewey, there was at least that much condemnation. By the 1920s progressive education was under attack. Dewey's pedagogy appeared to many to be nothing more than a series of slogans in search of child-centered fun. Progressive education, to its critics, seemed at best to be soft and at worst a waste of time.

The problems had more to do with the followers of Dewey than with his ideas. Consider how difficult it might be to read about concepts like freedom and experience and then try to make them real in an educational sense. Add to that the regrettable fact that Dewey did not write very well. He published a great deal, but what he wrote was never really clear. Not only was what he wrote tough to read, it was even tougher to understand and put into action. Far too many of his followers ignored—or were simply unable—to make real what Dewey had envisioned. Their classes were sloppy and unorganized and their students never learned how to understand experience the way Dewey had wanted.

Things got so bad that Dewey himself became a critic of much that called itself progressive education. He did believe that at times it was appropriate for a teacher to stand in front of the class and "teach," and there were things that a student should memorize, and it was sensible for students to practice the multiplication tables. He wrote that "it is not too much to say that an educational philosophy which professes to be based on the idea of freedom may become as dogmatic as ever was the traditional education which is reacted against."[40] In the end, Dewey was much more of a pragmatist than many of his progressive followers.

But progressive education increasingly became code for a kind of feel-good education without standards. By the second half of the twentieth century it had lost favor with most people. Still, there is too much genius in Deweys' ideas for them to ever be wholly ignored. His critique of traditional schooling still holds up, and his influence continues to be felt in most schools in the United States.

LIFE ADJUSTMENT AND LIFE REBELLIONS: 1940–1970

Progressive education was gradually replaced by something called life adjustment education. The thinking was that if 20 percent of the students were being prepared for college and another 20 percent were being prepared for a vocation, what could be offered to the other 60 percent? The answer was simple: Prepare them for life.

In 1944 the Educational Policies Commission issued a report titled *Education for All American Youth*. It was an updated version of the *Cardinal Principles* and described an ideal education.[41] It read, in part, "There is no aristocracy of 'subjects' . . . Mathematics and mechanics, art and agriculture, history and homemaking are all peers." What schools were asked to do was center their curriculum around basic human activity instead of traditional subject matter. The idea was that people needed skills for everyday situations more than they needed abstract knowledge or a "bookish" education. Whatever was taught needed to have real use.

---

[40] Dewey, Experience and Education.

[41] This discussion comes mainly from Ravitch, op. cit., pgs. 62–80.

Charles Prosser, a leader in life adjustment education, told a national educational conference that "Never was there such a meeting where people were so sincere in their belief that this was the golden opportunity to do something that would give to all American youth their educational heritage so long denied. . . . I am proud to have lived long enough to see my fellow schoolmen design a plan which will aid in achieving for every youth an education truly adjusted to life."[42] In 1947 the U.S. Office of Education was fully supportive of life adjustment education. It was remarkably popular.

It is important to have a sense of what this kind of education meant. It meant, for example, that few students took foreign language. The high point in foreign language enrollment was more than 83 percent in 1910. Enrollment had fallen to about 20 percent of high school students in 1955. By the mid-1950s almost half of the high schools offered no foreign language study at all, either ancient or modern. What was offered? In Denver, Colorado, high school students studied a unit on "What is expected of a boy on a date." It covered such problems as "Should you go in with a girl after a date (to raid the ice box?)." In Tulsa, Oklahoma, the junior high students learned what clothes were appropriate, the right shade of nail polish to wear, and how to improve their appearance.[43]

With the deemphasis of bookish knowledge came a change in national testing. In 1947 the College Entrance Examination Board that focused on testing a liberal education was replaced by the Scholastic Aptitude Test (SAT). The college boards had been individually graded and included many essay questions. The SATs were a standardized, multiple-choice test of verbal and mathematical skills that claimed to be curriculum-free. Because of the increased number of college applicants, they had the advantage of being machine graded. By 1948 exams included essay questions on life-adjustment topics.

I have no idea what you think about life adjustment education. While easy to make fun of, it was taken seriously by many in the field of education for more than a decade. It represents a kind of natural extension of the underlying philosophy of common schools and the idea that everyone deserves an education in the United States. Lawrence Cremin argues that many people believe that the phrase "popular education" is an oxymoron.[44] He argues that it is not unusual to believe that education, in its true meaning, is an elite activity. To put it differently, to popularize education is to vulgarize education.

What do you think? In its very nature, do you believe that true education belongs to the intellectual elite? That bias could not have been stated more clearly than Plato did in the *Republic*. His entire society depended on education and especially on the education of the most gifted children. While everyone was to have an opportunity to be educated, those who would lead were those with the skills we associate with the

---

[42] Quoted in ibid., pgs. 65–8.

[43] Ibid., pgs. 67–8.

[44] Lawrence A. Cremin, Popular Education and Its Discontents (New York: Harper and Row Publishers, 1989), p. 33.

brightest. Think about learning. We are expected to learn things and know them well enough to pass tests. Those who learn, retain, and test best get the highest grades, have a chance of going to the best colleges, and are on track to get the best jobs.

The very heart of that dynamic seems to indicate that schooling is an elite activity. Yet, the history of schooling in the United States is the history of common schools and the constant pressure to have our schools be more and more inclusive. Indeed, we have made school mandatory. But what do we do with the tension between those students who have the kinds of talents that are rewarded by schools and those students who have other kinds of talents?

When you think about popular education do you, as Cremins suggests, believe that the phrase is an oxymoron? When you hear the phrase "popular education," are you more on the *popular* or the *education* side? It is a question that cannot be dismissed; it is a question that will not go away. It is, in the end, a question each of us must deal with and eventually answer.

We know that life adjustment did not continue to dominate schooling. The world intruded and life became more important than life adjustment. The integration of public schools was finally taken seriously during the 1950s.[45] A brief background might be helpful.

Race

In 1896 the Supreme Court of the United States issued a ruling in the case of *Plessy v. Ferguson*. The case was about the constitutionality of a Louisiana law that allowed the segregation of rail passengers by race. Eight of the nine justices believed that as long as the facilities available to the two races were equal then there was nothing wrong with racial segregation. One justice, John Marshall Harlan, dissented. The *Plessy* decision legally recognized the doctrine of "separate but equal," which was simply segregation by another name. The emphasis was always on the separate because facilities were never equal. As we will see later, the education of blacks was always underfunded and second class.

By the 1950s cases involving segregated education began to be heard by the Supreme Court. Generally the cases involved graduate and professional education, cases in which it was easier to prove that separate education was not equal education. In a key case, a black mailman named Herman Sweatt applied for admission to the University of Texas Law School. The state of Texas denied him admission, but quickly created a law school for him. There were to be three part-time faculty and Sweatt was to be the only student. The state argued that with this school they had complied with the doctrine of separate but equal. In the case *Sweatt v. Painter* the Supreme Court ruled that the two schools were clearly not equal.

In a parallel case in a neighboring state, George McLaurin applied to the doctoral program in the graduate school of education at the University of Oklahoma. He was denied admission, and a federal court ordered that he be accepted—but went on

---

[45] We have seen that the education of blacks has been a part of our history since colonial times. In a later chapter we will study the education of blacks in some depth.

to rule that he was to be segregated from other students at the University. He could not be with other students in class, the library, or cafeteria. The Supreme Court finally ruled that McLaurin should be able to attend his state university as well as be free to engage with his fellow students in order to more fully learn his profession. The decisions in Sweatt and McLaurin were handed down the same day in 1950.

By 1952 the NAACP changed its focus from graduate education to public schooling. At the time, about 40 percent of students in the public schools were enrolled in segregated schools. A number of cases had been brought to challenge state-enforced education in elementary and secondary schools. The case heard by the Supreme Court was from Topeka, Kansas, and was *Brown v. Board of Education.* In 1954 the Court declared that states could not impose racial segregation in public schools. The decision was unanimous, and it changed history.

A year later the Supreme Court ruled that the implementation of the Brown ruling could be left to local school authorities. Many thought that this second ruling favored segregationists. It was not too much of a stretch to believe that many local school boards, especially in the South, would do their best to ignore the Brown decision. It was the job of the lower courts to make certain that did not happen. The local boards were to make "a prompt and reasonable start towards full compliance" and "to admit to public schools on a racially nondiscriminatory basis with all deliberate speed the parties to these cases." The word deliberate was, to many, the key to the phrase "all deliberate speed." The emphasis was certainly not on speed.

There will be a more full discussion of the Brown decision in chapter 6, but for our present purposes we can turn to the most dramatic early showdown of public school integration. It happened in Little Rock, Arkansas.

Arkansas was not the most militantly anti-integration state. It was not a part of the Deep South, and after Brown, it had slowly begun to allow blacks to attend white schools. In September 1957 the Little Rock school board agreed on a plan to desegregate the public schools. It was to be a gradual process and was to begin with the admission of nine blacks to Central High School. The plan was challenged by blacks for being too slow, and the federal court agreed. Whites then went to the federal court and argued that if things went any faster there would be violence. The court did not agree and ruled that there should be no interference in carrying out integration. The lines had begun to be drawn.

A day before classes began, Governor Orval Faubus sent the Arkansas National Guard to Central High in order to "maintain or restore order" and to prevent admission of the black students. A federal judge ruled that integration should proceed, the black students went to school, and were denied admission by the National Guardsmen. The scene was played out in front of an ugly mob of jeering, yelling whites.

The actions of Governor Faubus were opposed by just about every decision maker involved: the school board, the federal court, the mayor of Little Rock, the Supreme Court. Faubus met with President Eisenhower and pledged to accept the ruling of the court. The court issued an injunction and Faubus withdrew the Guard from Central High.

School opened September 23 and it was a mess. Almost a thousand demonstrators (and dozens of white students who left their classes to join them) were in front of the building making trouble for everyone: the press, the police, and especially the blacks who tried to enter. The police could not control the mob and things simply got worse. That evening President Eisenhower called the situation "disgraceful" and warned that rulings of the courts could not be disobeyed. The next morning he federalized the state National Guard and sent troops of the 101st Airborne Division to Little Rock to make certain that court orders were carried out.

Eisenhower, the old military man, sent plenty of troops to ensure success. The troops made certain that the black students could go to Central High. By November of that year they were no longer needed.

Faubus had another plan; he cancelled the 1958/59 school year for all four high schools in Little Rock. It took an entire year for the courts to finally decide that what Faubus did was illegal. In the end, Faubus was infamous for his resistance to segregation (famous to the segregationists), and the integration of schools in Little Rock is remembered as a low point in our recent history.

The incident also helped change the way school decisions were made. After that, the President and the federal courts were clearly asked to play a much more active role in some decisions regarding public schools. Courts were to become major factors in agreeing to, or modifying, the plans made by local school boards. The effects of some of their decisions (about busing for example) are still with us.

Other Changes

In addition to integration, there were other signs of change in the fifties. Women, who had done a great deal of work outside the home when their husbands had fought during World War II and Korea were now expected to stay home and raise children. In order to help women cope, the development and sales of tranquilizers became a major industry. Housework plus Valium was one Hallmark of the fifties. The conformity of the corporate worker was put in perspective by beatniks—dressed in black and full of angry poetry. The counterpoint of The Man in the Grey Flannel Suit was the "Rebel Without a Cause." The pressure to conform was too much for a generation raised by the feel-good, be-free philosophy of Dr. Benjamin Spock. By the sixties, everything would change—and that certainly included schooling.

Near the end of the fifties, October, 4, 1957, to be exact, the age of life adjustment education was challenged in the most serious way. On that day the Russians launched the first satellite—Sputnik. It is almost impossible to get a sense of just how traumatic that was for people in the United States. At that time, the United Soviet Socialist Republic (USSR) was the sworn enemy of capitalism in general and the United States in particular. We were spending (and would continue to spend) a huge amount of money on the military to protect ourselves from the USSR.

Sputnik was a remarkable, visible sign that the Soviet Union was ahead of us in areas that had military implications. Our enemies were in space and we were not. People in the United States were shocked, frightened, and not at all happy with what was—or was not—going on in schools. The argument was that life adjustment had robbed us of future scientists, engineers, and mathematicians. Schooling was about to change. The United States was at war (a cold one, but war none the less) and seemed to be losing. There needed to be changes and one of the first places to look was the schools. There was general agreement that it was in the national interest to make certain that the quality of public school education improved, and improved quickly.

President Eisenhower, traditionally against using federal funds to aid schools because it might lead to federal control, repeatedly asked for congressional approval for federal monies to go to school construction. Congress, in the wisdom that comes from a remarkable array of political interests, always said no. In 1958, a year after Sputnik, Congress passed the National Defense Education Act that provided money to encourage the study of science, math, and foreign languages, as well as money for the construction of new schools and equipment.

The response to Sputnik was not so much that the Soviet Union was better than the United States, but that somehow public schools had failed. In 1958 the Rockefeller Brothers Fund produced a report titled *The Pursuit of Excellence.* The essence of the report was that it was in the national interest to develop human potential and that could be done by encouraging both excellence and equality. Neither had to be sacrificed; each was necessary. A year later James Conant wrote *The American High School Today* in which he made the Rockefeller report real.

In his report Conant argued that a comprehensive high school needed to fulfill three tasks:[46] 1) it had to provide "a general education for all the pupils; 2) it should offer good elective nonacademic courses to those who were not going to college; 3) it should provide the academic talented students with advanced courses in math, science and foreign language." While opposed to separate curricula, he did see a need for ability grouping. Life adjustment education was all but dead by 1960, a time in which life itself seemed to change.

Politics and social change so dominated most of the sixties that just about everything else was of secondary importance. The Civil Rights movement became militant and the reaction to the push for equality was too often violent. Black and white Civil Rights workers were killed, state and local authorities blocked protests, poverty became an issue, and Northern cities were decaying along with their school systems. President Kennedy was assassinated, Martin Luther King was assassinated, Robert Kennedy was assassinated. A brutal and ugly war was being fought in Vietnam, but not by those who had college exemptions.

Society itself was under attack by the counterculture. Just as the first generation Puritans did not trust their children, so many parents did not trust their children during the sixties. Authority, anyone over thirty and almost any formally organized group of people, were not to be trusted. It was a youth culture with a vengence. The United States was awash with drugs, sex, and rock and roll, and boy was it fun, and boy did it make people mad. There was long hair and short hair and good dope and free love and all the while the Barry Goldwaters, Richard Nixons, and Ronald Reagans of the United States were unhappy and plotting revenge.

Schooling came under attack as being repressive. There were free school movements as well as anti-school movements. Critics (such as Jonathan Kozol, Nat Hentoff, John Holt, Ivan Illich, Paul Goodman) believed that schooling destroyed

---

[46] Ravitch, op. cit., p. 230.

students—all students. Given its nature, they argued that it was coercive for anyone, black or white, rich or poor or middle class, to sit for hours in a stultifying classroom until their spirits were broken. The lack of creative classrooms led to the spiritual death of students. We can get a sense of the difference between then and now by looking at why students were in college. "In the late 1960s developing a meaningful philosophy of life was the top value for students entering college, being endorsed as 'essential' or 'very important' by more than 80 percent." In 1996, more than 76 percent of the freshman were attending college in order to increase their earning power.[47]

There was a call for the end of compensatory education.

Other issues evolved from that time. In addition to the Civil Rights movement, women and cultural minorities began to find their voices. The classroom treatment of girls was questioned. Boys got more attention and seemingly had more career options than girls. There was the beginning of an effort to educate those students who did not speak English. The issue of bilingual education was introduced. Poor inner-city children required special help, and Head Start began.

All of these issues are still with us. We will take them up in later chapters.

What is difficult to do is somehow relate to the era in which these things came to our attention. The sixties is now, in a stereotyped way, silly bellbottoms and goofy looking people giving the peace sign and saying groovy. It is Woodstock, with all its rain and music and muck. It is, in part, difficult to relate to because of all the ways in which the counterculture won. The turn-of-the-century, relaxed, live-and-let-live attitude is the direct result of the sixties. The part of our liberalism that was so heavily involved with individualism is now playing itself out.

Schooling, as we shall see, did not quite know what to do with the remarkable freedom that was set loose during the sixties. The traditional strains were still there; the need to provide students with enough of a sense of culture and country to be productive and happy citizens sits right next to the need for each student to feel special and be free to be himself or herself.

Conservative Reaction

With the election of Ronald Reagan came a conservative reaction to what was seen as the moral breakdown of the sixties. For our purposes, the reaction came in the form of *A Nation at Risk*. It was published in 1983 by the National Commission on Excellence in Education, and in many ways continues to inform our debates about education. The essence of the report (details will come in later chapters) is this: education in the United States was in crisis. Students were ill-prepared, and the United States was vulnerable to foreign powers. Schools needed to get back to "the basics," to teach more math and science, to set higher standards and to strengthen gradua-

---

[47] A. Austin, W. Parott, S.A. Korn, and L.J. Sax, *The American Freshman: Thirty-Year Trends* (Los Angeles, Calif.: Higher Education Research Institute, UCLA, 1996), pgs. 29, 13.

tion requirements. The report urged the states to make, and pay for, these and many other changes.

The sixties were officially over in 1983. But the end of the sixties did not mean the end of our educational debates. The questions raised then remain with us: Should there be neighborhood schools—and that often means segregated—or should students be bused? Should we worry about what everyone is learning to the point of making sure they know enough by administering standardized tests? Should we spend money on bilingual education? Should girls and boys be put in different classrooms? Is television part of the answer or part of the problem?

These three chapters have simply been a background. They have been about our history, both the events and the philosophical problems. They are the background we need to know in order to better understand where our current issues began and how they have been answered in the past. They are what we share, whether we know about them or not. They inform who we are and how we got here.

MORALITY

In the rush of history we did not stop and ask many serious questions. Before beginning a more systematic look at schooling today there is at least one question that you need to answer. It involves an old question about the power of government and the role it might play in our schooling.

We know that President Eisenhower was against federal aid to schools. He, like many others both then and now, feared that federal power would follow federal money into schools and would dictate too many things. There is another critique of governmental power and it is this: You cannot legislate morality. Just because a "good" and "moral" law is passed does not mean that people will become better or more moral.

For example, there have been laws against prostitution probably forever. That does not seem to have stopped the practice. We know there are sellers and buyers and no amount of legislation is going to stop that. There are also laws against the use of certain drugs. Those laws have been on the books for generations and it would appear that they have little or no effect on the use of drugs. There are sellers and buyers and that has not changed for decades.

So much for legislating morality.

On the other hand, there were all of those laws about civil rights and integration and equal rights. What have they accomplished? More integration and equality and civil rights for more people than ever. While things are far from perfect, it would be very difficult to argue that those laws had no effect. Given the conditions of the fifties and sixties, American society is almost unrecognizable. Not perfect, but how much different would it have been without the legislation?

The question is easy enough: Can you legislate morality? If the answer is yes, do you want to?

SUMMARY

In this chapter we have seen education develop from the common schools of the nineteenth century to the conservative movement in the late twentieth century. We took time to review the changes in the social and cultural context in order to understand the new set of pressures on our schooling. It is important to remember that all of these changes took place on the foundation of our liberal/capitalist ideology.

By the turn of the twentieth century, schooling was involved in the dual tasks of educating immigrants in citizenship and educating newly discovered adolescents to become workers in the emerging industrial economy. As high schools became more important, there were intense debates about what their mission was. Esteemed groups issued reports that urged very different visions of education.

Philosophers and psychologists began to add their insights to the nature of children and the nature of knowledge. Each group had an impact on how people thought about schooling. With John Dewey and the Progressives, an entirely new model of education was suggested. The old methods of memorization and recitation were to be replaced with a student-centered classroom. Both the nature and the method of what was to be learned needed to be reexamined.

As society changed, and as the demand on what youth needed to learn to enter society, schools became more important. Parents, unsure of how best to prepare their children, granted more power to public schools. The nature of both parenting and schooling changed.

We were reminded that race, sex, and socioeconomic class have been political, social, cultural, and educational issues from the beginning. Often schooling is asked to solve these problems. Finally, by the mid-fifties, the problem of race was confronted openly and, in too many cases, violently. At about that time, schools were under pressure to begin to produce workers for what Eisenhower called the military/industrial complex. The cold war with the USSR meant that the federal government would begin to actively support certain kinds of education.

The critiques, criticisms, and political clashes of the sixties were aimed at breaking down what was understood as traditional, rigid schooling. Civil rights, anti-war, and general rebellion triggered cultural change. By 1983, with the publishing of *A Nation at Risk*, the conservative response to the sixties had won. That report has served as the basis of much of our national debates about education.

The roots of our current issues reach back through our history. Our liberal notions of the individual; our ideas about the role of the federal government in schooling; our faith in science; our questions about what to teach and the best way to teach it can be seen as reoccurring themes. The debates about what to teach in high school go back more than eighty years. How to best teach immigrants is a question we have debated for at last a hundred years.

Throughout our history, we have asked schools to solve our social and political problems. Throughout our history, our schools have been criticized for failing to, in many cases, be all things to all people.

We will turn away from the general progression of history to different topics of schooling and education. While there will be historical development in each chapter, the focus will be on a specific subject. In chapter 4 we will think about teachers.

THINK ABOUT

1. What do you think about the idea of adolescence? While possibly a necessary invention, do you think we should figure out a way to give more (or less) responsibility to younger people?

2. Do you believe that the federal government should be more involved with schooling?

3. Your parents (or, maybe your grandparents) were involved in the rebellions of the sixties. Do you envy that generation that seemed committed to social issues and acted on that commitment—or do you believe they were youthful fools who did more harm than good?

■ ■ ■ ■ ■

CHAPTER FOUR

IN SEARCH OF AN IDENTITY
Teachers

The educator by the very nature of his work is obliged to see his present work in terms of what it accomplishes, or fails to accomplish, for a future whose objects are linked with those of the present.

—John Dewey

Every 10 seconds of the school day a student drops out of school.

—Children's Defense Fund, 1991

In a real and everyday sense, schooling (and most often education) comes down to this: teachers and students. That is the fundamental dynamic. Emile and his tutor; Socrates and those he met as he wandered through life; the nun and her pupils. The bell rings, the door closes, and there you are—teacher and students. It is often a scary proposition.

Were it that easy. It would be comforting to know that once that door was closed, the teacher could teach the way he or she thought best, and that each student was an eager student, happy and anxious to learn. We know the influences on students are overwhelming, powerful, and complex. (For example, 49 percent of the 10–15-year-olds polled said they "learned a lot" from TV and movies. Learning from friends was second at 48 percent. Mothers were fourth with 38 percent.)[1] Families, friends, media, and culture do not always produce a happy student who is eager to learn.

We also know that each of us teaching is no more free from other influences than our students. Why is the pay so low, why do school boards and administrative staffs have so much power, where is the respect we honestly believe we deserve? There are few agreed-upon aims of education, and even the idea that teachers should be judged by how their students do seems to some little more than a giant trap. It is a giant trap.

This is a chapter about teachers. Because the context is so complex, there is no obvious and clear path to the discussion. There are powerful books written about

---

[1] *Newsweek*, October 18, 1999, p. 67.

good teachers and effective teaching methods. It is just as easy to find material about oppressive working conditions, bad schools, and wrong-headed administrators. While each approach is helpful, neither gives us a sense of teachers and teaching that is appropriate for our needs.

The more you read about teachers the more this point becomes clear: Teachers have a surprisingly difficult time understanding their role in society. In part, that is the result of the conflicts about what schooling and education are about. But there is more to it than that. There are questions surrounding who should teach, the education they should get, and the certification (if any) they should receive. Teachers want to be respected, want to be thought of as professionals, yet are members of strong labor unions.

Conceptually, the problem can be divided into two parts. In order to be respected professionals, as a group teachers must resolve their internal problems of consensus and consolidate their problem of external legitimacy. Until each has been worked out, neither problem will be solved. Put a little differently, while teachers may have honest and intense differences, they need to agree on the basic importance of education and the job they do. Strong professions, such as law and medicine, each have a consensus and legitimacy that teaching lacks.

In this chapter we will begin to sort out these questions. We will see who teaches, what their education is like, what their certification is about, if they should be considered professionals, the conditions of their work, why they teach, and why they quit teaching. There will be questions about some of the underlying biases (Do teachers really want to be like doctors? or Are certification tests simply expressions of the power of state politics?) so we can make better sense of teachers and teaching.

WHO TEACHES?

The long answer is that there are over three million teachers.[2] Of these, 66 percent are non-Hispanic whites; 17 percent are black; 13 percent are Hispanic; 4 percent are Asian American/Pacific Islander, and 1 percent are American Indian. In 1996 74.4 percent of the teachers were women. In 1960 the average annual salary for a teacher was $4,995, and in 1998 it was $39,385.[3]

There are over 52 million students in 87,125 public schools and 26,093 private schools. In 1996 approximately 11 percent of those dropped out (these are 16–24-year-olds out of school and without a high school credential). In 1995–1996 an average of $5,884 was spent per public school pupil. The federal government was responsible for 6.8 percent, the state 48.7 percent, and local areas 44.5 percent of the money spent.

We are, put differently, dealing with a huge number of people and a huge amount of money.

[2] From U.S. Department of Education, *Projectiions of Educational Statistics to 2007.*

[3] National Educational Association, *Estimates of School Statistics, 1997,* 8th ed.

The short answer to the question Who Teaches? is easy enough: the average teacher is a forty-four year old white female who is married with two children. She has taught for seventeen years. A third of these women are married to another teacher. In order to understand more fully why so many white, middle-class women teach, we need to review how that came about and what it might mean.

As we saw in the previous chapter, Horace Mann was the first strong and powerful advocate of having women become teachers. He argued that they would be good influences on children. Because of the combination of motherly instincts, having a less violent nature and being cheaper to hire than men, it was thought that women would be ideal teachers. They could somehow soothe restless young men and instill virtue in all their students.[4]

Teaching was one of the few occupations open to women during the last half of the 1800s, so in order to get out of the house many became teachers. In 1870 there were 123,000 female teachers and 78,000 male teachers. By the turn of the century almost 75 percent of the teachers were women, and in 1930 there were five times as many women teachers as men. Most of the men taught in upper grades.

There were several reasons for the increasing numbers of female teachers. The traditional pattern of family self-sufficiency declined as urbanization increased.[5] Work took place out of the house, so women became more responsible for both the raising and educating of children. Birth rates declined and the mechanization of farms freed more girls from the demands of helping raise large families. They were no longer needed for such tasks as helping with younger children or cooking for large numbers of farm laborers. Women began marrying later, and there were the beginnings of the women's movement that started the push for women to have more independent lives.

Between 1880 and 1925 there was a huge increase in immigration. At the same time there was a growing demand for more universal public education. All of these trends added up to a demand for teachers, especially elementary school teachers. The new teachers were women. They were often children of farmers or the urban lower class and many were not particularly well educated. In rural areas school districts hired teachers who were as young as fifteen or sixteen years old. Urban schools, which generally paid more, attracted more experienced teachers.

Public schools reflected the broader patriarchal patterns of the culture. Most of these female teachers had male bosses. Teaching was simply an extension of the traditional role of women, the difference being that it was done outside the home. In 1904 Professor Henry Armstrong, a British educator who was in the United States studying schools, wrote that, "Throughout the entire period of existence woman has been man's slave . . . Education will do little to modify her nature." In 1910 the sociologist Lester Ward wrote this about women, ". . . her sole duty is to bear children, keep her husband's house, and be ornamented according to his tastes . . . all labor . . .

---

[4] See Kathleen deMarrais and Margaret LeCompte, *The Way Schools Work*, 3rd ed. (New York: Longman, 1999), pgs. 155–8.

[5] This discussion comes from Gerlad Grant and Christine Murray, *Teaching in America: The Slow Revolution* (Cambridge, Mass.: Harvard University Press, 1999), pgs. 80–5.

is done by men and women found engaged in any of those pursuits are deemed violators of the social code . . ."[6]

Women, then, were subordinate to men. They were to keep the house and raise the children. As conditions changed it was clear that schools would take over the jobs of the family, and especially those jobs that were done by women. But because a woman can have children does not mean she wants to, nor because a woman could be a teacher did not mean she wanted to. Some women have babies because they feel they have to; some women became teachers because they had no choice. Around the turn of the century a woman teacher wrote an article in the *Educational Review* in which she speculated that, if asked, more than half of the teachers would say they did not like teaching.[7]

But if you were a woman and wanted a legitimate career, then teaching was just about your only choice. To be sure it was a low paying and low status career, but it was a career.

There was little effort to train blacks or other minorities to become teachers. Historically black colleges were mainly responsible for the education of black teachers. Later, we will see that many of the key court cases that led to integration revolved around all levels of education. While great efforts have been made to produce a more diversified group of teachers, as we saw earlier in this chapter the vast majority remains white.

Of course, to know, historically, why women came to dominate teaching does not explain why teaching is still a relatively low paying and low status career. To begin to understand that we need to take up the issues that surround teaching as an occupation.

IS TEACHING A PROFESSION?

As we read in chapter 3, schools that educated teachers were introduced in the United States before the middle of the nineteenth century. In 1838 Horace Mann persuaded the Commonwealth of Massachusetts to support normal schools. The first school opened a year later. It took decades for the education of teachers to become commonplace, for there to be any kind of certification, or for teachers to organize into strong political groups.

In *And Sadly Teach*, Jurgen Herbst argues that the education of teachers was of secondary importance to the idea that education should become a profession.[8] He uses Harvard, Teacher's College, and the University of Chicago to make the point that the education of teachers quickly became relatively unimportant to the leading schools of education.

Harvard decided to teach teachers in 1890. President Eliot appointed Paul Henry Hanus to direct teacher education. Hanus believed that only women and men

---

[6] Ibid., pgs. 83 and 82.

[7] Ibid., p. 85.

[8] Jurgen Herbst, *And Sadly Teach* (Madison, Wisc.: The University of Wisconsin Press, 1989), especially see chapter 7.

without ambition would want to be classroom teachers all of their lives, and he had no particular interest in either group. He wanted to train experts in the science of school administration; he wanted this career to be "worthy of a man's life-long professional commitment."[9] The program at Harvard brought specialization to the field of education administration, and by implication made classroom teaching less important.

Harvard accepted women in their masters program. Women and men sat in lectures together, but were put in separate discussion sections. The reason was simple enough, women would go into teaching and men into administration. Harvard did not disturb cultural norms.[10]

With a 2.8 million-dollar grant from the Ford Foundation, Harvard tried to build a program in education that would be the equal of medicine. Arthur Powell writes that the program envisioned "a career progression that ideally included the M.A.T. program, a period of teaching experience, and then doctoral study . . ."[11] The underlying dynamic was that those classroom teachers with skills and ambition would leave teaching for administration. Teachers took their place at the bottom of the hierarchy.

Teacher's College was founded in 1887 as a two-year school for the training of teachers. In 1893 it became associated with Columbia, and with the association began to raise the standards for its students. By 1905 it was no longer a two-year school, and in 1914 it became a graduate school. In the mid-thirties the school had divided into five divisions (foundations, administration, guidance, instruction, and measurement and research) and established a new professional degree—the Ed.D. As Teacher's College pushed more academic aims of research and the scientific study of education, training beginning classroom teachers was much less important.

The University of Chicago was the home of John Dewey. When Dewey was there he began his laboratory school in order to bring together scholarship and live experience in the classroom. When Dewey left in 1904 his successor, Charles Judd, wanted to transform education into a more "legitimate" university discipline. Given the times, that meant Judd wanted a science of education based on survey and research—he wanted to make it a "respectable profession for white men."[12] By 1933 the University of Chicago was no longer responsible for the training of classroom teachers.

While there continue to be a remarkable number of teacher education programs, what seems clear is that the higher-powered academic institutions are not in that business. Science and research remain the bias of our most prominent educational institutions. The professional aspirations of many of the faculty run counter to the training of new teachers. The focus on research and the training of administrators has had the effect of ignoring many classroom needs. How teachers should be trained remains an open question. In order to get to that question it is necessary to return to the question of teaching as a profession.

[9] Ibid., p. 177.

[10] Grant and Murray, op. cit., p. 223.

[11] Cited in Herbst, p. 179.

[12] Woody White, quoted in Herbst, p. 183.

Professions

Max Weber gave us the first, and probably the best definition of professional.[13] He used medicine, law and the priesthood as his models. As we shall see, those who discuss the possibility of teaching as a profession still use doctors and lawyers as their reference point.

Weber believed that individuals were somehow "called" to their professions out of deep personal commitment. And, through long and rigorous study, they became experts; they had great and "esoteric" knowledge that, along with their deep commitment, provided their qualifications. They dealt in serious and often life-or-death matters and were paid by their clients. Weber wrote that what went on between a professional and his or her client was legally privileged so that no court of law could require its disclosure. Finally, professionals were controlled by professional peers. These peers set requirements for entry, training, certification and review processes to ensure that competence was maintained.

In the literature about teaching a surprising amount of time is spent asking this question: Is teaching a profession? It is as if by being able to somehow place teaching on an occupational hierarchy, we will be able to answer a number of important questions. If we were able to say with confidence that teaching was a profession—like being a doctor or a lawyer—then it would be possible that the life of a teacher would change.[14]

There are some parts of being a professional that seem to fit with teaching. It may well be a calling for many; it may stem from a deep personal commitment to deal with serious issues of both individuals and the society. One is as likely to find as much commitment in being a teacher as in being a doctor. To do either job well is to have a genuine felt need to be doing that work.

From there, teaching does not quite fit Webers' definition of being a profession. To run through the traits quickly, we know that the relationship between teacher and pupil is not privileged; we know that the student does not pay the teacher; we know that teachers are not controlled by their professional peers in terms of entry, training, certification, and review. Finally, we know that there is no agreement about what teachers need to know. It is difficult to claim special knowledge when the field is so poorly defined.

Yet, teachers are the group that society trusts to raise its children. While we pay doctors and lawyers a great deal more than we pay teachers, it is up the teachers to make certain that the next generation is somehow on track to be productive and good citizens. We need to know more about teachers and their context.

There are certain things we know about teachers. For example, when at college they are rarely the "best" students on campus. Beginning in the 1960s there has been a decline in the quality of students who study to be teachers. The reason is easy enough to understand. As the movement politics of the sixties gained strength, occupations other than teaching opened up for women. As other more lucrative or interesting

---

[13] This discussion can be found in de Marrais and LeCompte, p. 150.

[14] The debate about being a profession is made more strange by the fact that most teachers are union members.

careers became viable options, many of the bright women who would have gone into teaching simply chose something else. Teaching lost its captive audience and with it some of its most talented people.[15]

In the 1980s *A Nation at Risk* was published. The report lamented that "not enough of the academically able students were being attracted to teaching" and "too many teachers are being drawn from the bottom quarter of graduating high-school and college students."[16] Teachers, and the education they received, were criticized. The Not-Very-Bright were learning Not-Very-Much from professors with Not-Very-High standards. The push for reform began in earnest.

Before going on it is important to remember that teachers were never very highly regarded in the United States, and one could guess that those fifteen-year-olds who taught in rural schools at the turn of the century were not well-educated. Studies show that prospective teachers during the 1920s and 1930s did not do well on standardized tests that judged academic ability. By the forties and fifties there was great criticism of the poor teaching in the United States. And as we saw, the academic skills of teachers began to decline during the sixties.

What I will suggest later is that maybe we have been focusing on the wrong things, but for now we need to examine teacher education and teacher testing more closely.

Should Medicine Be the Standard?

President George W. Bush believes that education needs to become more standardized. He believes (and we will discuss in this more in chapter 9) that research can provide education with the methods that will produce the best results. In his No Child Left Behind legislation, there is the requirement that students should be tested every year in both math and English. The best teaching methods are those that will produce the best test results.

There will be a What Works Clearinghouse that will establish standards for research and then determine which of the thousands of studies each year meet those standards. They will then distribute their findings. As one writer reports:[17] "The Bush administration is trying to make education more like medicine. . . . There is giddy talk in the research world of some day establishing the equivalent of the Food and Drug Administration, declaring educational doctrines safe and effective, or not."

If medicine sets the standard for what it means to be a professional, then it appears that teaching is not a profession. What doctors learn in medical school is pretty well standardized, how they are tested and certified are standardized, they are paid by their clients, for the most part they are respected and, generally, they are their own bosses. Those things cannot be said for teachers.

[15] Joseph Newman, *America's Teachers*, (New York: Longman, 1998), p. 82.

[16] Quoted in ibid., p. 81.

[17] James Traub, "Does It Work," *The New York Times Education Life*, Section 4A,/November 10, 2002, p. 24.

To study how medicine has developed is to get a sense of what teaching is not. Even an outline of how professional medicine has evolved in the United States should serve as a warning to those teachers who hold it in high regard: The profession of teaching may not be able to tolerate the flaws of the profession of medicine.

While it seems intuitive that "healers" have always been respected by their cultures, it turns out to simply not be true.[18] Doctors for the Romans were slaves, freedmen, and foreigners. It was a low-status occupation. In eighteenth-century England physicians were only at the margins of the gentry, and in the early twentieth century in France doctors tried to please the rich in order to get enough money to buy an estate and a title. In the Soviet Union most (70 percent) of the doctors were women and they earned less than three-quarters of the average industrial wage.

For centuries doctors in the United States were not treated with a great deal of respect. While their communities held certain doctors in high regard, it was more for whom they were individually than the fact they were doctors. Things began to change at the end of the nineteenth century and were locked in by the 1950s. The end of the nineteenth century was a time of remarkable events and inventions. We have seen that the changes influenced teachers, but the role of doctors changed even more.

There had been an American Medical Association (AMA) since 1851, but it was not very powerful. There was no licensing of doctors, medical schools were not very good (and were not graduate schools); in fact, doctors were not required to have medical degrees—or any degrees for that matter. There was serious competition from people who made potions, and many families took care of their own. Hospitals were for the poor and have almost nothing in common with the hospitals of today. The status doctors received were generally from the status of their patients. The "best" doctors would go to big cities and try to attract high-status patients. (While we still see magazine articles about "Doctors to the Stars," that is not the only way for doctors to have status.)

One thing that happened to help doctors gain respect was their belief in science and technology. We have seen that an underlying bias in the United States has to do with science. Our liberal founders believed in rationality and science, as did our doctors. The irony, as we shall see, is that this faith in science and technology would eventually undermine the autonomy of doctors. But, at the time, science and rationality was nothing but good for both physician and patient.

The most important first discoveries were in the 1860s and '70s and were in bacteriology. By the 1890s there was cleaner food and water and milk. Surgery became antiseptic and the nature of medicine changed. There was less and less "kitchen surgery" (doctors would go into homes and perform surgery in the kitchen) and more hospital surgery. Around the turn of the last century there was the first treatment of syphilis and there were major advances in immunology. Diagnostic techniques were invented: the stethoscope, the ophthalmoscope, standardized eye tests, X-rays, and instruments to take the temperature and blood pressure.

---

[18] Most of the following discussion comes from Paul Starr, *The Social Transformation of American Medicine: The Rise of a Sovereign Profession and the Making of a Vast Industry* (New York: Basic Books, 1982).

The list is very long, and the impact of these discoveries was important. The role of doctors changed, and their competitive position was enormously enhanced. Doctors now controlled the new diagnostic technologies and became the gatekeepers of medical care. The makers of potions and others without medical training simply could not make the claims of doctors. A physician could now literally look inside a person to see what might be wrong. The ability to diagnose using more information than simply what the patient reported was powerful.

Around 1900, almost anyone who applied to medical school was accepted. Some applicants had little or no college when they were admitted. But over the next ten years things changed. The first change was organizational: the AMA grew from 8,000 in 1900 to 75,000 in 1910. By 1910 half the doctors in the country were members of the AMA. Medicine was now "organized" and growing more powerful. They were gaining the international coherence they needed to become a strong profession.

As organized medicine got stronger its influence over medical education, medical schools, and medical boards increased. As private medical schools went out of business, the more powerful schools (like Harvard and Johns Hopkins) became more focused on the science of medicine than on medical education. It mirrors the trend in education that began to focus more on administration and research and less on teachers. By the mid-1930s medical schools rejected about half of the people who applied.

Doctors also had increased their power in hospitals. In the beginning trustees were the most influential group. They had donated and raised the money that had gotten modern hospitals started, but lost much of their power when income began to depend on admissions. Doctors controlled admissions, and with that gained power in hospitals. They became the key group.

We have, then, a kind of genuinely wonderful period for physicians. The medical profession might well be envied during this period. Until the 1970s organized medicine had almost everything its way. Doctors made a great deal of money, they were the gatekeepers not only to health care, but to who could join their profession. Why wouldn't teachers be attracted to that model?

Even during that time things were not always easy for organized medicine. Beginning in the late 1930s there was pressure for some kind of governmental involvement in health insurance. As technology became more expensive so too did health care. People needed insurance. The medical community was very much against any government involvement. By the time Harry Truman was President, the AMA was hiring expensive advertising agencies to fight health insurance. The doctors believed that any government involvement was socialized medicine . . . and if government could socialize medicine, what would be next?

The fact remained that people needed health insurance, and unions began to bargain for it. Costs of medical schooling (with an increased emphasis on training specialists) and medical technology made the cost of ordinary care almost prohibitive. It was in the interest of both unions and business to find ways to provide reasonably priced care. Health insurance plans were formed, as were health maintenance organizations (HMOs). While doctors were not particularly happy, they continued to control medical education and certification, and generally set their own pay scales.

Physicians had also lost some influence over hospitals. As medical technology became increasingly expensive and health insurance more widespread, hospital administrators became more powerful. As hospitals became complex organizations with huge budgets, their administrators were more and more important. (Later, administrators lost much of their power as managed care controlled what procedures patients could have and what they would pay for those procedures.)

Government had slowly gotten into the health-care business. After World War II veterans' hospitals expanded to take care of all the country's war veterans. Later, Medicare and Medicaid were established to help those who could not afford health care, as well as older citizens. By the 1970s there was a general economic crises (terrible inflation) and a particular health care crisis. Not only was the cost of health care unreasonably high for most people, the general trust in doctors was at a low.

Part of the problem was that medicine was highly organized and technology had a primary place in health care. Doctors became increasingly specialized, dependent on technology that was so expensive only institutions could afford it, and were seemingly removed from their patients. Women, who made up 25 percent of the doctors in 1900 were now only 9 percent. Doctors, generally, were white males. After the 1960s, those kinds of organizations were under attack. Also, for all of the money being spent, there was a perception that health care was not as good as it should be. Other remedies (alternative medicine) began being explored.

All during this period doctors continued to fight government intervention. Save the fact that they received an ever-increasing amount of government funding for research and even building hospitals, as well as Medicare and Medicaid payments, doctors resisted what they once called socialized medicine.

What organized medicine did, as we know, was trade governmental regulation for business regulation. Today, for-profit health companies compete for clients. While there are many models, a common one is for a business to help pay for an insurance plan for the worker. The worker may see a doctor on a fixed list, and the doctor must ask the company for approval for most things beyond normal health care. Not only that, but the amount the doctor (or hospital) gets paid is set by an agreed-upon contract.

Doctors have simply lost a huge amount of power. It is increasingly difficult for a physician to be in a practice alone. HMOs and group practices have taken over, and all doctors must deal with insurance companies and managed care companies. Technology and capitalism, at one time seemingly friends of organized medicine, finally took over. It may well be that a teacher in his or her classroom has more power than a doctor in his or her practice.

In the end, there are things that go on in medicine that teachers could never get away with. For example, 40 million people do not have health insurance. The importance of that fact is doctors (who are in private or group practice) can choose who they will care for, and very few care for people who cannot pay them.

Can you imagine if teachers refused to teach 20 percent of the children who came to their classes? Maybe those kids who caused trouble, or were poor, or were not very bright would be told to leave school. It would certainly make the life of the teacher easier—just as not treating people who cannot pay makes the life of a doctor more financially satisfying. For generations doctors resisted governmental intervention. One result of that is medicine was taken over by insurance companies that were much more interested in profits than patient care. Could teachers get away with that?

As we continue our experiment of substituting for-profit schools for public schools, we might get a better feel for what happened in medicine. I am not convinced that the public good is the sum of for-profit policies of private sector organizations. In the final chapter we review the current politics of education and see what the alternative private schools are doing.

And what about medical education? It has been barely twenty years since medical schools began to understand that the manner of a doctor might actually make a difference to the care of the patient. It is an insight that, in my experience, is still not fully shared by all physicians. Medical schools should have taken a lesson from schools of education. People have understood for a century that the relationship between the teacher and the student is central to learning. The model of professional medicine is deeply rooted in Western science, but until recently lacked a firm understanding of the importance of human relationships to the process of healing.

While trying to become a profession, it will be wise for teaching to remember what it does best.

Finally, about the time medical schools began to think about teacher/patient dealings, they started to train as many women as men to be doctors. They began to understand that doctors could be women, or black, or even from another country. While it is clear that teaching would benefit from more diversity, the lack of diversity is not a result of schools of education systematically keeping people out. Medical schools were pretty exclusive male clubs for generations.

The point we need to remember is that while it would certainly be a boost in the status of teachers to be thought of as a profession, there are reasons why holding up medicine as a shining example might not be a good idea. Medicine and teaching are special occupations, but high SATs and standardized certification tests hardly makes one better than the other.

There is one great and final irony to the idea of doctors representing the professional ideal. While I was writing this section there was a vote at a private hospital in Boston. The residents and interns (doctors in training) voted 177–1 "to be represented by a federally protected union."[19] A month earlier the AMA formed its own union—Physicians for Responsible Negotiations—in order to "counter managed care providers." The world, as doctors once knew it, will never be the same.

But doctors do have an enviable set of standards. Each must display a certain competency. While that competency may not make them good doctors, a patient can make the assumption the physician does know something. That is not always the case with teachers. One of the underlying questions about status has to do with the competency of teachers. Schools of education differ in what they teach, states have different standards to judge teachers, and there is no agreed-upon profile of a successful

---

[19] *Daily Hampshire Gazette*, Wed, Dec. 22, 1999, vol. 214, NO. 93, pgs. 1, 9.

teacher. Given these problems, it is not surprising that when teachers are criticized, one of the first things brought up is their education.

Educating Teachers—For What and How

The formal education of teachers began about 150 years ago. The Normal Schools gave way to state colleges and university programs. We know that in the course of the development of graduate education for educators decisions were made to deemphasize teacher training. The professional demands of university life quickly became the driving force of professional schools of education.

What should teachers know? How should teachers be judged? These two questions are probably impossible to answer. Too many things must be agreed on before there can be any answers that make sense. While there are groups of people who have suggested reasonable solutions, it is important to know that none of these suggestions has been accepted by a majority of people.

Consider the dilemma: before there can be agreement on what teachers should know, we need to agree on what students should learn. That only gets us to a deeper question—what is the role of education? Should schools be producing philosopher-kings, or Emile, or Sophie, or workers who will fit into a factory or an office, or rebels or obedient citizens? If we want, for example, to have thoughtful students then we need to figure out how to educate thoughtful teachers. If we want students who will do well on standardized tests, then we need teachers who will do well on standardized tests.

We can get at the question in another way if we begin with the idea that the ultimate test of any teacher is if he or she can actually teach—and, of course, how well students do. But even with this there are problems.

If teaching implies interaction with students, and if somehow we expect some kind of result from that interaction, then we need to look at who is being taught and what we expect.

Teaching as Results

What do we expect each child to learn? Is that an unfair question? Three books give us three different opinions about what schooling is for and what the student should learn. In The Manufactured Crises[20] we read that there are four expectations of public schools. They are: 1) intellectual tasks (teach cognitive and inquiry skills and substantive knowledge), 2) political tasks (make certain students will be good citizens, 3) economic tasks (prepare students for jobs), 4) social tasks (promote social and moral responsibility). The book argues that schools have actually been overburdened in what is expected of them. They say schools suffer from "the myth of unbounded instructional responsibility" and are bound to fail when asked to solve all—or even most—of society's problems.

---

[20] David Berliner and Bruce Biddle, *The Manufactured Crises: Myths, Fraud, and the Attack on America's Public Schools* (New York: Longman, 1997), pgs. 156–7.

In *The Way Schools Work*[21] we learn that in schools "education is believed to be essential to democratic citizenship" while acting as custodians of our children. Schools became the home of multipurpose social services for the youth of the country.

Life In Schools[22] tells us that schooling "generally serves to reproduce the technocratic, corporate, and capitalistic ideologies that characterize dominant societies . . . [and] . . . that educational programs are designed to create individuals who operate in the interests of the state, whose social function is primarily to sustain and legitimate the status quo social order . . . [finally] . . . teachers are reduced to what Henry Giroux calls 'clerks of the empire' . . ." While sharing the idea that schooling is related to the functions of the state, it is a long way from the idea that democracy is dependent on educated citizens.

Finally (at least for this discussion) there is a serious political fight about what students should know. In *Cultural Literacy: What Every American Needs to Know*, E. D. Hirsch, Jr., in an immodest and unapologetic tone details what it means to be "culturally literate . . . in the modern world."[23] In a truly remarkable (at oh-so-many levels) appendix, Hirsch offers a sixty-three page alphabetized list of what all of us should know. From adverb and the American Stock Exchange to Eli Whitney and the Y-chromosome we can quickly check our literacy for the modern world. Or, to be more accurate, to check Hirsch's idea of what we need to know.

What we need to understand is that it is very difficult to know how to educate teachers if we cannot agree on what they should be teaching.

Let's play out just one of these tracks—and a narrow one at that. What if we agreed that a teacher should be judged by finding out how well her or his students do on various tests and how successful (whatever that means) they become in later life? The notion has a vague ring of common sense, but is loaded with assumptions.

For example, if teachers are judged by "student outcomes" we are accepting the idea that schools are like factories and students are products. To make matters worse, good "raw" materials make the best "finished" materials. Put differently, kids from higher income and well-educated families are the "best" students. And the fix is in from the very beginning. One study looked at how often parents spoke to their children between the ages of thirteen months and three years. Parents in the professions spoke an average of 2,153 words per hour to their children, working-class parents spoke 1,251 words per hour to their children, and welfare parents spoke only an average of 616 words an hour to their children.[24] Infants who receive a great deal of attention generally do better in school.

---

[21] DeMarrais and LeCompte, op. cit., pgs. 72, 165.

[22] Peter McLaren, *Life In Schools: An Introduction to Critical Pedagogy in the Foundations of Education* (New York: Longman, 1998), p. 1.

[23] E. D. Hirsch, Jr., *Cultural Literacy: What Every American Needs to Know* (Boston: Houghton Mifflin Company, 1987).

[24] Richard Rothstein, *The Way We Were? The Myths and Realities of America's Student Achievement* (New York: The Century Foundation Press, 1998), p. 38.

What we know is that those kinds of advantages seem to accelerate as the children get older. The advantages of socioeconomic class begin early and remain strong. We know that the children of higher socioeconomic classes generally have higher test scores and have a better chance of doing well after they have graduated. If we decide to judge teachers by how well their students do, then we would come to the foolish conclusion that the best teachers just happen to be in school districts that have wealthy and well-educated parents.

Earlier we saw the argument that those districts pay more and, indeed, are able to attract the best teachers. While that is true, we could speculate that if those same teachers went into inner-city schools with disadvantaged students then they would appear to be less good teachers. After all, the scores and the futures of their students would have fallen dramatically.

So, before we even begin the discussion about what teachers need to know we find ourselves with a problem: If we judge by results—and we are increasingly asked to do just that—then the most important variable might not be the teacher at all. The most important variables might be families and neighborhoods and the values of the specific cultures from which the students come.

It gets much more complicated when we focus on the bigger issue of just what schools should be doing and realize we cannot even find agreement there.

Still, we need to push on. Even without basic agreement on what schools need to do, we have to acknowledge the fact that there are schools, and those schools need teachers, and those teachers need an education.

What Do Teachers Need to Know?

What do teachers need to know? There are different philosophies and batteries of tests that presume to offer answers. One would assume that teachers should know how to teach. But how much of an undergraduate education should be spent learning methods of teaching? Should future teachers take three methods classes or five? How much time should they spend in the classroom being observed and discussing how they have handled themselves? Is a semester enough, or two semesters?

And what about the subjects they teach? Does an elementary teacher need to know as much math as a high school math teacher? Is there anything they both should know? Do they need to have the same level of literacy skills? Do they both need to know the same amount of general information? Should that physics teacher be forced to have the same affective qualities as the first grade teacher? Does that first grade teacher need to know much—if any—physics?

There are those who argue that elementary teachers do need the same kind of academic training as high school teachers. They argue that all teachers are equally responsible for teaching a common culture and heritage. They believe that teachers should learn about teaching in graduate programs, and spend their undergraduate years learning liberal arts and sciences.[25]

---

[25] For a good example of this, see the report *A Nation Prepared: Teachers for the 21st Century* (New York: Carnegie Corporation of New York, 1986), prepared by Task Force on Teaching as a Profession.

In the end, this is what we know: "Teaching and learning are both largely mysteries."[26] While there are certain techniques that seem to work with some people some of the time, it seems impossible to explain exactly how anyone finally "gets" something. We don't know why something is a mystery one minute and perfectly understandable the next. But even given this unsettling truth about learning, there are certain things that can be said about good teaching.

A teacher needs to know his or her students. If teaching is a relationship between teacher and student, then that knowing is essential. It implies, of course, that different students need different things. A good teacher must, at some level, know with whom he or she is dealing. Even in a huge college class the lecturer needs to have a good idea about his or her audience—what they can hear, what they are able to relate to, and what they can be expected to understand.

Teachers need to be engaging and motivating. They need to not only ask important and interesting questions, but be able to have each student formulate his or her own questions. The process of educating needs to be engaging or it fails to be education. It ends up being worse than a waste of time, it turns students away from learning.

Teachers need to be role models. In a society that worships super models and sports stars, the fact remains that the law requires children to be with teachers for most of their growing-up. A classroom cannot be a neutral place. The teacher, the adult human being in charge of the class, needs to have the ability to breathe life into what goes on. How he or she does that is observed and lived by every student in that room. It means something. The teacher is a role model whether he or she wants to be or not.

Teachers must judge and evaluate their students. This means more than merely grading. There are all kinds of interactions between teachers and students that carry the weight of judgment. Advising, coaching, even the act of clarifying a point in class can reflect what a teacher thinks of a student. A teacher needs to help the student do the best he or she can, and part of that process is understanding what that best is and how well the student is doing.

Finally, a teacher needs to know stuff and be able to convey that stuff. That not only requires a good education in the subject to be taught, but also constant reflection and renewal. It is here, with good teacher preparation and development, that it is important to turn to teacher education.

Teaching Teachers

Teachers traditionally study liberal arts and sciences. They are taught to think in a clear and reasonable way, and in the process learn the basic values of our culture. While the question of just what those values are has been the center of bitter disputes in higher education, the idea of studying the liberal arts is still popular. Liberal education accounts for something between one-third and one-half of the content of an undergraduate education major.[27]

---

[26] This discussion comes from Grand and Murray, op. cit., Chapter 3.

[27] Newman, op. cit., p. 70.

Teachers need to study the area they will teach. Secondary teachers generally take about 25 percent of their courses in their teaching area. Is that enough? If a person is going to teach science in high school, will he or she be able to take enough courses in both physics and biology? Will the social science teacher be able to know enough about history and government to teach either very well? This is not a problem with faculty in higher education. Indeed, many new faculty members know too much about their slice of a field to be able to teach undergraduates. They are likely to know more about how the Congress works or esoteric branches of polymer science than undergraduates are interested in.[28]

On the other hand, knowing stuff does not mean people will be good teachers. Teacher education includes learning about educational methods. These are the "how to" courses for K–12 teachers and represent between one-fourth and one-third of an undergraduate course load. It is this set of courses that is of great concern to so many people. They ask the obvious question: What is the good of knowing how to teach if you do not know what to teach? While student teaching serves as a bridge between the how and the what, it seems too little too late for many critics.

Those who have tried to reform teacher education during the last twenty years have generally concentrated on three areas: 1) cut back the classes in professional education; 2) require students to take more classes in what they are going to teach; 3) try to recruit smarter people (those who have higher grades and do better on standardized tests) to become teachers. Two groups have pushed hard to reform teacher education, and we talk about them next.

Holmes and Carnegie

By the early 1980s, the "conservative restoration" of American education was strong enough to set the agenda for schooling. *A Nation at Risk*, with its critique of students, teachers, schools, and universities, was the context of what was being discussed. While there were responses to the critiques, it is important to remember that the agenda had been set by the conservatives.

During the 1980s two groups began major efforts to reform teacher education. Both the Carnegie Forum on Education and the Economy and the Holmes Group (later changed to the Holmes Partnership) issued reports in 1986. In *A Nation Prepared*, by Carnegie, and *Tomorrow's Teachers*, by Holmes, the proposition was made that undergraduate degrees in education should be eliminated. They argued that people with undergraduate degrees in the arts and sciences should be certified by the state, period. They needed no formal teacher preparation.[29]

Of course, they also envisioned that most teachers would eventually get master's degrees in teaching and some would even get their doctorates. What these groups argued for were "clinical sites" (what the Holmes group calls professional development centers).

---

[28] Regrettably, many new faculty members have neither studied teaching nor have they taught. Knowing a great deal and not understanding how to teach is hard on both the instructor and the students.

[29] This discussion comes mainly from Newman, op. cit., chapter 3.

Both experienced teachers and university professors would run these schools, and would help the "interns" or "residents"[30] learn the most recent knowledge about teaching.

These centers would be, in significant ways, the best kind of learning situations for the new teacher. The centers would let experienced teachers as well as professors at the cutting edge of research collaborate on the most effective methods of instruction. The assumption was made that the new teacher who trained at these centers would have a good basis of knowledge in the field in which he or she graduated.

While the reforms certainly appear to answer the criticisms of teacher preparation, they were only partly effective for a couple of reasons. First, the proposals were not wholly accepted by members of each group. There were those who defended at least parts of undergraduate teacher preparation programs. They argued that courses in methods, curriculum, educational psychology, and the like are necessary for anyone who becomes a teacher. They argued that to simply eliminate these traditional courses would be a foolish mistake.

The second reason is almost wholly political. There are vested interests in undergraduate degree programs in education. Not only would there be obvious problems with faculty that would lose their jobs, but those programs make a great deal of money for the institution. Few colleges or universities are willing to simply give up a good source of cash flow.

That is not to say that Holmes and Carnegie failed. About a dozen states required teachers to major in either arts or science. But by the mid-1990s, the proposals of the groups were essentially dead. In 1996 the Holmes Group reinvented itself and pushed for another kind of reform. Calling itself the Holmes Partnership, the group emphasized the development of new curriculum, new faculty, and new locations for their work. They called for universities to form partnerships with local school districts and develop at least one new professional development school. They wanted at least 250 institutions to be involved. The idea of 250 innovative schools that were run by a partnership of the local school district and university certainly sounds like a good one. These schools would have the potential to improve the quality of our teacher training.

But that is not the bottom line. The bottom line is that teacher training has never been able to get the funds needed for these kinds of expensive experiments. Even in the best of times, these partnership schools would simply cost more than most state legislatures or local communities are willing to fund. To take that a step further: Since the early twenty-first century, whenever the economy has taken a sharp downturn, education has been one of the first places that state legislatures choose to reduce funding.

Where does that leave us with teacher education? In truth, little has changed. There continue to be tensions between those who teach in education and their colleagues in other fields. Education as a field has never gotten much respect on campus and that has not changed. As we saw earlier, even within the field of education there is often little agreement about the aims of schooling/education, and that simply serves to weaken any agreement on what should be taught. Finally, the students who major in education are often not strong academically. Since the beginning of standardized testing they have tested poorly and they often enter college after making low grades in high school.

---

[30] As we can see, educators still seem strongly attracted to the medical model.

The idea of schooling, and what teachers should know, anticipates the next set of questions that centers on who gets to teach, should there be certification and, if so, how should certification take place?

CERTIFICATION

Who should judge teachers and who should certify them? If teaching were a profession in the Weberian sense, the answers would be pretty straightforward. All teachers would be expected to know the same basic things and would be certified and tested by a committee of their peers. While different doctors may be tested in different specialties, they are required to know the same basic stuff. There seems to be almost no "same basic stuff" for teachers. And we know that doctors are in charge of testing and licensing their own. Not only are teachers not in charge of testing and certifying themselves, as we shall see, there are cases in which no one is in charge.

It was almost two hundred years before certification became an issue in the United States. In those early days, certain general things were expected from teachers. They had to have an acceptable moral character, they had to know the subjects they were to teach, and they had to be men.[31] Each year the school board would "license" a teacher. The hiring was done on an individual basis and each person was hired for a year at a time. There were no general or established criteria; each school board did as it pleased. The pattern slowly changed as women replaced men and normal schools began preparing teachers. By the end of the nineteenth century the power to certify was taken from local school boards and became centralized by the states.

Practically speaking, a complete answer to the question of teacher qualification and certification is almost endless. Each state controls the requirements for its public schools. While local districts and school districts retain control over daily operations, real power belongs to the state.[32] In Michigan the court ruled that "The legislature has entire control over the schools of the state . . . The division . . . into districts, the conduct of the school, the qualifications of teachers, the subjects to be taught therein, are all within its control."[33] There can be, then, fifty different rules about how a teacher can be certified.

It is easy enough to generalize about certification. Most states, most of the time, require the new teacher to have a college degree with some courses related to teaching and pass a standardized test. Roughly 20 percent of the states require no testing. But even knowing that a state requires a test tells us little about what really goes on. Generalizations often hide more than they reveal.

For example, many states that require certification tests do not require those who teach in private schools to be certified. Probably the heaviest concentration of the

[31] Dan Lortie, *School Teacher: A Sociological Study* (Chicago: The University of Chicago Press, 1975), p. 17.

[32] Even this simple statement is misleading. There are, for example, no school districts in the state of Hawaii.

[33] Quoted in Steven Tozer, Paul Violas, and Guy Sense, *School and Society: Historical and Contemporary Perspectives*, 3d ed. (Boston: McGraw-Hill, 1998), p. 305.

top prep schools in the country is in Massachusetts. Elites from all over the world send their children to be educated at these highly regarded and very expensive schools. Interestingly, the Commonwealth of Massachusetts does not require teachers in private schools to be certified. Certainly those schools are very selective in who they hire, and while the standards vary from school to school, we know for certain that the people they hire do not need to be certified.

It is important to know that the certification tests are not uniform from state to state. In an effort to improve the quality of teaching in Massachusetts, the legislature decided to make the certification test more difficult. The new test, which, as I write, is less than two years old has had an immediate effect. While there is no evidence that teaching has gotten any better, about half of the new college graduates who wanted to teach failed the test and could not get a job. On the other hand almost no one fails the certification test in Connecticut. Would you be willing to bet that the quality of teaching in Connecticut suffers because their certification test is not difficult to pass?

Often substitute teachers do not have to be certified. It makes sense that when a school needs a teacher for a short time that certification might not be much of an issue. But we can put it in a different context. What if we decided that it was essential for teaching to be considered a profession and in order to do that it was necessary to change many common practices? Given those conditions, no one without certification could ever be allowed to teach. Would we be satisfied with a substitute lawyer who had not passed the bar or a substitute doctor who had not passed the medical boards? Teaching is all about exceptions.

Our generalization about degrees and certification makes the assumption that times are "normal" and there is an adequate number of teachers. The demand for teachers and the supply of teachers is at the mercy of many different variables. For example, when women had the opportunity to go into professions other than teaching it effected the supply. When the baby-boomers were in school, they affected the demand for teachers. Soon, many teachers will retire and there will be a demand for more teachers.

States have rules for those times when the regular rules need to be broken. If there is a shortage of math teachers, for example, states will allow people not certified in math to teach. A teacher certified to teach social sciences might end up teaching American history during one class period and first year algebra the next. This teaching out of one's field is not unusual. One source estimates time spent teaching outside of one's field is about 16 percent, while another writes:[34]

> In some states the 'percentages of high school classes taught by teachers who did not have a major, minor, or 20 quarter hours of preparation included Geography, 92%; Physics, 43%; Chemistry, 43%; Math, 36%; History, 32%; and English, 30%.' Thus, the areas most typically misassigned are in the core curriculum.

The percentages for junior high schools and middle schools are said to be even higher.

---

[34] Newman, op. cit., p. 22, believes it is 16 percent, and the quote is from deMarrais and LeCompte, op. cit., p. 152.

States do what they can to attract teachers. They allow people to teach without certification on a temporary basis, or they simply drop traditional teacher education requirements in some cases. New Jersey allowed people who had no teacher training to begin teaching in elementary and secondary classrooms as provisional teachers. Newman reports that "more than 40 percent of New Jersey's teacher recruits are now entering the occupation by the alternative route."[35]

When there is a teacher shortage, some states offer signing bonuses while others require few education courses and no certification exam to begin teaching. To discuss the remarkable variety of exceptions and tests and requirements (or nonrequirements) would simply illustrate this point: Teacher certification has little or no relationship with medical or legal certification. What seems unclear, and this is a genuine problem, is the relationship of certification and good teaching. Until we know what we want teachers to do, and what skills and knowledge they need to do it, then certification remains little more than a primitive political activity.

Judging Teachers

There are about 3 million teachers in the United States. If entry into teaching is only marginally difficult, then it is fair to wonder about what happens once they have a job. The question is interesting because it revolves as much around money as it does quality of teaching. It turns out that judging teachers and paying teachers are so tightly bound together that it is very difficult to talk about one without the other. The most intensive assessment of some teachers comes during their college days when they are student-teachers. As they begin to practice their craft everything they do—from lesson plans to grading papers—is discussed. They are observed as they teach and are able to learn from their experience.

The real question of assessment comes later, when a person has been teaching for some years. The teacher is now tenured and, it is assumed, doing a good job. But how would anyone know? How would it become a question?

The most obvious way for teaching to become a question is if someone was doing a very poor job and there were constant complaints. There are, of course, those who are acknowledged as wonderful teachers by their colleagues and students. Finally, it would be common sense to simply tie salary to how well someone teaches. The best teachers get the most money.

While it is simple (and good business) to give a bonus to the realtor who sold the most property, or the chemist who developed the new drug, or the CEO who helped the company produce a huge profit, there seems to be a completely different dynamic going on with public school teachers. The idea that money and performance are related has yet to be fully accepted in education. The reasons are historical and political.

The traditional contracts for teachers are not difficult to understand. After the first year, a raise is given for each year a person teaches. These increases are fixed and automatic. Every year you teach you know exactly what your raise will be. Raises are

---

[35] Newman, op. cit., p. 23.

also given for earning more college credits, for getting a master's degree, for earning credits beyond a master's degree, and for earning a doctoral degree. Again, the raises are automatic and fixed.

In the context of the discussion, money has not been used as a way to assess and reward teachers. Salaries have nothing to do with how well a person teaches or how well his or her students do. The contract sets the rules for how teachers are to be compensated, and for what, and there is not room for individual judgment.

The idea of merit pay has, from time to time, been a source of serious disagreement. The argument is simple enough: reward good teachers with bigger pay increases. It makes perfect sense. Well, perfect sense unless you are a teacher. It has been the teachers who have been most opposed to merit pay, and their reasons have everything to do with politics. They have successfully argued that to institute merit pay would soon come to mean that administrators would be able to reward their friends and punish their enemies. To understand the politics of many public schools is to have sympathy with the fears of the teachers.

There are also the very complex issues of the relationship of teaching and learning, and how that is assessed. How do we measure outcomes, and who do we reward? For example, do we reward those teachers whose students do well on state exams? If we did that, we know teachers in the more wealthy school districts would get the most money. Should the rewards be based on whose students are most improved? In that case, the teachers in the lowest performing (poorest) districts would get the most because their students have the biggest chance of improving. Before people agree to the idea of merit pay, they have to first agree on what merit is.

There are other ideas about how to pay teachers. Some argue that career ladders make sense; that teachers should be able to do extra tasks for more money. There is also the idea that different levels of certification could mean higher pay (we will review this idea in a later section).

What is important for this discussion is that, in public schools, the assessment of a teacher has nothing to do with pay. Unlike most occupations in the United States, compensation is not related to evaluation. Because there is so little agreement on what schools should be doing, and what teachers should be teaching, and just how fair administrators might be, it is easy to understand why teachers continue to like the traditional pay scale.

Money, then, does not help us understand how to assess teaching. Earlier, we read about what people needed to be able to do in order to be a good teacher. They needed to know each of their students, be able to motivate them, know their subject, and the like. In 1994 the National Board for Professional Teaching Standards outlined five general things it took to be a good teacher. The standards said teachers need to: 1) be committed to students and their learning; 2) know the subjects they teach and how to teach them; 3) be responsible for managing and monitoring student learning; 4) think systematically about their practice and learn from experience; 5) be active members of learning communities.[36]

---

[36] National Board for Professional Teaching Standard, *What Teachers Should Know and Be Able to Do* (Detroit: NBPTS, 1994).

Tests (specific for different teaching areas) were created around these principles. The object was to develop a national certification for those who had been teaching for some time. It was to be a "badge of merit" for the country's best teachers. A National Board Certified Teacher would be the "highest honor the profession has to bestow." The first national certificates were awarded in 1995 (81 teachers from 23 states), and the process is still being refined.

There are two things that should be noted. First, the idea of a national certification using the above five criteria is a good one. That there might be at least one national assessment with appropriate values and standards for those already in the field can rightly be understood as a positive thing. Second, to devise an appropriate and accessible test for this "badge of merit" will be difficult, at best.[37]

The original test was comprised of several parts. Each candidate spent a school year compiling a portfolio of his or her work. The portfolio consisted of examples of their students work, reflective essays, and a videotape of their teaching. During the summer they went to an assessment center where they took written exams, defended their portfolio and were interviewed by those doing the assessments. In sum, the process seemed to cover all the necessary areas and seemed a reasonable approach.

What the National Board did not count on was the time and money involved. During that first year, it took as long as twenty-three hours to evaluate each candidate's materials. Even then, the evaluators complained that they were getting only "glimpses" of each candidates work. The board had two evaluators go over each portfolio and, in some cases, more evaluators were used. Each candidate paid an application fee of $950 to take the test. The board paid $4,000 to evaluate the first round of each candidate. Clearly, something had to change.

In 1995 the Board raised the application fee to $2,000 in hopes that states or school districts would agree to help pay some of the fee.

This national assessment is an impressive step toward better understanding teacher evaluations and establishing a kind of certification that might be taken seriously. As opposed to the remarkable variation in state certification, this national test has the potential to begin to systematically recognize and honor good teachers.

Different Tests and Certification

Lawyers need to know the law, and doctors need to know about the body. Teachers need to know what to teach and how to teach it. While there is generally agreement about how to certify lawyers and doctors, as we have seen there is little or no agreement on how to certify teachers. Even if there was agreement about what education should be, there is no agreement about the skills and knowledge teachers need.

The complicated problem of what teachers need might require a simple (but hugely difficult) answer. Possibly, one test does not come close to solving the problem. To find another answer we need to begin looking in another place.[38]

---

[37] The following discussion comes from Newman, op. cit., p. 91.

[38] This, as were many ideas in this book, was suggested by my colleague Andy Effrat.

Howard Gardner proposed the idea of multiple intelligences more than a quarter of a century ago.[39] He argues that it is foolish to believe that all intelligence can be reduced to linguistic and logical-mathematical. Those, of course, are on what most testing—from basic IQ tests to college entrance exams—is based. From reading and writing and arithmetic in elementary school to verbal and math scores that mean so much to those people in college admissions, we are taught early what we need to know to score well on standardized exams, and to be thought of as smart.[40]

To repeat, according to Gardner, there are more than two types of intelligence. As a prerequisite for deciding something is an intelligence, he writes:[41]

> To my mind, a human competence must entail a set of skills of problem solving—enabling the individual *to resolve genuine problems or difficulties* that he or she encounters and, when appropriate, to create an effective product—and must also entail the potential for *finding or creating problems* —thereby laying the groundwork for an acquisition of new knowledge . . . The prerequisites are a way of ensuring that a human intelligence must be genuinely useful and important, at least in certain cultural settings.

Gardner goes on to describe eight "signs" of an intelligence. His effort is to both show and prove that there are other intelligences.

In addition to linguistic and logical-mathematical intelligence, there are also musical, spatial, bodily-kinesthetic and personal intelligences. A short description of personal intelligence will be most helpful for our purposes.

Gardner explains there are two parts of personal intelligence. The first is "the development of the internal aspects of a person. The core capacity at work here is *access to one's own feeling life* —one's range of affects or emotions: the capacity instantly to effect discriminations among those feelings, and eventually, to label them, to enmesh them in symbolic codes, to draw upon them as a means of understanding and guiding one's behavior."[42] This is an intrapersonal trait, it is about introspection and the ability to develop a deeper understanding about self.

The other personal intelligence is about others and is turned outward. Gardner writes that "the core capacity here is *the ability to notice and make distinctions among other individuals* and, in particular, among their moods, temperaments, motivations, and intentions."[43] A good therapist would need this kind of intelligence, as would a good politician, parent and, in some cases, teacher.

What I would like to suggest is that we teach different things at different levels of school. The wonderful third grade teacher simply does not need the skills of a won-

---

[39] The following discussion comes from Howard Gardner, *Frames of Mind: The Theory of Multiple Intelligences*, Tenth-Anniversary Edition (New York: Basic Books, 1993).

[40] I do not want to leave the impression that this is the only problem with tests. In Peter McLaren *Life in Schools*, 3d edition (New York: Longman, 1998), p. 26, we read that the "groundwork for the SAT" was racially biased. We will take this up in a later chapter.

[41] Gardner, op. cit., pgs. 60–61.

[42] Ibid., p. 239.

[43] Ibid., p. 239.

derful college lecturer. If we take the idea of different intelligences seriously—and I think we should—then we need to rethink our testing.

Generally Gardner's work has been used to make us sensitive to the fact that our students have different skills and abilities and it is important to attend to those differences. It is a good reminder that the best teaching goes on when we understand our students as individuals, and are able to present things to their strengths. Whole curriculums have been developed around these different intelligences and the idea of multiple intelligences has an ever-increasing number of supporters.

What Gardner has done, in part, is take what we know intuitively—that there are different kinds of abilities and talents—and systematically develop it into a working set of ideas. Contextually, different abilities—intelligences, if you will—gain and lose importance. If you want to be a basketball player, the need for musical intelligence does not seem too important. If, to take a Gardner example, you were a Puluwat youth who must learn to sail long distances by using the stars, spatial intelligence would be a necessity. Logical/mathematical intelligence would be of little help.

What we have, then, are two concepts that might serve as the basis of somehow assessing and certifying teachers. First, there are more than two kinds of intelligence. Different tests need to be devised so we can judge a variety of intelligences. Second, context is important for helping to know which intelligences are needed. It may well be that one or neither of the traditionally tested traits of language and math is necessary for all teachers.

The answer to the question, How should teachers be assessed and certified? would become this: The assessment should be on what skills and abilities a teacher needs to do his or her job. The answer is also almost hopelessly complex: What intelligences do teachers need for each subject at each grade level, and who will be able to invent the tests for them?

This is not the place to obsess about who needs what to be a good teacher. One way to think about it is a continuum from pre-kindergarten·to graduate education. At the pre-kindergarten level it would seem that a priority would be personal intelligence. That teacher would need an exquisite sense of who the children were; their moods and temperaments and intentions. Teachers simply need to be tuned to younger children. While that is not a bad trait for those teaching graduate students, it seems essential at lower other levels.

At the other end of the continuum is doctoral education. The image, and it does get played out in our research institutions, is of the professor lost in an esoteric world of his or her discipline trying to make that one discovery that will change the world—or at least gain some personal status and maybe even a little fame. That graduate student working with that professor learns a great deal about his or her subject. While the personal intelligence of the professor may help learning, it is not central to the process.

Assessments of the first grade teacher and the professor working with a graduate student would have almost nothing in common. What would make one perfect for a doctoral dissertation advisor may make that person totally unable to teach first grade. That doesn't mean the professor couldn't teach first grade, it simply means that skills to direct dissertations do not generalize into the skills it takes to teach a seven-year-old.

Genuinely helpful teacher assessment and certification will not happen until there is some acknowledgement that one or two skills, and one test, does not fit all. The reality is that schools of education need to somehow begin to sort out who has the intelligence to teach what. There should be a way to make some reasoned judgment about those students who want to teach. While they may make good grades and even do well on current certification tests, that does not mean they have the intelligence needed to teach.

Of course, certification exams need to test the right intelligences for the right levels and subjects.

We have seen that many teachers do not do well on standardized tests. That has been so since standardized testing began. The argument here is that that might not mean much of anything. It would be much better for teachers if they could be tested on the strengths they needed to do their jobs well. One suspects that many would score very high on those tests—and their self- and public-image would at least have a chance of being correspondingly high.

What traits will you need to be a good teacher, and will anyone ever test for them? What subject will you need to know, and will you be able to take the courses you need to learn it?

In the face of questions about what teachers need to know, and are they professionals, and how are they to be certified, it is wrong to think that teachers are without power. For almost a hundred and fifty years teachers have been organized. The history of their unions and associations gives us another way of understanding teachers in the United States.

UNIONS

Before there were teachers unions there were teachers associations. The first associations were statewide and had little or no power. These organizations were, not surprisingly, run by males. At the 1853 meeting of the New York State Teachers Association the women teachers, who made up about two-thirds of the delegates, were only allowed to observe the proceedings.[44] The topic of the meeting, after a couple of days, finally turned to a discussion of why teachers were not as respected as lawyers and doctors.

For the first time at any teachers convention a woman spoke. Imagine the shock. A woman asked the presiding officer for permission to speak. "What will the lady ask?" asked the chair. "I wish to speak to the question under discussion," replied Susan B. Anthony. The chair did not know what to do so asked what "the pleasure of the convention" would be. He was talking to the men, because only they could vote, and he could easily have a discussion with them because men sat in the front and women sat in the back. It was moved and seconded that Ms. Anthony should be allowed to speak. After a half hour debate, the motion carried by a small majority. Susan B. Anthony then said:[45]

[44] Grand and Murray, op. cit., p. 83.

[45] Ibid., p. 84.

> Do you not see that as long as society says woman has not the brains enough to be a doctor, lawyer or minister, but has plenty to be a teacher, every man of you who condescend to teach, tacitly admits before all Israel and the sun that he has no more brains than a woman?

Her biographer writes that she intended to make the point that the only way to make teaching level with the other professions was to either let women enter those professions or exclude women from teaching, but she was too nervous and she had to stop.

After the meeting, many women were upset that she had spoken. Only a few supported her.

The story gives us a remarkable sense of the social environment at the time the first national teachers association was formed. Women were beginning to take over classrooms while men continued to have power. Teaching was not a high status occupation to begin with, and as the percentage of women teachers increased, the status of teachers decreased.

The National Education Association (NEA) was formed in 1857. Its founding work was to nationalize the state educational associations. For much of its history it focused on shaping the American school system. It was the NEA, in 1892, that formed the Committee of Ten on Secondary Schools (see chapter 3) under Charles Eliot. The work of that committee was finished by the NEA Commission on the Reorganization of Secondary Education that issued a report in 1918 and helped shape our current high school system.

From the late nineteenth century the NEA worked to standardize teacher education. By 1925 teacher training was "rather systematically standardized" and the NEA claimed a large share of the credit.[46] Over the first hundred years of its existence, NEA conventions were a key place for discussions about curriculum changes in public schools. The NEA changed in the 1960s.

For those first hundred years the NEA thought of itself as a professional association. Its concerns were with school organization and teachers. For many years the NEA was controlled by administrators, college professors, and school superintendents, and its focus was educational policy. It was not a union and did not want to be a union. It did not deal with traditional union issues such as pay and working conditions. Its members, for example, would negotiate their salaries individually. While the NEA was an important force in sharing and distributing information that helped nationalize and standardize schooling, the issues of teachers were largely ignored.

There was a teachers union that prided itself in taking care of the issues of workers. In 1897 the first union local, the Chicago Teachers Federation, was organized. It did the traditional work of unions, and had early success in fighting for pensions and higher salaries. By 1902 it joined the Chicago Federation of Labor (AFL) and, as the American Federation of Teachers (AFT) put itself in the mainstream of the labor movement. Unlike the NEA, the AFT has traditionally been more inclusive than

---

[46] Joel Spring, *American Education*, 8th ed. (Boston: McGraw-Hill, 1998), p. 58.

exclusive. Its membership includes "public and private school teachers, paraprofessionals and school-related personnel, higher education faculty and professionals, employees of the state and local governments, nurses and health professionals."[47]

Key leaders of the early AFT were women who strongly favored feminist causes such as the right to vote and social and economic equality. Again, unlike the NEA the AFT traditionally drew a line between managers and workers. The AFT was a worker organization that believed their interests were fundamentally different from those of management. Although men (traditionally, the school managers) eventually took over the leadership of the AFT, the focus of the organization remained on worker's issues for decades.

The tension between the organizations is instructive. Professionals do not unionize; they do not understand themselves as "workers," so basic bread-and-butter issues would be somehow considered beneath them. In that regard the NEA made a great deal of sense. It was an association of people involved and interested in educational issues and set about to influence and help make national policy. One could imagine MDs doing much the same thing.

On the other hand, teachers had low status, were treated poorly, and made very little money. Being *that* kind of professional hardly pays the bills. What the AFT did certainly made as much sense as what the NEA did. The AFT took on the everyday issues of those who labor in schools and militantly tried to make working conditions and pay better for its members. While it lacked the luster of being a professional organization it certainly made up for it by helping to improve the everyday life for its members.

I do not want to suggest that teacher's lives were ever wonderful; indeed, we know that teachers continue to be relatively poorly paid. The AFT had no organizational control over a local school system until 1944 when it signed a collective bargaining agreement in Cicero, Illinois. Until the middle of the twentieth century it had almost no impact on school systems. To get a sense of the country during the 1950s, in 1956 there were still 34,964 one-teacher schools in the United States.[48] Big city schools were a world away from rural America, and while teachers were organized, some were isolated and most were powerless.

The change began during the end of the 1950s. In New York City the AFT began to organize the schools. The fifty thousand teachers in the system belonged to a baffling number of organizations that centered on subjects and grade levels taught. The AFT argued that one union that focused on the bread-and-butter issues shared by all teachers could be a powerful force. The organizer was Albert Shanker, a former high school teacher. There was a bitter struggle over the right to organize.

The Shanker group voted to strike over issues that today are accepted facts in most school systems. They wanted to be able to conduct a collective-bargaining election, have a dues checkoff plan, give teachers fifty-minute lunch periods, change the salary schedules, and provide sick pay to substitutes. On November 7, 1960, fif-

---

[47] Ibid., p. 56.

[48] Dan Lortie, op. cit., p. 5.

teen thousand teachers did not go to work, and seventy-five hundred picketed around the schools.

The Board of Education finally agreed to a collective bargaining election and in 1961 New York City teachers voted to be represented by AFT Local 2, The United Federation of Teachers. By a 3–1 margin Local 2 won the right to bargain for the entire teaching force in New York City. That was the beginning. During the 1960s and '70s the AFT grew four times as fast as the NEA. In 1966 there were 125,421 members of the AFT; in 1981 there were 580,000 members.[49] Teachers, like so much of the population during that time, became militant and one way to act that out was through a union. The issues stressed by the AFT spoke to many of legitimate and long-standing concerns of teachers.

There was, of course, a remarkable number of ways teachers were militant during the sixties. While most agreed with the aims of the AFT, there were many pedagogical issues that were outside of the scope of both the NEA and the AFT. The free and alternative schools that were created had little to do with any national organization. The discussion about the NEA and the AFT is about mainstream public school teachers and administrators.)

The New York City strike was the beginning of teachers organizing to gain power. While there had been teacher strikes following World War II, collective bargaining agreements put a different spin on these actions. The most serious strike was in Buffalo, New York, in 1947. The teachers, members of the AFT, went on strike for higher wages. While strikes, no matter what the circumstances, are often dramatic and difficult things, the stakes seem higher when a national union is involved. Union action gains automatic sympathy from other unions. A teacher's strike, for example, may easily lead to the Teamsters deciding not to cross picket lines.

The Buffalo action was a model of an effective strike. Other unions supported the teachers. Local drivers, to take a specific example, delivered only enough heating oil to keep the pipes in the schools from freezing. Although the AFT had a no-strike policy, what happened in Buffalo clearly signaled that it was the obvious group to fight for the demand of the teachers.

The dynamic from the sixties to the eighties was simple enough: teachers organized, demanded collective bargaining, and if they needed to they would strike. The most active period for teacher strikes, 1979–80, was a time when the cost of living was rising much, much faster than teachers' salaries. The AFT, which had long since abandoned its no-strike policy, sanctioned 34 strikes that year; NEA affiliates went on strike 208 times. As wages began to catch up with the cost of living, the number of strikes decreased. There was an average of 100 strikes a year from the mid- to the late eighties.

An interesting thing happened during that time, and the numbers give us a clue. The NEA became more militant while the AFT seemed to become more conservative. The switch in positions signaled a change in the way teachers presented themselves to the world.

By the end of the 1950s the role of the NEA in shaping national educational policy had been greatly reduced. The National Defense Education Act of 1958 increased

---

[49] Spring, op. cit., p. 62.

the role of the federal government in the discussion of national educational policy. The NEA also seemed to be losing touch with teachers as the AFT was increasingly successful initiating collective bargaining agreements for its local chapters. It became clear that to remain the largest and strongest teacher association the NEA had to change its attitude about unions.

If prior to the sixties the NEA thought it was unprofessional to belong to a union, by the 1970s the organization had changed its collective mind. It joined the Coalition of American Public Employees and endorsed its stated purpose of "supporting legislation to provide collective-bargaining rights to all public employees, including teachers."[50] By the 1980s the NEA became fully involved in politics. It supported candidates who were pro-education and pro-union. At the Democratic National Convention in 1996, about 12 percent of the delegates were members of one of the two teachers unions.[51]

The NEA has reconfigured itself. It is now a politically active organization that is much more concerned with social issues than the AFT. For its part, the AFT began criticizing the NEA for being too politically active. Somehow, the AFT has lost its traditional labor-union radicalism. By the mid-eighties to the mid-nineties the AFT endorsed the Reagan/Bush view that one of the major purposes of education was to help the United States compete in the emerging international economy. While the AFT endorsed neither Reagan nor Bush, their endorsement of education that seemed to carry out the business of business was a significant marker in their evolution.

By 1994 the AFT was even willing to discuss merging with the NEA. There is general agreement on issues such as vouchers: Both are against any public support for private or for-profit schools. But generally the NEA is a much more progressive organization that would like to rethink the role of schools and teachers. The AFT continues to support more traditional ways of organizing schools and teaching.

At the turn of the century, there were simply too many problems for a merger to take place. The NEA continues to be nervous about affiliating with the AFL-CIO, and the AFT is still worried that the merger would produce a "monster" union that could easily be attacked as simply another special-interest group. Both groups are in agreement that bread-and-butter issues will remain important to their members.

How teachers have chosen to organize may help us understand who they are. While teachers are union members, it seems wrong to say they are workers in the traditional sense. As we saw earlier, there are ways in which teachers fit even the most conventional definition of professional. But if teaching is a profession, it is one that is more difficult to define and more diffuse than either law or medicine. Teaching has too many bosses and goals to fit into easy categories. When serious social and cultural changes need to be made, all too often it is schooling, and teachers, who are told to be in the forefront. When it was time to industrialize, schools got students ready for

---

[50] Ibid., p. 59.

[51] At the Republican Convention, nominee Bob Dole said: "And to the teachers unions, I say, when I am President, I will disregard your political power for the sake of parents, children, the schools and the nation . . . If education were a war, you would be losing." Ibid., p. 55.

that life. When families seemed poorly equipped to provide their own children with the skills needed for a changing world, schools were asked to take over those responsibilities. So too with integration, the idea that girls and boys were equal, that a diversity of cultures could be a positive thing . . . and on and on.

Beyond the demands of society are the demands of parents and the needs of each student. And, for the classroom teacher, there are the directives and memos from school boards, superintendents, and principals.

All of this takes place in the context of often less-than-ideal schools and less-than-adequate pay.

The unions mirror these tensions. There is still a great desire to have the respect that comes from being a profession. Certainly teachers take great pride in the job they do and acting in a professional manner. But it is more than that. There is the desire of many teachers to make a difference, and the biggest teachers union is now wholly involved in politics. The political effort is a natural outgrowth of the personal everyday efforts of teachers to make a difference to at least one student.

Along with the idealism is the simple fact that in this remarkably prosperous country it is not a bad thing to enjoy its flood of consumer goods. It's nice to live in a pretty house, drive a cool car, dress well, and be able to send your kids to college. If you are a teacher it is almost impossible to do all those things. Unions will continue and try to make the physical life of teachers better.

TEACHING: WHY AND WHY NOT

The remaining two questions are at either end of the continuum: Why do people teach and why do people quit teaching? As you should expect, there are multiple answers to each question.

In order, people teach because they: 1) enjoy working with students, 2) like academics—the subject they teach, or learning in general, 3) like the job advantages, 4) believe the job has social value, and 5) appreciate the influence of other teachers.[52] Almost half the people surveyed had "enjoying working with students" as their first choice, about 20 percent liked academics most, while only 5 percent thought the influence of other teachers was the most important reason for teaching.

All that we have seen in this chapter supports the idea that people who teach both enjoy and have concern for their students. More than 150 years ago the role of schools began to change and Horace Mann argued for the feminization of America teaching so that the effect in the classroom would be different. If teachers were to become mothers to their young students then it made good sense that teachers should be women. Today, 88 percent of all elementary school teachers are women. In a 1995 survey, 84 percent of the teachers talked about their students when asked what they liked best about their work.

---

[52] This list comes from Newman, op. cit., p. 5.

Certainly enjoying an academic life, having job security as well as summers off (although almost 20 percent of the teachers surveyed worked during summers) make teaching attractive. Doing something of social value is, it seems to me, simply another aspect of getting satisfaction by working with students.

Teachers are happier now than they have been in the recent past. During the 1970s and '80s the percentage of teachers who said they would certainly or probably choose to become teachers again was as low as 46 percent. It is not a good thing when less than half of those teaching thought, essentially, that they had made the right career choice.[53] By the 1990s nearly 70 percent of those asked said they would choose to be teachers again. Indeed, most said that they looked forward to going to work, and only 8 percent would change their job if they could.

That teachers are now happier indicates that their working conditions have improved. In the early 1990s, Karen Louis found that there were seven conditions that teachers found important:[54]

1. Respect and status from their community
2. To participate in decision making that influences control over their work setting
3. Frequent and stimulating professional interactions among their peers within their school
4. Have the opportunity to make use of their skills and knowledge, be given the chance to develop new ones, and the opportunity to experiment
5. Develop ways for teachers to obtain frequent and accurate feedback about the effects of their teaching on student learning
6. A pleasant physical working environment and adequate resources to do their job
7. A sense of congruence between personal goals and the goals of the school. The teachers want a low degree of alienation.

In her interview, Louis found that respect and status in the larger community was easily the most critical factor. It is interesting to note that salary was not on the list. While certainly not overpaid, it is clear that one effect of the activism during the 1970s and 1980s was to raise teachers pay. We need not overstate the case. Feeling respected has not resulted in huge economic gains for teachers. Further, as more states require standardized testing the implication is that teachers do not know what is best for their students.

There are other ways to understand working conditions. Teachers average a forty-five hour work week. They are required to be at school for an average of thirty-three hours a week, and spend the rest of the time in preparing for class, reading papers, meeting with parents, and, doing other school related activities. Elementary school teachers spend less time grading papers, and private school teachers spend more time at school and doing after-school work.[55]

---

[53] Grand and Murray, op. cit., p. 15.

[54] Karen Seashore Louis, "School and Community Values and the Quality of Teachers' Work Life," pp. 18–19, quoted in Tozier, Violas, and Sense, op. cit., p. 315.

[55] Spring, op. cit., p. 48.

The average teacher works for a male principal, teaches an average of 181 days each year, and only about 5.5 percent have teacher aides.[56] In 1993 the average size of a public school class was about 23 students. The average high school teacher taught 5.6 classes per day in public schools, and 6 classes per day in private schools.

We can look at the conditions of labor to understand why teachers drop out.[57] Teaching is fragmented by the structure of school life. There are announcements over the intercom, students leaving class, students changing classes, fights between periods, requests from other teachers, fire drills, assemblies, and so much more. School can be sensory overload for everyone involved. For teachers, the structure of school often interrupts the flow of teaching. It is difficult to arrange joint activities with other teachers. There are some schools that have completely restructured around collaborative teaching. But they are the exceptions; in most schools the conditions for teaching fragment learning.

Most teachers are isolated from other adults. They teach in schools that look to motels for their architectural model: many rooms off a long hallway that seem to ensure isolation. Teachers see their colleagues before and after school, between classes, and at lunchtime. Only where there is team teaching do teachers seem to have the time to talk together.

There is, clearly, an issue around students and discipline. There is a range of teacher attitudes and levels of teacher comfort when it comes to how students conduct themselves in class. It seems that the more experimental classrooms are less structured. Classrooms are also less structured in many upper-middle and upper-class schools. Discipline, to generalize, often increases as one goes down the socioeconomic scale. As public attitudes and laws have changed, it is seemingly more difficult for teachers to enforce classroom discipline.[58] The changes over the years have been difficult for some teachers.

There is a lack of tangible results for teachers. We read: "Teaching is a labor process without an object. At best, it has an object so intangible—the minds of the kids, or their capacity to learn—that it cannot be specified in any but vague and metaphorical ways . . . [teaching] does not produce any things, nor . . . does it produce visible or quantifiable results."[59] The lack of a concrete product is a relatively unacknowledged problem that is as real as classroom violence. While there is certainly satisfaction when students do well, and pride when students remember and acknowledge a teacher's good influence, the fact remains that teaching produces few tangible results. Teaching does not change the physical, visible world. The lack of actually seeing a product can be surprisingly wearing.

[56] DeMarrais and LeCompte, op. cit., p. 166.

[57] Much of this following discussion comes from ibid., pgs. 167–73.

[58] We will take up the topic of vionence in a later chapter. This is not the place for the full discussion that it needs.

[59] R. W. Connell, *Teachers Work* (North Sydney, Australia: George Allen & Unwin, 1985), p. 70, quoted in ibid., p. 169.

Finally, teachers are asked to do a variety of things. They teach, they coach, they develop instructional materials, they monitor the hall, they watch the lunch room, they supervise extracurricular activities, they serve on committees, they tutor and counsel and sometimes act as social workers for families. There are often too many things to do, too little time to do them, and too few resources to do them right.

The conditions of labor, then, do not seem to be ideal. So, why do teachers say they leave teaching? In a 1996 Phi Delta Kappa poll of teachers, the top four reasons were: 1) lack of student discipline, 2) low pay, 3) lack of student interest, and 4) lack of parental support.[60]

We can understand more by what those who left teaching had to say. In a 1986 survey, 57 percent of those who had stopped teaching said they had been under "great stress" while in the classroom. Only 22 percent found great stress in their new jobs. Almost two-thirds said that they had not received the kind of respect they had expected when they were teachers and, while 58 percent said that they missed teaching, 83 percent doubted they would ever return to teachering. In the end, almost all those surveyed were satisfied with their new careers.[61]

There is a third way to think about why teachers drop out. Teachers are stressed.[62] The conditions of labor (and we will see other lists of these conditions in different contexts) are aggravating, isolating, and sometimes overwhelming. Teachers burnout. Tension builds up as work is added to the job description and, seemingly, power is taken away. There are those teachers who feel there is an overload of work and it is impossible to do all that is asked. They feel inadequate and want to withdraw.

The sociological concept is called alienation. An alienated person feels the world is meaningless and is powerless to change anything. Those ways of dealing with things in the past no longer seem to work, and in the end the individual feels personally estranged and culturally isolated. In 1986, a third of the teachers in a major study felt that their work was meaningless and were powerless to do anything about it.[63]

The good news is that teachers feel better and more positive about their work. The bad news is that burnout and alienation remain a part of teaching.

SUMMARY

While we now know more about teachers, there is much that is still a mystery. Some of what we learned was obvious. Teaching continues to be a job for white middle-class (and increasingly middle-aged) women. The most important reason that people teach is because they like their students. Over the years, the pay has gotten better, as have the working conditions. On the whole, teachers like their jobs.

---

[60] Quoted in Newman, op. cit., p. 13.

[61] Ibid., p. 13.

[62] This discussion comes from deMarrais and Lecompte, op. cit., pgs. 170–1.

[63] A.G. Dworkin, *Teacher Burnout in the Public Schools* (Albany, N.Y.: State University of New York Press, 1986), quoted in ibid., p. 173.

The problems of teachers were divided in two parts: internal consensus and external legitimacy. If we use Weber's model of professional, then it is clear that teachers need to agree on what is needed to be done in order for the larger community to give them the respect and legitimacy they desire.

The search for consensus leads to difficult questions. What are the aims of education (or, schooling) in the early twenty-first century? If teachers could answer the question, the next series of questions is just as difficult: What should be taught? Who should teach? What should those teachers be taught? Should they be certified and, if so, how? How should their work be assessed?

What we learned was that there was no consensus on any of those questions. Our history in the United States is one of constantly changing aims and no agreement on standards. Each state makes its own rules and it seems that every state has exceptions to those rules. While doctors do not have those problems, I tried to suggest that they have problems of their own that teachers should try to avoid. I also suggested that we reexamine how we think about the tests we give those who want to go into teaching as well as those who want to be certified.

Much of the problem of external legitimacy comes from the lack of internal consensus. But the social context of teaching is more complex than that. Different people want different things from public schools. It has always been a political issue, and what makes it more messy is that the experts—educators—do not agree on what needs to be done.

The result is that teachers occupy a strange place in American life. The population feels strongly enough about education to make children go to school. Billions of dollars are spent yearly on education. Yet teaching is not a high status occupation, and it is relatively commonplace for politicians to criticize current educational practices and suggest plans for better schools. These same politicians (especially Democrats) want to be friends of the NEA and AFT. Teachers who, individually, are not very well paid and without much status, have organized themselves into a powerful union.

This chapter raised more questions than it answered. The rest of the book is about classroom issues a teacher must face, and the broader cultural context with which he or she must deal. By sorting through issues with the problems of this chapter in mind we may, by the end, be closer to answering our questions.

THINK ABOUT

1. What should teachers know?

2. Why aren't teachers more highly regarded?

3. In your life as a student, how many teachers have you had that you believe should not be teaching?

CHAPTER FIVE

SUGAR/SPICE/SNAKES/SNAILS AND TESTOSTERONE
On the Matter of Girls and Boys

From the expectations and guidance communicated by parents early on, children can see in time that one set of characteristics is desirable for females and another set is preferred in males. Their peers are receiving similar messages.

Quoted by Carolyn Pillow

[Texas] did raise the age of consent for a woman from 7 to 10 in 1890—but it went a little smoother after we got some say in it. Until June 26, 1918, all Texans could vote except "idiots, imbeciles, aliens, the insane and women."

Molly Ivins

My generation was taught that little girls were made of sugar and spice and everything nice, and little boys were made of snakes and snails and puppy tails. Over the years there have been a remarkable number of studies to find out the accuracy of these descriptions. Some findings suggest they are (at least metaphorically) true, while others refute them. Biologists and psychologists and social scientists come at the issue of boys and girls in different ways, and their answers point us in different directions.

When you walk into a classroom and see boys and girls, what do you think? Do you assume they are the same and should be treated in identical ways? Or, do you think that they really are different in important ways; ways that need to be considered in everything from lesson plans to classroom interactions?

Good teachers will say, and we must believe them, that they treat every student as an individual. Each person is unique and sex has nothing to do with it. On the other hand, if we talk with those same good teachers long enough we will find that from the minute kids walk into kindergarten they bring with them the notion of what a boy is and what a girl is. We know that this knowledge just expands, so by the time of middle school, girls are losing self-esteem, and boys are an awkward mix of hormones, fear, and power—and sexual differences seem to be at the center of what goes on.

To treat every student as an individual means that a teacher needs to take into account how that student sees her or himself. Sex—and much of what we are really talking about is identity—is too important to ignore.

There is a great deal of research and a huge literature about boys and girls. Regrettably, the problem of how we should deal with boys and girls does not seem to have a scientific solution. The studies tell us a great deal, but in the end what we are dealing with is a complex mix of politics, biology, and culture. Our myths interact in powerful ways with our biology. As we will see, to sort everything out seems to be beyond our current capabilities.

It is important to remember that sex and gender are not the same thing. Sex has to do with the part you play in reproduction, while gender is mostly learned from and reinforced by society. We will see how sex and gender are related, but keep in mind that they are not the same thing.

In this chapter we will review what the theorists say about girls and boys, what the studies show about how the sexes do in school, and finally ask the question: Is the equal treatment of the sexes fair treatment?

We begin with what the psychologists tell us.

PSYCHOLOGY

For most of the life of mainstream psychology, men have been the standard of healthy growth. Men, biologically, have always been understood as being physically superior to women. That physical superiority—and it is actually only physical strength—was somehow translated into psychological superiority. Men were superior, were the role models; women were inferior and dependent. It was simply assumed that male traits were best. In chapter 1 we saw it was true for Rousseau and, as we shall see, it was true for Sigmund Freud.

Sigmund Freud

Freud believed that a person's psychological development was most deeply effected by his or her physiological interactions in early childhood.[1] To experience normal development a boy needed to experience great anxiety during early childhood, and develop a great hatred for his father. As the conflict (this is the Oedipus complex in which the boy competes with the father for the love of the mother) gets resolved boys begin identifying with their fathers. In doing so they develop both a conscience and morals. By doing this boys are able to take their rightful place in society. They are able to participate in the advantages of being male in a patriarchal society. Boys who

---

[1] L. Brannon, *Gender: Psychological Perspectives* (Boston: Allyn & Bacon, 1996). Much of the first half of the chapter relies on work originally done by Carolyn Pillow, *Teaching Gender: A Qualitative Study of How Gender Appears in the Thinking of Four Elementary Teachers* (Doctoral dissertation, U. of Massachusetts, Amherst, 2000).

do not completely break with their mothers remain too feminine and, according to Freud and the culture of his day, inferior.

Think about the theory for a minute. Here is Sigmund Freud, the father of modern psychology, a person who was wholly committed to science,[2] giving us what is at least an understandable account of how a healthy boy should grow up.[3] Let me put it a little differently. The first love of every baby is its mother. It seems reasonable that little boys might resent their fathers when the mother gives him attention. There might be "competition" for the mother. But soon the boy understands that he has much more in common with his father than his mother and, indeed, will grow up to be a father. In order to form a masculine identity the boy needs to break away from his mother.

In the course of doing this, in the course of identifying himself as a little man, the boy develops certain moral dimensions. For Freud this was the very definition of normal. Indeed, it was the standard by which development had to occur.

The question, of course, is what about little girls? By definition they could not develop normally. Freud wrote that because of women's failure to develop a complete super-ego "that they show less sense of justice than men, that they are less ready to submit to the great exigencies of life, that they are more often influenced in their judgments by feelings of affection and hostility."[4] Freud wrote that women were less ethical, more concerned with personal appearances, and had more self-contempt then men. They were also jealous of men's accomplishments.

Freud was not only the father of modern psychology; he was also the father of Anna Freud. He encouraged her when she wanted to become a psychoanalyst, and he readily accepted women as colleagues. Anna became a powerful person in the field, and was an early voice of protest about some of her fathers' ideas. There were other voices: Karen Horney, Helen Deutsch, and Melanie Klein developed important critiques of the work done by Freud. Each attacked Freud in different ways, and all believed his ideas about female inferiority were wrong. Horney wrote:[5]

> The girl is exposed from birth onward to the suggestion of her inferiority . . . It seems impossible to judge to how great a degree the unconscious motivates for the flight from womanhood are reinforced by the actual social subordination of women.

Women were caught in a vicious circle of strong social prejudice that demanded certain kinds of behavior. When women behaved in those socially demeaning ways that were prescribed by the culture, they simply reinforced the idea that they were inferior.

---

[2] "Wholly committed" is an overstatement. Apparently he also liked cocaine a great deal.

[3] Of course this is not new to Freud. The "complex" gets its name from the Greek myth Oedipus Rex.

[4] S. M. Okin, "Thinking Like a Woman," in D. L. Rhode, ed., *Theroretical Perspectives on Sexual Difference* (New Haven: Yale University Press, 1990), p. 148.

[5] S. Quinn, "Awakened to Life: Sources of Independence in the Childhood of Karen Horney, in M. M. Berger, ed., *Women Beyond Freud: New Concepts of Feminine Psychology* (New York: Brunner/Mazel, 1994), p. 6.

While the work these women psychologists was important (but not to a majority of their colleagues) professionally, it wasn't until the 1970s that Freud's (and society's) views about women were successfully challenged.

Nancy Chodorow and Carol Gilligan

In 1978 Nancy Chodorow argued that gender development was different for girls and boys.[6] She theorized that parenting, especially during the first two years of a child's life, was done primarily by the mother. The baby has no real sense of self and is, essentially, one with the mother. It is during this period that girls develop a sense of being self-continuous with others. When it is time to separate from the mother the child is already identified as a female. Girls grow up with the care-taking abilities of the mother with whom they have fully identified. These abilities are understood by the girl as positive, and became an important part of her identity.

That is the part Freud failed to mention. Chodorow does agree that boys need to reject their mothers in order to develop an identity that is different and separate. She believes that boys have a more difficult task than girls do. But Chodorow went beyond Freud by arguing that one of the lasting effects of the boys' rejection of the mother (and that which is feminine) is that they develop a mistrust and sometimes fear of femininity.

With this turn, boys are no longer the standard of psychological development; indeed, boys have a tougher time finding their identity than do girls. Jean Baker Miller continued the case for girls and women.[7] She argued that the traditional traits of women should not be understood as negative but as positive. In a male dominated world, qualities such as affiliativeness, relatedness, empathy, and nurturance are systematically devalued and distorted. (We should remember that traditionally our liberalism and capitalism preached the virtues of individualism.) Miller writes that girls learn very young that they need to depend on others for their individual development. She argues that the female traits are both powerful and positive, and should be the model of behavior.

Until Carol Gilligan, studies of human development were of white, upper-class boys and men. As we know, males had been the models of human beings in Western culture for as long as that history has been recorded. Gilligan studied females.[8] Her findings led her to believe that there was a woman's way of thinking. She found that a constant theme of the women she studied was "caring for others." Gilligan believed that this caring was a natural part of a woman's development, and it should be understood not as a weakness but a strength that allowed women to act responsibly towards themselves and others.

It is easy to see how Gilligan's work fits nicely with that of Chodorow. We saw that Chodorow believed that boys had a difficult time separating from their mothers,

[6] Nancy Chodorow, *The Reproduction of Mothering* (Berkeley, Calif.: University of California Press, 1978), p. 38.

[7] Jean Baker Miller, *Toward a New Psychology of Women* (Boston: Beacon Press, 1976), p. 38.

[8] Carol Gilligan, *In a Different Voice* (Cambridge, Mass.: Harvard University Press, 1982), p. 40.

while girls keep a feeling of connection with the mother with whom they identified. It follows almost naturally that while boys would value separation, girls would value connection. The conclusion is easy enough: girls think differently than boys. They develop differently, they grow up differently, they think differently: Girls and boys are different.

In this view of the world, boys grow up with a strong sense of autonomy, finding their power by being competitive, being judgmental, and having a great deal of faith and command of the rules. The girls build alliances and partnerships, and try to empower others. To put all this in a little different context, boys grow up preparing to go into bureaucratic structures that minimize the connections between people, while girls grow up with other kinds of abilities.

These psychologists have helped change our world. While there remains a sense that girls and boys should be treated the same, much has changed. What should the teacher do about the differences? The studies show the obvious: It is dangerous to overgeneralize. Generally, girls might think differently than boys, but that does not tell us how any particular boy or girl might act. But, how do teachers not make assumptions before they know each student well?

It is also interesting to note that many of these female traits are exactly those that lead Horace Mann and others to begin to feminize teaching. What were thought of as weaknesses a hundred and fifty years ago are now considered strengths. As parts of our world become linked technologically, and as speed and change seem to be the central elements of many of our dealings, it is exactly these newly recognized and described female traits that seem best suited for the future. The bureaucratic model of organized life seems too awkward, too rule-bound, and too slow for the twenty-first century. The psychology of women, in no small part, seems to be the psychology of our post-industrial age.

The final question that needs to be asked is this: Are these psychological traits a product of conditioning or physiology? Are boys and girls different because they are taught to be or because they were born that way? This has been a discussion of the idea that gender, in part, is based on sex. What these studies do not tell us is the role society plays in enforcing these views (and stereotypes). Later, we will discuss how gender is taught, and rewarded, but first we turn to biologists who have tried to answer that question.

BIOLOGY

There are biological studies that indicate physiological differences between boys and girls (beyond the very obvious differences) and may explain why they have different abilities. While there is no widely held consensus that biology is intellectual destiny, there are those in the field who believe strongly that many differences between boys and girls have their basis in physiology.

Studies show that girls are perceived as having better language skills than boys, while boys are perceived as doing better in math and science. (Later in the chapter we will discuss these and other differences.) In studies of the brain, it was found that women use both hemispheres of their brain in language and spacial functions (reading and geometry) while men tend to use the left hemisphere for language and the right for spacial functions.[9] This indicates that women have more generalized brain use for language while men might be able to specialize more in math and spatial abilities. Some believe that the way men and women use their brains have some degree of influence on female/male cognition.

When babies are born, infant girls have a greater sensitivity to sound, more skin sensitivity, better fine motor performance, and a greater ability to handle sequential movements than infant boys.[10] Girl babies seem to be more reflective than boy babies, while the boys are more emotionally expressive (girl babies will suck their thumbs when they are unhappy, while boy babies tend to cry).[11] If that were true, then it would be normal for parents to treat girls and boys differently. If girls are more sensitive and attentive it would make sense to talk to them and hold them more frequently than they do boys.

The tension is set-up: If girls and boys show different traits at birth, it seems reasonable for adults to treat them differently. However, as society continues to treat boys and girls differently, and in less than subtle ways forces them to act differently, at what point does nurture become more important than nature?

Testosterone

Boys are drawn to movement of larger objects and it would be natural for parents to play more, and rougher, with them. It could well be that the difference begins in the womb. Every embryo is female and unless it is altered by testosterone it remains female. Testosterone masculinizes the brain and body of the fetus. Boys experience a flood of testosterone twice: the first time in the womb about six weeks after conception and the second at puberty.[12] The chemical has serious effects on how we look and how we act.

Boys have higher levels of testosterone and lower levels of serotonin than girls. It is believed that serotonin inhibits aggression and impulsivity. Nearly 95 percent of kids with ADHD (attention deficit hyperactivity disorder) are boys.[13] Four times as many boys are dyslexic and are learning disabled as girls. If that is the way boys and girls begin life, then it should be no surprise that they are different by the time they get to school.

Much of what tests show depend, of course, on the test itself. For example, boys are supposed to be superior to girls in spatial perception. The **rod and frame test** has

[9] The work was done on stroke victims; Brannon, op. cit.

[10] M. Notman and C. Nadelson, "A Review of Gender Differences in Brain and Behavior," in their edited book, *Women and Men: New Perspectives on Gender Differences* (Washington D.C.: American Psychiatric Press, 1991), pgs. 23–41.

[11] Barbara Kantrowitz and Claudia Kalb, "Boys will be Boys," *Newsweek*, May 11, 1998, p. 56.

[12] Andrew Sullivan, "The He Hormone," *The New York Times Magazine*, April 2, 2000, p. 49.

[13] This and the following data comes from ibid., pgs. 59 and 69.

always been the standard way to study spatial perception. To make this point we need to understand the test.

For the rod and frame test the subject is asked to adjust the position of the rod (which is simply a line) to a horizontal or vertical position while ignoring the position of the frame it is in. Usually boys and men did better than girls and women on this test. One could conclude that boys and men had superior spatial ability. However, when the test was changed the results also changed. A human figure was substituted for the rod, and the subject was told that the task was a measure of human empathy. With those changes, women outperformed men.[14] What do we make of that? Do the results of this test tell us about the influence of biology on human abilities, and if so, exactly what?

We know that levels of testosterone account for differences in human activity. Higher levels in men seem to be associated with winning athletic competitions and, sometimes, aggression and other antisocial behavior. People with higher levels of testosterone are more willing to be competitive. While testosterone exists in both men and women, the fact is that men produce ten to twenty times as much testosterone as women.

But human biology is never simple. It is possible that there is a feedback loop between competing and winning and levels of testosterone. In other words, the more a person competes and does well the higher the levels of testosterone will be, so the more the person will want to compete, which will lead to more testosterone and on and on. It is easy to see in athletes and also with actors. Studies also show that women in professional, technical, and managerial jobs have significantly higher levels of testosterone than housewives or clerical workers.

Indeed, we find that some measures of aggression seem to become more alike when women and men have similar roles.[15] We know that as women climb the corporate ladder they display more "masculine" ways of thinking about justice. Even a woman's size and strength change when her actions and environment change. As we will see in the next section, we have no clear idea just what the biological limitations are for women.

What can we make of this? Is biology destiny? One of the things that seems clear from the testosterone example is the relationship between biology and environment. Our bodies are capable of changing given the context; or, we may change our environment given who we are—and in turn the environment will change us. Later in the chapter we will pick up the testosterone discussion again and see that its effects remain surprisingly strong.

While there are biologists who are firmly convinced that the differences between males and females begin with biology, the case is not nearly convincing enough for agreement. Before we turn to the effect of the environment on gender, it is important to take a step back and think about what we know about raising our young.

---

[14] Brannon, op. cit., and A. Fausto-Sterling, *Myths of Gender: Biological Theories About Women and Men* (New York: Basic Books, 1985).

[15] David Schuman, A Preface to Politics, 5th ed., p. 84.

EARLY HUMAN LEARNING

What we know about infants and babies, whether they are girls or boys, has changed over time. As we understand more about how the human brain develops, and as we study the results of different ways of raising children, we are slowly letting go of some myths. That does not mean we are raising and educating our children well, it just means that it is possible to look forward to the time when we might reasonably agree on what is best for most children. This section is centered on some of our myths about babies, and why they are wrong.

The first thing we need to understand about babies is that they are not wholly "egocentric."[16] While all too often we think of young children as having no appreciation of others, just the opposite seems to be the case. Jerome Bruner writes that not only is there intense interaction between parents and child, there is no other species on earth in which "the young point things out to bring them to the attention of an adult, even looking back from the things pointed out to see whether the adult 'got it.'"[17]

There are a remarkable number of everyday examples that show us the ties between the young and their parents. Parents teach their babies speech by simplifying their syntax to match what the baby can understand. Virtually from birth mothers and infants share attention and are able to work together in an intersubjective way. Human learning starts very early. The parents want to teach and the babies want to learn.

As educators (and parents) we are concerned with that learning. For some time the questions have been these: What should be learned, and by when? Interestingly, those may be the wrong questions.

It may well be that a basic part of being human is to try and understand what it means to be human. That task begins in the crib and the learning process is instructive. According to Alison Gopnik, Andrew Meltzoff, and Patricia Kuhl, babies are born with a kind of "start-up" knowledge that is inherited from our evolutionary past.[18] That knowledge gives them a way to begin to figure out what they encounter. Once a baby has made sense of something, that new experience modifies his or her initial knowledge and leads to a better understanding of other things.

There is, in other words, a consistent stream of new knowledge that loops back and changes a baby's basic mental construct. And much of this is a social activity. Language is a good example. Language is learned because of a steady dialogue with parents and adults, but that could never take place without the particular development of a child's nervous system.

Bruner tells us that the development of a baby's mind is like Ulysses's ship during his ten years of wandering. During those ten years the ship needed continual repair. By the end of the journey the ship had been almost entirely replaced with new material. It was, in a sense, not the same ship at all. Piece by piece, the ship had to be

---

[16] Much of the following comes from Jerome Bruner, "Tot Thought," *The New York Review of Books*, March 9, 2000, vol. XLVII, no. 4.

[17] Ibid., p. 27.

[18] See *The Scientist in the Crib: Minds, Brains, and How Children Learn* (New York: Morrow, 1999).

rebuilt. There was little left of the original ship by the time Ulysses returned. On the other hand, it looked exactly like the ship he set sail in and that he always thought of as his ship. The human brain is much like that: While it is always the "same" brain, there are ways it is constantly being replaced and the most recent brain is not like the early brain at all.

What research shows is that while babies begin to learn almost from birth, and they do so in a social manner, not much is gained by pushing them to learn more and sooner. According to John Bruer[19], early stimulation has almost no effect on brain development during the first three years. He argues that early growth is genetically programmed and is self-driven. While a lack of stimulation might hurt development, more stimulation has no positive effects.

In an $88 million study done by the National Institute of Child Health and Human Development, it was found that a host of early child care programs had only minor positive effects. "Psychologically well-adjusted mothers and sensitive, responsive mothers had the most securely attached infants . . . But the 'amount, stability, type or quality' of child care beyond what a mother provided has little effect on a child's attachment to her mother."[20] Again, the exception was for children raised in economically disadvantaged families. High-quality child care at least helped make up for poor mothering.

The bottom line is that children who had good parenting ("frequent, affectionate, responsive interactions") during their first three years developed better cognitive and linguistic skills. High-quality day-care added little or nothing to that development.

We as a society push to make certain our children learn more and learn it sooner. But do we know, for example, when it is appropriate to teach children to read? Western Europe provides surprising illumination. Hungarian schoolchildren do not start reading until they are seven. In preschool they do a great deal of oral work (learning nursery rhymes, songs, playing show-and-tell and the like), but do not begin to read or write.[21] The result is that they are behind children in other nations.

The most "hurry-up" country in Europe is Britain. They teach their children to read very early. By the age of twelve, the Hungarian children are near the top of the European League, and the British have steadily dropped to lower levels. That is not the only case. "In German-speaking Switzerland, kids who start reading later and are given lots of oral training are more literate by age twelve than their French-Swiss cousins, who begin reading at four."[22]

This is not the place to speculate about why we push our children so hard. Certainly all of us can connect our ideological push to succeed (as well as our fears of having our children drop in social class) with wanting our young to succeed ever faster. The most powerful preschool and grade schools in New York City are the most diffi-

[19] *The Myth of the First Three Years: A New Understanding of Early Brain Development and Lifelong Learning* (New York: Free Press, 1999).

[20] Bruner, op. cit., p. 29.

[21] For a thoughtful discussion about orality, see Barry Sanders, *A Is for Ox.*

[22] Ibid., p. 29.

cult of all schools to get into. Later, we will see that admission to Harvard College is easier than admission to some of these preschools. We are also aware of the studies that tell us about how deprivation can somehow "mark" a child for life, and we might over-compensate to make sure our family has every opportunity.[23]

What we find, in part, is that infants are much brighter and more social than we had ever thought. The very young are "cognitively active" in their cribs during their first year of life. They are like that naturally, and what helps most are attentive and loving parents. For our purposes, we can focus on two very important things. First, even first-rate childcare that provides wonderful stimulation does little to help a normal child who has had good parenting. Second, we see that pushing kids to learn "school things" like reading and writing when they are young is not helpful.

The fact is that there is no general agreement about what to teach children and when. The reason for spending time on this general argument (that children are capable of a great deal without being pushed) is that gender might be involved in the equation. It is possible that if we let children learn at a slower pace, with an emphasis on different things, then girls and boys might develop academically in less gender-specific ways. Possibly, if we wait, learning might be more even between boys and girls—not to mention, waiting will put off the pressure to perform that we routinely add at a younger and younger age.

The longer we delay teaching specific skills, the longer we set aside our prejudices about what boys and girls can do best.

Of course, even though this is mere speculation, it is something that we need to think about. As we will see in the next section, socialization has played a huge part in defining gender by the time children get to kindergarten.

ENVIRONMENT AND SOCIALIZATION

We can begin with something that seems obvious: Socioeconomic class influences many traits we think are natural. For example, males are generally bigger than females. We also know that in most cultures male children are more highly valued and treated better than female children. What we can expect, then, is that in those countries where there is a big class difference, the children of the privileged classes will be taller than those of the lower classes. We know that drug-addicted babies are smaller than average babies. We also know that babies born by malnourished mothers, as well as babies who are malnourished, are smaller than average babies. Immigrant families to the United States show surprising increases of height from one generation to another. And, of course, we can't forget the obvious: Tall parents are likely to have tall children.

Environment matters. There are studies of how people raised in round homes (for example, teepees) have a different sensitivity to vertical and horizontal than do Europeans, who are raised in rectangular rooms. The inferential leap here is that

---

[23] Ibid., p. 30. Interestingly, these studies do not always tell us what we think they do. The studies on deprivation, according to Bruner, are centered on such extreme deprivation that they tell us almost nothing about the human experience.

brains can be shaped by environment. If women are raised as if they are fit for only certain jobs (house jobs, for instance), then their brains may not be suited for many other jobs. What if it turns out that the many hours some kids spend in front of video games result (as many parents may hope) in greater ability in learning to use more complicated computers in school and at work? If that happens, we may lament the strongly male orientation of the video-game industry. (Nearly all of the subscribers to the main video-game magazines are male.)

If the shape of your room may make a difference in your sense of reality, think of how remarkably strong socialization might be.

While we know that there have been great efforts to erase gender socialization, and in some ways the efforts have been successful, there is still a long way to go. We can begin with adults. In a series of tests, two groups of people were asked to evaluate particular works—articles, paintings, resumes, and the like.[24] The names attached to each item were clearly a woman's name and a man's name. The names were reversed for each group. In other words, one group was told something was a woman's and the other group was told that the same work was a man's.

In both groups, work that was believed to be a man's was rated higher than when it was believed to be a woman's. In all of the studies, women were as likely as men to downgrade the women's work. In another study, female college students rated scholarly articles higher if they believed the articles were written by a man than if they believed that they were written by a woman.[25]

Those are remarkable studies. They indicate disturbing things about our culture and ourselves. We need to ask when they begin to develop, and how these attitudes shape us.

GENDER SOCIALIZATION

We begin treating girls and boys differently from infancy. We will see that by the time boys and girls start school they are already acting like boys and girls. While schoolteachers certainly do their share of teaching gender-appropriate roles, the first teachers are parents.

Boys are interacted with more often by both parents, are held more by both parents, and are played with more roughly. Mothers talk with girl babies more than they talk with boy babies. Finally, in spite of the fact that there is no difference in sturdiness, strength, or response in early infancy between girls and boys, girls are handled more gently and are thought of as more fragile than boys by both parents.[26]

When young children were dressed in the clothes of the opposite sex, adults reacted to infants and toddlers based on stereotyped notions that were represented by

[24] Schuman, op. cit., p. 98.

[25] Ibid., p. 98.

[26] B. Ring, "Early Childhood Sex Role Socialization," in A. Carelli, ed. *Sex Equality in Education: Readings and Strategies* (Springfield, Ill.: Charles Thomas, 1988).

the clothing. The boys dressed in girls' clothes were perceived as "quiet and sweet" and were played with more gently, while the girls in boys' clothes were spoken to more loudly and seen as "tough little guys."[27]

Parents responded significantly more positively to children who acted in "correct" stereotypical ways. For example, they approved of the assertiveness of young boys and attempts to communicate by young girls. The adults did this despite the researchers' observation that both the girls and the boys were equal in their assertiveness and attempts to communicate.

Girls are given soft and cuddly toys and boys are given materials to build things with. Boys begin their active life from the beginning while girls are expected to be nurturing. From eighteen months to three years, the training continues:[28]

> From the expectations and guidance communicated by the parents early on, children can see in time that one set of characteristics is desirable for females and another set is preferred in males. Their peers are receiving similar messages. These messages are reinforced by toys, books, advertising, television, and extended family and friends. In short, sex role expectations pervade the social environment of babies and children from birth.

By the age of two research shows that children tend to select toys and play games that are understood as gender appropriate. Children at this age have also learned that there are appropriate settings for the play to take place. Girls play with girl-toys inside, and boys play with boy-toys outside. While it is clear that there are girls who play with boy-toys and boys who play with girl-toys, the research shows that by the time children get to preschool, powerful gender lessons have been learned. ("We gave the boys dolls and they used them as guns."[29]) Generally, boys and girls get to preschool knowing how boys and girls are expected to act.

Studies show that preschool teachers interact with boys and girls much the way parents do.[30] Like parents, these teachers treat girls more gently and boys more robustly; they talk more loudly and are more directive with boys; they encourage girls to play quietly with dolls, coloring materials, and the like, and give boys toys like building blocks that require more activity.

But it might not matter much what the teachers do. Even when teachers set up gender-neutral environments and encourage the children to initiate their own play, it turns out the girls choose domestic themes (setting up a room) and the boys are full of action (looking for a lost animal).[31] When it came to computers, there were

---

[27] J. Streitmatter, *Toward Gender Equity in the Classroom: Everyday Teachers' Beliefs and* Practices (New York: State of New York, 1994).

[28] L. Perry and H. Sing, "Differential Differences in Young Children's Sex-Typing: Automatic versus Reflective Processing" (ERIC Document Reproduction Service, No. ED 356888).

[29] Kantrowitz, op. cit., p. 56, quoting Michael Gurian, *The Wonder of Boys*.

[30] Streitmatter, op. cit.

[31] J. Cook-Gumperz and B. Scales, *Girls, Boys and People: Gender and the Discourse of the Nursery School*, 1993 (ERIC Document Reproduction Service, No. ED 360074).

no differences in either interest or competency. However, boys were more assertive about gaining and controlling access. When the girls were asked why they finally stopped trying to use the computes, they said things like "other people [boys] use it," or "I did want a turn but there were always other people [boys] there all the time."[32]

Preschool boys are more physically and verbally aggressive than preschool girls. They are generally more critical, insulting, and challenging in their interactions with their peers. Girls, by preschool, have become more interactional in their style. They question, request, invite, and are more inclusive than boys. To a remarkable extent, boys are boys and girls are girls by preschool.

Kindergarten and Grade School

When kids get to kindergarten they are ready to somehow convert what they know about gender roles into who they are. "Kids of this age [five and six] are the worst chauvinists, because they are trying to define the really rather fuzzy categories of male and female . . . They have just learned that the exclusive categories of boy and girl are exclusive. So they think that if you're a boy, you do boy things and *not* girl things. The same goes for girls. In trying to make sense out of these categories they make them much more separate than they need to be."[33]

Generally, girls learn well in teams, they prefer to avoid confrontations, and they compromise in order to reach solutions. Boys seem to be more competitive and want to resolve problems by getting their own way. This is the accepted wisdom and is generally supported by research. What we don't know is how much was determined by biology and how much by the social context. We certainly know that these generalities do not describe any single person. What is clear is that by kindergarten, gender plays a major role.

We can see an interesting tension between those who believe in the notion that girls and boys are the same, and the forces of capitalism.[34] At the turn of the twentieth century, Toys "R" Us decided to redesign their stores. They were going to group products most likely to be bought by the same types of customers. They called this approach "logical adjacencies." Not surprisingly, it was almost entirely based on what we think of as gender. Girls World was full of Barbies and Easy-Bake Ovens, and Boys World was full of action figures and trucks.

The research done by Toys "R" Us showed that gender differences began as young as two, and it was redesigning its stores to make shopping easier for everyone. There was such a negative public response that they cancelled their plans.

In the year 2000, the Fox Family Network planned to begin two new networks: girlzChannel and boyzChannel. Their research showed that girls were more interested in "entertainment that was more relationship-oriented" and boys were more

---

[32] J. King and N. Alloway, "Preschooler's Use of Microcomputers and Input Devices," *Journal of Educational Computer Resarch*, 8, 1992, p. 463.

[33] Nancy Seid, "The Gender Gap: Why Sexism Flourishes in Kindergarten," in Linda Orozco, ed., *Perspecives: Educating Diverse Populations* (Boulder Colo.: Coursewise Publishing, 1998), p. 2.

[34] The following examples come from Sullivan, op. cit., p. 59.

"action-oriented." The new channels would make it more efficient for Fox to attract both advertisers and consumers.

The two examples are interesting on several levels. There are ways in which capitalists need to be very sensitive to what people believe. To offend the public is the easiest way to go out of business. Both Toys "R" Us and Fox clearly believe that boys and girls are different. But politics got in the way of what they believed. When thinking about gender, sex, and socialization, we need to remember that the facts of a case may never be as powerful as the politics that surround them.

By elementary school, teachers expect boys to be more active and aggressive than girls. Boys interrupt teachers more than girls do, and it seems to be all right. One study found that boys called out eight times more than girls, and the teacher called on them whether the comment was relevant or not. When girls called out the teachers corrected the girls' behavior and reminded them of the rule about raising your hand before talking. The girls were immediately put in their place while it seemed that boys were just being boys.[35]

Elementary school teachers expected girls to take "caretaker" roles. Girls were expected to be well behaved as well as helpful to both the teacher and classmates. Girls even fought for the privilege of staying inside during recess and helping the teacher. For their help, the girls were given great praise.[36] It should be noted that race and class were rarely variables in these studies. When race was considered, white girls were generally considered the model students. Teachers praised white girls, and these girls were loyal to their teachers. They avoided challenging their teachers and generally accepted what the teachers said.[37]

GENDER AND ACADEMIC WORK

How teachers treat boys and girls means something academically. In elementary school, boys get more attention—both positive and negative. While most of the positive attention is about their academic work, it turns out that most of the time boys get more response to their work. If it is praise, correction, help, or even criticism, it all helps foster achievement. Most negative response for boys is because of their behavior. Teachers give praise to girls for being neat or quiet or having good handwriting or for their behavior. Girls get most of their negative responses for their academic work. Put differently, boys seem to get better instruction than girls.[38]

---

[35] M. Sadker and D. Sadker, "Sexism in the Classroom: From Grade to Graduate School," *Phi Delta Kappan*, 67, 1986, pgs. 512–5.

[36] Ibid.

[37] White females were least reprimanded and black males were most heavily reprimanded. See R. Best, *We've All Got Scars: What Boys and Girls Learn in Elementary School* (Bloomington, Ind.: Indiana University Press, 1983).

[38] Sadker and Sadker, op. cit., p. 57.

When teachers talk to girls about their appearance, the conversations are usually longer, and the focus stays on how pretty the girl looks. Sometimes the emphasis moves from personal appearance to papers and work. When boys are praised, it is most often for the intellectual quality of their ideas. Girls are twice as likely to be praised for following the rules of form. "I love your margins" is the message.

How teachers treat students might be based, in part, on gender stereotypes that we have discussed. It is possible that teachers avoid giving more negative comments about academic topics to girls because they believe that girls are more vulnerable and emotional and less able to handle criticism. Boys, if we believe the stereotypes, are given more academic feedback because they are thought to be strong and capable of improving their work because of help from the teacher.[39] (If we add race, white male students received more feedback than white, black and Hispanic girls, and black and Hispanic males.)

Elementary teachers believe that the academic ability of girls and boys is different. They project higher grades for middle-class Asians and female students, and white girls are believed to have higher academic skills than black females and males of either race.[40] Not surprisingly, students who were perceived as being behavioral problems were thought to have lower academic skills regardless of their actual skill level or gender.[41]

Girls and boys are understood in different ways by their teachers. Boys are often seen as doing well because of their ability and the help of their teachers. Boys' failures are understood as the result of a lack of effort. Girls are seen as doing well because of their efforts, not because of their ability. If a girl does poorly, or is a behavioral problem, that is often seen as an indication of her true ability.

Entering the second grade, a study showed that there were no differences in the math and reading abilities of boys and girls. During that year, teachers spent more time with girls during reading lessons and more time with boys during math lessons. By the end of the year, the girls were better readers and the boys were better at math.[42] So what's going on here? From what we read before, by the end of the second grade our image of the way things should be turned out to be true: Girls were better readers and boys were better at math. What we do not know is how much of that is self-fulfilling prophecy. Would it be different if our stereotypes changed and that led teachers to spend more time with boys learning how to read and more time with girls learning math?

[39] J. J. Irvine, "Teacher-Student Interactions: Effects of Student Race, Sex, and Grade Level," *Journal of Educational Psychology, 78,* 1986, pgs. 14–21.

[40] D. Tom, H. Cooper, and M. McGraw, "Influences of Student Background and Teacher Authoritarianism on Teacher Expectations," *Journal of Educational Psychology, 76,* 1984, pgs. 259–65.

[41] R. Bennett, R. Gottesman, D. Rock, and F. Cerullo, "Influence of Behavior Perceptions and Gender on Teachers' Judgments of Students' Academic Skill," *Journal of Educational Psychology, 85,* 1993, pgs. 347–56.

[42] G. Leinhardt, A. Seewald, and M. Engel, "Learning What's Different: Sex Differences in Instruction, *Journal of Educational Psychology,* 71, 1979, pgs. 432–439.

What is true for math is also true for science. A number of studies show that girls and boys received different treatment when learning science. Boys used the science equipment, performed more experiments, and participated in science activities more than girls. They were also asked to help assist with experiments more than the girls.[43] Interestingly, there is no significant difference in the attitudes of male and female teachers when it comes to science. And we wonder why there are fewer girls in science classes by the time they get to high school.

We can back up a little and think about math and science in a different way. What we know is that very young boys are much more likely to have experience in problem solving and action play than girls. Boys are encouraged to explore. Very young girls have more experience doing tasks. Their play is much more structured than boys, and they are less encouraged to explore. It's entirely possible that the cognitive skills of boys is helped, in no small part, by their knowledge of "building things." The cognitive skills of girls has to be influenced by their experiences of "cleaning up" and being neat. If that is true, then girls and boys may well approach math and science in different ways.

The tests that measure computational skills (adding, subtracting, multiplying, and dividing) generally favor girls/women, and tests that measure mathematical concepts or problem solving generally favor boys/men.[44] While those results should not surprise us, there is still no clear answer about which came first—the skill or the socialization.

We began this chapter by speculating about what the teacher saw when he or she walked into the classroom. We know, in most schools, there are boys and girls. To generalize, those boys and girls have a clear sense of what that means, and most of them, most of the time, do their best to act in character. One of the other things we know is that boys and girls mean something to teachers; it is one of the first cuts teachers make before they have learned what each student is like individually.

The bottom line is this: Teachers generally believe that the girls will do better academically in elementary school, but that the boys have more "ability." The boys will act out, and the girls will be better behaved. The girls will read better, and the boys will have better skills with math and science. While it would be foolish to believe that all teachers, at some pre-conscious level, work with these stereotypes, it would be equally foolish to believe that these attitudes play no part in what goes on in the classroom. Teachers are in a position to make their perceptions come true.

To Review

Before going on to middle school it makes sense to do a short review. It is a way to see, in one place, the very uneven development of boys and girls that has gone on during their first ten years.

---

[43] C. Mills, K. Ablard, and H. Strumph, "Gender Differences in Academically Talented Young Students' Mathematical Reasoning: Pattern Across Age and Subskills." *Journal of Educational Psychology, 85,* pgs. 340–6.

[44] Ibid.

Boys are born with bigger (about 5 percent) brains than girls, and proportionately larger bodies. Both disparities increase with age. (We should remember that the size of the brain does not affect intelligence.) At birth, girls have a higher proportion of nerve cells that process information. More regions of girls' brains are involved with language production and recognition.[45]

From ages four to six, girls are ready to go to school. They are relatively calm, they get along with others, they are able to pick up social cues, and reading and writing come more easily to them than to boys. At the same age, boys are still trying to deal with their aggressiveness. Generally, they lag behind girls in reading skills. Hyperactivity might become a problem. This means, to put it differently, that school is tough for boys.

The next three years are even better for girls. On average, they are better students than boys. They continue to excel at reading and are even with the boys in math. From seven to ten the boys now have good gross motor skills, but still lag behind the girls in finer control. While some of the best students might be boys, nearly all of the poorest students are boys. What we have seen is that many social and environmental adjustments are made so that boys and girls have a relatively even chance at school.

What we will see are dramatic changes during the next eight years, and the changes are not necessarily good for either boys or girls.

MIDDLE AND HIGH SCHOOLS

Most teachers believe that they teach their students in the same way. That is true no matter what grades they teach. What we find is that the differences in boys and girls seem to increase as they get older, and some of that might have to do with how they are treated. The following is an example of how students are treated.

In 1994 Catherine Krupnick videotaped twenty-four secondary classrooms in the Boston area.[46] She wanted to find out who spoke and who was heard by the teacher. In an advanced math class, the teacher said that the boys and girls participated equally, that an equal number of girls and boys participated during the lesson. There were sixteen girls and nine boys in the class, so that meant there would be more girls participating than boys for "equal participation."

The reality was that only one boy and many of the girls did not participate. In this class there was a female student who had scored 800 on her math SAT. Although she knew the answers she never volunteered them, and the teacher never called on her. There was a male "B" student who made it a practice of calling out the answers. In one instance, the answer he gave was wrong, so the teacher went over and told him he could solve the problem in another way. The teacher and student talked about the

---

[45] Kantrowitz, op. cit., pgs. 57–8.

[46] C. Krupnick, "Gender, Speech, and What Teachers Hear in Secondary School Classrooms," in The Women's College Coalition (sponsor) *Studies in Success: Applying Effective Models to Educating Women and Girls* conference at Mount Holyoke College, 1994.

problem for eight minutes. During that time the 800 SAT girl sat and discussed the problem with the girl behind her.

This can be understood as a double-edged example. The teacher reinforced the notion that the boys have math ability. By going over and spending time with him, we can speculate that the first lesson is that it is important for boys to be right. The second lesson is that by not attending to the bright female student, the signal is for her to be quiet. It might even reflect on her ability.

It is certainly fair to be wary of overanalyzing and overgeneralizing from one example. Maybe this teacher, this time, was simply using good pedagogy and trying to bring a slower student up to the level of better and brighter students. But there are too many examples of teachers believing boys are better at math and science and working harder with them on those subjects. The example is good enough that it can be a metaphor for what happens all too often in middle and secondary schools. What feels like equitable treatment might not actually be equitable treatment.

Middle school is tough. At one end of the scale the dropout rate for boys begins to climb, and at the other end the good male students begin to pull ahead of the girls in math skills and are catching up in some of the verbal ones. Girls become more vulnerable because of the start of puberty. Many girls in this age group (eleven to thirteen) experience depression and as many as 15 percent may try to kill themselves.

Middle School and High School

In this section we will discuss girls, and then boys, in middle school and high school. This section is meant to give a sense of how some experience those years; it deals with broad trends and statistics and will tell you nothing about any particular person. Still, it would be surprising if you did not recognize either some of what you went through, or at least the lives of some of your friends.

Girls' confidence drops in middle school, and they deal with their problems differently than boys. By adolescence the boys turn their aggression outward while girls turn aggression against themselves.[47] In one study, it was found that girls in general are more likely (between one-and-a-half and two times) to feel stress than boys.[48] Not surprisingly, by high school almost half the boys strongly agreed with the statement "I am happy the way I am," while less than a third of the girls did.[49]

One of the reasons seems to be that boys have ways to deal with their problems that do not seem available to girls. We find, for example, that "There is a significant body of research showing that, among their peers, high-achieving boys compensate by clowning or through athletics; these options are ineffective for girls."[50] We know girls

---

[47] David Levit, "Gender Differences in Ego Defenses in Adolescence: Sex Roles as One Way to Understand the Differences," *Journal of Personality and Social Psychology, 61*, 6 (1991), p. 995.

[48] Found in Peggy Orenstein, *School Girls* (New York: Doubleday, 1994), p. 310.

[49] Ibid., p. 279.

[50] Ibid., p. 288.

are more involved with athletics than ever before and what we learn from that tells us something about the dynamic of sex and gender.

Girls who are physically active do have higher self-esteem than their less active counterparts. But the more revealing finding is that when the sports activities are coed—such as in school gym classes—the girls' confidence in their athletic abilities falls dramatically.[51] For girls as well as boys, high school athletics can also cause problems. By training too hard, some females will stop having their periods, and in sports such as gymnastics eating disorders are not unusual.

By the time Latinas reach adolescence, the percentage who say "I like the way I look" drops 36 points, from 47 percent to 11 percent. Those who believed they are "pretty good at a lot of things" drops from 51 percent to 18 percent.[52] In high school, 58 percent of the black girls strongly agreed with "I like the way I look," while 12 percent of the white girls and 11 percent of the Latinias agreed.[53] An interesting insight into the subcultures in the United States.

We know that girls this age develop eating disorders. By the ninth grade, almost 10 percent of the girls have used laxatives or have vomited in order to lose weight.[54] There is evidence that girls do not wait until high school to worry about their weight. Some studies indicate that there are girls in grade school, girls as young as seven, who "have adopted prevailing adult perceptions of beauty, including an unnatural standard of thinness."[55]

Weight is a remarkable issue. One study shows that 51.9 percent of non-obese high school girls went to college, while only 31.6 percent of clinically obese girls went.[56] By the time women get into the work force, severely overweight women are 20 percent less likely to get married, and earn at least $6,000 a year less than women who were more slim.[57] As a logical extension of the fact that white girls did not like the way they looked, they are the group most likely to have eating disorders.

By the time girls get to middle school, they begin to lose confidence. Even though they perform as well as boys in math, girls' confidence drops significantly. Girls who believe that math is a boys' subject consistently perform less well than girls who do not hold that view. Because confidence is a variable that is strongly correlated with achievement in math, the very idea that it is a boys' subject seems to hurt girls' performance.[58]

---

[51] Lynn Jaffee and Rebecca Manzer, "Girls Perspectives: Physical Activity and Self-Esteem," *Melpomene Journal, 11*, 3, 1992, p. 14.

[52] American Association of University Women, *Shortchanging Girls, Shortchanging America: Full Data Report,* (Washington, D.C.: American Association of University Women, 1991), pgs. 22–3.

[53] Ibid., p. 25.

[54] Kantrowitz, op. cit., p. 60.

[55] Quoted in Orenstein, op. cit., p. 297.

[56] Ibid., p. 298.

[57] John Schwartz, "Obesity Affects Economic, Social Status: Women Fare Worse, 7 Year Study Shows," *Washington Post*, September 30, 1993, p. Al.

[58] Orenstein, op. cit., p. 283.

Of course, confidence is not merely about math. A study showed that black girls' sense of pride in their schoolwork dropped 43 percentage points between elementary school and high school. By high school, only 12 percent of the black girls believed that their teachers were proud of them.[59] And a study of eighth-grade science classes reinforced what we know. The videotaped classes showed that in science labs, even when there were a majority of girls, they deferred to the boys, and the boys discouraged dissenting opinions. When there was a majority of boys, they insulted and ignored the girls until the girls finally stopped participating.[60]

The bottom line is that there is no social advantage for a girl to be smart in high school. Gifted girls were the least popular of all groups no matter what ability or gender.[61]

None of the above studies is at all encouraging. We need to ask serious questions about what happens after elementary school that so effects girls in school.

Boys

When boys get to middle school and high school they are beginning to struggle with some of the same issues as girls. For example, while it is not unusual to associate body image problems with girls, it would be foolish to believe that boys are not affected. The middle school seems to be the worst time for boys. During those years the boys and girls are most out of sync with each other in terms of development. What we are finding out is that boys have not escaped the problems of body images. The popular media is an interesting way to get into the problem.

We can begin to see this with the action figures GI Joe and his friends Batman and Wolverine.[62] The original Joe was projected to be a man of average height with a 32-inch waist, 44-inch chest and 12-inch biceps. By the time we get to Batman, he has a 30-inch waist, 57-inch chest, and 27-inch biceps. If Wolverine was the height of an average male, he would have 32-inch biceps. Those biceps (the size of my waist) would be larger than any bodybuilder in history.

If the ideal for girls is unrealistically thin, then the ideal for boys is unrealistically muscular. Girls stop eating while boys begin to work out and take steroids. And boys are mean to each other.[62a] In a 1994 study, it was found that the majority of kids in middle school were bullied by their peers, that the shaming was sex-based and much more intense for the boys.[63] In another study, it was estimated that an average high school student hears twenty-five antigay slurs a day.

[59] Ibid., p. 305.

[60] Cited in ibid., pgs. 286–7. Sadly, they found that girls lacked confidence even in all-female groups.

[61] Richard Luftig and Marci Nichols, "Assessing the Social Status of Gifted Students by Their Age Peers," *Gifted Child Quarterly, 34*, 3 (1990).

[62] Much of this discussion comes from Stephen S. Hall, "The Bully in the Mirror," *The New York Times Magazine*, August 23, 1999.

[62a] I do not mean to suggest females are not mean to each other. As I write, a group of high school girls in Illinois faces criminal charges for hazing younger high school girls. The hazing was simply violent.

[63] Adrian Nicole LeBlanc, "The Outsiders," *The New York Times Magazine*, August 23, 1999, p. 38.

A sixteen-year-old-boy who decided to work out in order to change his body (at one time he was 5'6" and weighed 210) describes his life before he got in shape. "When I was fat, people must have gone home and thought of nothing else except coming in with new material the next day. They must have had *study groups* just to make fun of people who were overweight. . . . My parents—God bless them, but they would make comments *all the time*. My father would say, 'If you eat like that, you'll be as big as a house.' And I'm like: 'Dad, it's a little late for that. What am I now? A mobile home?'"[64]

The culture has an idealized male body just as it has an idealized female body. As kids go through adolescence, and their bodies are in some kind of developmental hell, the further away they are from the ideal the worse their lives seem to be. While not new, it seems that the perfect male body is showing up in ads more often and in more aggressive ways. Boys are now catching up with girls in terms of insecurity and even psychological pathology.[65] And we can see a trend. Between 1996 and 1998 the number of men who had cosmetic surgery rose almost 34 percent.

In 1995, 23,000 girls between the ages of five and fourteen attempted suicide. Only twenty-three were successful. In that same year, 3,000 boys of the same age attempted suicide. But 260 boys killed themselves, more than ten times the number of girls.

In 1993 there was a study of steroid use among male weightlifters. Of those studied, 10 percent "perceived themselves as physically small and weak, even though they were in fact large and muscular."[66] The researchers called the syndrome "reverse anorexia nervosa" and, two years later renamed it "muscle dysmorphia." It is a condition that revolves around "an obsessive preoccupation with muscularity." The man who did the research, Harrison Pope, says:

> . . . people who are insecure about their body appearance are unlikely to come out of the woodwork to confess that they're insecure about their body appearance. And so it is an epidemic, which by definition is covert. But it has become a much more widespread concern among men in the United States.

This affliction can start becoming serious about the time a boy is eleven. That is the time when males experience their second great rush of testosterone. For boys, the amount of testosterone in the bloodstream rises roughly 100-fold during puberty. It is a flood of hormones that leads to a series of bodily changes, and can make that time sometimes impossibly difficult for young men. Middle school, as we have seen, is the worst time. Not only are boys and girls changing, but their changes are out of sync. Girls develop earlier, so that the pressure on boys—and especially those boys who change most slowly—can be unbearably great.

The numbers are discouraging. There has been a fivefold jump in the suicide rates of boys in the last forty years. Experts blame the problem on increasing male

---

[64] Hall, op. cit., p. 32.

[65] Ibid., p. 33.

[66] Hall, op. cit., p. 35.

depression and anger as well as easier access to guns.[67] The male–female arrest rate (this is all arrests) is 4–1 which is, interestingly, close to the testosterone difference between males and females. In 1998, 55 percent of everyone arrested was under the age of twenty-five. Andrew Sullivan points out that those are the years in which male testosterone levels are at their natural peak.[68]

In what could not have been a mistake, *Newsweek Magazine* did a revealing thing. In their cover story article they tried to make sense of boys—the current pressures on them and the best ways to raise them. It was a good piece, one that I used for this chapter. Of course there was a discussion of the pressures of society (and testosterone) on boys for them to perform like men. It was made very clear that the life of a boy, given all those pressures, could be tough. The very next article, and it was a long one, was about Viagra. The message seemed to be this: Gender expectations effect everyone and there seems to be a chemical solution to help meet every expectation.

We know that by high school there are male students who have caught up and sometimes surpassed female students. Classroom dynamics do not change a great deal from middle school, with boys remaining more outspoken and more dominant. By the end of high school males have progressed a great deal and society has found ways to reward them. Boys, who clearly begin school behind girls academically, receive 64 percent of the merit scholarships.

A SHORT REVIEW

What follows is a list of sex-role stereotypes found in an educational psychology textbook. It gathers many of the points we have been reading in a particular way. The list is introduced like this: "Think back to some of your experiences as a student or reflect on a classroom with which you are familiar as a visitor or observer. Which of the following practices did you observe?"[69]

1. Textbooks (or other curriculum materials) portray females as housewives and males as outside-the-home wage earners.
2. Teachers use the female gender with the roles of teacher, nurse, or social worker, but the male gender when referring to engineers, doctors, and lawyers.
3. Girls and boys grouped for certain types of activities during recess that reflect sex-role biases.
4. Teachers call on boys more for answers during math or science but girls more during language arts.
5. Different career advice given to girls and boys.

---

[67] Ibid., p. 38.

[68] Sullivan, op. cit., p. 58.

[69] Gary D. Borich and Martin L. Tombari, *Educational Psychology: A Contemporary Approach*, 2d ed. (New York: Addison-Wesley, 1997), p. 524.

6. Teachers address boys from across the classroom but girls from an arm's length distance or less.

7. Teachers reprimand boys more sharply and in front of students more often than girls for the same behavior.

8. Teachers praise girls when they choose activities associated with traditional gender roles.

9. Female teachers express misgivings about math more often than do male teachers.

10. Boys are more often corrected for academic mistakes and more often told to get it right than girls who make similar mistakes.

11. Teachers call on boys more often than on girls.

The authors are trying to get you to focus on how sex-stereotyping looks in an average classroom on a daily basis. The points are not very profound, but to see a list of eleven fairly common behaviors is a way to get us to an underlying tension of the chapter: If girls and boys are different, should they be treated differently in school? It is a question with no easy answer.

GIRLS AND BOYS

When it comes to issues of sex and gender there is a series of questions good classroom teachers need to sort through. For example, teachers need to decide if girls and boys are different. If they are, is the difference biological or because of socialization or a combination of each? Do the reasons for the differences matter? Or is sex, in the words of Martin, "like baldness, [a] difference that makes no difference"?[70] Finally, and this is the nub of the teachers' dilemma, if there are differences should we treat girls and boys differently? We can put the matter in another way: Would identical education mean unequal education?

We have a chapter full of facts and a lifetime of experience with these questions. There are studies that indicate girls and boys respond to things in different ways from the very beginning. Those differences lead adults to treat even infants differently which, of course, serves to exaggerate those early inclinations. By the time of kindergarten girls and boys have developed a sense of gender appropriate behavior. It is not clear if those behaviors are the result of biology or intense socialization.

We do know that by the time kids begin school, girls are ahead of boys developmentally, and teachers treat girls and boys differently. Even though teachers believe they are treating everyone the same, the data shows teachers generally reward girls for "girl" behavior and boys for "boy" behavior.

And when it comes to classroom behavior, most of the time girls act better than boys.

Jane Roland Martin believes that we must consider how females are treated outside the classroom before we make any decisions about how they should be treated in

---

[70] Martin, op. cit., p. 14.

the classroom. Her point is that it is almost impossible to believe that the cultural construction of gender has no effect on how a person learns. If that is correct, then it would make some sense to treat females differently in class.

As we read earlier, the psychologists have made the case for women having different ways of understanding and being in the world. Females naturally tend to be more collaborative and connected with other people than are males. Males, we are told, are more often driven by issues of justice and tend to be more individualistic and competitive. If that is correct, then it would make some sense to treat females differently in class.

The argument is that much of teaching is designed by males to teach males. Classes encourage competitive and individualistic learning and behavior, and downplay the desire for group leaning and connectiveness preferred by females. Is identical education equal education if people are different?

These arguments might sound just a little strange to a population that has been taught to believe in equality. Almost instinctively there are people who pull back from the idea that we should be treated differently. While we all want to be seen and understood as individuals, there seems to be a greater comfort in believing that individuality is a personal trait and should not be based on gender or sex.

To follow each of these arguments out in a reasonable way, in order to find an answer that is essentially true, seems nearly impossible. There is a great deal of good evidence that is, in the end, mutually exclusive. And when we put that evidence in the context of our ideological beliefs, clarity seems even further removed.

We can easily see how arguments become awkward by showing how similar arguments can make, if you will, strange bedfellows. Those who argue that males and females are different and should be treated differently, are in philosophical agreement with Rousseau. In the first chapter we saw that there was no doubt in his mind there were significant differences in the sexes and those differences should be reflected in how they were educated. Martin quotes Rousseau:[71] "A perfect woman and a perfect man ought not resemble each other in the mind any more than in looks . . . One ought to be active and strong, and the other passive and weak . . . [The partnership between man and woman produces] a moral person of which the woman is the eye and the man is the arm."

While clearly not the particular differences advocated by contemporary writers (and especially feminist writers), Rousseau does make the case for treating people differently and according to their sex. Rousseau believed girls and boys should be educated separately, just as there has been a history of people making strong arguments in favor of women's schools in the United States. While Rousseau demeans women and almost all contemporary educational thinkers hate what he had to say about them, the great irony is that many agree with him that girls and boys are different and that difference needs to be taken into account when we think about how we teach.

[71] Martin, p. 53.

IS IT THE RIGHT QUESTION?

I hope you did not expect an answer to the questions about sex and gender. While there is a remarkable amount of material that helps us understand those differences, in the final analysis there are fundamental mysteries that are no closer to being solved now then they were 5,000 years ago. In this section I would like to suggest that the differences (or lack of differences) between girls and boys are neither the only, nor possibly even the most important, questions that the classroom teacher must answer. It is entirely possible that the differences among girls and among boys may be more useful to us than the idea that all girls are different from all boys.

In the beginning of the chapter the teacher walked into class and saw boys and girls. That is one of the most obvious and easiest observations. More difficult, but possibly more important, the teacher can see neither the type of intelligence each student has, nor his or her thinking style.

We will begin with the idea that there are different types of intelligence. This idea was introduced when we discussed teachers, and how to think about testing them. It was used as much as a critique of current testing as an alternative method. The suggested testing would have been so complicated that, for the foreseeable future, it is simply fantasy. But different intelligences currently serve as the basis of teaching in many places, so it is important that we review some of what we know.

Howard Gardner developed and is the strongest advocate of the idea that there are multiple intelligences.[72] Gardner writes that there are two assumptions about intelligence he believes are wrong: "first, that there is a single, general capacity that every human being possesses to a greater or lesser extent; and that, however defined, it can be measured by standardized verbal instruments, such as short-answer, paper-and-pencil tests." [73] He urges us to forget we had ever heard of the idea that intelligence is a single property of the human mind or that there was any such thing as an intelligence test.

For Gardner, this is a better way to define intelligence: "An intelligence is the ability to solve problems, or to create products, that are valued within one or more cultural settings—a definition that says nothing about either the sources of these abilities or the proper means of 'testing' them." [74] Gardner's definition is inclusive. It is his intention to help us understand that there are many different kinds of intelligences.

The truth of the matter is that, traditionally, we admire only certain kinds of intelligence. As we saw earlier, the West has put the highest premium on a certain type of reason and rationality. While other skills, such as music and art, might be praised, we know that our schooling is primarily aimed at helping students think more rationally. It forms the basis of our science and is at the heart of our beliefs that intelligence can be tested for and measured.

---

[72] The following argument comes from his *Frames of Mind: The Theory of Multiple Intelligences, Tenth-Anniversary Edition* (New York: Basic Books, 1993).

[73] Ibid., p. x.

[74] Ibid.

If Gardner is correct there are many different kinds of intelligence. To name those found in Frames of Mind (periodically, others have been discovered): linguistic, musical, logical–mathematical, spatial, bodily–kinesthetic, and personal. Each of these types of intelligence is easily seen as key to different skills and abilities. The argument is, for example, there are wonderful athletes who have a high degree of bodily–kinesthetic intelligence. A brilliant basketball player, for example, might be able to not only see where every other player on the court is, but also able to tell where each one is going to be. That player is able to make a pass that would simply be impossible for most other human beings.

And it is entirely possible that same player might not do well on a standardized intelligence test. If we chose not to believe Gardner then we would say that the player was not intelligent. What Gardner would argue is that the player is very intelligent, just not intelligent in the restrictive sense of there being only one, testable intelligence.

Most of us have a combination of intelligences. Some combinations are common: The musician might also have logical-mathematical intelligence, while an architect might be a combination of mathematical and spatial intelligences, and the teacher might combine linguistic and personal intelligences. The world, if we are to believe Gardner, is much more complicated than we have been taught. If he is correct, we must make ourselves understand, appreciate, and teach to the idea that people are intelligent in different ways.

Gardner writes that "an increasing number of researchers believe . . . there exists a multitude of intelligences, quite independent of each other; that each intelligence has its own strengths and constraints; that the mind is far from unencumbered at birth; and that *it is unexpectedly difficult to teach things that go against early 'naïve' theories or that challenge the natural lines of force within an intelligence and its matching domains.*" [75]

The emphasis on the last couple of lines is to make the point that no matter who we are talking about . . . either girls or boys . . . if we believe that there is simply one kind of intelligence and teach only to that then we will be bad teachers for those who have different kinds of intelligence. If it was difficult to teach the old way, and we decide to take Gardner seriously, then teaching will become much more complicated. There can be no one right way to teach if there are eight or nine different intelligences. There can be no two right ways (for girls and for boys) if sex is less significant than type of intelligence.

It would be easy to end the chapter here and say that there is much work to do. Regrettably, additional theories exist that further complicate teaching. Robert Sternberg argues that there are different *thinking styles.*[76] In a book of that very name, Sternberg wants us to understand that "A *style* is a way of thinking. It is not an ability, but rather, a preferred way of using the ability one has . . . An ability refers to how well someone can do something. A style refers to how someone likes to do something." [77]

---

[75] Ibid., p. xix, emphasis added.

[76] Robert J. Sternberg, *Thinking Styles: Theory and Assessment at the Interface* (Cambridge, U.K. Cambridge University Press, 1997).

[77] Ibid., p. 8.

Basically, thinking styles are divided into three categories: functions, forms, and levels/scopes/learnings of thinking styles. Sternberg, a psychologist, decided to use the vocabulary of government to explain styles. So, the functions of thinking styles are called legislative, executive, and judicial styles. The functions roughly correlate to the institution it is named after. The forms are the monarchic, hierarchic, oligarchic, and anarchic. Finally, the levels, scope, and learning of thinking styles are the global, local, internal, external, liberal, and conservative.

Each of these functions, forms, and levels means something about how a person thinks and learns, and the profession for which he or she might be best suited. Some styles are best for working on independent projects while others are most suited to highly structured environments. Someone who does not do well with structure will often do very poorly in those classes with a great deal of discipline and carefully constructed tests of memory. We are told that "we repeatedly confuse styles with abilities . . . [and] . . . school children who are viewed as stupid often suffer from nothing more than a style that mismatches that of their teacher."[78]

It is not difficult to find everyday examples of this. While in high school, I was not in the college track. I would sit in class and daydream while teacher after teacher would lecture about things that did not interest me in the least. I did much better in college. I was more free to do my own work, and by the time I got to Berkeley to do graduate work in political science, I did better still. While I assume my abilities did not change from my late teens to my early twenties, I just kept doing better and better. If we are to believe Sternberg, it is because I was able to find more teachers who fit my thinking style. I could "hear" them more clearly, I could understand them more easily, and I could do the kind of work they assigned.

We can take the idea one more step: "[W]hat happens to us in life depends not just on *how well* we think, but also on *how* we think. People think in different ways, and moreover, our research has shown that they over-estimate the extent to which others think the way they do. As a result, misunderstandings can develop—between spouses, parents and children, teachers and students, and bosses and employees."[79]

As teachers it is sometimes difficult to remember the lesson of teaching styles. Periodically, I take tennis lessons. I take them from different people but always for the same reason: I want to remind myself what it is like to be a student. It does not matter if the teacher is a woman or a man, because basically they all teach the same fundamentals. There is a physics to the game that does not change.

What is interesting is that there are some people I understand perfectly well and others who make almost no sense to me. It has nothing to do with what they are telling me and everything to do with how they are saying it. Taking lessons forces me to remember that no matter how clear I think I am being in class, there are some people who will respond like I am teaching in some ancient, dead language. Others, of course, understand exactly what I am trying to say.

[78] Ibid., p. 12.

[79] Ibid., p. 18.

The same is true with this book. I assume that some will respond well to the effort to make this a conversation. They will "hear" what I have to say and accept the invitation to think about the questions and come to their own conclusions. Others may not like informality at all and dismiss even the good information because of the way it is presented. That would certainly fit the argument made by Sternberg.

SUMMARY

In this chapter we reviewed a great deal of literature about boys and girls. We began with the idea that, while related, sex and gender are different things. Sex has to do with biological reality and gender is more of a social construction. What seems to be true is that some gender differences are directly tied to sex differences.

The data indicated strong social reinforcement for gender differences. First from parents, and then from teachers, a child is taught gender differences. By the time a child enters kindergarten, the idea of what girls do and what boys do is firmly in place. We saw that the social context furthered stereotypes.

Throughout school, we saw that gender roles were played out in ways that sometimes hurt both girls and boys. From how one is supposed to look, to how one is supposed to think and act, gender dominated reality.

Finally, it was suggested that the differences between girls and boys might not be as important as the differences between girls and other girls, or boys and other boys. Types and intelligences, as well as types of learning styles, may be more important to the classroom teacher.

The centering questions of the chapter were these: It is important to figure out if boys and girls are different. If you believe they are different, then do you need to figure out if boys and girls should be treated differently in class? But those might not be the most important questions. It is entirely possible that not all girls think alike nor do they have the same kind of intelligence, and that is equally true of boys.

The real bottom line of the chapter seems to be this: Given the remarkable number of variables we must consider as teachers, it is possible that the real differences between girls and boys are just the beginnings of our problems if we want to become good teachers.

The lesson, in the end, may be this: to generalize about boys and girls is to miss the point about how best to approach teaching.

THINK ABOUT

1. There are genuine differences between boys and girls, and only a fool would dismiss the obvious.

2. Would you rather teach a class of boys or girls . . . why?

3. Do you believe it is possible to treat girls and boys the same? Do you think it would be a good idea even if you could?

ANDRÉ: *It's like what happened just before my mother died. You know, we had gone to the hospital to see my mother, and I'd been in to see her, and I saw this woman that looked as bad as any survivor of Auschwitz . . . and I was out in the hall sort of comforting my father, and this doctor who was a specialist in a problem that she had with her arm went into her room and come out just beaming and said to us, "Boy, don't* **we** *have a lot of reason to feel great? Isn't it* **wonderful** *how she's coming along?" Well, all he saw was the arm. That's all he saw. And I mean, he's another person who's existing in a dream. Who on top of that is a kind of butcher who's committing a kind of familial murder, because he comes out of that room and he psychically kills us by taking* **us** *into a dream world, you see, where we become confused and frightened, because the moment before, we saw somebody who looked already dead, and now here comes the specialist who tells us that everything is great. I mean, they were literally driving my father crazy, because here was an eighty-two-year-old man, who's very emotional, you know, and if you go in one minute, and you see that the person's dying, and you don't want them to die, and then the doctor comes out five minutes later and tells you they're in wonderful shape—uh, you know, you can go crazy.*

WALLY: *Right. I know. I know what you mean.*

ANDRÉ: *I mean, the doctor didn't see my mother.*

My Dinner with André
Screenplay by Wallace Shawn and André Gregory

■ ■ ■ ■ ■ ■

CHAPTER SIX

RACE

Statistically, the factor that best predicts a U.S. adult's income is his or her: a) race; b) IQ; c) father's occupation; d) level of education; e) number of years in the workforce. The best public schools in the United States. spend over $15,000 per pupil and have an average class size of about 15. What is the average per pupil spending and class size in the worst schools? a) about $7,000 and over 40 students per class; b) under $3,000 and over 60 students per class; c) about $6,000 and over 100 students per class.

(The answers are *c* and *b*.)

It is the first day of class. You walk into your classroom and see your new students for the first time. For most of you, the faces you see will be different colors. What will you think? Will you consciously take note of those colors and somehow adjust your thinking depending on what the colors are? When asked, teachers routinely say that they pay no attention to the color of a student. Should we believe them? Is it a good or bad thing not to pay attention?

Race is, quite possibly, the most difficult problem in the United States. It is as real as it is confusing. Our past is cluttered with racism, and even today there are people who seem as bigoted as those who had slaves, or hanged blacks, or denied Hispanics schooling, or drove American Indians off their land or killed them, or brought Chinese over to build the railroads, or put Japanese in concentration camps.

On the other hand, there are ways in which the United States has struggled harder to eliminate racism than most other countries. There is a deep sense of fairness that went from being a quiet sub-theme in American politics to a loud and very major cause when it came to racism. The Civil War was the most costly war, in terms of human life, that was ever fought by the United States. And, after the courts finally got involved in the idea of equality, there was a second powerful movement during the late fifties and early sixties to help make things better.

There is a sense that the future of the United States depends on our ability to solve the problem of racism. One cannot imagine how we, as a nation, could continue to survive as "the land of the free" without constantly working to reduce the amount of intolerance and injustice and violence that seems to have always been with us.

151

It is not easy to sort out the problems that are directly tied to race. As we shall see, everything from social class to the size of a class, to the education of one's grand-parents, seems to be involved with how a person will do in school. And while racism is a broad term, every minority seems to have a special history and set of problems. While it is not unusual to think of blacks when one thinks of race, the fact is that there are many different minorities in the United States. Blacks, to now, have been the largest minority and have had to deal with the fact that white Americans made them slaves. Hispanics are about to become the largest minority and have other issues—as do American Indians and Asian Americans. And, of course, it is unfair to even think of a single minority as the same. There, for example, is no "typical" Asian American. Asian Americans come from scores of different countries with different personal his-tories and different cultural advantages and disadvantages.

To think of race in a simple-minded, single way is as foolish as it is inaccurate.

And underlying the whole issue of race is that it is a political category and not really a biological one. While we can "see" race, it is important to understand and acknowledge that race is something we have made up. Biologically, we are all humans. The differences between us are almost nonexistent and certainly unimportant. We are packaged differently—tall, short, fat, skinny, black and tan and a remarkable number of tints. But the fact remains that we are all pretty much the same.

There are those who confuse ethnicity with race. It is a topic we need to discuss. Ethnicity is about culture, and race is about biology (or, more specifically, about color). In the next chapter we will focus on ethnicity.

This chapter is about race. As with many issues in the United States, we believe that education can make a difference. We will spend time understanding the problems faced by minorities and what has been done to solve them. There will be a look at his-tory as well as what is going on now. We will review the theories and issues of contem-porary thinkers and sort out what the data seem to indicate about our current situation.

What drives the chapter are these questions: Why do some minorities do so poorly in school and what can be done to change that?

We will begin by looking at race, and what it is not.

RACE

As mentioned, while race seems very straightforward, the more you think about it, the less clear it is.[1] Research on racial differences has led to agreement on these three points:[2] First, skin color, hair texture, and facial features are only three of many dif-ferences between people. There are dozens of physical differences ranging from body chemistry, to shapes of bones, to consistency of ear wax.

The second agreed-upon point is that one of the reasons for the great evolu-tionary success of the human species is because of its genetic variability. Put differ-

[1]This discussion comes from Schuman and Olufs, *Diversity on Campus* (Boston: Allyn & Bacon, 1995).

[2]These are found in Boyce Rensberger, "Racial Odyssey," *Science Digest* (Jan/Feb 1981).

ently, as humans moved around the globe, their large variety of physical traits greatly enhanced their chances of surviving.

Finally, no one has ever discovered a reliable way of distinguishing one race from another. That seems hard to believe. We all have our ideas race and what it might mean. The author Kurt Vonnegut, in his novel *Hocus Pocus*, writes that human beings come into the world color-coded. Well, what's right for *Hocus Pocus* might not be exactly right scientifically. Skin color does not tell us everything about race. This is where science makes things hard for our ordinary stereotypes and prejudices.[3]

Although we know that most Africans from south of the Sahara, and their descendants around the world, generally have darker skin than most Europeans, that does not tell us much. There are millions of people in India who are classified as Caucasoid (or "white") who have darker skins than most Americans who call themselves black. Biology books and professors will probably tell you that skin color is determined by *polygenes*, or on several locations in your DNA, and the effect of the many genes is roughly additive. Humans run along a continuum of skin colors, with no clear lines between light and dark.

There are Africans who have skin no darker than Greeks or Lebanese or Italians. The point is that skin color cannot be the universal test for race. Neither is height, eye color, or the shape of your nose. Biologist tell us that there is no way to distinguish one race from another.[4]

Notice how the discussion began with race and ended up talking about color. That is no accident. It is all too common for us to equate race and color and get on with a discussion of racism based on skin color.

It might help to sort out some of the colliding ideas about race by starting at the beginning. The basic fact is this: There is one human race, *Homo sapiens*. We're all it. Anthropologists use terms such as "group" and "tribe" because they allow flexible definitions to fit actual human populations without some of the baggage that goes along with the term *race*. There is a huge amount of variation in sizes, colors, shapes, technologies, mobility, histories, religions, family practices, and on and on. But we are all one race. As you read about what the scientists say about race and racial differences, keep this in mind: The Human Genome Diversity project has proved that the darkest-hued African and the lightest-skinned Scandinavian are 99.99 percent identical in their genetic makeup.

We know that there are people who make much of the many human variations. It is important to see what the studies have to offer.[5]

---

[3]It is important to remember that "science" can be put to the service of racism. *The Bell Curve*, by R.H. Herrnstein and C. Murray (New York: Free Press, 1994) is a current example. In a later chapter, we will see how "science" helped control immigration. Science, to put differently, has never been a neutral discipline.

[4]The movie *Mississippi Masala* is about a black man who falls in love with an Indian (Indian-born) woman. One of the points is that it is a love story about two people of roughly the same color, and color is not the issue. The problems of identity and conflict are illuminating about our culture, and how misleading and meaningless and meaningful race can be.

[5]See the debate in *Scientific American 266*, no. 4 (April, 1992) between: Allan Wilson and Rebecca Cann, "The Recent African Genesis of Humans," pgs. 68–73; and Alan Thorne and Milford Wolpoff, "The Multiregional Evolution of Humans," pgs. 76–83.

There are two main schools of thought about how humans evolved. One holds that humans evolved in several regions around the Earth, pretty much where they are now in Europe, Africa, East Asia, and Australia. Strong genetic similarities among these populations result from connections between populations over the last million years.

The second theory suggests that an "Eve," a single common ancestor, lived in Africa about 200,000 years ago. All human populations, goes the argument, can be traced back to one woman. That's why she's called Eve. The humans all over the globe spread out from Africa and replaced previous populations in the new regions they settled, and human variation is the result of recent evolution.

Why is this a controversy? That might be the most interesting question. The means of calculating Eve is uncertain (it is based on estimates of the rate of change in mitochondrial DNA), and could easily be off by more than a half a million years. The estimate of the time of parallel evolution could be off as well. The two theories could be talking about the same thing, only Eve lived a lot earlier. Both theories agree that populations evolved and continue to evolve.

There is a controversy because of the way people interpret the theories. Would you take the existence of a recent Eve to mean that all humans are more closely related than previously believed? Or, to take the other side, do you believe that the groups that evolved in the different regions are at different levels of evolution—some having evolved more than others? Would you take the parallel evolution theory to mean that races were distinct and, at some point "pure," or that the parallel quality of the evolution shows a long-term pattern of genetic mixing among the regional groupings of population?

If you are one of those people who are worried about race, the theories raise a lot of questions.

Most questions about race begin with distinctions made between groups of people. There is an explanation for most of them.

Color provides us with a good example. Generally speaking, if you start at the equator you will find people who have the darkest skin. The farther you get from the equator, north or south, the more pale the skin. Your skin color is a function of the intensity of a dark brown pigment called melanin. Skin cells have varying amounts of melanin granules. All races increase the melanin in their skin by exposure to the sun. Populations that evolved closer to the equator produce more melanin.

We have known for some time (as the ozone layer is getting holes in it, we are painfully aware of the fact) that the human body can tolerate only a narrow range of intensities of sunlight. Too much sun causes sunburn and cancer, too little deprives the body of vitamin D and can cause rickets.[6] Albinos who live near the equator have a high rate of skin cancer, and dark-skinned children living in northern latitudes had a high rate of rickets before their milk was fortified by vitamin D.

The dark skin limits the skin's production of vitamin D in northern latitudes, while light skin lets in more of the sun. Dark skin protects against too much sun near the equator, and light skin lets in too much. (The white of polar bears lets more sun in than the fur of black bears.)

It boils down to this: One reason we survive as a species is that our skin color has adapted to different regional demands.

---

[6]Resenberger, op. cit., p. 50.

And what about the nose on your face? Accident? Racial characteristic? Religious choice? Maybe a kind of adaptation? The job of the nose is to warm and humidify air before it gets to sensitive lung tissue. Given the job, it is no great surprise that people native to colder or drier climates tend to have longer, more beak-shaped noses. The colder or drier the air, the more surface area is needed to make sure that the air gets to be the right temperature and humidity.[7]

There seem to be explanations for height and eye pigmentation and scent glands and so on. But scientists are far from understanding why there are so many differences between us. Why do the bushmen of Kalahari, the !kung, have small noses? Why do many of Nigeria's Wodaabe have more beaky noses? Why are Aleut noses more like African or Asian noses than like Lapp or Celt? There seems to be no compelling reason why Indian men in one part of South America have blue penises.[8] Maybe it is just a genetic mutation that women found wildly attractive.

The idea that there may never have been "pure" races fits well with the fact that contemporary races continue to mix. For example, it can be argued that American blacks are a distinct race. They are a combination of African blacks and European whites. According to Bruce Rensberger, it has been "calculated that whites contributed 21 percent of the genes to the American black population. The figure is higher for blacks in northern and western states and lower in the South.[9]

Indeed, in many Latin and South American countries, the native populations are stable mixes of two or three races. They have become new races. These races, like all successful ones, are continually adapting to their environment.

The point of all this information should now be more clear: *Races are not fixed biological categories.* Indeed, there is very good reason to believe they may never have been. Races are intermingling and interacting and evolving all of the time. We need to keep in mind that constant evolution is one of the reasons why the species has been so successful. Given that all people are the same species, it seems silly to try to classify people according to race. When it comes right down to it, racial classification is much more a political classification than a scientific one. Racism seems to be based on pure prejudice, and all of the reasons for discrimination because of color seem to be an emotional response unhindered by facts.

Yet, while race is a nebulous idea—maybe even a nonidea—what we know is that it is a remarkably important nebulous nonidea.

WHO DO WE MEAN?

Discussions of race rarely stand alone. In any serious conversation it is almost impossible to talk about race without adding the notions of socioeconomic class and multiculturalism. It is not unusual to have race talked about as an issue of equal rights or minority rights, and other groups are added to the mix. It is logical to add women and the disabled in any discussion of equality. The questions are these: When you talk

[7]Ibid., p. 51.

[8]Ibid., p. 50.

[9]Ibid., p. 53.

about race in the United States, where do you begin and where do you end? The answers seem to depend on whom you ask.

While a clear theme underlying race has to do with equality, this chapter will not deal with either women or those with disabilities. We live in a time when the push for equality has led to remarkable changes. It would be foolish to argue that we have reached an acceptable level of equality of opportunity for everyone. We know that simply is not true. But this chapter will include neither women nor those with disabilities. In the preceding chapter we began to understand the role of sex in school. In a later chapter we will deal with how schools treat those with disabilities.

Near the end of this chapter we will review the tensions between those who want to focus on race and those who are concerned with multiculturalism. Some of the issues seem to overlap. For example, a discussion of Hispanics in a chapter about race seems reasonable, but what about a discussion of how schools should deal with the issue of English as a second language? Is that a problem of race or culture? For the purposes of dividing chapters in this book, it is a problem of culture.

It is more difficult, at least for me, to separate out the topic of socioeconomic class. A good argument can be made that, in the end, it belongs in a chapter about politics. If we think of race as a biological concept, then the notion of class would not fit in this chapter. But what we know is that race is, in the end, probably more of a political concept than a biological one. When we begin to discuss the problems of minorities and schooling, and different solutions, it will be impossible to get away from the effects of social class. While there is an increasing number of successful people of color, there continues of be a disproportionate percentage of minorities who suffer the problems that stem from poverty.

Socioeconomic class, then, will be part of this discussion. The problems connected to class are not limited to minorities and are not limited to the inner cities. There are whites who are poor, and some of the worst poverty in the United States is rural. But in this chapter the main focus is on race, so our discussion of class is limited to how it impacts on race.

Finally, race is an inclusive term and each particular group is unique. Put differently, any discussion of race in the United States needs to begin by acknowledging that there are many races, and each has its own history or histories.

Hispanics

By the year 2010 it is estimated that the largest minority will be Hispanic.[10] There are now approximately 32 million (expected to grow to more than 40 million by 2010) Hispanics in the United States, and they have one of the lowest—if not the lowest—per capita income level in the country.

Hispanics are not a single group. They come from 17 different countries (from the southernmost tip of South America to the part of Texas that was once Mexico) and have settled in different parts of the country. For example, many Mexican Americans live in Texas, California, and other parts of the Southwest, while Cuban Americans have concentrated in Florida and especially Miami. With all of the immigration,

---

[10] Marco Portales, *Crowding Out Latinos: Mexican Americans in the Public Consciousness* (Philadelphia: Temple University Press, 2000), p. 32.

75 percent of the Hispanic population was born in the United States.[11] To overgeneralize, Hispanics share a common language—Spanish—and a common religion—Catholicism. In 1990 there were 17 million Spanish-speaking people in the United States. The second largest English-as-a-second-language group was "all other languages combined," and that added up to 4.3 million people.

Spanish-speaking students were traditionally segregated from other students, but as we will see, the courts have ruled that practice illegal. Mexican Americans (Chicanas and Chicanos) have the lowest educational attainment of all Hispanics. Cuban Americans have the highest. Puerto Ricans are closer to Mexican Americans in school achievement. If we put that in the context of socioeconomic class, it is no surprise that Cuban Americans are the most prosperous and Mexican Americans are the least prosperous Hispanics.[12] It is estimated that 38 percent of Mexican American children grow up in poverty.

Hispanics, who will soon be the largest minority, need better schooling. Less than 10 percent of the Hispanic population between the ages of twenty-five and twenty-nine have a college education. Almost 10 percent of the Hispanics come to school with limited proficiency in English.[13] Many are very poor. It is clear that something needs to be done, specifically, to help Hispanics break out of the cycle of poverty and poor education.

While Hispanics are about to become the largest minority, there are less than two million American Indians. (It is not easy to know exactly what to call each minority. There are different names for Hispanics, and even a greater number of names for blacks. Each group claims the right to name itself, but that does not guarantee that each group can agree on what it should be called. In many parts of the Midwest, for example, American Indians call themselves Indians. In other places they call themselves Native Americans. Still others call themselves Indigenous People. While Native Americans seems to be the current name of choice, there are two reasons I will use American Indians. First, it is now unclear just who the first people were who populated the continent. Skeletons found in Washington State now indicate different groups came to this part of the world at around the same time. Second, the use of language compels me to believe that anyone who was born in the United States is, technically, a Native American. While I do not believe that American Indian is the best name, it will have to do until there is general agreement on a better one. I certainly have no intention of offending anyone.)*

From almost the very beginning, American Indians were brutalized by the Europeans who explored the "New World," and then systematically destroyed by those who settled here. Almost 90 percent of the native population died from diseases brought by Europeans. (Lord Jeffery Amherst, after whom a town about ten miles

---

[11] These figures come from Steven Tozer, Paul Violas, and Guy Senese, *School and Society: Historical and Contemporary Perspectives*, 3 ed. (Boston: McGraw-Hill, 1998), pgs. 383–4.

[12] An important variable about how well a group will do is how successful they were before they came to the United States. Many of the Cubans who came to the United States were well educated and successful.

[13] Joseph Newman, *America's Teachers: An Introduction to Education*, 3rd ed. (New York: Longman, 1998), p. 255.

*For example, in the *New York Times* magazine section of August 3, 2003, there is a full-page ad with a nice looking young woman smiling at the reader. The caption is this: *HAVE YOU EVER SEEN AN INDIAN?* It is an ad for the American Indian College Fund.

from where I sit writing is named, was given property as a reward for killing natives by giving them malaria-infected blankets.)

During a series of wars from the 1620s to 1890, whites won nearly every battle. They took the land and forced the natives to live on reservations—often hundreds of miles from their original homes. An effort was made to destroy the native culture. The results were physically and psychologically devastating. The life expectancy of an American Indian is ten years shorter than the national average, and almost thirty years for members of some tribes. They are about three times as likely to die from accidents, including automobile accidents, from cirrhosis of the liver, and diabetes. The quality of life is the worst of any minority. About 40 percent live on reservations, and unemployment on reservations is around 50 percent.[14]

Schooling reflects the poverty and problems of American Indians: they have the lowest test scores, the highest dropout rates, and the college completion rates of any group. At least 9 percent enter school with limited proficiency in English.[15]

For decades the government of the United States educated American Indians in reservation schools. These schools did much to try to destroy native culture. They were often brutal places where little if any learning took place. In the last thirty years, tribes have begun to take control of local education. By 1988 Congress passed a Tribally Controlled Schools Act that gave grants to tribes to support the operations of their own schools.

Also, for more than a decade American Indians have become more active and effective in local and national politics. Slowly, they have gained more control of their lives both financially and politically.

Asian Americans

If American Indians represent a particularly ugly example of how minorities have been treated in the United States, Asian Americans would seem to represent a success story. In the literature, they are often referred to as the "model minority." The label, not surprisingly, hides at least as much as it reveals.

As we have seen, Hispanics come from different countries and there are hundreds of different tribes of American Indians. There is an even greater diversity of Asian Americans. The largest Asian American groups, in order of size, are Chinese, Filipinos, Japanese, Asian Indians, Koreans, and Vietnamese. There are another seventy smaller groups. Asian Americans generally live in urban areas. About 40 percent live in California, and another 30 percent live in New York, Illinois, Texas, and Hawaii.[16]

There is great variation between groups and, of course, between individuals. That variation, as we shall see, has lead to a surprising educational problem. Some Asian Americans (mainly Chinese, Filipino, and Japanese) have been here since the

[14]See Schuman and Olufs, op. cit., pgs. 216–8.

[15]Newman, op. cit., p. 257.

[16]Ibid., p. 255.

early 1800s or early 1900s. Many of these well established Asian-American families are at the top of the economic and educational scale.

Those Asian Americans who have come more recently to escape political repression (Southeast Asians such as the Vietnamese and Cambodians) are among the poorest families in the nation. In 1991 77 percent of the Cambodian and Laotian households in California received public assistance.[17] More than 15 percent of students from Southeast Asia begin school with little English.[18]

Asian Americans have been discriminated against in the United States. California segregated Asian Americans. By the turn of the twentieth century, the California State Legislature passed a law that enabled the San Francisco Board of Education to operate segregated schools for "Mongolians." The segregation slowly ended over a fifty-year period. During World War II Japanese Americans were put in concentration camps and their property was seized. Even now, Asian Americans are not often chosen for high management jobs, although many companies pursue them for technical jobs.[19]

To look at one set of figures it is easy to understand why Asian Americans are the "model minority." Many have been remarkably successful at the best universities in the United States. Indeed, so many have done so well that the elite schools began instituting quotas on the number of Asian Americans they would accept. The University of California, Berkeley, was sued because so many bright and talented Asian Americans were not accepted. From coast to coast, from Berkeley to Harvard and Cal Tech to MIT, for more than a decade there have been more outstanding Asian American students applying for admission than there have been places for them.

The problem, of course, is that not all Asian Americans are model students. Not all are bright or motivated or even speak English. Too many teachers walk into their classroom, see an Asian American face, and simply assume it is the face of a talented student. A surprising number of Asian American students are neglected because of the color of their face and the wrong-headed assumption of their teacher.

For example, not too many years ago a study of the Seattle schools showed that 39 percent of the Asian Americans were "at risk." That is the same number of at-risk Hispanic students.[20] Sucheng Chan writes:

> . . . Asian Americans, more so than black or Latino Americans, live in a state of ambivalence—lauded as a "successful" or "model minority" on the one hand, but subject to continuing unfair treatment, including occasional outbursts of racially motivated violence, on the other.[21]

There is, then, a strange and unfortunate dynamic with even the most successful minority. It seems that good stereotypes as well as bad are not at all helpful.

---

[17]Spring, op. cit., p. 131.

[18]Ibid., p. 255.

[19]Tozer, op. cit., p. 381.

[20]Tozer, ibid., p. 381.

[21]Ibid., p. 383.

A SHORT REVIEW

A short review might be helpful. In this chapter we have discussed the idea that race is probably more of a political concept than a biological one. That we are all members of the same race, and to make judgments on the basis of skin color seems a particularly silly (and destructive) way to think. We then turned to different-colored minorities in the United States. Each, we saw, has its own history and set of problems. To make things even more complicated, each large color grouping is not at all monolithic. There are different problems within each group.

And, on purpose, there has been no discussion of blacks. It is not unusual to equate racism with blacks, and it is important to acknowledge the reality that racism in the United States is not limited to one color. One reason why blacks are so closely associated with racism is because of slavery. While whites killed a huge number of American Indians, and have systematically been biased towards most minorities, only blacks were brought to the United States as slaves.

Blacks were brought over here early, they were defined as partial human beings in the Constitution, they were not allowed to learn to read, they were brutalized, humiliated, raped, killed—and later simply segregated and treated as second-class citizens.

In an earlier chapter there was a summary of court cases that led to the desegregation of schools in the United States. The history of the movement from slavery to citizenship and equality is a remarkable one. It is remarkable not only for the courage and bravery of the blacks involved, but also for the whites who fought bigotry throughout this period. The bottom line is that over time the United States has become more and more committed to civil rights and equality. That the words of Jefferson had little to do with his actions seems less important than the fact they have served as a moral imperative for future generations. It took good faith, a civil war, an understanding Supreme Court, civil disobedience, and everyday acceptance for equality to become more and more of a reality.

And at the center of many of the battles were blacks.

BLACK EDUCATION

Before the statistics about how blacks are doing educationally and economically, it is important to understand one part of our history. It is the debate between W. E. B. DuBois and Booker T. Washington, two black men. The debate, and what happened in the South with schooling after the Civil War, will help us understand in a practical sense what it was like for many blacks.

W. E. B. DuBois was born in 1868. Great Barrington, Massachusetts, his home, did not have slaves, and he was brought up as unaware of the great prejudice against blacks as was possible at that time. Growing up, he wrote for different newspapers and graduated valedictorian of his class. The town, collectively, raised the money to send him to Fisk University in Nashville, Tennessee.[22] During the time at Fisk, DuBois dis-

---

[22] We should note two things. First, that a town of whites would send a black man to college was exceptional. Second, DuBois was disappointed—he wanted the town to send him to Harvard.

covered racism (he called it the Veil) and, in the summers, taught in Southern rural school districts.

In 1888 DuBois enrolled at Harvard as a junior. He got his degree, cum laude, and began graduate school there. His was the first black to get a doctorate from Harvard. Dubois was a genuinely remarkable person. He taught, wrote, helped found the National Association for the Advancement of Colored People (NAACP), was active in international affairs, was a member of the Communist Party, attended the founding conference of the United Nations, ran for Senate in New York as a member of the Progressive Party, was indicted and acquitted of subversive activities (the Justice Department was after him), won the Lenin Peace Prize, was chosen to edit the Encyclopedia Africana, and in 1963, became a citizen of Ghana. DuBois died on August 27, 1963, at the age of 95. The next day he was eulogized by Martin Luther King in his "I Have a Dream" speech at the march on Washington.

If you could choose only one book about blacks in the United States, I suggest you read *The Soul of Black Folks*. It is a beautifully written, clear-headed reflection of our culture.

Please understand that the previous paragraphs do little justice to the life of DuBois. He was smarter, cared more, was more active, and lived longer than even the most extraordinary people of his time. The reason he is important to us is because of his ideas about education.

The bottom line for Dubois was that blacks needed to be well educated. He argued that the best education possible be given the brightest students. For him, the "talented tenth" should be given the kind of education that would help all blacks. The best and the brightest were to be given the education and power to become effective leaders.

The formula was simple enough: "Teach workers to work . . . teach thinkers to think . . . make carpenters of carpenters, philosophers of philosophers, and fops of fools . . . . The worker must work for the glory of his handiwork, not simply for pay; the thinker must think for the truth, not of his fame. And all this is gained only by human strife and longing; by ceaseless training and education; by founding Right on righteousness and Truth on the unhampered search for truth . . . "[23]

While it is not difficult to understand and agree with what DuBois writes, it is important to remember the context in which he wrote. There were few well-educated— or even minimally educated—blacks following the Civil War. As we saw earlier, slave owners thought it was not in their best interests to have slaves who could read and write. But DuBois was not suggesting remedial work; what he wanted was an appropriate education for people at all levels. There are ways in which it sounds almost Platonic; that the brightest would get an advanced education and become the leaders.

DuBois was called an elitist. If that meant he believed the smartest people should get the best education and probably become leaders of society, then DuBois could be called an elitist. But he was certainly more complex than that. Remember, he was also a member of the Communist Party that was all about egalitarianism, and he believed that everyone should have an "appropriate" education.

---

[23]W. E. B. DuBois, *The Soul of Black Folks* (New York: Dover, 1994), p. 54. The book was published originally in 1903.

At the turn of the twentieth century, it was not easy for a black person to be well-educated in a classic sense: "I sit with Shakespeare and he winces not. Across the color-line I move arm in arm with Balzac and Dumas, where smiling men and welcoming women glide into gilded halls . . . I summon Aristotle and Aurelius and what soul I will, and they come all graciously with no scorn nor condescension. So, wed with Truth, I dwell above the Veil. Is this the life you grudge us, O knightly America? . . . Are you so afraid lest peering from this high . . . we sight the Promised Land?"[24]

While DuBois did not deny that educating blacks for a trade was a good and necessary thing, it was clear to him that there should be no limit on what a black should be encouraged to learn. Living with the great thinkers was living in the "Promised Land." The world of ideas was beyond racism, it was above the Veil. It was a place of gilded halls and searching for the Truth. For the talented tenth to be denied that kind of education was, for DuBois, one of the nastiest parts of prejudice.

That particular vision of education was not a popular one. Booker T. Washington not only disagreed with DuBois about education, but also about politics. As we shall see, Washington's thoughts dominated the times, but in the end it has been the ideas of DuBois that strike the more modern and familiar cord.

Booker T. Washington was born a slave in West Virginia in 1856. He was dirt poor growing up. He heard of the Hampton Institute and decided to go there: "I started out one morning to find my way to Hampton, though I was almost penniless and had no definite idea where Hampton was. By walking, begging rides, and paying for a portion of the journey on steam-cars, I finally succeeded in reaching the city of Richmond, Virginia. I was without money or friends. I slept under a sidewalk, and by working on a vessel next day I earned money to continue my way to the institute, where I arrived with a surplus of fifty cents."[25]

Washington became a student at Hampton, and worked as a full-time janitor to pay his expenses. Hampton taught practical skills; that hard work developed moral virtue, and that each Hampton graduate needed to learn manners, cleanliness, morality, and practical life skills. Washington took the lessons to heart and he constantly preached about the virtue of hard work. He even found something good about the ugly past: "In spite of the evil, the negro got the habit of work from slavery." [26]

In 1901 Washington wrote his biography *Up From Slavery*. In it, he described how he grew up and the importance of his education. After Hampton, after he fully understood how effective that kind of education could be, Washington founded a similar school—Tuskegee Normal and Agricultural Institute. He became its first president. Years later, he received an honorary degree from Harvard.

Washington was very successful. With an emphasis on an industrial education, and a practical curriculum, Washington offered what was seen as a reasonable approach to the problem of black education: "Nothing else so brings about right rela-

---

[24] Ibid., p. 67.

[25] Booker T. Washington, "The Awakening of the Negro," *The Atlantic Monthly*, September, 1896. From *Atlantic Unbound*, p. 2.

[26] Ibid., p. 4.

tions between the two races in the South as the industrial progress of the negro. Friction between races will pass away in proportion as the black man, by reason of his skill, intelligence, and character, can produce something that the white man wants or respects in the commercial world."[27]

Washington was also an advocate of seeking accommodation with whites by the acceptance of the limited opportunities available to blacks. By cultivating the values of patience, enterprise, and thrift, Washington believed that blacks could slowly and steadily gain equality in the United States only if they did not rush things. He assumed rights were a privilege that had to be earned. While the Civil War freed the slaves, it was Washington's view that the next step for blacks was to earn the equality promised to all citizens. He believed a practical education was the most reasonable way of doing that.

In 1895 Booker T. Washington gave a speech that we know as the Atlantic Compromise. In it, he explained his ideas about the place of blacks in American society. Basically, he believed that it was in the best interest of blacks to: 1) be educated in crafts and industrial skills; 2) to cultivate patience, enterprise, and thrift; 3) to abandon efforts to win full civil rights and political power and concentrate on skills necessary to attain economic security; 4) to assume that rights were privileges to be earned; and finally, 5) that social segregation was the best environment in which to do these things. In the speech he said: "The opportunity to earn a dollar in a factory just now is worth infinitely more than the opportunity to spend a dollar in the opera house."

With the speech in Atlanta, it was agreed that Washington had become the spokesman for the blacks. His message was at once passionate while doing almost nothing to change the status quo. The underlying theme was that blacks had been deprived of rights and education for so long that it was just good sense that they go slowly and develop those habits that would someday make them productive and conscientious citizens. It was a very conservative message that contained nothing threatening to any part of society. The vision that blacks should be segregated and be schooled in the industrial arts was a step above slavery but one that was well below equality. As we will see, the underlying economic thrust was to encourage blacks to become part of a stable work force.

For DuBois, who found comfort in the great minds, Washington's ideas could not have been worse. DuBois encouraged action, and wanted equality, the right to vote, and education according to ability.[28] His experience of growing up in a white town that accepted him made the idea of segregation, of the Veil, all the more repulsive.

DuBois believed that Washington's ideas were directly responsible for: "1. The disenfranchisement of the Negro. 2. The legal creation of a distinct status of civil inferiority for the Negro. 3. The steady withdrawal of aid from institutions for the higher education of the Negro."[29] But it was Washington's vision that was accepted. He was a very bright man, a powerful speaker, and wrote convincing articles and books. He

[27]Ibid., p. 5.

[28]DuBois, op. cit., p. 32.

[29]Ibid., p. 31.

showed the South that educated blacks could become a critical source of cheap, skilled workers. The most compelling problem, according to Washington, would be if there was no education for blacks and they became a burden because they would be unable to contribute anything to society.

The debate is a classic example about the best way to fold a minority population into the mainstream. What makes DuBois/Washington so instructive is that there are ways in which the integration of society has yet to fully take place. We continue to hear echoes of the gradual approach of Washington and the more pressing, progressive points of DuBois.

In the following section we will look at the reality of debate. We will see exactly what it meant that Washington's views became policy.

SOUTHERN EDUCATION AND NORTHERN MONEY

To a greater or lesser extent, all schools in the United States were affected by the Civil War.[30] Government spent most of its money in the war effort. In the North most schools stayed open, but with fewer teachers and resources. In the South the war devastated education. Recall that public education was never as important in the South as the North. Plantation owners either had their children tutored or sent them away to school. Little or no education was provided for the slaves. After the war, if it was possible, the idea of public education had even less support.

Government in the South broke down after the war. Northerners and former slaves (carpetbaggers) tried to take over but never got the support of the white majority. The whites were bitter that they lost the war, were not happy at the way they were treated in the post-war period, resented Northerners, and were afraid of blacks taking over. The economy that was dependent on slavery was generally weak. While there were some stronger segments of the economy (like textile mills, tobacco, lumber, and even steel mills), the mainstay of the South was always agriculture, and Southern agriculture needed slaves. The region was full of poor blacks and poor whites.

Immediately following the war a great number of black adults were enthusiastic about education, but soon it became clear that they had neither the time nor preparation for schooling. There was an initial response from the North. Almost nine thousand teachers went South to work in the newly established schools for former slaves. But the economic support was sporadic, the whites were nervous about educating blacks, and the schools were low quality. Pulliam writes that "for all practical purposes the states of the South were bankrupt, so that little more than a paper system of education existed in 1870."[31]

---

[30]John Pulliam, *History of Education in America*, 5th ed. (New York: Merrill, 1991), pgs. 83–8.

[31]Ibid., p. 86.

What developed by the turn of the century was a relationship between charitable foundations in the North and rural black education in the South.[32] During the first two decades of the twentieth century there was a remarkable expansion of public education in the South. The number of schoolhouses increased, illiteracy decreased, school terms expanded and teachers' salaries increased considerably.[33] The change came from a combined effort of Southern white educators and industrial philanthropists.

Between 1900 and 1913 a man named Robert Ogden was very active in Southern education. Earlier, he had helped establish Hampton Institute, and served as a trustee and then the president of the board of trustees of that college. He believed blacks should be educated to be industrial workers, and convinced others to join in supporting black education. George Peabody, for example, headed a campaign that raised $8 million for Hampton and Tuskegee Institutes. The money came from Northerners like John Rockefeller and George Eastman. It is no mistake that they supported the kind of education and the very institutions connected with Booker T. Washington.

The motive of the Northern money seemed to be this: "The Northern philanthropic reformers also regarded an economically efficient and politically stable agriculture as a necessary underpinning for national industrial life . . . their concern for an efficient and stable Southern agriculture forced a close study of the black laborers who operated many of the region's farms. . . . . 'Our great problem,' said Ogden, 'is to attach the Negro to the soil and prevent his exodus from the country to the city. . . . . The prosperity of the South depend[ed] upon the productive power of the black man.'"[34]

To that end, a huge amount of money was donated. The General Education Board (GEB) gave over $129 million to the board between 1909 and 1921. The official policy of the board was the promotion of black industrial education.

During the 1930s W. E. B. DuBois was interviewed by the great historian Merle Curti. DuBois said that there was "a provable correlation between the migration of Northern capital to the South for industry, and industrial education." DuBois recalled that the great Northern industrialist and educational reformer William Baldwin Jr. had stated that "his plan was to train in the South two sets of workers, equally skilled, black and white, who could be used to offset each other and break the power of the trade unions."[35]

The GEB got involved in Southern schooling. They established three major programs, the most significant involving placing supervising industrial teachers in hundreds of Southern counties. They were known as Jeanes Teachers and were named after Anna Jeanes, who contributed money to the project. These teachers dominated the development of Southern rural education for the first part of the twentieth century. Put more precisely, they dominated black, rural education.

---

[32]The following depends heavily on James Anderson, "Northern Foundations and the Shaping of Southern Black Rural Education, 1902–1935" in B. Edward McClellan and William Reese, *The Social History of American Education* (Urbana: University of Illinois Press, 1988).

[33]Ibid., p. 287.

[34]Ibid., p. 290.

[35]Ibid., p. 292.

The heart of the teaching was the industrial arts: From sewing and housework to broom-making and gardening, the Jeanes Teachers helped show the rural school teachers how to teach their black students practical skills. During summers, schools taught mostly "domestic science" and "manual training." It was the actualization of Washington's dream. It was the playing out of what Northern money wanted from Southern education of blacks.

But there was tension. The philanthropic reformers were not happy that many black rural schools moved away from "the demands of the agricultural economy and the "needs of Negro life,' by emphasizing the classical aspects of the curriculum . . ."[36] A state supervisor of training school installed a "well-ordered kitchen" in one of his schools. His reasoning was instructive: "This will better prepare the girls to do cooking for the white people of the town."[37] Northern reformers seemed to believe that Southern blacks were best served by an education that emphasized agricultural skills and domestic training.

But the blacks fought for a more academic curriculum. They wanted education to emphasize reading, writing, and arithmetic. They wanted a life different and better than the ones of their parents who had been slaves. It is important to understand that most blacks in rural areas of the South, through the 1930s, rarely went to secondary schools. And the secondary education that was available was mostly centered on vocational training. The county training schools dominated secondary education for rural blacks, and Northern philanthropists greatly influenced what was taught.

Earlier, we read about the court cases that finally desegregated American society and eventually led to the effort to do more than give lip-service to the idea of equality. But even after the court decisions well-intended people disagreed on how to desegregate society.

What I want to argue is that some of the basic positions about integration and equality were in place by the turn of the twentieth century. The Washington/DuBois debate was a clear forerunner of what continues in our time. There are those people who have always wanted to take it more slowly while others want to speed up change as fast as they can. In education, that meant either training blacks to be workers in the local economy or offering a broader (and more meaningful) education.

It is easy to look back at the philanthropy of the North and see a kind of prejudice and racism. It is hard to imagine that, at some level, those in the North did not view blacks as inferior. It is also clear that Booker T. Washington's sense that blacks needed to go slowly, be careful, and stay segregated would be the ideas of choice of bigoted and fearful white America. But those are not the ideas that are important for us right now.

What is clear is that race was central to the thinking in those times. Color made a big difference. It played a part in just about every segment of society. Hispanics, for example, were not allowed in white schools because English was their second lan-

---

[36]Ibid., p. 302.

[37]Ibid., p. 303.

guage.[38] But it is more probable that they were not allowed in white schools because they were brown. Certainly blacks were denied entry into white society simply because of their color.

We know that things have changed. Since 1954 schools have been integrated, the idea of separate but equal is illegal, we had (and continue to have in some areas) affirmative action, and to deny anything to anyone on the basis of color is neither legal nor condoned in most parts of the culture.

Does that mean there is no racism? What was I thinking when I said that race is the most difficult issue in our country? If you are a college student in your mid-twenties or younger, the idea of race, no matter what color you are, may not seem as compelling to you as it did to older generations. Certainly the world you grew up in was full of different colored people. And, if you are a person of color, should it be assumed that you are not prejudiced against white people? Segregation is a historical concept for many whites—but does that mean racism is dead? Prejudice seems to be a part of daily life for people of color—does that mean they are entitled to be prejudiced in return?

Maybe much of the traditional racism is no longer with us. Maybe not. But there are facts we need to consider before we pat ourselves on the back, declare victory over racism, and decide to not mention it again.

RACE AND CLASS

These days we get figures that are often tied to socioeconomic class. In 1990 the average white family income was almost $37,000; the average black family income was about $21,500. On the average, black men earned 20 percent less than white men given the same level of education. By 1996 white and Asian American income was up to $39,000 while black income was about $26,500 and Hispanic income was about $24,300. In 1990 a little over 11 percent of black men were unemployed while only about 4 percent of white men were unemployed. In 1992 more than 15 percent of the Puerto Rican-American males were unemployed, while only 7.1 percent of Cuban American males were unemployed.

In 1992, when family wealth was measured, it was found that white families' mean net worth was $58,500, with half of all white families having a net worth of over $203,000. Nonwhite families had a net worth of $4,000, with half having a net worth of a little over $45,000. At the other end of the scale, in 1994 blacks and Hispanics each exceeded 30 percent living in poverty while only 11.7 percent of the whites lived in poverty.

The United States has the highest infant mortality rate of any industrialized nation. Black infants die at a rate twice as high as white infants.[39] In some inner-cities

---

[38]See an interesting article about how Texas segregated Mexican Americans in Guadalupe San Miguel Jr., "The Struggle against Separate and Unequal Schools: Middle Class Mexican Americans and the Desegregation Campaign in Texas, 1929–1957," in McClellan and Reese, pgs. 334–49.

[39]See Tozer, op. cit., pgs. 372–4.

(for example, Chicago and Detroit) the death rate for infants is higher than Jamaica, Costa Rica, and Chile. Forty-five percent of black children, 39.8 percent of Hispanic children, and 16.1 percent of white children lived in poverty in 1991.

By 1996 things had improved for blacks.[40] For the first time since records began being kept in 1959, less than 30 percent of the blacks lived in poverty. Married black couples earned 87 percent of what white couples earned, and that is up from 79 percent in 1979. The rate of black murder victims fell by 17 percent, and the proportion of blacks, ages 25–29 with high school degrees was the same as whites.

One interesting part of these figures is the emphasis on economics. It is something we can count and something we all seem to agree is important. The American Dream, in no small part, is entangled with economic well-being. As much as any time in our history, our individual ability to consume is an important indication of how each of us is doing. At this point in our history, economics and education seem to have almost merged.

Most students think about higher education as the path to economic success. The better the school, the smarter the career training, the more likely there will be a well-paid job in your future. In the mid-'80s, the Carnegie Foundation funded a study that discovered 90 percent of college-bound high school students said they were going in order to have a "more satisfying career." Eighty-eight percent of their parents agreed.

The tension between training and education has been around forever. DuBois argued that the classic curriculum was, in the end, the most satisfying one. To converse with the great thinkers, to enjoy the beauty of the best ideas, and understand the depth of the human experience should be denied no one who was capable of learning it. But it was Washington who won that battle. Blacks were given the kind of training that would assure them a paying job, but assure them little more. Another way to understand the distinction is this: Some of our most elite colleges are liberal arts schools. They focus on teaching their very bright students to think, write, and get a clear overview of problems. Being small and concentrating on liberal arts, they do not have the number of faculty it takes to provide the kind of specialized courses that a large research institution is routinely able to do.

But those powerful little schools produce highly successful people. While they do not necessarily graduate with a clear career path open to them, what they do have are the skills that will eventually make them leaders in whatever they decide to do. What was true for Plato remains true today: Those with the best and deepest educations have the best chance of becoming part of the elite.

If that is so, what does it have to do with socioeconomic class? Children of poor people tend to go to school with others who are poor. Their schooling is generally regimented (they pay a great deal of attention to discipline, for example) and tend to teach cut-and-dry material. Students are generally taught that there is one right answer and then they are tested to see if they actually have remembered the answer. For poor students, high school is often a place where there is a weapons search at the

---

[40]These figures come from Spring, op. cit., p. 111.

door and there is a military-tough discipline. Counseling is marginal and career choices are limited. While there are always examples of exceptional students who go on to excel, basically students who attend these schools have only a very limited chance of moving up the socioeconomic scale.

The bottom line is that schools in poor neighborhoods seldom send their graduates to college. Indeed, they are schools that have the lowest graduation rates.

The suburbs offer another kind of education. They often offer tracks of education where the top-level students are in the college track, there is good counseling, and most foolish childhood mistakes are forgiven. College is taken for granted by the best students, and even the other students are encouraged to continue their education after they graduate.

In the better, more affluent schools the idea of getting the right answer is replaced by teachers asking students their opinions. An effort is made to help students learn to think conceptually, and to apply their ideas and concepts to different situations. If a right answer is called for and a student doesn't get it, it is not unusual for the teacher to ask the student to "think about it some more."[41]

Schools in richer districts get more qualified teachers and have more resources. They have better science labs, libraries, computers, and well, just about everything else. Parents who are middle and upper middle class are often very active in their children's education. They know their kids' teachers, are comfortable in the schools, and are willing to make some kind of contribution to their children's education. They expect their kids to learn a great deal and, ultimately, do well. That is not the case with lower-class parents. They frequently feel alienated from the process and are not prepared (or do not know how) to help their children. Schools have higher expectations of middle- and upper-class students than they do lower-class students. Too often students who have lower-class parents are not expected to know much or to learn much. The expectations become self-fulfilling prophecies.

Clearly, this is all generalization. There are remarkable teachers who do amazing things in the poorest and most dysfunctional schools. There are lower-class students who become world leaders through hard work and because various people have helped them. Certainly there are lower-class parents who insist that their children have the best possible education while there are middle- and upper-class parents who ignore their children. But it is not helpful to focus on the exceptions. While many deserve high praise for the work they do and what they accomplish, the other and more powerful truth remains: There is a genuine correlation between money, class, and quality of education.

The last kind of schooling is done by private schools that offer an entirely different kind of education. These schools are about preparing students for college and, if successful, leadership positions. While there is certainly not military discipline at these schools, they are possibly more demanding than the inner-city schools. Students are forced to work hard. The reward for the majority of those in inner-city schools who graduate is that they do not have to go to school anymore. And why would they

---

[41]Jean Anyon, "Social Class and the Hidden Curriculum of Work," in Kevin Dougherty and Floyd Hammack, *Education and Society, A Reader* (New York: Harcourt Brace Jovanovich, 1990), pgs. 426–8.

want to after their high school experience? The reward for those at private schools is a network of powerful friends, a good college, and a genuine head start as they become young adults. Private schools help students achieve and excel; they provide an extraordinary preparation for life. Not all students who attend private schools are rich—but being rich is very helpful because tuition for elite prep schools is sometimes more than $30,000 a year. Private schools teach us an important thing about our society: Elites are not necessarily permanent. There is a revolving elite in the United States. We can see that easily enough with our presidents. Franklin Roosevelt was a member of an established elite family. The 2000 presidential candidates George W. Bush and Al Gore come from families we understand as elite. Both were prep school boys who went to fine colleges and whose families had both power and money. On the other hand, Bill Clinton and Ronald Reagan were from poor families and anything but privileged.

Prep schools provide one way for very bright and ambitious kids to begin to work their way into elite circles.

Back to public schools.

The statistics show that disadvantaged students (in terms of parental income, occupation, education, and presence of consumer goods in the house) are three times *less* likely to be in the academic track than affluent students. The disadvantaged are three times *more* likely than affluent students to be in the vocational track. *Social class is a more effective predictor of future opportunities than race.*[42] These are very distressing facts.

In the context of our discussion, the dilemma is this: Is the real problem in schooling race or class? Those who focus on race believe the problem is race. It is no mistake, they argue, that so many of those inner-city schools house racial minorities. Indeed, "segregation by race is strongly related to segregation by poverty."[43] They believe that to focus on class is an effort to make people ignore the racism that clearly still exists. To think through the problem tells us much about our present culture.

Bulworth

Have you seen the movie *Bulworth*? The short description is this: A United States Senator decides to have himself killed. Through a process of being exhausted, drinking, doing drugs, and not eating much, he becomes liberated enough to talk about how he understands politics. He becomes involved with a beautiful young black woman who helps educate him—and finally falls in love with him—as he has fallen in love with her. The ending is true to American culture, and is sad. The movie is a remarkable piece about money and color. [It is, I believe, more and better than a movie simply about money and color. For our purposes, the discussion is limited to these two topics.]

---

[42]Tozier, op. cit., p. 384.

[43]G. Orfield, *The Growth of Segregation in American Schools: Changing Patterns of Separation and Poverty Since 1968* (Cambridge, Mass.: Harvard University School of Education, 1993), p. 1.

See *Bulworth* twice. Once, just listen to it and don't watch it; the other time, watch it without listening to it. If you just listen to it, it is easy to believe that the basic problem in the United States has to do with the uneven distribution of wealth; if you simply watch it, it is easy to believe that the basic problem in the United States has to do with race.

Senator Bulworth, liberated from the constraints of electoral politics by drinking, not sleeping, and getting ready to die, rants about economic inequality. Listen to what he says. His is an economics lesson we rarely hear. But if you just watch the movie, you will see the division of society based on color. His Hollywood is white and wealthy; Halle Barry's Compton is black and poor. If you have time, rent the video.

We know that class is the best predictor of the future while it is clear that a disproportionate number of the lower class are people of color. Which came first; which is the most important? It is my sense that the class/race problem is an indication that we are in the middle of a transitional period. My generation (I am an old guy) was very involved in the Civil Rights movement. It was as simple as black and white in those days; there was clear prejudice, and it was all about race.

I am reasonably sure things are not that simple now. If you are now in your twenties, or younger, your world has always been more full of integrated images than any other generation in our history. The easy questions have been answered. There can be no segregation. From schools to restaurants to where professional golfers play their tournaments, there must be integration. Colleges have made efforts for years to somehow have their student bodies reflect the culture as a whole. Later, we will see how affirmative action helped the progress of equality. Prejudice is now not simply illegal, it is generally socially unacceptable. It is possible that we are gradually approaching a time that class might be more important than race. I do not believe for a minute that racism has been eliminated.[44] I still believe that it is the single most difficult problem with which we must deal. But it may well be that we have yet to find the way to educate people about racism.

It is entirely possible that one way to get at race is through class. Those who teach in kindergarten will tell you that race is not an issue with their kids. Racism is often at attitude passed on from one generation to the next. If you have grown up in a multiracial environment, then your idea of race, and the problem of racism, might well be different than that of your parents. Racism has not gone away, but neither does it dominate everyday life for most Americans. If you are poor and a minority, then it is very difficult to separate race and class. If you are trying to eliminate the considerable differences in class as well as education between whites and some minorities, maybe the best way to do that is to concentrate on class. Too many advances have been made in race relations to continue to make them our only focus.

In the next chapter we will take up multiculturalism. While it seems a harmless thing to say that if we concentrate on eliminating some of our class differences then many of our problems might disappear, the underlying prejudice is that if we were just

---

[44] In 2003, then Republican Majority Leader of the U.S. Senate Trent Lott publically lamented that a segregationist did not win the 1948 presidential election. In his mind, it would have prevented so many current problems. His is a mind of the past. He was forced to resign his position.

all like white, middle-class people then there would be no problems. But what if a person wants to keep his or her own cultural identity? Should we penalize that person with bad schools and little or no chance at economic success? These are problems we will take up in the next chapter. Now, we need to turn our attention to what people call second-generation segregation and the various attempts to restructure education to make it more equitable and accessible to all groups.

Put differently, we will return to the topic of racism with a short history about how we have tried to eliminate it, and how it currently seems to be manifesting itself.

ELIMINATING RACISM

Earlier we traced the history of how the courts finally did away with segregation. From separate but equal to *Brown v The Board of Education of Topeka*, segregation was finally found illegal by the Supreme Court in 1954. Chief Justice Earl Warren wrote that segregating black children simply because of their race could create "a feeling of inferiority as to their status in the community that may effect their hearts and minds in a way unlikely ever to be undone. . . . Separate educational facilities are inherently unequal."

Not surprisingly there was active resistance to the Court's mandate to desegregate the public schools with "all deliberate speed." Some schools were simply closed while others tried different schemes to keep the races apart. We saw that President Eisenhower sent federal troops to Little Rock, Arkansas, to make certain the high school accept black students. While many communities continued to resist, in 1971 the Supreme Court ruled unanimously that the busing of students was a legitimate way to achieve desegregation in public schools. The Court made it clear that it was intent on making sure that the greatest possible degree of desegregation was obtained.

Busing became a serious issue. All of a sudden the long-respected and cherished idea of the neighborhood school seemed in great danger. There were horror stories about students who were forced to be on buses for hours when they were only minutes away from their former school. President Nixon said he was against busing. There were boycotts, protests, and even violence aimed at busing. The opposition took place in both northern and southern cities.

Busing brought change. Before busing, white families had been moving out of urban areas. As busing became a legal way for school boards to integrate, more white families than ever moved to the suburbs. As we will see in the next chapter, urban education during the last quarter of the twentieth century became education for minorities. Schools in the suburbs were generally well-funded and white. While there is little doubt that busing was successful in forcing people to face the issue of integration, there is also the awful irony that it helped recreate segregation. In the end, busing is at least partially responsible for the current condition of our inner-city schools.

There have been a series of ways school systems have tried to desegregate. These methods have created what critics call second-generation segregation. It is the kind of segregation that takes place in integrated schools. Before we look at second-generation segregation, the fact remains that in many places real segregation still exists. For example, in California 78.7 percent of blacks and 79.1 percent of Hispanics attend schools with between 50 percent and 100 percent minority population. In

New York 86.1 percent of Hispanics, and in Illinois almost 89 percent of blacks, attend such schools.[45] There are school systems all over the country that have schools that are almost all white, or almost all minority.

Many of these systems are legally desegregated because they have put in place different desegregation plans. In some districts, for example, there are magnet schools. These schools were started during the '70s and '80s as an alternative to busing. Magnet schools often had the best teachers in the system and were concentrated on teaching different skills. Some schools taught mainly fine arts, some science, and some were back-to-the-basics that focused on strict discipline, dress codes, and an emphasis on helping students fit into the system.

While magnet schools were never the full answer to integration, they certainly helped. They represented a voluntary kind of desegregation that was appealing to a great many people. Some of these schools were, in fact, wonderful. But they have not been enough to desegregate school systems. In some places, magnet schools have been dismantled. While they have helped with racial integration, they have regrettably seemed to increase class segregation. They often appealed to middle- and upper-middle-class students and left lower-class students to what many thought were second-rate neighborhood schools. In the final chapter, we will look at more current proposals for change. The concept of school choice might have some impact on segregation, but the agenda is more complicated than that.

Presidents Reagan and Bush were not interested in the idea of desegregating schools. From the mid-1970s, the Supreme Court has decided not to be involved with the issue. By the 1990s the Supreme Court decisions indicated that it was all right to ignore the fact that many students went to segregated school.

One focus, from the middle of the '70s to now, has been on the idea of "effective schools." The idea was to focus on those schools with high minority enrollments and make certain that there were clear goals, there was not an oppressive environment, and that the students would be able to score well on standardized tests. Teachers were to have high standards, and administrators needed to be effective instructional managers. There was an emphasis on basic skills, frequent evaluations of student progress, and efforts to strengthen the ties between the schools and home.[46]

In principle, there is little to criticize about effective schools. The qualities of these schools are simply the qualities of all good schools. Good teachers and managers, clear goals, close ties with the family, and high standards and test scores in a welcoming and encouraging environment. What's not to like? The downside of effective schools is what some believed has been the unstated agenda: To reinstitute the idea of separate but equal and make certain that it worked. It seems to many that effective schools is simply a way to reassure people that segregated education is equal education. What we know is that there is a strong sense that segregated schools can never provide equal education. In the Brown case the Supreme Court was very clear that there are things that are impossible to get from segregated schools. While the stated goals of effective schools should be the underlying principles for all schools, in reality

---

[45]These are 1992 figures found in Spring, op. cit., p. 117.

[46]Newman, op. cit., p. 264.

schools can be truly effective only if they are at least roughly representative of the population.

Second-Generation Segregation

One should not assume that all integrated schools are either good or effective. There are ways to keep segregation alive even if schools are integrated. We have come to know these ways as second-generation segregation. The three most popular methods of separating students are through tracking, ability grouping, and misusing special education.

Like effective schools, there is much good to be said about the basic ideas behind these methods. It seems to make sense, for example, that students who are going to college be put in a track that will provide them with the courses they need to get into college. Or, why should students who are capable of doing advanced math be held back by students who are not mathematically gifted? Or, why shouldn't those students who are going into a trade be given the opportunity to take those math courses that will be of practical use to them?

Certainly those students who need special help should be given the right to get that help. (Special education is the topic of a later chapter.) That sometimes students are mistakenly put into special-ed classes does not mean that those classes are bad. Using special-ed classes as a way to segregate by race should simply be considered an administrative abuse of power.

There are those who argue against tracking and ability grouping. There are students who prosper in classes that are supposed to be too advanced for them. It is possible that the brighter students help the less bright in those classes, and everyone is better for it. In some studies, it has been shown that ability grouping has no significant effect, positive or negative, on test scores of students in the middle or bottom third of the distribution. If these groupings help the high-scoring students, the effect is very small. There is enough conflicting data that we really do not know if tracking and ability grouping is sound educational policy.

What we do know is that in integrated schools these plans often result in segregating students by race. What is the use of having integrated schools if minorities are going to be grouped together in classes that are "lower" than those for whites? We can read the findings of a 1989 report:[47]

> [In urban school districts] a black student is nearly three times more likely to be placed in a class for the educable mentally retarded than is a white student. A black student is 30 times more likely to be assigned to a trainable mentally retarded class than a white student. At the other end of the sorting spectrum, a white student is 3.2 times more likely to be assigned to a gifted class than is a black student.
>
> In terms of discipline, a black student is more than twice as likely as a white student to be corporally punished or to be expelled. [And, at the other end of the road] a black student is 18 percent more likely to drop out of school and 27 percent less likely to graduate from high school.

[47]Found in David Berliner and Bruce Biddle, *The Manufactured Crisis: Myths, Fraud, and the Attack on America's Public Schools* (New York: Longman, 1997), p. 230.

The bottom line is that minorities continue to have a difficult time in public schools. While there are some indications that the gap between blacks and whites is narrowing (IQ scores is one example[48]), it is still painfully clear that students continue to be sorted by race—as well as economic status. The methods people use to separate students are now more sophisticated than they were before the Brown decision, but they are almost as effective as when segregation was legal.

There are two more topics that need to be discussed. One deals with testing, and what variables really seem to affect student achievement. In the last section, we will focus on race one more time.

WHAT AFFECTS TEST SCORES

Before you begin to disagree with the whole notion that test scores are valid measures of education, let me assure you I agree. In a later chapter we will deal with testing, and its various strengths and even more numerous shortcomings. The reason test scores are interesting for our purposes is that they represent something that can be studied with relative reliability. It is possible to not only compare scores but to understand those variables that are responsible for these differences. *The Black-White Test Score Gap*[49] is a book of essays concerned with trying to help us understand what needs to be done for more equal test scores for all students. It is concerned with how to raise blacks' test scores to be equal to scores of white students.

On the average blacks score lower than whites on vocabulary, reading, and math tests. These differences appear before the children enter kindergarten and persist into adulthood. While the gap has narrowed since 1970, the typical black continues to score below 75 percent of whites on most standardized tests. It is necessary to remember that these kinds of figures tell us nothing about anyone in particular. There have always been many blacks who score above many whites. All these figures do is give us an idea of the whole picture.

What can be shown is that the differences have nothing to do with the innate intellectual abilities of either blacks or whites. For example, when blacks are raised in white rather than black homes, their preadolescent test scores rise dramatically.[50] Also, we know that even nonverbal scores on IQ tests are sensitive to environmental change. "Large environmental changes can have a large impact on test scores."[51] Finally, as schooling has improved for blacks, the black–white differences in academic achievement have narrowed.

If we put this in the context of racism, what we see is that race—genetics—is not what has caused the difference in achievement. In the beginning of the chapter the

[48]Richard Rothstein, *The Way We Were: The Myths and Realities of America's Student Achievement.* (New York: Century Foundation Press, 1998), p. 85.

[49]Christopher Jencks and Meredith Phillips, editors (Washington D.C.: Brookings Institution Press, 1998).

[50]Richard Nisbett, "Race, Genetics, and IQ," in ibid.

[51]Jencks, ibid., p. 3.

argument was made that race was, in the final analysis, a political concept. We can begin to see that more clearly. Given political, economic, and educational equality that has traditionally been deprived of racial minorities we could assume that there would eventually be no differences in achievement.

Economic differences play a role in black–white differences. While black and white school districts often spend about the same amount of money per student, whites continue to have higher test scores. Interestingly, the difference in those schools that seemed to be most important to test scores was that teachers in predominately black school had lower test scores themselves.

Along with the idea that poverty plays a role is the fact that many students come from a one-parent family. There is a sense that two-parent families provide the kind of environment needed for children to be successful in school. What actually seems to be the case is that the mother's family background, her years of schooling, and test scores turn out to be much more important than whether she is poor, or living with another adult. Indeed, the family background of parents is important. Students with grandparents and parents who have been academically successful have a better chance of doing well than students whose parents have not done well.[52] Put differently, academic achievement often takes two generations. Educated grandmothers count.

Parenting practices also affect how well students do. We know that parents' educational achievement and income are important. What is more difficult to know are the things built into that calculation. If elimination of the disparity in income was accompanied by the elimination of the causes of that disparity, then it seems reasonable to assume the black–white gap would disappear. What does seem clear is that parenting practices are even more important than parental income. That makes the argument about which is more important—class or racism—less compelling. While it can be argued that parenting skills are affected by both racism and class, it is equally clear that good parenting can be done by anyone.

We know that heredity plays a role (for example, most of the variation in white IQ scores is genetic, especially in adults), but environment might play a more important role for blacks. In one study, it was found that blacks adopted by white parents had IQ scores 13.5 points higher than blacks who were adopted by black parents. Children of mixed race averaged 11 points higher on IQ tests if they had a white mother rather than a black mother. The color of the father made no difference.[53] Because the average difference in black–white IQs when the studies were done was 15 points, the implication is that four-fifths of the difference were family-related factors such as schools and neighborhoods.

The white–black test gap has narrowed since 1962. Black reading and math scores have risen substantially, while white scores have remained about the same. Still, in 1992 white high school seniors were about ten times more likely to score in the top 5 percent on a composite test of academic skills than blacks. The speculation is that the Civil Rights movement, the War on Poverty, and affirmative action, along

[52]Ibid., p. 25.

[53]Ibid., p. 17.

with better schools, helped change both black parents' and students' attitude about schooling.[54]

There is an interesting and serious question about the narrowing of the scores. The question is this: Which scores does one measure? The gap in scores is much less for students just beginning school than for those finishing high school. What happens between the ages of six and eighteen? Are the schools to blame? Does the social context—both inside and outside of school—explain why black–white scores widen as the students get older? We do know that some of the explanation has to do with economics. We do know the test score gap between economically advantaged and economically disadvantaged children widen when they are not in school during the summer. But that tells us little about why the black–white gap increases.

One possible answer is that teachers are, in part, the cause.[55] Ronald Ferguson concluded that teachers had lower expectations for blacks than for whites, that their expectations had a greater impact on black performance than on white performance, that teachers base their expectations on children's past performance and behavior—thereby perpetuating racial disparities, and finally, that "exhorting teachers to have more faith in black children's potential is unlikely to change their expectations." On a more hopeful note, teachers may change their attitudes if they actually see disadvantaged children performing well.

As mentioned earlier, the test scores of the teacher is the best available indicator of the teacher's ability to raise students' test scores. The data that has been gathered (none of it has been gathered in randomized experiments) show that teachers with high test scores are more effective than teachers with low test scores. The interesting dilemma with this bit of information is that black teachers tend to test lower than white teachers. If the standards were raised, and teachers with lower scores were not allowed to teach, one result would be that black students would have very few black teachers. Is that a reasonable thing to do?

In the final section we will return to the question of what might happen to students from the time they are first tested to when they graduate from high school.

Part of the black–white gap test score gap can be explained by the tests themselves. The first problem is "labeling bias." Those who give these tests claim they measure one thing but actually measure another. Generally, the claim is that these tests are able to measure either intelligence or aptitude. Both of these words are linked to ideas of innate potential or developed ability. Both, then, may somehow indicate that there are innate differences that can be shown by test results. The problem, of course, is that the psychological community now agrees that "intelligence tests measure developed rather than innate abilities, and that people's developed abilities depend on their environment as well as their genes."[56]

[54]David Grissmer, Ann Flanagan, and Stephanie Williamson, "Why Did the Black–White Score Gap Narrow in the 1970s and 1980s?," in Jencks and Phillips, op. cit.

[55]Ronald Ferguson, "Teachers' Perceptions and Expectations and the Black–White Test Score Gap," in Jencks and Phillips, op. cit.

[56]Jencks and Phillips, op. cit., p. 13.

The tests, in other words, show much more about the background of the person than his or her innate skills and abilities. When a minority tests low on an intelligence test, it says more about how that person was raised than his or her native abilities.

The second bias is content. This does not necessarily mean language. In a standard vocabulary test, if the obvious black–white word differences are eliminated, the black–white test results remain about the same. What does make a difference is when black children are raised in white homes. Their test scores go up dramatically. The suggestion is that there might be a way in which blacks and whites are taught to learn and to deal with new situations differently. We are back to the point that test scores are often a reflection of the way children are brought up.

This brings us to the last topic: being a color.

COLOR

In 1992, 88 percent of the teachers were white. Discussions of racism in the United States have almost always meant that whites were part of the discussion. (While minorities discriminate among themselves, and racism in other nations often has nothing to do with whites, it is safe to say that most racism in the United States involves white people.)

Alice McIntyre defines whiteness this way:[57] " . . . a system and ideology of white dominance that marginalizes and oppresses people of color, ensuring existing privileges for white people in this country." She then quotes J. E. Helms when she writes about white racial identity as "a sense of group or collective identity based on one's *perceptions* that he or she shares a common racial heritage with a particular racial group."

One argument is that whites do not identify themselves as white, and often seem to avoid the use of whiteness in discussions. This becomes important when a teacher is white, and he or she falls into these patterns. We read that whites will define themselves as, for example, Irish or Italian or Catholic or Jewish. A white will rarely say he or she is simply white. Because ours is a white-dominated culture, the overwhelming advantage of being white goes unstated.

There are also ways in which whiteness is a critical variable that is often not mentioned.[58] For example, take the sentence "Racism forced urban housing to deteriorate." While more or less accurate, Duarte and Smith point out that the sentence does not indicate who was responsible for the deterioration of urban housing. Clearly racism was involved, but so too were white people. We read: " . . . passive sentence constructions allow us to talk about racism without ever naming our own complicity." While certainly a valid point, one can also ask a question about the writers' sentence construction. When they write about "our own complicity" are they making the case

---

[57]Alice McIntyre, *Making Meaning of Whiteness: Exploring Racial Identity with White Teachers* (New York: SUNY Press, 1997), p. 3.

[58]This comes from Eduardo Manuel Duarte and Stacy Smith, *Foundational Perspectives in Multicultural Education* (New York: Addison Wesley Longman, 2000), p. 129.

that all whites were involved in the deterioration of urban housing? Are they telling us that all whites are racist?

While it sounds that way, I am not sure we need to get into the merits of their point right now. More basically, the argument is that white people try hard to avoid discussions of racism. That was an underlying problem when race and class were talked about. The same kind of problem can be seen with the topic of multiculturalism.

Multiculturalism is understood by some as just another way of not discussing race. The argument is that while multicultural education may address "culture, race, ethnicity, and gender," it also serves to "mute attention to racism . . . focusing mostly on cultural differences . . . we frame our perspective of multicultural education in such a way that it loses its original critique of the multiple levels of miseducation of children of color, and of white children as well, and the unequal distribution of wealth and power that exists in our nation and is partially lived out within the confines of our educational institutions."[59]

In the end, this is what we read about being white: "What is crucial to American identity . . . is not that Americans hate black people. Rather the fundamental feature of their identity is that *they do not know who they are without black people. Without the Black Other, the American [white] Self has no identity.*"[60]

This kind of analysis can lead to many interesting insights. It is a way to conceptualize a social reality that helps clarify the role of both the powerful and the powerless. The problem, of course, is that it may be interesting analysis but a poor vision of reality. One wonders if it is an accurate view of the United States in the twenty-first century. There are, I suppose, those white people who need blacks in order to have an identity. One thinks of the Ku Klux Klan, or the small and destructive Aryan militants that periodically make themselves heard. What these groups have in common is that they take their identity from their hate—and they do not even hate blacks exclusively. They hate the "mud people," who includes all people of color as well as Jews and sometimes Catholics.

Why would people make the argument that multiculturalism is, in a sense, destructive because it takes us away from racism, or argue that whites have no identity without blacks? It is difficult to fully understand. Should we try to generalize the idea? Are we to assume that there is *no* identity without an oppressed Other? Does the Other have to be black? Did Africans have no identity until whites showed up? Do those small tribes who live on isolated islands in the Pacific have no identity? Finally, does this kind of analysis do any good? It must accomplish something with some group, and might have even been partially accurate in some places during certain times, but I am not prepared to embrace it for all whites for now. It may well provide us with interesting insights, but is a map of reality for only a few.

The anthropologists tell us that all cultures name themselves something like "the people." No matter how isolated they are, no matter if they have never seen any other humans, each culture seems to define itself as special. It seems to me the point

---

[59]McIntyre, op. cit., p. 13.

[60]Ibid., quoting D. Wellman, p. 17. Emphasis added.

is cultures are biased in that they see themselves as special. As somehow chosen. People do not need an Other in order to claim an identity.

Let me repeat what I have said before: I believe that race is the most difficult issue we have in the United States. But I am pretty certain that I am not who I am because there are black people. I tried to suggest one way to get at an answer to this question by quoting from "My Dinner with Andre" at the beginning of this chapter. It is possible that those who make the argument are, at least metaphorically, making the same mistake as the doctor who was looking at Andre's dying mother. All the doctor saw was the arm. Maybe what we all need to do is look at the entire situation.

It is quite possible that I am simply wrong.[60a] It is not out of the question that I do not know what I am talking about. It is in that spirit I suggest you think about the following: Who would you be if you were white and there were no blacks in your country? How big a difference would that make? Would you like it more or less than you like living in the United States? Or, another question: Would you even have an identity if you were a member of the only race in your country?

It's an interesting exercise. If done carefully, it is entirely possible to get at least some insight into what the "whiteness people" are all about.

"Acting White"

There is another literature about schooling that is about the perceived problems blacks have if they "act white."

In a remarkably influential study by Signithia Fordham and John Ogbu[61] the idea of "acting white" became a standard fixture of how people thought about blacks in school. Their study focused on one school in Washington, D.C., that was almost entirely black. Both Fordham and Ogbu have continued to write about what it meant to act white. What follows is from Ogbu that is quoted by Peter McLaren:[62]

> Specifically, blacks and other minorities . . . believe that in order for a minority to succeed in school academically, he or she must learn to think and act white . . . to think and act white enough to be rewarded by whites or white institutions like the schools, a minority person must give up his or her own minority-group attitudes, ways of thinking, and behaving, and, of course, must give up or lose his or her own minority identity . . . striving for academic success is a subtractive process: the individual black student following school standard practices that lead to academic success is perceived as adopting a white cultural frame of reference . . . as "acting white" with the inevitable outcome of losing his or her black identity, abandoning black people and black causes, and joining the enemy, namely, white people.

[60a] Indeed, a "whiteness" person who read an early draft of this chapter thought this was the most accurate sentence in this section.

[61] Signithia Fordham and John Ogbu, "Black Students' School Success: Coping with the Burden of 'Acting White,'" *Urban Review 18* (3), 1986, pgs. 176–206.

[62] Peter McLaren, *Life in Schools: An Introduction to Critical Pedagogy in the Foundations of Education*, 3d ed. (New York: Longman, 1998), p. 202.

This is a powerful argument. If true, it represents an almost impossible dilemma for those interested in schooling and, maybe even more importantly, education. How could anyone, in good conscience, ask someone else to give up his or her identity? Would you give up who you are on the promise that by making good grades you would somehow live a better life? And even if making good grades might lead to a better life, just who would you be if you no longer had an identity? If your best friends thought making good grades was somehow almost evil, would you have the strength to go ahead and make good grades anyway? When you are in school, is there anything more important than figuring out who you are, and being accepted by those with whom you want to be friends?

It is not as if the idea of acting white is entirely out of the realm of possibility. We know that the word oreo can mean something other than a cookie—black on the outside, white on the inside has never been considered a compliment. The popular press has dealt with the idea, and the problems, of acting white. In 1992, *Time* magazine wrote, "Social success depends partly on academic failure; safety and acceptance live in rejecting the traditional paths for self-improvement." In 1994 the *Wall Street Journal* had an article about a summer program for minority teenagers. They wrote: "At a lunch table, over cold-cuts on whole wheat, talk turns to the ultimate insult: 'wanting to be white.'"

There have been some studies that seem to indicate that Fordham and Ogbu were right, that there might be some data that shows there is a cultural force influencing how well blacks do in school. But, interestingly, those studies are not close to being convincing.

In 1997 there was a study that cast genuine doubt on the idea that good grades were equated with acting white in the black community. It is unclear if times had changed from 1986 and 1997 so that acting white might have been true at the time, but was no longer important. Or, possibly the school that Fordham and Ogbu studied was an exception even then. What is interesting to our discussion is that the idea of acting white has been an important concept, and it just might not be true.

In 1997, Philip Cook and Jens Ludwig took information from the National Education Longitudinal Study (NELS) that was sponsored by the U.S. Department of Education. The study began in 1988 and the sample covered 814 public schools and 237 private schools. In all, 17,544 students were involved. The paper written by Cook and Ludwig was taken from the data gathered in 1990 when most of the students were in the tenth grade.[63]

Cook and Ludwig asked three basic questions: 1) Do black adolescents report greater alienation from school than non-Hispanic whites; 2) Does academic success lead to social ostracism among black adolescents? and 3) Do the social costs and benefits of academic success differ by race? Their answer is this: Apparently not.[64]

Here are some of the conclusions Cook and Ludwig came to after looking at the data from the NELS:[65]

---

[63] The original article was in the *Journal of Policy Analysis and Management*, 1997. This version is Cook and Ludwig, "The Burden of 'Acting White': Do Black Adolescents Disparage Academic Achievement?," in Jencks and Phillips, op. cit.

[64] Ibid., p. 376.

[65] Ibid., pgs. 390–2.

1. Black students are not particularly alienated from school. Like whites, they expect to graduate from high school, enter and complete college. Given the same socioeconomic background, their rate of graduation is the same as whites.
2. Blacks and white spend about the same amount of time on homework. The hardest working whites spend about ten to fifteen minutes a day more on homework than blacks, but the hardest working blacks are more likely to be members of the honor society or win academic awards.
3. Black and white tenth-graders who excel in school are no more likely to be unpopular than other students. While black students sometimes taunt high-achieving blacks for acting white, it appears that the benefits of doing well more than offset the social problems. (It was noted that white students who are high achievers are often identified by others as nerds, or worse. But "nerd" does not carry the slam power of "oreo.")
4. There is little difference between the attendance and graduation rates of whites and blacks.
5. It appears as though the social costs and benefits of doing well seem to offset each other.

The bottom line, for Cook and Ludwig, is that what is called the "oppositional culture" is not as important as more fundamental issues such as improving schools and providing more support and guidance for students who live in poverty.

While these findings might not be in dispute, there are ways in which they might not tell the entire story. For example, it is possible that pressure might be seen in other places. A black might hesitate raising his or her hand in class because of social pressure, or one's speech might get moderated in order to fit in better. In a study using data from the same study, it was found that teachers rate black students as more disruptive and putting forth less effort than white students. Does that indicate blacks fear "acting white" and decide to act out? (Or, does that reinforce the idea that white teachers continue to believe in old stereotypes about black students?)

It seems we are at a familiar point: Our conventional wisdom does not quite seem to fit our current reality. Yes, there continues to be racism; no, the idea that there is a black subculture in schools that systematically forces blacks to not achieve much academically appears to be wrong. Yes, race is an issue; yes, class might be an even bigger issue.

It is time to turn to our last topic. What has been done and what needs to be done?

TAKING ACTION

As we have seen, there have been different attempts to narrow the minority/white gap in schooling. Our short review began with in the post–Civil War South, proceeded through busing, and ended with what has been called second generation segregation.

Had this been written in the early '90s there would have been a long section on affirmative action. The idea behind affirmative active is simple enough: It means that an extra effort should be made to make certain a class of people (a minority group, or women) is protected and given a reasonable chance to get a job or a promotion. It was the law that organizations needed to look at the sex, race, and other attributes of those people who were hired, promoted, and fired.

It was an effort to make certain that those groups that had systematically been discriminated against in the job market (or in getting into college) would be given a fair chance. It was very clear that minorities and women had been routinely excluded in these areas, and affirmative action was understood as a way to compensate for past injustices and their lingering effects.

In practice, it went something like this: There is rarely an absolutely "best" job applicant or college applicant. Different people have different skills and attributes, so the idea of a one best person is generally not a sound notion. Affirmative action made people consider categories such as race or sex when hiring, admitting, promoting, and the like. That way, if other things were more or less equal, then a minority or a woman would get the job, college acceptance, promotion, or whatever. Even if there was a written test, a person who scored a 95 might not be any better qualified than a person scoring an 89. If things were that close, then affirmative action policies could come into play. In a practical way, a 95 or an 89 cannot be the entire difference between two individuals.

Not surprisingly, there were heated objections to the policy. Philosophically, affirmative action chose to look at people in groups, while American liberal thought always favored the idea that people should be judged individually. And when "all things" were equal, those white males who had traditionally been chosen were very unhappy not to be chosen *because* they were white males. A frequently heard argument was that those white males, individually, had never oppressed anyone. Why should they pay for the sins of other generations?

While progress under affirmative action was slow, it was progress. Not only were minorities and women given a fair chance, but probably equally importantly, those in organizations became aware of the systematic biases of the past. The idea of routine discrimination has certainly not gone away, but one suspects that it would be remarkably difficult to be reinstituted—it would be almost impossible to go back to those very bad old days of our work and college worlds being a club of only "white old boys."

On the other hand, affirmative action is no longer the law of the land. While it is still illegal to discriminate, many of the old affirmative action policies are also illegal. Just as it is almost impossible to think we will return to obvious discrimination, it is equally difficult to believe we will soon return to an active policy of affirmative action. [66] But one of the bottom lines is that we tried it, it was effective in certain ways, and we are better off for it.

What are other things that we might do? Regrettably, it is my sense that there are no, great, sweeping answers that will be acceptable to a majority of the country. Busing and affirmative action were grand answers. In many ways, they were effective. They were instituted in the face of great opposition and they helped bring change. After a great deal of contention and bitterness, the opponents of affirmative action finally won. It should be noted that some of the most outspoken opponents were people of color who thought the policy had run its course and was, in no small way,

---

[66] The Supreme Court will rule on two affirmative action cases from the University of Michigan. It is generally agreed that these rulings will set the direction of affirmative action for years to come.

becoming detrimental to minorities. One powerful opponent of affirmative action is George W. Bush.

So, what can be done? Cutting class size and weeding out ineffective teachers works. It actually works better for black students than whites. What that means is that black students' test scores improve more than the scores of white students in these conditions when classes are small. We can raise teacher expectations of minority students. When teachers see how well minority students can do, they are more likely to change their expectations.

We can change the preschool experience of minority students. Parents can be taught different behaviors that impact on their students. Also, Head Start can begin to emphasize cognitive development so that those children will be ready to begin school.

While these ideas do not seem as sweeping or as grand as other ideas, it does not mean they would be easy to institute. If classes for minorities were small, there would certainly be a call for all classes to be small. That would mean hiring more teachers, and taxpayers do not frequently vote for higher taxes.[67] And how receptive would any parent be when someone came into their home and told them there were different, and better, ways to be a parent? Few of us readily accept the advice of strangers. The point is obvious: Even the seemingly simple suggestions about how to help make education more equal might be difficult to implement.

The twist to all of this is that one of the things that makes the United States special, that makes the United States unusually strong, is that it is a multiracial society. The effort to make certain that people can live together, equally and in peace, has helped create some of the best parts of our society. As teachers, we know that society expects that we, somehow, provide the solution. When you walk into your classroom and see different colored faces, you are walking into one of our most profound problems—and you are expected to solve it.

SUMMARY

To begin the discussion about race, we were reminded of two important things. First, we saw that race was a political concept, not a biological one. There is only one human race; that, at the least, we are all 99.9 percent the same. Second, we reviewed the idea that a discussion about race in the United States is more than simply a discussion about blacks and whites. We read about the different races that make up our population—and how each group has its own history and own set of issues.

The ideas of W. E. B. DuBois and Booker T. Washington were examined. Their views were important and influential in how the education of blacks was understood following the Civil War. We also saw how money from Eastern foundations supported a particular kind of vocational education for Southern blacks.

The relationship of class and race was seen from several points of view. There is evidence that class may be a more important variable than race when it comes to edu-

---

[67] The economic downturn that began at the beginning of the twenty-first century has meant less money for schools, and fewer rather than more teachers. It is exactly what our schools did not need.

cation. Time was spent on how race and class related to test scores. We also reviewed the idea of "whiteness" and the insights gained from that analytic construct. We looked at the literature on "acting white."

Finally, we reviewed the actions taken to help eliminate racism (busing, magnet schools, affirmative action), as well as things that might currently be helpful in our schools.

THINK ABOUT

1. Do you believe your children will grow up in a less racist society? Why or why not?

2. Can you explain why, during Desert Storm, Iraq called all Americans "White Satans"—no matter what color they were?

3. Would you ever want to be another color? Why or why not? What does that say about the color and how it is viewed in the United States?

CHAPTER SEVEN

TRAINING AMERICANS
Urban, Multicultural, and Bilingual Education

Dare the schools build a new social order?

George Counts

Those council people from Los Altos should be made to understand that they are advocating their law in occupied Mexico [referring to the U.S. conquest of Mexican territory, including California] . . . They should move back to England or learn how to speak the language of Native Americans.

Quoted by Joel Spring

You walk into your classroom and see boys and girls of different colors and backgrounds. Some might be first or second generation immigrants. A language other than English might be spoken at home; indeed, English might not be the first language of some of your students. These students come from different cultures, have different ethnic identities, and it is entirely possible that they see the world in ways that are mystifying to their classmates and maybe even to you.

What do you plan to do with different cultures and different languages? As we will see, there are some who are very sure about the right thing to do. Luckily for them, the issues are so clear that the answers are obvious. It may well be that some of them are right and that there are clearly superior ways to think about multicultural and bilingual education. But before you walk into your first classroom, there are many things that need to be sorted out. There are decisions you need to begin to make.

This chapter is divided into three major parts. The first focuses on urban education. The reason is simple enough: Issues of multiculturalism and bilingual education were first dealt with in our big cities more than a hundred years ago. Immigrants settled in the cities and it was believed that the job of the public schools was to somehow make them citizens of the United States. It was up to the schools to solve the emerging interrelated dynamics of immigration, industrialization, and modernism that were changing our national identity. The changes began in our urban areas.

The job of urban schools was to prepare a very unprepared population for a new kind of life.

The second and third sections center on multicultural and bilingual education. These two topics are intensely political. While there are some studies that indicate the pedagogically most successful ways to deal with these issues, the bottom line is that "most successful" also includes political aims. As we sort through the data about how diverse we are, where immigrants come from and when, what languages we speak and the variety of ways Americans understand the world, we will finally get to this point: What is there about diversity that can make us stronger, and when does diversity somehow become division and make us weaker? We need to ask how the needs of an individual might conflict with the needs of a society, and which we should favor in such a conflict. Do we believe that individual differences are more important than social solidarity?

In order to make sense of multicultural and bilingual education, it is important to review the purposes (there are many) and the proposals (there are many) for how to best teach our diverse students in our society that is increasingly sensitive to differences.

These topics give us an unusually good opportunity to become more clear in how we understand the nature of our society. And although these questions have been around for a long time, they seem more difficult to answer now than they ever have been. There are at least three ways to conceptualize the basic question. We have already mentioned the first: How do we balance individual and social needs? In a sense, it is a matter of minority rights and majority power. A second way is much like the question we asked about boys and girls: Is equal treatment fair treatment? And third, there is a little different way of asking the first question: How diverse can a society be and still agree on basic principles?

What we will see is that, in the end, this chapter is about you—and what you think and just where you fit in our diversified society. As a teacher, you will have an important say in what goes on.

URBAN EDUCATION

For more than a hundred years immigrants have been a large part of the collective life of the United States. While there have been periods during which immigration slowed, much of the twentieth century was marked by waves of people moving here from different parts of the world. As we shall see, the job of helping these new citizens assimilate (at least for a time) fell to the public schools.

When we turn our attention to the current (and often highly confrontational) debates about multicultural and bilingual education, we will see that the older idea of assimilation has been under attack for at least forty years. Indeed, it is now very out of fashion in many parts of the educational world to endorse the idea of assimilation. The things we ask our schools to do seem to be ever-changing and never finished.

Between 1880 and 1914 there was a huge flow of immigrants. They came and settled in what quickly became big cities. In 1890, 30 percent of a population of 63 million people lived in cities; by 1920, half of the 106 million Americans lived in cities; by 1950, two-thirds of 150 million people lived in cities, and by 1980 three-fourths of a population of 227 million people lived in cities.

Until around 1900, immigrants to the United States were mostly from Northwest Europe and Germany. For the following twenty years there were an increasing number from other parts of Europe and Asia. Some of the numbers help us see the remarkable changes. Between 1881 and 1885 more than 6,700,000 people immigrated to the United States, and from 1901 to 1915 more than 11,800,000 people came.[1]

More specifically, in 1880 Catholicism was the largest single church, with over 6.25 million members. (Of course, it was still a minority religion. The United States was firmly Protestant.) By 1910 there were 16.3 million Catholics, in 1920 there were 19.8 million, and by 1960 there were about 42 million Catholics in the United States. In 1960 more than 5.5 million Catholic children were enrolled in more than 13,000 elementary and secondary parochial schools. Most cities of any size had parochial schools.

In 1880 there were about 230,000 Jews in the United States. In 1914 there were 2 million living here. And most of those Catholics and Jews settled in big cities. They entered the United States often knowing little or no English, and having no sense of what to expect from life in the New World. They did not come from democracies and had little sense of what life would be like in an increasingly industrialized/capitalist democracy. To make things more difficult, immigrants all too frequently experienced intolerance. In Boston, the Irish were an abused minority by the Protestant majority, and there was not so subtle anti-Semitism in all phases of American life.

Blacks added to the diversity of the cities. At the end of the Civil War more than 90 percent of the blacks lived in the South. During the 1890s they began moving north to big cities. While they escaped the poor and sometimes nonexistent education of the South (Lawrence Cremin writes that the missionary schools in the South were much like the missionary schools in India, China, and Japan[2]), what they found in the North was not a great deal better. The cities were segregated. The schools in the black districts were much inferior to schools in the white districts.

New York City, about which most has been written, added 21,000 new students each year during the 1920s[3]. The pressure on schools to somehow adapt to those numbers was great. In 1927, for half of the students in the Brooklyn high school, English was not spoken at home. By 1930, 25 percent of the population between ages 7 and 20 did not attend school. Clearly, the officials of the school system had mixed feelings about the law that made schooling compulsory.

In 1910, 78 percent of the school population in the city of Chicago had at least one foreign-born parent—and the figures were about the same in New York City and

---

[1] Found in Steven Tozer, Paul Violas, and Gary Senese, *School and Society: Historical and Contemporary Perspectives*, 3d ed. (Boston: McGraw-Hill, 1998), p. 85.

[2] Lawrence Cremin, *American Education: The Metropolitan Experience 1876–1980* (New York: Harper & Row, 1988), p. 119.

[3] Kate Rousmaniere, *City Teachers: Teaching and School Reform in Historical Perspective* (New York: Teachers College Press, 1997), p. 55.

Milwaukee.[4] In 1911 over half of the students in urban schools were from immigrant families. [5] To repeat the point: Urban schools were the first to deal with issues of multicultural and bilingual education.

It is important to note that urban schools were not the only places where the issues of language and culture came up. During the late 1800s to the 1930s, the federal government decided that American Indians needed to be Americanized and assimilated into mainstream culture. The government systematically took children away from their families, taught them English at the expense of their native languages, and forced white, middle-class values on them. It was a remarkably culturally destructive effort.

In 1882 Congress passed the Chinese Exclusion Act that stopped immigration to the West Coast. The act served as a model for excluding immigration. By the mid-1920s Congress passed a series of laws that limited and almost stopped European immigration.

To better understand what was going on, we need to know about the environment of the emerging cities during those days of rapid growth and increasing immigration. It was an unsettled, uninviting, and often incomprehensible period of American history. Too many parts of society were changing. Too many things were developing. There were too many traditionalists who resented change of any sort, and what seemed like too many emerging dynamics that would change the world.

In that setting, it was up to schools to figure out an effective way to educate and produce a new citizen for new times. As a part of the change, laws were passed that forbade child labor and shut down sweatshops. Also, education became compulsory. The effect of these changes cannot be underestimated. The entire dynamic of entire classes of people was effected.

Even families changed. In 1890 the average number of children in a household was 4.9; in 1920 it was 4.3, and by 1980 it was 2.8.[6] Everything seemed to change. Fathers went out of the house to work and were paid to work in newly organized factories. Children were no longer needed to help the economy at home. Instead, they needed to go to school in order to prepare themselves for the new industrial world.

The first (and very understandable) thing many immigrants did was move into neighborhoods with immigrants like themselves. They spoke the same language, shared the same past, and generally understood the world in the same way. Their instinct was to reproduce the village life they had left. Irish Catholics in this section, German Jews in that section, Southern Blacks in another part of the city. While it was possible that the adults could live the rest of their lives in this kind of environment, it was all but impossible for their children to do so. Indeed, it was typical for their children to reject everything from the old world and do their best to become Americans. [7]

---

[4] Tozer, op. cit., p. 86.

[5] S.Alexander Rippa, *Education in a Free Society: An American History*, 8th ed. (New York: Longman, 1997), p. 139.

[6] Cremin, op. cit., p. 525.

[7] Interestingly, their children—the grandchildren of the original immigrants—often wanted to rediscover their heritage; the first generation wanted to get as far from the old world as they could.

After the Civil War, the United States began to export its culture and civilization,[8] while internally there was an emerging struggle between traditionalism and modernity. One way to understand this internal struggle is to remember the Scopes Trial. A high school teacher was put on trial for teaching evolution. In the emerging world of science, the Darwinian idea of evolution was something that could be proven, but it seemed directly counter to the Biblical version about how God created people.

It was science versus religion; traditionalism versus modernity. We know that the evolutionists won (with the exception of the State of Kansas in the 1990s), and the Scopes Trial provides good insight into the stakes of the fight. To control what was taught in public schools was to help control the direction of the country. There remain remnants of the struggle. For example, while the Supreme Court has ordered that there can be no prayers in school, there are continual challenges to those rulings. The traditionalist belief in religion (and that means Christianity) will, it seems, always be in conflict with the modern/secular/scientific vision of the world.

Other things were changing. Big cities (and this discussion is mostly about New York City) were dirty and crowded and noisy. Some neighborhoods were filthy and ongoing health hazards. The way cities worked—the dynamics that made them grow and allowed them to prosper—became more and more interdependent. No longer could people take care of themselves. Industrialism began to eliminate face-to-face communities. People left their homes to work, they depended on public transportation to get them to their jobs, where they worked for people they did not even know. There were telephones, automobiles, radios, typewriters, and mass production. The spiritual heart of community—the kind of community that only sometimes existed in liberal America—was all but eliminated in our urban areas by the 1920s.

The turn to industrialism, modernism, and urbanism was celebrated by the political and pedagogical progressives. Before the Progressives, the politics of the big cities—as well as the public schools—were controlled by political machines. The schools were not centralized, and each school district provided opportunities for bosses to grant favors for their supporters. Schools were a good source of patronage and political graft.

Progressives

It was the Progressives who fought the old machine politics. As we have seen, the ideas of John Dewey provided the pedagogical basis of progressive schooling. They were a radical challenge to the traditional classroom. But there was more to the Progressive movement than John Dewey. At its core, it was about politics. By the turn of the twentieth century, there was a successful move to replace local power with a centralized system. During the first third of that century the Progressives tried to remake schools. They changed both what schools were to do, and the administrative structure that they thought would best achieve the new aims.

The Progressives believed that administrators should be professionals. Administrators needed to understand the latest theories of how organizations worked (which

[8] Cremin, p. 9.

was scientific management—a much respected, wrong-headed theory of human behavior), needed to be nonpartisan, and needed to have a working knowledge of scientific information. To make this last point more clearly, the new administrator needed to understand Darwinism, evolution, and the functional approach to biology.[9]

Progressives believed that the emerging professional middle class could best run the emerging American culture. They wanted to replace the political bosses with the "best" people. Progressives believed that the new professionals needed to have the kind of exact, scientific, impersonal skills that would be able to produce schools (and other parts of society) that would be run efficiently and effectively.

Imbedded in the Progressive beliefs was the idea that schools should begin to teach middle-class values. They assumed students were not equal, so began to track students. For the less academically able students there was a track to teach them how to be good workers. These students learned about personal cleanliness and factory-like discipline. Brighter students were placed in an academic track.

During this time the Progressives became great supporters of the newly developed intelligence tests. With these tests, they believed that the abilities of students could be known and each could be put in his or her proper track. In a later chapter we will have a full discussion of testing. But there are important things that need to be understood about testing during the first part of the twentieth century. The tests were, to be generous, very crude. These tests were just being invented and they probably did more harm than good.

There were ways in which these tests were used to confirm that some groups of people were genetically inferior. The racism was not limited to color, but included many immigrants. Part of the argument to restrict immigration during the 1920s was based on the idea of genetic inferiority. In a popular text of 1916 we read: "the new immigration . . . contained a large number of the weak, the broken, and the mentally crippled of all races drawn from the lowest stratum of the Mediterranean basin and that Balkans . . ."[10]

The strong feelings about immigrants were finally felt in legislation. In 1921 Congress began restricting immigration based on nationality. In 1924 and again in 1929 Congress passed even stronger restrictions. The laws limited the immigration from southern and eastern Europe. Immigration would not be a factor of great importance until the end of World War II and again after the war in Vietnam.

For immigrants, the new schools taught citizenship. Democracy was a concept that depended on a kind of discipline, participation, and nonviolence that Progressives thought immigrants needed to learn. Schools worked hard to help (or make) new citizens assimilate. Schools began to change from a more academic curriculum to one that would somehow "Americanize" students.

In an earlier chapter there was a discussion about the National Education Association's Cardinal Principles Report of 1918. It might be helpful to look at that again in this context. The report was a statement by educators about the purpose of high

[9] Rippa, op. cit., p. 144.

[10] Madison Grant, *The Passing of the Great Race*, quoted by Tozier, op. cit., p. 85.

schools in the emerging modern world. Among other things, the teachers believed that high schools should teach students about healthy lifestyles, how to have productive leisure time, help them develop ethical character, and learn "worthy home membership."[11] Schools needed to do all of that, along with teaching academic subjects.

In 1921 the National Educational Association created a Department of Immigrant Education. They called for "comprehensive Americanization programs for immigrant children."[12] The report they issued relied on an earlier report that claimed to show that immigrants were "inferior." Given this basic prejudice, the Department of Immigrant Education recommended programs that would not only teach middle-class values, but also to disdain immigrant heritage. Schools were to teach socialization with a vengeance.

Students learned what it was like to live in a democracy and in a capitalist system. The Progressives wanted to make certain that students would become good citizens and support the system. Social studies focused on civics, history, economics, and geography in order to show the ties between academic study and social behavior. It should be no surprise that homerooms were invented to teach students the basic lessons of democratic participation.

Schools were asked to do other things. During World War I, it was found that American males had surprisingly poor eyesight and low physical stamina.[13] Public schools began modest physical education programs and became more aware of the physical and psychological problems of their students.

Progressives in the Classroom

At that time, most classes continued to be dominated by the teacher.[14] Urban educators believed that the most pressing classroom problem was discipline, so they were very strict. They demanded silence and order. As they had done since before the Revolutionary War, students were expected to stand up in class and recite their lessons.[15] The discipline was, in many cases, done in a military manner. (The irony, of course, was that teachers could not hit students . . . but the students were often hit by their parents.[16] Lawrence Cremin wrote that urban schools were dominated by "mindless, rote learning."[17])

The Progressives believed that classroom teaching needed to change. As we saw, both John Dewey and Jane Addams worked very hard to produce something different. The Settlement Houses that were inspired by Addams were a direct result of her

---

[11] Kate Rousmaniere, op. cit., p. 57.

[12] Lawrence Cremin, op. cit., p. 237.

[13] Rousmaniere, op. cit., p. 59.

[14] Rousmaniere, op. cit., p. 112.

[15] For a good description of teaching, see Larry Cuban, *How Teachers Taught: Constancy and Change in American Classrooms 1890–1990*, 2d ed. (New York: Teachers College Press, 1993).

[16] Ibid., p. 125.

[17] Cremin, op. cit., p. 226.

dislike of the how people taught. It was an effort to help people who hated schools find constructive places in the community. In Chicago at the same time, Addams's good friend John Dewey was also working on new methods of education. They kept in close touch.

While John Dewey believed that some education should remain the same, he is best known for his emphasis on student-centered teaching. He thought students should work more in small groups, that they should (with help from their teacher) concentrate on things that interested them, that there should be field trips and research projects and what we would call a more open classroom.[18] Dewey believed that these things were not only better pedagogy, but they would also make schooling more interesting and "real" for the students.

We know that two things happened. First, there were changes in how students were taught. Many teachers used progressive methods, and classrooms became more interesting. Second, and sadly, Dewey was often misunderstood by his followers. The changes he wanted were not easy to implement. Teachers had to develop different skills and priorities in order to teach progressive classes. All too often those who wrote about Dewey's methods failed to fully understand the rigor needed to make progressive education work. After a promising beginning, progressive education was undermined by inferior Dewey advocates and fell out of favor. Even Dewey disassociated himself with much of what was being done in his name.

The basic push was to make urban education more appealing to its remarkably diverse student population. City life was seductive. There was always something new going on—and those things always seemed more interesting than what was going on in school. There were gangs, which could give young people identities, and peer groups who literally spoke their language. New York City was vibrant for everyone, and there was constant action in the streets. Schools needed to somehow motivate their students. They needed to keep kids from dropping out and living life on the streets—or in factories. To do these things, schools had to stop being irrelevant and somehow concentrate on those things that their students were interested in.[19] These were not easy tasks.

In terms of multicultural and bilingual education, the push was for assimilation. The metaphor was the melting pot. People who immigrated to the United States were to become Americanized. All the citizens were to somehow be melted and blended into the same kind of person with the same kind of identity. During the first third of the century, that worked surprisingly well. The children of those waves of immigrants wanted to be socialized, wanted to be Americanized, wanted to be just like everyone else.

The result was that the job of the schools became pretty clear-cut. Teachers, while having to do many things (for example, learn about progressive education and become social workers for the families of their students), could concentrate on teaching English and teaching middle-class values. As we now know, there have been genuine long-term

[18] For a description of how teachers changed during these times, see Larry Cuban, op. cit.

[19] Tozer, op. cit., p. 105.

problems with assimilation, but that was the original way multicultural and bilingual education was handled.

Later, metaphors changed along with our ideas of how to understand our country as a nation of immigrants.[20] After the melting pot came the idea that we were more like a mosaic. That was followed by the metaphor of a kaleidoscope. A current metaphor is that we sit at a common roundtable. As we take up the debates about multiculturalism, it is important to keep these metaphors in mind. The basic tension revolves around the needs of an individual and the needs of a society. What, to put that differently, is the best mix of different cultures and social stability? Clearly we have moved away from the idea that we should all be the same, and toward the idea that our social stability depends, in part, on a mix of different cultures. What is not clear is just how that works in practice, and exactly what roles public schools should play.

MULTICULTURAL EDUCATION

As we noted earlier, by the middle of the 1920s immigration began to slow down and schooling was no longer a major focus. Certainly things were changing and evolving, but the national agenda was full. In 1929 the Great Depression began and it took World War II to get us out of it. After the war, the United States tried to return to some kind of normalcy during the 1950s. Normalcy was Dad worked, Mom stayed home with the kids, and there would be a great deal of prosperity.

While the '50s were "slow" there would never again be the kind of normalcy people had fantasies about. There was a warlike experience in Korea, Valium was invented for all those moms who were slowly going crazy because they were forced to stay at home, *Brown v. the Board of Education of Topeka* began the integration of public schools, and beatniks dressed in black and spread their interesting, insightful gloom to the general population.

During the '60s, changes that had their roots deep in our past became the focus of intense political activity. We continue to deal with the same issues today. Civil rights, the war in Vietnam, and feminism radicalized different segments of American culture. Between the late 1960s and the 1990s there was another huge wave of immigration.[21] The new immigrants were from different parts of the world and were let in for different reasons. The legislation in 1965 established preferences for people with family already living in the United States, and for those with higher professional and educational training. But many of the immigrants were illegal aliens who crossed the border to find work in California and the Southwest.

The well-educated also came looking for work. Joel Spring tells the story of the entire graduating class of a medical school in Thailand that chartered a plane and flew to the United States because they could find higher paying jobs. During the mid-1970s more the half of the interns in municipal hospitals in New York City were immigrant Asian doctors.

[20] This comes from Cremin, op. cit., pgs. 116–7.

[21] These figures come from Spring, op. cit., pgs. 148–50.

Unlike earlier times, the majority of the new wave of immigrants were neither European nor Chinese. The largest group was from Mexico. During the eighties the Asian population grew from 3.8 million to 6.5 million. The large number of Cuban and Vietnamese immigrants that came during the sixties and seventies were given preference because of political repression in those countries.

The new immigrants were not particularly like those who came during the first part of the twentieth century. They were not Europeans. Many did not speak romance languages nor did they have a Western sense of the world.[22] That is an important variable to which we must pay attention.

To make the point most simply, the reality we live in is a creation of how we socially construct it. As a culture, or a subculture, we agree on what things in the world mean. Everything simply *is*, and as humans we add meaning to those things that surround us. What we see and what we do have no meaning in and of themselves. Actions and things simply are. Homes and pets and skin color and religion and material belongings and . . . and everything has a particular value only because we have decided what that value should be. In those places where there is little or no diversity then there is almost complete agreement on how things are valued. In a place where there is a great deal of diversity then agreement on what reality means is much more difficult to attain.

During the last part of the twentieth century, as movement politics became powerful and as immigrants with different worldviews came to the United States, it has simply become less and less easy to agree upon a common set of values. When we talked about how people in the early twentieth century were in favor of assimilation and becoming Americanized, part of that meant that those who had different ways of seeing the world would begin to see the world like the middle class did. American Indians and Italians and Irish Catholics and German Jews were taught to judge things the way middle-class, Protestant Americans judged the world.

It is important to be clear. The argument is *not* that agreement is necessarily a good thing or even a desirable thing; all I am saying is that social norms that were strongly enforced a hundred years ago are much less powerful today.

But beginning in the 1960s more and more people began to construct the world differently. As Asians and Mexicans came in greater numbers, and as women and minorities began to fight actively and successfully for equal rights, and as different groups began to try and reconnect with their ethnic or religious past, reality as it had been traditionally defined in the United States came under attack.

In no small part, how people understand multicultural and bilingual education is about how to best define reality. Do we need a common reality? How much diversity can be tolerated in a society before the lack of agreement on values undermines the culture? What are the rights of minorities in these cases, and how can these rights be protected? Is providing an identical education for everyone the same as providing an equal education? Clearly the questions are critical, and the stakes are high for everyone involved.

---

[22] For how these ideas are connected with multiculturalism, see Jack Nelson, et. al., *Critical Issues in Education: Dialogues and Dialectics*, 4th ed. (Boston: McGraw-Hill, 2000), p. 259; and Leonard Davidman and Patricia Davidman, *Teaching with a Multicultural Perspective: A Practical Guide* (New York: Longman, 1997), p. 4.

Conceptualizing Multiculturalism

To begin to fully understand these problems we will begin by conceptualizing different models of multiculturalism. The discussion will be brief, and we will return to it later in the chapter. In this section we will review the different ways people would like for us to define multiculturalism.

William Newman writes there are four main theories of pluralism.[23] The first theory is assimilation: $A + B + C = A$. In the formula, A represents the dominant group. In our context, that would mean German Jews and Irish Catholics come to the United States and are Americanized. The reality of white Protestant culture (and liberalism) simply dominated immigrant groups.

The second theory is amalgamation: $A + B + C = D$. This is the melting pot theory. Everyone who comes to the United States adds a little something to society, and the result is a culture that is more than and different from any of the cultures in the mix. We have friends who have Chinese food every Thanksgiving. The melting pot idea is more serious than that, but the idea is the same.

The third theory is what Newman calls classical cultural pluralism: $A + B + C = A + B + C$. That would mean that each immigrant group would retain its identity. The Vietnamese who immigrate to the United States would remain Vietnamese, those from Chile remain Chilean, and so on. In big cities there are places like "Little Italy," or "China Town" in which cultural identities from the old country are meant to be kept.

But Newman believes that cultural pluralism does not really apply to the Untied States. He believes that this is a more accurate way to think about it: $A + B + C = A1 + B1 + C1$. The argument is that American culture is powerful, and anyone who moves here is affected by it—so that Italian Americans are different than Italians who live in Italy, and African Americans are different (and not only genetically) than Africans who live in Africa. Put differently, a certain amount of assimilation goes on no matter what. If there was no assimilation, then cultural pluralism would lead to the kinds of divisions that divide nations into warring factions.

These formulations represent good ways to think about multiculturalism. But before we think in depth about what they mean, it is necessary to see how people define multiculturalism and diversity.

Kit Machado argues that there are several things students need to know about cultural diversity.[24] First, there are a number of bases for cultural diversity (for example, race, nationality, religion, caste), and cultural diversity is a widespread and common phenomenon. There are many different patterns of cultural diversity, and each has particular values and ways of handling conflict and dominance. Finally, these patterns are not static but dynamic, and different societies deal with cultural diversity in different ways.

---

[23] Found in Christine Sleeter and Carl Grant, *Making Choices for Multicultural Education: Five Approaches to Race, Class, and Gender,* 3d ed. (Upper Saddle River, N.J.: Prentice-Hall, 1999), pgs. 159–60.

[24] "Teaching about Cultural Diversity: International Comparative Perspectives," found in Liucija Baskauskas, editor, *Unmasking Culture: Cross-Culture Perspectives in the Social and Behavioral Sciences* (Novato, Calif.: Chandler & Sharp Publishers, 1986), p. 3.

What Machado wants us to remember is that faculty and students in the United States are limited in how they understand cultural diversity. Instead of simply thinking about people of color or women as "diversity," it is important to look at the full range of the ways in which groups of people differ. There are a remarkable number of cultural patterns in the world and each has a unique set of values that is always changing. Everyone, we are told, needs to remember the entire range of ways in which people live in the world.

Peter McLaren begins thinking about multiculturalism at a very different place.[25] McLaren believes that it is best to develop the concept of multiculturalism in the context of discussions about colonialism and post-colonialism. The audience he wants to reach is, in his words, the "colonial theater" known as the United States. What he argues is that the ideas behind mainstream multiculturalism work under the assumption that justice already exists in the United States and all that needs to be done is for it to be evenly appropriated to different groups.

The fact, according to McLaren, is that we do not even have a language of analysis that is necessary to create a democracy. What is needed is a "politics of refusal that challenges the institutionalization of formal equality based on the prized imperatives of a white, Anglo, male heterosexual world."[26] We are told that in order to truly understand multiculturalism, one must be able to find a perspective outside of the dominant values of our society.

While the language of McLaren will offend some, there is something we can learn from him. Later in this chapter we will return to his ideas. What we will see is that there might be tensions between different groups. For example, we will explore this question: Is multiculturalism bad for feminism?

Sonia Nieto[27] believes that multiculturalism "*can* have a substantive and positive impact on the education of most students." She argues that multiculturalism should be included in every part of the curriculum so students can understand and become tolerant of other cultures. If multiculturalism is successful, students will learn other frames of reference and actively work to create social justice for all groups.

Education, then, would continue its tradition of social reform. Instead of the old focus of creating a melting pot, the new focus would be to ensure tolerance and social justice. It would require a complete redoing of how most subjects are taught, and the emphasis on what cultures are taught would vary from region to region in order to reflect the diversity in each place. Nieto is a strong and articulate voice for reform.

(To stop for a moment, we can ask a question that was raised in an earlier chapter: What do teachers need to know? In addition to everything else, should teachers understand and know how to teach about a world of cultures?)

---

[25] Peter McLaren, *Life in Schools: An Introduction to Critical Pedagogy in the Foundations of Education*, 3d ed. (New York: Longman, 1998), pgs. 251–6.

[26] Ibid., p. 256.

[27] Sonia Nieto, *Affirming Diversity: The Sociopolitical Context of Multicultural Education*, 3d ed. (New York: Longman, 2000), p. 3.

But the toleration called for by Nieto may be too modest a goal. According to Amy Gutmann, "toleration is an essential democratic virtue" and is important for students to learn.[28] She goes on to argue that toleration is not enough. What schools must aim for is a condition of mutual respect. "In a democracy, proper regard for the position of citizens includes the mutual recognition that all persons, regardless of the accomplishments of their ancestors, are entitled to equal political and civil liberties and fair equal opportunities to live a good life."[29]

The points Gutmann wants to emphasize are: 1) by focusing on what a person does instead of his or her past, the idea of racial superiority will be eliminated, 2) to focus on each person will mean that they are honored or dishonored by what they do and not by the acts of their ancestors, 3) true mutual respect rests not only on the recognition of cultural diversity but "needs to be accompanied by a willingness and ability to deliberate about politically relevant disagreements."[30]

There is, of course, an interesting emphasis on liberal individualism in these points. John Locke would be happy to see that each citizen is to be judged by his or her own acts, and that group claims—either positive or negative—count for very little. While Gutmann insists that differing cultural views be respected, in the end, individual acts count most heavily.

Multicultural education is understood by some, in the end, to have very personal results. There are ethnocentric schools that are organized around different cultures. For example, there are Hispanic and Afrocentric schools. They are designed to teach students about their cultural heritage and help preserve traditions of each "dominated" group. In the end, though, these schools want to build the self-esteem of each student. Many of these ethnocentric schools have been very successful in taking students who have done poorly in public schools and giving them the confidence and pride to perform well academically.

Finally, Davidman and Davidman believe that multicultural education, in no small part, helps empower students. They argue that K–12 education needs "to provide *all* students with experiences, attitudes, and skills that better enable them to cope with, and serve as catalysts for, change and/or preservation in their own lives and communities."[31] They argue that unless students and their families feel empowered, then they will be unable to be happy and productive citizens.

Among the different parts of an "empowering environment" that a school needs to provide is this: "*validation*—that is, acceptance of and support for the cultural identities and languages they bring to class and choose to maintain."[32] As examples of groups, they mention Japanese American, Jewish American, African American, Nigerian American, Italian American, the deaf or gay student, the Christian, Sikh, or Muslim student. But the Davidmans do not mean that all cultural identities or lifestyles

---

[28] Amy Gutmann, "Challenges of Multiculturalism in Democratic Education," in Eduardo Manuel Duarte and Stacy Smith, op. cit., p. 314.

[29] Ibid., p. 313.

[30] Ibid., p. 315.

[31] Davidman and Davidman, op. cit., p. 18.

[32] Ibid., p. 19.

should be tolerated. They mention the white and black supremacist, the Neo-Nazi cultural group and the drug-supporting lifestyle as examples of groups that should not be supported.

Personal empowerment based on lifestyle or culture seems to be a kind of last logical step in the progression of multiculturalism. It has been a hundred-year road from assimilation to pluralism to tolerance to mutual respect to empowerment.

Skeptics

There are those who remain skeptical about how people have come to understand multiculturalism. Two of the most well-known of these critics are Diane Ravitch and Arthur Schlesinger Jr.[33] Their arguments are simple enough. They believe that the core of the culture in the United States has to do with European thought and tradition. Our government, language, and ideology all have their roots in Western civilization. They believe it would be a mistake to destroy the foundation of our civilization in the name of multiculturalism.

A second and equally important concern is that the teaching of cultural pluralism will lead to intense antagonism. They argue that we must be concerned about the loss of tolerance because of the teaching of various cultural ways of understanding the world. While it makes sense to them for schools to teach about other cultures it only makes sense if differences are taught within the context of American culture that is the result of what we have gotten from European culture.

Finally, the critics ask if it is the job of schools to teach the cultural heritage of different countries. Traditionally, in the United States, if families wanted to preserve another language of a different set of values, they either sent their children to private schools or to after-school lessons. It is, critics argue, the job of schools to teach the cultural values of the United States. It is fair, they continue, to have others provide education in different values.

There is support for their arguments. It should not be surprising that many people who have grown up with a respect for the culture of the United States (and that certainly includes a healthy dose of European culture) believe it needs to be preserved. On the other hand, those same people need to be reminded that almost all groups were, at some point in history, part of an immigrant group.

I would like to repeat one of the basic points of this chapter: I do not believe it is at all easy to figure out the best way to deal with diversity and teach multiculturalism.

The Schlesinger and Ravitch critique is only the beginning of the questions that need to be answered about multicultural education. For example, does it make sense to make generalizations about groups of people? Do all blacks, for example, believe the same things? Is there, in other words, a black position? If you think there might be, then consider Jesse Jackson and the Supreme Court Justice Clarence Thomas. This is what we know: Jesse Jackson has always been on the very liberal end of the

---

[33] For example, see Arthur Schlesinger Jr., *The Disuniting of America: Reflections on a Multicultural Society* (Knoxville, Tenn.: Whittle Direct Books, 1992), and Diane Ravitch, "Multiculturalism, Yes, Particularism, No," *The Chronicle of Higher Education*, October 24: A44. William Bennett shares their concerns, but is often discounted as a less-than-open-minded ideologue.

scale, Clarence Thomas has always been on the very conservative end of the scale, and they are both black.

Is there a Catholic point of view, or an Italian one, or a Jewish one? If the answer is no—and it is easy to agree the answer is no—then what does that exactly mean for multicultural education? Do we, for example, teach that all American Indians believe the same thing, when we know that is simply not true?

And we must answer the question about what should be taught about different cultures. While there is general agreement that it is important to teach about the problems that have existed (and continue to exist) in the United States, is it also necessary to be that honest about other cultures? When we teach about Africa, for example, would it be important to teach about how some tribes captured people from other tribes and sold them into slavery? Or teach about the social customs that have made the spread of AIDS so horrible in Africa or Haiti? Do we teach about the terrible violence in Ireland or the racism in Japan and China?

These are genuine questions. If we rightfully insist on exploring the strengths and weaknesses of the United States, it seems reasonable to explore the strengths and weaknesses of other cultures. And what do you believe would happen if a teacher both praised and criticized other cultures? Do you think that teacher would be attacked by the groups involved? What would that do to the self-esteem and empowerment of those children who wanted to hold on to a different culture or lifestyle but did not know about the problems of those cultures or lifestyles? In the name of empowerment, should we ask our teachers to be only partially truthful? If we do that for some countries, should we do it for all—including our own?

Conflicting Ideals

We can understand some of these issues in a more concrete way. To be more specific, how do we handle the tension of teaching about cultures that have conflicts with other cultures? If we want our students to be proud of their cultural heritage, what do we do with those parts of the heritage that seem to go against agreed-upon norms? For example, those in favor of multicultural education generally include women. The idea is that women need to be fully understood and respected as human beings. But we can return to the question asked earlier: Is multiculturalism bad for women? In a book of the same name, Susan Okin argues that it is.[34]

Early in the introduction to the book we read, " . . . thus understood, multiculturalism condemns intolerance of other ways of life, finds the human in what might seem Other, and encourages cultural diversity?"[35] While some would quibble with her definition because it might not go far enough for them, it basically reflects what most believe. What Okin argues is that some groups, some cultures, treat women badly, and that we should be less focused on these groups' rights and more attentive to women's

---

[34] Susan Moller Okin, with respondents, *Is Multiculturalism Bad for Women?* Joshua Cohen, Matthew Howard, and Martha Nussbaum, eds. (Princeton, N.J.: Princeton University Press, 1999).

[35] Ibid., p. 4.

rights. As she writes: "[W]hat should be done when the claims of minority cultures and religions clash with the norm of gender equality that is at least formally endorsed by liberal states (however much they continue to violate it in their practices?)"[36]

What Okin reminds us is that, while cultures do have "meaningful ways of life," that does not mean all people within those cultures are treated fairly. In the all-inclusiveness of a culture it is important to understand what goes on in private. For example, sexual and reproductive practices are central to all cultures. Those practices are especially important to women, but they are practices that are not discussed often enough.

Of the many examples she offers, three are enough to see the point she is trying to make. First, what about cultures that practice clitoridectomy? The woman's clitoris is cut out to help "insure a girl's virginity before marriage and fidelity afterward by reducing sex to a marital obligation." Do proponents of multiculturalism believe that the practice should be kept because it is a viable part of the cultures of Togo and Egypt? Is the argument that group rights are more important than individual rights in this case?

In many Latin American countries, in rural Southeast Asia, and parts of West Africa it is part of their culture to pressure or even require a rape victim to marry the rapist. In Peru, members of a gang rape are exonerated if one of the participants asks the victim to marry him. According to one Peruvian, "Marriage is the right and proper thing to do after a rape. A raped woman is a used item. No one wants her. At least with this law the woman will get a husband."[37] How should we put this pretty horrifying example together with the argument that it is important to respect all aspects of different cultures?

The third example is polygamy. While there are some Mormons who still practice polygamy (illegally) in the United States, is it a custom that we should respect? Okin quotes an immigrant to France: "When my wife is sick and I don't have another, who will care for me? . . . One wife on her own is trouble. When there are several, they are forced to be polite and well behaved. If they misbehave, you threaten that you'll take another wife."[38]

While Okin offers other arguments, these make her point well enough. She asks us if it is wise to grant special rights to cultural minorities. If these cultures are oppressive in their private spheres, then why should we somehow respect and allow that? Okin believes that everyone in the United States, all cultural minorities, need to promote basic liberal rights. In the end she thinks that there are parts of multiculturalism that are bad for women.

It would be wrong to leave the impression that her views are unopposed. Bonnie Honig, for example, takes on the example of polygamy. Reading from the same article as Okin, she quotes the wives of the immigrant as saying that they would leave him if he brought home another wife. "In this instance, the institution of polygamy put the women in a situation of solidarity."[39] While there is not quite the support for rapists

[36] Ibid., p. 9.

[37] Ibid., p. 15.

[38] Ibid., p. 15.

[39] Bonnie Honig, "My Culture Made Me Do It," ibid., p. 38.

and clitoridectomy, most of what Okin writes is challenged. Her critics believe Okin stereotypes the groups she criticizes, believe she uses too many secondary sources in her research, and believe she does not fully understand the religions she attacks.

As in most scholarly work, arguments are tightly made and all sides of an argument can sound correct. Also, as in most scholarly work, there is an assumption that there are rules that apply to arguments and if there is even one piece of an argument that is wrong then it invalidates everything that has been said or written. What we know, of course, is that carefully thought out and closely argued points might have little or nothing in common with human reality. This is simply a way to remind you to consider not only what you read, but basically what you understand reality to be. If four wives of a French immigrant have bonded together in a good way, is that enough to make you believe in polygamy? Maybe so. All I want to suggest is that the rules of scholarly debate—while interesting and important—may mask more important points.

What many point out is what they understand as an interesting contradiction in Okin's argument. While she clearly favors liberal principles, and opposes special group rights for groups, as a feminist she believes in special rights for women (like affirmative action). It is a problem in her thought that, according to her critics, weakens her argument. Earlier in the chapter we discussed some of the ideas of Peter Mclaren. He argued that it was impossible to truly understand multiculturalism because the reality of the United States was simply the reality of white, Anglo-Saxon males. It was necessary, he thought, that we escape from that perspective.

What is important to our discussion is that Okin, as a feminist, wants us to think carefully about multiculturalism, and her perspective is that of a person with liberal sensitivities. Is Okin, a woman and possibly a pretty radical woman at that, simply the mouthpiece of white, Anglo-Saxon males? That sounds awfully strange—but there might be a kind of reality that we need to consider. While there is much more to her argument, for our limited purposes she helps us focus on genuine problems. As teachers, these are tensions with which you will need to deal. How you decide what to teach is never an easy decision.

One of the genuine problems about multiculturalism arises when liberal principles are attacked. While it is certainly easy to defend the idea that it is very important for all of us to respect the cultural heritages of everyone who has come to the United States, the underlying problem is this: Should we accept everything about those cultures? Liberalism, while wildly unfair at times, is also remarkably open to many things. Like all ideologies, it has shortcomings and strengths.

Are there certain strengths that you, personally, are unwilling to compromise about? Are there some practices that you believe should be protected no matter what other cultures believe? Is there some level of tolerance beyond which you will not go? Is anything all right if it can be defended as being an important part of another's culture?

Is there some essence of the United States that you believe should not be compromised? If people choose to come and live in this country are there some rules you believe they need to observe?

In the end, how you answer these questions will determine how you will teach multiculturalism. They are tough questions, but before you walk into your classroom it is necessary to begin to answer them.

BILINGUAL EDUCATION

There are different kinds of bilingual education just as there are different kinds of multicultural education. There are disagreements about the reasons for bilingual education, the ways in which it should be taught, and what the results should be. The decisions you make about the reasons we teach bilingual education go a long way in determining how it should be taught and the results you want. Those decisions will also reflect how you feel, in part, about the culture of the United States.

Ramona Cutri and Scott Ferrin suggest different ways of understanding bilingualism.[40] They write that language may be seen as a problem, as a right, or as a resource. Those who see it as a problem think that linguistic diversity is not good for the country. The solution is to make certain everyone speaks English well—while abandoning his or her original language. Those who believe that language is a right, believe that language diversity is a basic human right. Finally, to understand language as a resource is to believe that it "should be conserved and used for multiple reasons, including economic or utilitarian rationales."[41]

That is not the only way to understand bilingual education. Joel Spring, for example, writes that it can be divided into maintenance, transitional, and two-way bilingual education. Maintenance means just that—maintain the native language while learning English. Transitional means having the student stop using his or her native language after learning English. Two-way bilingual education means mixing English speaking and non-English speaking students, and the result would be true bilingualism for everyone involved.[42]

There are different approaches to bilingual education and they roughly fit the different reasons for it. Leonard Valverde and Gloria Armendariz write about five common bilingual programs. They are: pullout, structured immersion, transitional, maintenance, and dual language. We read that "The first three fail to promote or facilitate bilingualism and are therefore considered less desirable in many communities. The remaining two are often recommended because of their proven success in fostering bilingualism, academic achievement, and cultural pluralism."[43]

The pullout program describes what it is—students with limited English-speaking skills are pulled out of the home classroom and tutored in English. Students who speak different languages are often in the same class and because of the different needs of different students, this kind of program is often not very effective. In this environment, English is learned slowly, if at all. Valverde and Armendariz do not believe that this is even a "true bilingual program."

---

[40] Ramona Maile Cutri and Scott Ferrin, "Moral Dimensions of Bilingual Education," *Bilingual Research Journal*, 22(1), Winter 1998.

[41] Ibid., p. 34.

[42] Spring, op. cit., p. 157.

[43] Leonard Valverde and Gloria Armendariz, "Important Administrative Tasks Resulting from Understanding Bilingual Program Designs," *Bilingual Research Journal*. 23 (1), 1999, p. 1.

In a structured immersion program, the teacher provides instruction of academic lessons in English and "accepts responses and contributions from children in their native language." Because different languages are heard in the classroom, we are told that an "overall positive learning environment" is the result. The idea is that instruction is more effective and "a greater understanding and trusting relationship" is formed between teacher and student. One of the weaknesses cited by Valverde and Armendariz is that this kind of environment "imminently and inherently leads to assimilation."

There is a shift of emphasis in transitional bilingual education. In this program, students are encouraged to use a language other than English. The purpose is for them not only to learn English, but also to enhance their knowledge of their native language. Bilingualism is both accepted and promoted by this approach. We read that the problem with this program is that these students do not stay long enough to attain biliteracy. " . . . [T]here is an implicit devaluing of the native language" if there is not true biliteracy.

Maintenance/developmental programs are designed to both preserve and enhance a student's native language while that student is learning English. These classes are for students with the same native language and allow them to fully participate in instruction. The National Research Council, in 1997, issued a report that "indicates" students with a strong background in their home language do better learning English than those without "such a primary language advantage." Interestingly, Valverde and Armendariz list no weaknesses to this approach.

Finally, the two-way/dual language programs consist of classes made up of native English speakers and non-English-speaking students. The split is 50–50. It is aimed, in part, at producing full bilingual proficiency for both native and nonnative speakers. We read that it "promotes a positive attitude toward both cultures, which, in turn, helps reduce racism within the formative minds of children." Valverde and Armendariz list many strengths of these programs while giving no indication of any shortcomings.

Of course, given your preference, there may be no shortcomings in the bilingual proficiency program. For our purposes, what is important to keep in mind is not which approach is best, but the underlying idea that these are not particularly pedagogical problems. As it is played out in the United States, bilingual education, like multicultural education, has everything in the world to do with politics.

Bilingual education has a political past. Court rulings and legislation provide a clear picture of the development of bilingual education. Before 1964 most bilingual education was about providing non-English-speaking students with English proficiency. The goal, from the time of the common schools, was to help these students assimilate and become Americanized.

In 1964 the U.S. Congress passed the Civil Rights Act. Title VI of that legislation set a minimum standard for the education of language minority students.[44] The

---

[44] While this history can be found in many places, I have drawn most heavily from Ann-Marie Wiese and Eugene Garcia, "The Bilingual Education Act: Language Minority Students and Equal Educational Opportunity," *Bilingual Research Journal*, 22 (1), Winter 1998, pgs. 1–18.

act prohibits discrimination on the basis of, among other things, national origin. In 1974 the Supreme Court added substance to the law. In *Lau v. Nichols* the court ruled that the Unified School District of San Francisco discriminated against the Chinese-speaking minority. In the court's words: "It seems obvious that the Chinese-speaking minority receive fewer benefits than the English-speaking majority . . . [and it] . . . denies them a meaningful opportunity to participate in the educational system . . ." San Francisco was in violation of the Civil Rights Act of 1964.

While giving no details, the court ruled that the school district needed to "take affirmative steps to rectify the language deficiency . . ." How that was done would be a matter of local choice. In 1974 Congress passed the Equal Educational Opportunity Act. The law made Title VI of the Civil Rights Act applicable to all educational institutions. Like *Lau v. Nichols*, the law lacked details. In the language of the law: A school should "take appropriate action to overcome language barriers that impede equal participation by its students in its instructional programs."

We need to remember the level of political activism that began during the 1960s. Key to understanding the development of bilingual educational programs was a shift in thinking about why children had trouble in schools. The old theories were based on the idea that some children were simply biologically inferior. There were those who believed that almost all immigrants and people of color were genetically inferior. These racial theories that were so popular during the first quarter of the twentieth century that they retained a surprising amount of their power. Indeed, there are groups who continue to believe theories of racial superiority and inferiority.

By the sixties a counter-theory was becoming popular. The discovery behind the new theory was the existence of a "culture of poverty." The idea was that instead of genetic inferiority, children did poorly in school because of environmental reasons. In short, "specific types of attitudes, language styles, work values, and other behaviors dampened the abilities necessary to overcome poverty."[45] President Lyndon Johnson began waging his war on poverty to help break the cycle in which the poor were caught. Clearly, there needed to be remedies for what was understood as "language deficiencies."

Congress was busy passing legislation that dealt with bilingual education. Specific legislation was passed in 1968, 1974, 1978, 1984, 1988, and 1994. In the 1994 legislation Congress defined bilingual education. Congress wrote that bilingual education is "instruction given in, and study of, English, and, to the extent necessary to allow a child to progress effectively through the educational system, the native language . . ."

There is an interesting political note about the Congressional definition. One of the reasons that the students were to be given instruction in their native language was because of the bilingual programs in southern Florida. Those programs were developed by Cuban immigrants who believed that they would soon leave the United States and return to a post-Castro Cuba. South Florida was simply their temporary home. It was in their best interests for their children to retain Spanish, as well as keep their Cuban customs, so returning to Cuba would not be traumatic.

---

[45] H. Levin, quoted in ibid., p. 5.

The politics of the United States had changed by the end of the 1970s, and with the change came revisions in the laws about bilingual education. As immigration increased and the population became nervous about possible political instability, the next federal legislation had a new focus. In 1978 the law called for more English acquisition and a greater emphasis on assimilation. The objective of bilingual education was now to "assist children of limited English proficiency to improve their English language skills." The emphasis was away from encouraging any maintenance of the native language of the student.

The 1984 law brought even greater changes. While Congress believed that "bilingualism is a laudable and worthwhile outcome," they also passed legislation that said the "ultimate goals of bilingual education are that the students learn English" and that the only way to judge the benefits were "in terms of English-language acquisition and subject-matter learning." There was even a time limit on how long a student could be in a bilingual program. Congress decided, and President Ronald Reagan agreed, that "No student may be enrolled in a bilingual program . . . for a period of more than three years."

In political terms, the 1984 legislation was part of the conservative agenda. The pedagogical issues seemed to be laced with a kind of Americanization agenda that was the political fashion of the day. The patriotic ways of Reagan, and the fear of increased immigration, were certainly underlying causes for the idea that students needed to learn English, and learn it quickly.

Remember that Reagan had been governor of California and that state has a remarkably diverse population. By the 1980s there was a backlash against bilingualism in California.[46] Almost a third of Hispanic Americans live in California, and more than half of all students are minorities. California even amended its Constitution to make English its official language. The amendment was directed against bilingual ballots and certain forms of bilingual education. One suspects Reagan's policies were little more than the playing out, at the national level, the reaction California had to diversity.

By 1994 there was a new president with a different agenda. The result was legislation that again changed how we were to think about bilingual education. The Clinton legislation authorized new grant categories, promoted bilingualism, created enhancement programs for indigenous languages, and encouraged a systemic reform effort.

These changes were important. Bilingual education was to no longer simply serve as a method of assimilation and Americanization. A student could now preserve his or her native language. The enhancement program for indigenous languages was even more interesting. While many languages do not seem to be in danger of disappearing, that is not the case with "native languages." There are American Indian languages and Native Alaskan, Hawaiian, and Pacific Islander languages that will cease to exist if no effort is made to preserve them. The political weight of the Clinton administration was behind an effort to save these languages.

The systematic reform part of the reauthorization bill had three main components. There was the call to 1) establish what students should know and to upgrade the quality of the programs, 2) help align state educational policies and 3) give schools more resources and responsibility for preparing students to learn.

---

[46] This data comes from Newman, op. cit., pgs. 267–9.

In 1999 a revision of the bill was before Congress. Part of the proposed law stressed accountability for bilingual programs. There was a great deal of conflict over just how much accountability there should be. The bottom line of accountability was testing, and it seemed that there would be a great deal of testing in bilingual programs. Indeed, critics (the National Association for Bilingual Education) believed that to stress testing would detract from effective instruction. The worry was bilingual students would be over-tested compared to English-speaking students. The other concern was that bilingual education would once again focus on learning English while bilingualism and biliteracy would be deemphasized.

In 2002 the voters of the Commonwealth of Massachusetts voted overwhelmingly to provide students with one year of immersion in English, then put them in English-only classes. It was a clear political statement about the importance of English to the voters.

What Works

There have been some studies about which bilingual models work best.[47] The Reagan Department of Education conducted a study in 1986. The study found that the maintenance model was most effective for both learning English and keeping the native language. The more instruction students had in their native language, the better their skills were in both English and that language.

The Bush Department of Education (1988–92) found that all three programs—structured immersion, transitional, and maintenance—were effective. Those who favored more instruction in students' native language endorsed the findings of this study.

Finally, in 1995 the largest of the three studies was concluded. The researchers found, over a thirteen-year period, that students who were pushed out of bilingual classes too early were effectively "left out of the discussion in their mainstream classes." Students who had taken at least six years of well-designed bilingual classes had significantly higher test scores in English by the eleventh grade. That cast a great deal of doubt on the three-year maximum set by the 1984 law.

While there are few studies about the best kind of bilingual education, it seems that data is not as important as politics. What drives the debate has just about everything to do with what one believes the goal of bilingual education should be. It has to do with what a person thinks about citizenship and cultural diversity. I would guess that it also has something to do with what a person believes the nation owes an immigrant, and what an immigrant owes the nation.

And, of course, it is more complicated than that. Do you believe that there should be different rules for different languages? For example, we saw earlier there seems little danger that Spanish or Chinese or Russian will disappear if they are ignored in bilingual classes. The same cannot be said for languages native to the United States, many of which have already disappeared. Should there be a special effort to keep these indigenous languages alive?

---

[47] Ibid., pgs. 269–70.

And what should be done with Ebonics?[48] In 1996 the school board of Oakland, California, adopted a resolution that stated black language/Ebonics "was a legitimate, rule-based, systematic language, and that this language was the primary language of many African-American children enrolled in the Oakland school system."[49] Teachers were told that Ebonics was to be affirmed and maintained and not stigmatized. These are genuine questions; questions that will need to be answered.

The result, in part, was a remarkable reaction against what the school board had done. People whose politics could not be more different, people from Jesse Jackson to Rush Limbaugh, agreed that Oakland had done something terrible. While the school board kept saying that it was not abandoning standard English, almost no one paid attention. Basically, the critique was that Ebonics represented a kind of internalized racism and was the expression of a "colonized consciousness." Ellen Goodman, a liberal columnist, wrote that black language was a "second-class language for a second-class life."

But is there something to the argument for Ebonics? Is there something to the rhythm and rhyme of black language? Does metaphor and repetition in the speeches of Martin Luther King and Jesse Jackson have a power and beauty that we need to preserve? Are Toni Morrison and Zora Neal Hurston able to convey their thoughts in remarkable ways because of their use of black language?

And what of the black students who come to school having grown up with black language? Is it appropriate to constantly correct their language? Is it right, or is it good pedagogy to make them feel as if they should not even open their mouths for fear of saying something in the "wrong way"? Is teaching about meeting students "where they are," or is it about imposing another culture on them?

Is the critique of Ebonics about racism, or is it about understanding that Ebonics will not serve the student well when he or she grows up? Should Ebonics be understood as a legitimate native language that falls under the category of bilingualism, or is it a trap that will ultimately serve as a kind of glass ceiling for those who speak it?

Were I so bright as to have an answer. It seems to me that there is some truth to each side of the argument. That is the perfect condition for political debate. While I am certain that some on each side of the argument might have "bad" motives, it is also clear that there are well-intentioned people on both sides. As I write, the argument for Ebonics seems to have been beaten down. That does not mean we have seen the last of it.

What do you believe is the right way to teach bilingualism, and what are your reasons? In the following section the effort will be made to at least be able to agree on some of the important questions that need to be asked.

SUMMARY

At the beginning of the chapter there were comments about people who seemed to be certain about what the right answers were for multicultural and bilingual education. While I am not at all clear about what the best things to do are, I am clear about this:

---

[48] See, Theresa Perry and Lisa Delpit, editors, *The Real Ebonics Debate: Power, Language, and the Education of African-American Children*, (Boston: Beacon Press, 1998).

[49] Ibid., p. 3.

Everyone who teaches needs to have some sort of answer. The answers are in no small way political.

Earlier in the chapter there were different ways to understand multiculturalism: assimilation—$A + B + C = A$; amalgamation—$A + B + C = D$; cultural pluralism—$A + B + C = A + B + C$; and the realistic cultural pluralism—$A + B + C = A1 + B1 + C1$. I would argue that the issues of bilingual education are subsets of these models.

Which model are you most comfortable with? Do you believe that people who make a decision to live in the United States should be taught the basic values of the culture? Do you believe they should learn to speak English? Do you believe that there are certain things that define the culture that everyone must accept? If that is the case, then you probably endorse the assimilation model.

If you believe that everyone and every group brings something special to the United States, and those special things should go into the big mix that is our culture, then the second model—the melting pot—would seem appropriate. But even here you need to be clear about what you think is basic to the culture. It is possible that you might want groups to add certain things to the mix, but not others. For example, you might believe that everyone has equal rights, and to treat women as second-class citizens might not be tolerated. On the other hand, it is very possible to believe that everything should be added to the pot and that the culture stays open to all ideas.

Finally, we can think about the last two models of cultural pluralism. Do you believe that immigrants should be able to keep as much of their native culture (and language) as they wish? If we are genuinely interested in true diversity, isn't this the position we need to take? Is it fine to let people live exactly as they wish in order to preserve their cultural identity? Do you think this will actually add strength to our culture and not ultimately lead to great divisions?

And when you think about these questions you need to ask one more: Are you thinking more about an individual student or the culture—or are they so interconnected that you believe what is best for one is also best for the other?

All of these questions have important pedagogical implications. How we answer these questions go a long way in determining what we teach and how we teach it. The politics surrounding each position have become more and more intense. While not ideal, the truth of the matter is this: Political issues have always been at the heart of our public schools, and multicultural and bilingual education are no exceptions.

THINK ABOUT

1. You emigrate to France. You love the culture, the people, and your high-paying, high-powered job. You want to become a citizen. You send your children to school. There is no bilingual program. How does this make you feel?

2. You notice that almost all Harvard graduate students have the ability to speak and write in a certain, "educated" way. Do you have any desire to be able to communicate that same way?

3. As a math teacher, do you think it is important to take courses in multicultural education?

CHAPTER EIGHT

DEALING WITH DIFFERENCES IN THE LAND OF EQUALITY
Special Education

Or who maketh the dumb or deaf, or the seeing or the blind? Have not I, the Lord?

Exodus

Thou shalt not curse the deaf nor put a stumbling block before the blind . . . [and curse those] . . . that maketh the blind to wander out of the path.

Leviticus

Since 1975 there has been a major effort to provide appropriate education for students with special needs. That is both the good news and the bad news. What it implies, accurately, is that while there were efforts to help before 1975, they often ranged from not very effective to wholly inadequate. Indeed, as we shall see, human beings have historically institutionalized, demeaned, and even killed people who were different. To understand what humanity has done to people with disabilities is to feel shame.

Once the courts became involved with the matter in the mid-'70s, every school district in the United States has tried to understand what is best for students who need special education. What we will learn is that these issues, like just about every educational issue, are part pedagogical, part political, part moral, part regional, and part biological and ideological.

Because we, as a society, have only recently taken up these problems, and because they are remarkably complex, there seems to be no apparent resolution to many of the questions educators face. While there are strong advocates for different positions, there seems to be neither the research that points to a "right" answer nor the finances to provide a full range of options.

As different solutions are suggested, the pressure increases on teachers to know more and do more. If, for example, the most appropriate solution is to have students with special needs study in general education classes (be mainstreamed), then how much more does a teacher need to know in order to teach everyone? And what will the role of special education teacher become as answers evolve?

When we hear the term *special education* it is not unusual to assume that the discussion will be centered on those students with some kind of problem—a learning disability or a physical problem or a behavioral problem. It is important to remember that there are two ends of the special continuum. There are also gifted students. We need to understand the best methods to educate those who are the brightest and most talented.

There is one last issue that needs to be mentioned. It is important to understand, as well as we can, why some students are put in special education classes. We know that there are genetic explanations just as there are problems caused by injury. What we are beginning to realize is that there are also economic and racial reasons why students are labeled (or not labeled) as special needs. Studies show that too many minority and poor students are put into special education classes, and too few minority and poor students are put into the gifted classes.

In this chapter we will study the history of how those with disabilities have been treated. It is a brutal and sad history. Things changed dramatically when the courts and the federal government became involved. During the last quarter of a century remarkable changes have taken place. We will get a sense of the types of disabilities students have, as well as who those students might be. There is also a section about gifted students. We often forget that the gifted and talented might also be put into special classes. Finally, we will discuss the idea of full inclusion into regular classes for students with disabilities. It is a very contentious issue, and will provide a way for us to get some insight into the topic of special education.

THE HISTORY

What we know is that there has been a series of bitterly fought battles about how to educate students with special abilities. While there seem to be almost as many fights about how to deal with special students as with gifted and talented students, this history is not about the very bright. Most of the problems of the gifted do not seem as pressing as the problems of those with disabilities. Later in the chapter there will be a discussion about the gifted and talented.

It is my sense that no matter how enlightened we are as a society, there is a remarkable amount of misunderstanding about those who do not have what we consider "normal abilities." By seeing how the people we consider special students have been treated in the past, it is possible that we might get some insight into the remarkable struggle this group of people has gone through. When I say "group of people" I mean it to include the families of those special students. Parents and siblings are often an important part of the struggle. In order to understand the present, we need to at least glimpse a part of the ugly past of human behavior.[1]

In prehistoric times, it is safe to assume that unproductive members of a tribe were left to die. Life was brutally tough and, in a hunting and gathering society, there were too few resources to share with the weak and unproductive. There is

---

[1] This history is limited to Europe and the United States.

some evidence that cave-dwellers practiced a primitive kind of medicine on those who behaved in aberrant ways. In addition to the strange things found in amulet bags that were thought to contain magic (snake vertebrae, animal teeth, and the like) there was also surgery. One kind of surgery was to chip holes in the patient's skull in order to let the evil spirits out. Regrettably (or possibly thankfully), there are no records about the success of these methods.[2]

The ancient Greeks had clear policies about how to handle special children. In warlike Sparta, the elders would routinely examine babies for their fitness as soldiers and citizens. Those who seemed unfit were left in the wilderness to die. In the more civilized Athens, the unfit were simply killed outright, or set in clay vessels to die by the wayside. Indeed, Aristotle wrote: "As to the exposure and rearing of children, let there be a law that no deformed child shall live."[3]

The dynamic in Rome was a little different. In Rome, families played a more important role. It was the father's role to deal with children with disabilities. Generally, it was the father who threw the baby into the Tiber River so he or she would drown.

The early Christians believed that the devil was responsible for handicapping individuals. Disabled people were seen as polluted and their disabilities were believed to be evil omens. Because they were understood as being dangerous to others, they were shunned by society. By the Middle Ages, things would only get worse.

Possibly the most reasonable early historical example of how a culture treated those with disabilities came from the Old Testament and the Hebrews who believed in it. This is found in Exodus: "Or who maketh the dumb or deaf, or the seeing or the blind? Have not I, the Lord?" And in Leviticus: "Thou shalt not curse the deaf nor put a stumbling block before the blind . . . [and curse those] . . . that maketh the blind to wander out of the path." While not the best of all worlds, at least those with disabilities enjoyed a kind of benign legal protection from the Bible.[4]

With the fall of the Roman Empire came the rise of Christianity. By the sixth and seventh centuries, monks and nuns lived in cloisters and were responsible for most of what little learning went on. During that time the handicapped were also cloistered. These cloisters kept the handicapped (at least some of the handicapped) from the general population that would have simply mistreated them. By the eleventh century things became a little more settled in Europe. As Christianity became stronger and more centralized, secularized society followed its lead.

Church law discriminated against those with handicaps, and "nearly every European country imposed strict civil disabilities on handicapped people—they were deprived of the rights of inheritance, forbidden to testify in a court of justice, and not allowed to make a deed, contract, note or will."[5] At that time, belief in the power of the devil grew. In 1484 the Pope declared war on witches. It is estimated that there

---

[2] This section relies heavily on Margret Winzer, *The History of Special Education: From Isolation to Integration*, (Washington, D.C.: Gallaudet University Press, 1993), p. 12. The book is remarkably good.

[3] Ibid., pgs. 13–14.

[4] Ibid., p. 19.

[5] Ibid., p. 22.

were more than 100,000 trials about witchcraft. Witchcraft was especially hard on women. Almost 80 percent of those accused were women, and witchcraft was a capital crime.

Those who were mentally ill were thought to be "agents of the devil." They were taken to the clergy or to secular powers who would burn them at the stake as punishment. Martin Luther believed the mentally handicapped were "filled with Satan." There is a report that he suggested one retarded child be taken to the nearest river and drowned.

By the Renaissance things began to change for the better. During the mid-1700s England repealed its penal laws against witchcraft. There was also an attempt to deal with problems medically. One medical book, written in 1689, dealt with "the usefulness of voluntary beatings in many diseases of the head; beatings in meloncholia; in frenzy; in paralysis; in epilepsy; in facial expression of feebleminded; in hardness of hearing; in toothache; in dumbness; hysterical crying; in nymphomania."[6] The point is not that the medicine was bad, but that there was at least the attempt to find medical solutions.

The beginning of special education took place in Spain. In the sixteenth century, a Benedictine monk named Pedro Ponce de Leon began to teach boys who could not speak to "speak, read, write and reckon; to pray, and to assist at mass, to know the doctrines of Christianity, and to know how to confess themselves by speech . . ."[7] Religion clearly served to motivate this effort. John Cleland, an Englishman, took a different tack and tried to find a universal language for the deaf. In order to fund his research, Cleland wrote *Fanny Hill*, which was a bawdy novel that horrified religious leaders.

Basically, Western Europe was changing. As we saw in earlier chapters, science and rationality began to dominate the way people understood the world. Deeply superstitious beliefs gradually lost their ruling grip on the population. Humanism evolved alongside the rationalism of the times. In chapter one we saw how Rousseau believed that children had a natural goodness that needed to be respected and encouraged. Slowly, the enlightenment seeped through the culture and finally worked its way to those with disabilities.

There are too many important turning points in this history to discuss. Remarkable people with remarkable perseverance and insight did their best to understand disabilities and how they might be overcome. The roots of some of our current debates began hundreds of years ago. For example, by the late eighteenth century a central conflict in the deaf community had begun. In Paris, Abbe Charles Michel de l'Epee began teaching deaf children sign language, while in Germany Samuel Heinicke believed that deaf children should be taught to speak. There are schools devoted to oralists and others that are manualists—and neither can convince the other to change.

As we enter the twenty-first century, there continue to be oralist and manualist schools, and the debate is as intense as ever.

[6] Ibid., p. 28.

[7] Ibid., p. 32.

We will end this short history with mental illness. By the early sixteenth century the mentally ill were simply put in what were called lunatic hospitals. They were put there, the reasoning went, to protect society. Those asylums were brutal places. The mentally ill were considered insensitive to pain, so they were "chained naked in rat infested cubicles below ground and fed on bread and soup.[8]" They were "brutalized, treated like animals, and, legally speaking, they had the status of animals."[9]

While people no longer believed that mental illness was caused by demons, there was a popular belief that it was caused by masturbation. Mental illness, then, was something that could be self-inflicted. Some thought that masturbation caused epilepsy, reduced the flow of blood to the brain, and generally caused insanity. In *Emile*, Rousseau warned about the dangers of masturbating.[10]

By the end of the eighteenth century Phillippe Pinel both rethought and reformed how the mentally ill were treated. Pinel began by rejecting the agreed-upon explanations for mental illness.[11] He believed that the following were *not* the reasons for insanity: the devil, witchcraft, the moon, libertinism, liquor, or masturbation. Nor did he believe it was caused by some inner nature of the individual.

Pinel's idea was that the most significant cause of mental disorders was the failure of society to provide the proper conditions necessary for good mental health. The result was that stress produced breakdowns. He believed that those who were ill would not respond to the violence of mental hospitals. He thought that kindness, creative activity, minimum restraint, routine, and structure would be the best course of treatment. In 1793 he began to test his ideas and, as we know, he was basically correct.[12]

The purpose of this history is not to fully examine any single problem. To do justice to these problems would take book-length discussions, and even then there would be much that we would not know. Pinel, for example, was certainly on the right path; however, we are still far from knowing all there is to know about the causes and best treatments for mental illness. What this brief section shows is how long it took to even begin to carefully consider the causes and the best/most humane ways to deal with those who have disabilities.

Our history stops at 1793 not because things got better all of a sudden, but simply to show how recently even the most basic insights into problems began to occur. The truth is that barbaric conditions continued to exist well into the twentieth century—and still exist in too many places. Some of the worst public institutions were closed in my lifetime. Some of the most important chemical breakthroughs have happened in your lifetime.

With that in mind, we turn to special education.

---

[8] Ibid., p. 61.

[9] Ibid., p. 60.

[10] Thankfully, there were ways to prevent excessive masturbation. By avoiding salt meat, taking cold baths, and using various ointments and manual restraints, this moral and medical problem could be solved. As a last resort, there was radical surgery. Ibid., p. 62.

[11] This discussion is found in ibid., pgs. 62–3.

[12] The old ideas have not died. A friend recently told me that she took a mentally retarded man to the dentist. The dentist was not going to give the man novocaine before he drilled because "these people don't feel pain."

RECENT HISTORY AND THE LAW

From about 1910 students with disabilities in the United States were moved out of institutions and into public schools. They were put into segregated classes in those schools, but the move was an important one. The theory was that these special classes best served the needs of disabled students because of the low student–teacher ratio and the homogeneous nature of the group. The idea was for these classes to provide remedial instruction so that the students could someday return to regular classes.

During the 1930s little was done for exceptional students. The Depression caused so many strains in every part of the culture that the problems of students who needed special help was simply not a priority. While it is possible to understand why there was little enthusiasm for rethinking and innovation, it is regrettable that conditions for students with special needs got worse.

In just about every important way, the gap between those in regular classes and those in special classes widened. The special classes concentrated less and less on education and became more of a holding area. There was a stigma connected with these classes. The special needs students were educated poorly and rejected socially. Their teachers were not well trained and often did little more than be an adult presence in the classroom. Special education was merely the lowest track in public school during the '30s.

While there were some changes during the post-war '40s in the United States, the most significant event had nothing to do with disabilities. In 1954, as we know, the Supreme Court of the United States, in *Brown v.Board of Education of Topeka*, ruled that separate education was not equal education. The parents of children with disabilities took that logic and applied it to their own families. They asked, rightly, if the isolation of their children represented an education equal to that of other children.

The result was that parents began bringing their complaints to the courts. Three issues emerged:[13] 1) the fairness of intelligence tests and the legitimacy of placing students in special education classes on the basis of these tests; 2) the cultural bias of the tests and the language in which the tests were administered; and 3) the arguments that schools could not afford to educate special students.

In 1972 a court in Pennsylvania[14] ruled that because the Commonwealth could not prove these children were uneducable, then they were entitled to a free, public education. Other courts followed suit and included, for example, children with disabilities. In a broad sense, the rulings were based on the proposition that all people were protected by the Fourteenth Amendment. That amendment provides, essentially, that a person cannot be deprived of his or her basic rights because of any classification such as race, nationality, or religion. The courts decided that disabilities could not be a classification of exclusion.

By 1975 the Congress passed Public Law 94-142. It was the Education for All Handicapped Children Act (but we know it as the Individuals with Disabilities

---

[13] These come from William Heward and Rodney Cavanaugh, "Educational Equality for Students with Disabilities," in James Banks and Cherry McGee Banks, editors, *Multicultural Education: Issues and Perspectives*, 4th ed. (New York: Wiley, 2001), p. 303.

[14] *Pennsylvania Association for Retarded Children v. Commonwealth of Pennsylvania*

Education Act, or IDEA). The legislation is based on six major principles. Even with important additional legislation (that we will review later in the chapter) these principles have remained unchanged.[15]

The first requirement of the law was that schools had to educate all students with disabilities. Clearly, the policy that all students—no matter what their disabilities—must be accepted by public schools was a huge change. That no student could be rejected meant that every school district in the country was affected. When President Gerald Ford signed the bill into law, the role of public schools dramatically expanded.

The law affected every person between the ages of six and seventeen. But it did not stop there. If a state provided educational services for children without disabilities from the ages of three to five, then it was obliged to provide education for all children between the ages of three and five. Finally, each state was required to locate, identify, and evaluate all children in that state from birth to the age of twenty-one who had or were suspected of having disabilities. This *child find system* was to help ensure that each child with a disability could have an appropriate education.

The second principle of the law was that students with disabilities should be assessed and evaluated fairly. For example, children who did not speak English, or did not speak it well, needed to be tested in their first language. Because most tests have cultural biases (it is no mistake that white, middle-class students tend to do best on standardized tests), the law requires that no one can be placed in a special education program on the basis of one test. Over the years, a series of different tests have been developed to more accurately evaluate student ability and achievement.

The third important part of the law is that each child should have a free, appropriate public education. The heart of this principle is the *individualized education program* (IEP). It is important to understand what makes up an IEP. Put simply, the IEP calls for each student to have individualized goals and objectives with timelines. It must contain a description of the child's current skill abilities and a list of services to be received in order to achieve the goals and objectives.

The IEP is the result of a collaborative effort. The IEP team consists of at least one parent or guardian of the child, at least one regular education teacher of the child, at least one special education teacher, as well as a representative of the local school district and, if appropriate, the child. While the details are not terribly important at this point in the discussion, it is easy to imagine the problems that IEPs have caused.

While the inclusion of parents is critically important, parents may not always be the best judges of their own children's potential. Yet, they may well know much more about their child than anyone else. The tension between parents and experts is one that is a constant theme in any discussion of IEPs and what is best for any given child.

There were other issues. For example, in order to be an effective part of the team, teachers who taught in regular classes needed to learn a great deal about special education. At that time, and even now, those who teach in regular classrooms have little training in special education. Should we add to our "what should teachers know" list? Also, special education teachers are not always experts on all types of disabilities,

---

[15] See H. R. Turnbull and A. P. Turnbull, *Free Appropriate Public Education: The Law and Children with Disabilities*, 5th ed. (Denver: Love Press, 1998).

so other specialists are often brought in to consult. Finally, it is the job of the local school district to monitor funding, and while it is the law that all educational services will be provided, we know there is a practical limit on funding.

To further complicate the process, there is an outline that all IEPs must follow. The law calls for a great deal of detail, and the amount of time it would take to carefully construct an IEP is simply prohibitive. The way the law read, it was impossible to fully comply with the requirements of the IEPs. The argument was never that IEPs were a bad idea; the argument was that, as a practical matter, it was impossible to create the millions of individualized plans that needed to be written.

The fourth requirement of the law was that each student with disabilities be educated in the least restrictive environment (LRE). The principle was that the educational environment should be normalized for those with special needs. Normalization calls for programs in which the culture of the education reflects the culture in which the learners are a part.

The range of settings for students with special needs is great.[16] There are seven different types of educational services: 1) Private, specialized facilities. This is the most protected environment for the student. 2) Special schools within the public school system. 3) Full-time special classes. The student receives a prescribed program given by a special education teacher. 4) Regular classrooms and resource rooms. The student has a special program but is in a regular classroom. He or she might also go to a special resource room with special teachers. 5) Regular classrooms with supplementary instruction and services. Again, the instruction takes place in a regular classroom but there are special services available. 6) Regular classrooms with a consultant. The student with special needs is in a regular classroom and has the ongoing support of specialists. Finally, 7) the student has a prescribed program under the direction of the regular classroom teacher.

The law calls for the least restrictive, appropriate environment. The idea of least restrictive, appropriate environment—the policy of inclusion—deserves a more complete discussion. We will return to it at the end of this chapter.

The fifth principle of the law deals with due process safeguards. The law does not allow schools to act in an arbitrary way. Parents were given the right to be notified if the school decided to take any action that might alter the child's program. They were given the right to see all their child's school records and could give or withhold permission to have their child tested, reevaluated, or placed in a different classroom or program. They had the right to a hearing before an impartial party to resolve disagreements with the school, and could appeal the findings of the hearing to the state department of education.

This part of IDEA did two things. First, it provided students with disabilities with an important set of legal rights. In doing so, it also empowered the parents of these students. Schools and professionals could no longer make decisions without the consent and approval of parents. It represented a huge shift in power.

The sixth principle is really a different way of understanding what was just said. The due process safeguards meant, in no small part, that the parents and students were important participants in the process, and that the most important educational decisions had to be shared.

[16] See Heward and Cavanaugh, op. cit., pgs. 307–10.

We need to note the remarkable nature of IDEA. For the first time, children with disabilities were given the rights of all other children. It became a matter of federal law that each child not only be given a free, public education, but that education had to be appropriate, individual, and as least restrictive as possible. As of 1975 it was not only policy but law that all children were to have an equal education. Given what we know about how these children have been treated historically, the law stands as a genuine milestone of human rights.

While the law was remarkable, it certainly was not perfect. In the next section we will review what has happened since 1975, and deal with the issues it helped create.

CHANGES AND REVISIONS

Two other pieces of federal legislation have helped provide rights for special needs children. The Rehabilitation Act of 1973 protected the rights of persons with handicaps. It said, basically, that an individual could not be discriminated against "solely by reason of his handicap." The law was primarily concerned with the public sector.

The Americans with Disabilities Act of 1990 extended the rights of persons with disabilities to the private sector. The civil rights of those with disabilities was broadened to cover almost all areas. One provision of this law required that all new public accommodations (those places where people go—like grocery stores, hotels, restaurants, theaters, public universities) must be made accessible for those with disabilities. It also required all existing public accommodations be made accessible if the cost was reasonable.

Think about this one section of a relatively complicated law. Close your eyes and remember what you did yesterday. Now think about what yesterday would have been like if you happened to be in a wheelchair, or happened to be blind. Were there ramps leading to every building you entered? There is a very good possibility that, if this was 1989, simple access to those buildings would have been very difficult for you. Or, think about crossing a street if you were blind. Did you hear that little ringing when the light changed? If you were blind you certainly would have heard it—and in 1989 there would have been nothing to hear.

As you relive your yesterday, what you will find, I suspect, is that while there have been efforts of make the world better for those with handicaps, the work is not complete.

Certainly the laws concerning disabilities have helped all students. In 1997, a new Individualized Education Program was added to the Amendments to the Individuals with Disabilities Act.[17] There were a number of problems with the IEP under the earlier law:[18]

> Among the concerns . . . are a lack of adequate teacher training, mechanistic paper compliance, difficulty with the team process, burdensome paper work, and excessive time demands . . . the *pedagogical* problems [were] the emphasis on measurable

---

[17] Much of the following discussion is taken from Dixie Snow Huefner, "The Risks and Opportunities of the IEP Requirements Under IDEA '97," *The Journal of Special Education*, Vol. 33/No. 4/2000. pgs. 195–204.

[18] Ibid., p. 195–6.

short-term objectives and criteria for evaluating their achievement . . . minimal coordination with general educators . . . failure to link assessment data with instructional goals and objectives . . . and failure to include social and behavioral goals [for] students with emotional disturbance.

Among the *legal* errors were failure to report current levels of performance . . lack of short-term objectives and evaluation procedures . . . and absence of key personnel.

The problems were so widespread, and the mandated procedures so complex, that during the 1980s people began using computer-generated IEPs. There is more than a little irony that individualized study plans were being produced by technicians who were using formulas and following rules to make certain the plans were legal. The bottom line is that these standardized IEPs saved schools both time and money. The problem, of course, is that they ignored the spirit of the law.

While it is clear that the 1997 law was intended to solve as many of the problems of the earlier IEPs as possible (the most recent law was in 1990), it was also intended to make certain that children in need of special education would get the best possible education. The changes in 1997 made the law more complex, which may not have been the best way to solve the problems.

There were at least eight major changes in the law. They dealt with the content of the IEP, special factors that needed to be taken into account and the makeup of the IEP team. One change, for example, required that the annual goals must be measurable, but that the short-term objectives could be considered benchmarks. The law expanded the inclusion of special services while requiring students with disabilities be with "nondisabled children to the maximum extent appropriate."[19] In the new IEP team, the role of the general educator is expanded. This would seem to be a natural extension of the idea that students with disabilities will probably be spending more time in general education classes.

The details of all the changes are not our immediate concern. From the clear direction of the law, the idea is that inclusion and normalization is only going to increase, so it is necessary to understand what that might mean.

The problems, both political and moral, are tough. Assuming that inclusion and normalization are the best educational policies,[20] it would seem wrong and heartless to resist them. But as a practical matter, it is important to consider what the changes mean to the classroom teacher. As a teacher, while your heart may say that the most moral educational policy is one of inclusion, what does that mean as a practical matter?

Because the law is more complex, it means that you will be more involved in team meetings, in goal setting, and in doing paperwork. Doing that means extra time is added to teachers who we know are overworked. The hours are long, the job is stress-filled, and the threat of burnout is never too far away. If that is true, how much sense does it make to add complicated and sensitive matters to a teacher's responsibility? More meetings? More paperwork? More students who are, by definition, difficult to teach? That hardly seems the formula for successful teaching.

---

[19] From the law, quoted by ibid., p. 198.

[20] That they are the best policies for everyone is not clear. We will take them up later in the chapter.

But the burden for the regular teacher is really much more than that. What is clear is that, given the new law, teachers will need to know much more about special education. The less they know, the worse-off students with disabilities will be. If a regular teacher has a limited knowledge of special education, then placing students with disabilities in a general classroom amounts to little more than dumping them in an inappropriate setting.

The situation might improve if the budget for special education is large enough to provide enough help for those students in need. There might be pullout settings, aids and services to help each student, and enough resources to ensure a good education. But the question—while practical, it sounds a little tacky—is unavoidable: Where do those funds come from? If all the provisions of the new law are fully funded, does that mean that funding will be taken away from other segments of the student population? That is certainly possible, but we can assume, politically, that will never happen.

And how will the teachers in general education learn about students with special needs? We know that, in order for the law to be effective, our teachers must be better-educated in this area. The answer is that teachers will need to take additional courses in their programs. Schools of education must make it their business to make certain their students know about and are comfortable teaching students of all abilities. The legal, pedagogical, moral, and practical aspects of teaching are much more demanding and complicated now than they have ever been.

For public schools to be inclusive, and being inclusive is in the very best tradition of our schooling, then teachers must understand their new responsibilities.

WHAT AND WHO

In this section we will deal with three problems that are both political and pedagogical. The *What* question has to do with some of the types of disabilities we have been discussing. The *Who* is exactly that—who are we talking about?

What Are the Disabilities?

The first set of problems is concerned with what, exactly, are we talking about? What is the range of disabilities that one might come in contact with in a publc school.[21]

There are **physical disabilities.** Hearing and visual disabilities are not uncommon. About one out of 1,000 children have visual problems so severe that his or her educational needs cannot be met in a regular classroom. A much, much larger number of students need glasses. About three or four out of 1,000 have at least partial hearing impairments. Many of the oldest schools for special students are for the deaf. Indeed, deafness is the disability that has traditionally been the first to be accepted by the larger culture.

---

[21] Much of this comes from Borich and Tombari, Gary Borich and Martin Tombari, *Educational Psychology: A Contemporary Approach*, 2nd ed., (Deading, MA: Longman, 1997) op. cit. pgs. 475–91.

To take deafness as an example, what we find is an intense conflict about the best method of education. The conflict, as we read earlier, goes back to the eighteenth century. One group believes that it is best for deaf students to learn sign language, while the other group believes that it is much better for deaf students to learn only how to read lips. There are powerful schools dedicated to one or the other type of education. The tensions, in part, revolve around which community (hearing or nonhearing) an individual wants to be trained to live in.

As in most cases, there is no answer that is right for everyone. Like all groups of people, it is foolish to believe that everyone in the group has the same feelings, thoughts, and ambitions.[22] The point here is not to somehow give a "right" answer to the problem, but to simply point out that bright people acting in good faith can disagree. As we have seen over and over, it is not surprising that educational questions are all too often political questions. That certainly seems to be the case in education for the deaf.

There are other physical disabilities. There are students in wheelchairs, students who need crutches or walkers, and students who have different injuries. We know that, legally, public places must be accessible to those with physical disabilities. We also know that teachers need to be sensitive to students who are unable to participate in all of the activities those without disabilities participate in.

There are communication disabilities. There are different forms of speech disability in which the student has problems with articulation. They may distort, omit, or substitute one sound for another. Another form of communication disability is stuttering. In all these cases a speech therapist can be very helpful. There are also students who have language disabilities. They have difficulty understanding English. These are not students for whom English is a second language, but students who may have physical problems or may be mentally retarded.

The second category has to do with **behavioral disorders.** These are not the normal range of behavioral problems that almost every student has at one time or another. These are problems that generally last six months or longer. It is estimated "that 3 to 5 percent of learners ages 0 to 10 experience attention deficit disorder, 5 to 7 percent experience conduct disorder (such as aggression), and 2 to 10 percent experience severe depression. In other words, 14 to 20 percent of learners experience some form of behavioral disorder during their school-age years."[23]

During the last several years much has been written about attention deficit hyperactivity disorder (ADHD). While psychologists use a relatively long list of symptoms to diagnose ADHD, there are four primary behaviors that point to the disorder: 1) the inability to sustain attention. Someone with ADHD is easily distracted from what he (twice as many males have ADHD than females) is doing. It seems that just about everything, or anything, is interesting—for at least a short time. 2) being impulsive. Too often, a person with ADHD fails to think about a task before he begins. The

[22] In the most unscientific way, I can report that those people I know who went to those schools where they learned to read lips—almost to a person—learned to sign as soon as they got out of school.

[23] Ibid., p. 485.

impulse is to start. 3) hyperactivity.[24] The person is more active and restless than his classmates. He cannot sit still. 4) problems keeping rules. Given the other traits, it should be no surprise that the person with ADHD has a very difficult time behaving.

If you become a teacher, the odds are good that you will have students with ADHD in your class. By understanding the issues involved, it is possible that issues related to other problems might be more easily dealt with. It is just about impossible to have gotten to college and not known people with ADHD. They might have been bright and talented, but they were also prone to get into trouble. For teachers, they were the students who were most likely to interrupt the class, talk without raising their hand, and always seem to be on the edge of breaking the rules.

The discussion of ADHD, at least in the popular press, generally centers on the drug Ritalin. The notion is that the drug is overprescribed to kids who are just naturally (and normally) active as a way to calm them down. One suspects that Ritalin, like many subscription drugs, may be abused. But I would like to focus on those people who seem to condemn the use of any drug for children, but especially Ritalin.

Consider this: You have a wonderful son. Bright, funny, a pleasure to be around. But around his seventh birthday he starts having trouble in school. While he is smart enough to continue to do well, his teachers keep writing you notes that he is acting out in class. Naturally, you become concerned and, at the suggestion of the school, he takes a series of tests to see what is going on.

The psychologist the school has hired to do the testing contacts you. She says that your son has ADHD and believes that Ritalin will help him a great deal. Then she says this: ADHD is generally genetic; that if a child has it so too does one or both parents. The doctor recommends that the parent with ADHD should also take Ritalin.

That night, when you talk with your mate, you bring up what the doctor has said. Your mate, as well as your son, agree that you are the parent with ADHD. They remind you of your behavior and, like the doctor, strongly urge you to try Ritalin. Now you are faced with two questions: Will you have your son take Ritalin? Will you take Ritalin?

It is my impression that surprisingly few people are either willing to give their child Ritalin or are willing to take it themselves. The range of reasons is fairly broad, but it often comes down to a misunderstanding of ADHD and a mistrust of the drug.

It seems to be a normal impulse to try and find ways in which ADHD can be handled without taking a drug. Less sugar, more structured time, fewer extraneous demands, and more individualized attention all seem to be ways to moderate the effects of the disorder. People also try to find other reasons for behavioral problems: your child has just entered a new school or class, another sibling is leaving home, the dog died—the list of excuses is almost limitless.

But the bottom line is this: ADHD is simply a chemical imbalance. While experimenting with the behavioral variables in a young person's life might be of some limited help, the only thing that will absolutely help is to normalize the chemical balance. The argument that Ritalin is used to quiet normal kids who are simply high-energy ignores reality. Ritalin, in street terms, is speed. To give a "normal" person speed will

---

[24] There is also ADD, which are the same problems without the hyperactivity. In ways, ADD is more difficult to spot because the person will simply appear to be very quiet and, possibly, not very smart.

do nothing less than speed him up. To give a person with ADHD speed will have the opposite effect—it will slow him down. In other words, to give Ritalin to a person who does not need it is to create an even bigger behavioral problem.

What is remarkable about Ritalin is that the person who takes it will know within twenty minutes if it is the right drug. The effect of Ritalin is like turning a switch. Click. The light goes on. The drug works. While it is certainly well within the realm of probability that the drug is overprescribed, and it is equally probable that too many doctors do a poor job of monitoring their patients. That does not reflect badly on the drug—it reflects badly on the doctors.

Finally, even those people who might be willing to give their children Ritalin are often much too cautious to take it themselves. Several years ago it was thought that people simply outgrew ADHD. It turns out they were wrong. What happens is that while people graduate from the more tightly controlled environment of school, they do not escape their symptoms. Some things seem better simply because an adult has a little more control over his or her life. Also, as people grow older they learn more and more ways to compensate for their problems, but compensation is not the same as getting rid of the problem. There is a natural defensiveness on the part of adults to judge their lives as successful and resent the idea that medication could make daily life better. What is rarely considered is the effort it takes to compensate for their chemical imbalance.

Enough about ADHD. It is an instructive example for several reasons. In addition to being relatively common and not exceedingly complicated, there are actually ways to eliminate the symptoms. But when it is personalized, when it involves your family, it suddenly becomes different. All kinds of misinformation, prejudices, and personal issues come into play. If those types of emotions occur in relatively easy problems that can be taken care of, imagine what it must be like when something much more serious is the issue. Imagine if the disability is more severe and there are fewer and less-effective cures?

The third and fourth categories of disabilities are **mental retardation** and **learning disabilities.** While there is certainly overlap in these categories (people with mental retardation may also have learning disabilities), the two are not always connected. We will begin with mental retardation.

It was only with the passage of PL 94-142 that children with mental retardation were allowed in schools. For the most part, it was thought that they were incapable of benefiting from education and were simply placed in large institutions. Little attempt was made to educate them; mostly, they received custodial care. That changed in 1975 when the federal government mandated that each child had the right to the least restrictive education possible. Since then a huge amount of effort has been spent understanding how best to educate the mentally retarded.

There is a range of definitions for mental retardation.[25] The American Association of Mental Retardation (AAMR) definition has three major components. First, there is subaverage general intellectual functioning. That means a person is at least two standard deviations below the mean in an individually administered, standardized

---

[25] This discussion comes from Gale Morrison and Edward Polloway, "Mental Retardation," in Edward Meyen and Thomas Skrtic, editors, *Special Education and Student Disability: Traditional, Emerging and Alternative Perspectives*, 4th ed. (Denver: Love Publishing, 1995).

intelligence test. (We will see how different scores are understood by schools later in the discussion.) The second part of the definition of mental retardation is that there is an impairment in adaptive behavior. In other words, it is difficult for the individual to "effectively adjust to environmental demands." And the final component of the definition is that these traits are seen during the development period from birth to the age of eighteen. The onset of these traits after the age of eighteen is not considered mental retardation.

Here are the general reasons for mental retardation:[26] 1) genetic disorders; 2) chromosomal disorders; 3) prenatal complications; 4) infections, and 5) social and environmental factors. The first four causes "generally affect brain development by causing premature closure of the skull bones, abnormalities in the formation of certain brain structures, or biochemical disorders that affect brain nourishment." But most mental retardation, almost 75 percent, is caused by social and environmental factors. Psychological and social deprivations in a child's early life have devastating effects. We will take this up later in the chapter.

Children with lower IQs are also more likely to have other disabilities such as hearing or visual problems. They also are more likely to lack coordination.

In terms of schooling, in the last three decades we have found that students with an IQ range from about 50 or 55–70[27] can learn some basic academic skills. These students are considered mildly retarded and classified as educable. An IQ range of about 30–49 is considered moderately retarded and classified as trainable. This person can learn self-help skills and routine work skills. One scale suggests that between 26–40 a person is severely retarded, and anything below that is profoundly retarded. On another scale, a person with an IQ below 30 is severely retarded and will always need full-time supervision and care.

The effect of enlightened law, increasing data, and the willingness to acknowledge the humanity in each person has brought about remarkable changes in how the mentally retarded are treated. The central concern of the public schools is now to make certain that the mentally retarded receive instruction. While the amount and intensity of that instruction is obviously related to the severity of the retardation, the goal is to help each person become independent. Although there are those who will always be in need of some level of supervision, in most cases public schools are committed to at least training and teaching skills to every student.

As a teacher, you can expect that those who are mildly retarded will be in general education classes some, if not all, of the time. In 1996–97 there were more than 5.7 million children with disabilities.[28] That means 7.7 percent of the school-aged population received special education services. Since the law took effect in 1976, the number of students in special education has risen every year. Almost twice as many boys as girls were receiving special education.

---

[26] Borich and Tombari, op. cit., p. 476.

[27] There are several ways to classify IOs, and several different scales. The numbers I am using are generally a compromise of different scales. They are, at best, approximate.

[28] These statistics come from Heward and Cavanaugh, op. cit., p. 299.

Of those in special education, the majority (51 percent) have learning disabilities; 21 percent have speech and language impairment; 11.4 percent are mentally retarded; and 8.6 percent are emotionally disturbed. Of those who are mentally retarded, 85 percent have only mild disabilities. Beginning in 1976, the percentage of students with learning disabilities has risen dramatically (20.1 percent to 51.1 percent) while those with mental retardation has decreased (24.9 percent to ll.4 percent). These last numbers are a reflection of the amount of research that has been done, and the increasing sophistication of assessment.

In a very general sense, this is the range of disabilities that is found in special education programs. In the following section we will see just who we are talking about.

Who Is in Special Education

One would expect that the percentage of children in special education programs would mirror the percentage of children in the general population. If that were the case, we should expect to find about the same number of girls and boys who need these services. What we find is that there are twice as many boys as girls in special education. While we have seen that girls seem to mature faster than boys, and there are some chemical differences that come into play, even taken together those things do not account for the two-to-one ratio.

The second thing we would expect, for example, is that since black students comprise about 16 percent of the school population, then about that same percentage would be in special education. It is surprising to find that 31 percent of those classified as mildly retarded and 23.7 percent of those with severe emotional disturbance are black. Both Chicanos and American Indians are overrepresented in special education. In this section we will focus on the relationship between disabilities, race and socioeconomic class.

For the last three decades the number of Americans living in poverty has steadily increased.[29] In 1969, 24.2 million people lived below the poverty line; in 1997, the number was 35.6 million. The increase effects children. In 1973, 10.8 percent of American families below the poverty line had children; in 1997, nearly 16 percent of poor families had children. It is worse for minority children. Nearly 40 percent of African American and Hispanic children live below the poverty line, and the majority of these are female-headed, single-parent households.

We find in the 1997 Report to Congress that "as poverty among children has increased in the United States, the number of children with disabilities and receiving special education has also increased."[30] The dynamic seems to be this: There is an increase in disabilities among those most vulnerable to poor socioeconomic conditions. For example, we know that inadequate (or no) prenatal care or health care can lead to mental retardation. We know that poor health care can be a cause of chronic illness, mental disorders, and learning disabilities. As we just saw, a disproportionate number of minorities live in poverty.

---

[29] Much of what follows comes from Glenn Fujiura and Kiyoshi Yamaki, "Trends in Demography of Childhood Poverty and Disability," *Exceptional Children*, Vol. 66, no. 2, pgs. 187–99.

[30] Quoted in ibid., p. 188.

The data does not indicate that the most important variable is either race or single-parent families. From 1983 to 1996, the increasingly high level of minority children with disabilities "appears to be largely associated with the disproportionate representation of poor . . . households in the minority community . . . Poverty emerged as a significant predictor of disability status in 1996."[31] While there have not been enough longitudinal studies to show this is absolutely the case, certainly the data is highly suggestive.

There is a more philosophical way to understand the problem.[32] Alfredo Artiles argues that those who are put into special education classes are somehow understood as being different. These differences have traditionally rested on the assumption that differences are linked to abnormality or stigma. In other words, sameness is the measure of equality. If you are different, if you are not the same, then you do not "measure up."[33]

It has always been the case in the United States that minorities have been seen as different. White culture has traditionally set the norm in America. The white culture, the dominant culture, defines how to think, how to act, and how to feel. Minority groups, race/ethnicity/cultural, who define the world in other ways are, according to Artiles and others, in danger of being defined as different in a school setting. He writes:[34]

> We need to acknowledge, therefore, that human difference has been seen as problematic in our society, that ethnic minority groups have been traditionally seen as "problem people," and that discrimination, prejudice, and racism are subtly and openly enacted every day in our country.

While acknowledging the "documented negative effects of poverty," Artiles argues that we cannot ignore the effects of prejudice. He urges us to remember that the idea of difference is a comparative one and that those with power get to define what is normal and what is not. It is important to ask further questions like, when does difference count, under what conditions, in what ways, and for what reasons?[35] If we proceed in this way, it is possible that we may be able to redefine who needs special education.

One suspects that both poverty and prejudice feed into the fact that there is a disproportionate number of minorities in special education classes. When we discuss special education for gifted children we will return to the theme of prejudice. But before leaving this subject it is important to think, practically, what this means.

---

[31] Ibid., p. 191.

[32] Alfredo Artiles, "The Dilemma of Difference: Enriching the Disproportionality Discourse with Theory and Context," *The Journal of Special Education*, Vol. 32/No. 1, 1998, pgs. 32–6.

[33] Ibid., p. 32.

[34] Ibid., p. 33.

[35] Ibid., p. 35.

First, if poverty is the most significant variable for determining those who are in special education, then it is clear that the problem is social and political, and schools have almost no chance of making a substantial difference. While it is clear that schools can do a remarkable job teaching and training those with special needs, if the root of the problem is poverty, then the best the school can do is make a bad situation a little less worse. Any social policy that puts money into schooling but ignores the context of poverty, will never solve the problem.

Second, if there are students in special education programs because of our cultural diversity, then there are important things that schools can do. There needs to be a new set of tests and assessments that are sensitive to cultural and language differences. Every effort must be made to take out the biases in the referral practices. Finally, as always, teachers will be asked to learn more. Just as students are asked to learn and adjust to a new or different culture, so too must teachers understand, act, and teach in an appropriate way that will be sensitive to other cultures.

THE GIFTED

Like children with disabilities, it is not unusual that gifted children have been "feared as possessed because they know and understand too much too early. Like retarded children, gifted children have been feared as strange, as oddballs, as freaks."[36] It is important to at least have a working definition of who we are talking about when we mention gifted and talented students. In 1978 the government passed the Gifted and Talented Act. It said, in part:[37]

> Gifted and talented children means children . . . who are identified . . . as possessing demonstrated or potential abilities that give evidence of high performance capability in areas such as intellectual, creative, specific academics, or leadership abilities, or in the performing and visual arts, and who by reason thereof require services or activities not ordinarily provided by the school.

There are different ways to understand the gifted and talented. Ellen Winner believes there are three atypical characteristics shared by the gifted.[38] First, she believes gifted children are precocious. The first trait is that they begin to master some domain (math, music, chess, tennis, and so on) earlier than average and much more quickly than average. The second trait is that these children "march to their own drummer." They not only learn quickly, but in a qualitatively different way. They are, by definition, creative. Finally, they are intrinsically motivated to make sense and conquer the domain in which they show precocity. They are intense and even obsessive and have a remarkable ability to focus. Winner writes, they have a "rage to master." A gifted child is more than a bright child, and a prodigy is an extreme example of someone who is gifted.

[36] Ellen Winner, *Gifted Children: Myths and Realities* (New York: Basic Books, 1996), pgs. 3–4.

[37] Public Law 95–561, Section 902.

[38] Winner, op. cit., pgs. 3–4.

A standard textbook tells us there are four characteristics of the gifted.[39] The gifted child has a high general intelligence, a high level of achievement, is creative, and has a high level of task persistence. The lists of Winner and this standard text have much in common. The reason to mention both is to help us remember that there are different levels of knowing something. For those who teach in a general classroom, the gifted child might be as much of a mystery as a child with disabilities. What I mean is that, just as there is a great deal to learn about those with disabilities, there is much to learn about those who are gifted. *As a teacher, you may be in the awkward situation of being the only adult in the classroom—but not being the smartest person.* Being older helps, knowing more helps, but the fact may remain that one of those kids might be smarter.

The first trait offered by the standard text is general intelligence. Yet, in a book only about the gifted there is something the author calls "the myth of global giftedness." She writes: "The underlying assumption here is that gifted children have a general intellectual power that allows them to be gifted 'across the board.' . . . Children can even be gifted in one academic area and learning-disabled in another."[40] There are several things that seem to go against our common perceptions that might help us better understand gifted children.

First, as we just read, children may be gifted in one area and average or even learning-disabled in another. Abilities are independent of one another. Second, having a high IQ is irrelevant to some kinds of giftedness. Art and music are examples. Third, biology plays a powerful role. Gifted children start out with extraordinary brains. Fourth, families play a more important role in the development of the giftedness of their children than do schools. While parents cannot take ordinary children, or even bright children, and make them gifted, they can do a great deal to help those with gifts develop them. Sixth, giftedness, like disability, can lead to unhappiness and social isolation. And finally, personality attributes are better predictors of what will happen to a gifted child than is the degree of giftedness.[41] In other words, for a gifted child to grow up to be an extraordinary adult, he or she needs to have enough social skills to relate to others. Even a great deal of giftedness is not enough to overcome negative personality traits.

About the time that IQ tests were first being used, a Stanford psychologist named Lewis Terman decided he would study gifted children. He wanted to show that high-IQ children not only had superior intelligence, but also were socially and physically superior. He wanted to show that these kids were neither social outcasts nor physically awkward.

He chose children who were born between 1900 and 1917. They all had IQs of 135 or above. Indeed, the great majority of them scored better than 140 on the tests. (Average on these tests was between 90 and 110). While there were problems with his selection (most were nominated by teachers and were "school-house" gifted, most

[39] Borich and Tombari, op. cit., pgs. 492–7.

[40] Winner, op. cit., p. 7.

[41] Ibid., pgs. 12–3.

were white and from at least middle-class and professional families, and so on) there are some interesting things to note about his work.

He found that these students were, as he had hoped, surprisingly well-rounded and well-adjusted socially. They were even "somewhat" superior in their physical development. But here is the most remarkable aspect of the study: In 1995, 79 years after the initial results were published, the sixth volume of Terman's study was published. (The series is *The Genetic Studies of Genius.*) The remaining subjects are now well into their eighties and continue to be studied and written about. For those interested in the very definition of a longitudinal study, I recommend this study of people with high IQs.

One of the things that has changed dramatically from Terman's sample of gifted children is the notion of who should be included.[42] No longer is intelligence the only variable. Indeed, there are cases in which IQ does not count at all. The shift is to an emphasis on talent "as the primary defining characteristic of giftedness and focuses on the identification of special talents and aptitudes." As we have seen throughout the book, the more we learn and understand, the more complex (and often inclusive) the world becomes.

The idea of genius was formulated in the late nineteenth century by Sir Francis Galton. He offered the first definition of genius from his study of famous adults. It was his thought that the largest proportion of human intelligence was "fixed and immutable." A hundred years later that idea became the central feature in the theory that a person was born and died with the same amount of intelligence, no matter what their life experiences had been. As we know, about this time IQ tests were invented to measure intelligence. For decades the results of these tests remained the ultimate authority in judging a person's ability.[43]

The greatest challenge to the supremacy of IQ tests has come from the work of Howard Gardner. As we saw earlier, Gardner believes that there are multiple intelligences. One of the outcomes of his way of understanding the world is that because there are different kinds of giftedness, there need to be different methods of testing to measure these gifts. Like those before him, Gardner acknowledges the importance of both biology and environment in intellectual functioning, but he points out that there are a variety of gifts that are special.

As an educator the question, of course, is what does this mean for education? What is best for these gifted and talented students? Should they be put in accelerated classes or should they be in general classes? And should something be done differently for girls than for boys who are gifted? And what about gifted students who have disabilities? What is best for them? (One can think of Stephen Hawking, who is possibly the most gifted theoretical physicist in the world. He has not been able to walk for years, and can speak only with the aid of a computer. Do you think it is possible that he is a better theoretical physicist because of his physical disabilities?)

---

[42] William Heward, *Exceptional Children: An Introduction to Special Education*, 5th ed. (Englewood Cliffs, N.J.: Prentice-Hall, 1996) pgs. 536–7.

[43] We will spend more time on tests in a later chapter.

There are differing opinions about what is best for the gifted. The National Association for Gifted Children calls for: 1) a greater effort to identify them early, and 2) group them in "accelerated classes, enrichment programs, advanced placement programs, etc."[44] Others believe that placing gifted students in general classes not only does not hurt them academically, but actually helps the other students. Later in the chapter we will discuss the idea of inclusion in more detail.

We know that a disproportionate number of minorities are put into special education programs. There is also a disproportionate number of minorities at the other end of the gifted and talented scale. The difference is that there are too many minorities in the special education programs and too few minorities in the gifted and talented programs.

One minority group, Asian Americans, is overrepresented in gifted and talented programs. They are overrepresented by 43 percent, while whites are overrepresented by 17 percent.[45] In 1992, black students represented a little over 21 percent of the school population, but only 12 percent of gifted education—an underrepresentation of 41 percent. Hispanic students were underrepresented by 42 percent. There seem to be several reasons why minorities are placed in gifted classes.[46]

The tests that are used to screen for and identify gifted children do not seem to be inclusive. The Wechsler Intelligence Scale for Children, for example, is not effective in identifying gifted minority students, but it continues to be used. If minority students fail to do well on certain tests, then there is no valid reason to keep using those tests.

The procedures used in the screening and selection of gifted children needs to be broadened. Multiple factors need to be used in the assessment process. In addition to standardized tests, as much qualitative and quantitative information as possible needs to be available. To simply select those who make high scores on a single test is to miss the variety of talents and gifts that students possess.

Parents need to be more involved in the process. They need to not only be able to nominate their children, but to help keep their children in the programs. This can be a class, race, and/or cultural issue. It is important that the gifted from all backgrounds are comfortable in classes for the gifted and talented. While it somehow seems more natural for the children from well-educated, professional families to be in those classes, that is probably just a comment on our biases when we think about what we consider gifted.

As with most things in schools, it is important that teachers know more about the general category of being gifted and more specifically about gifted minorities. From the nomination of these students for special classes, to the ability to teach minorities, it is necessary for teachers of general education to better understand a variety of issues. (The issues, generally, are those we discussed in the race and multicul-

---

[44] Ibid., p. 567.

[45] Donna Ford, "The Underrepresentation of Minority Students in Gifted Education: Problems and Promises in Recruitment and Retention," *The Journal of Special Education*, Vol. 32/no.1, 1998, p. 5.

[46] The following points are made in ibid., pgs. 10–12.

tural chapters.) As gatekeepers, teachers are central to recognizing and encouraging the gifted.

Finally, it is necessary for some minorities to be given additional support services and educational opportunities. For decades, minorities have come from less rigorous schools. No matter how gifted and talented they might be, if their preparation has been poor then classes for the academically talented will be too difficult and stressful. While one answer is more help, another answer is a fifth year in high school. Interestingly, there are elite prep schools that have programs for these students. These schools provide full funding for a postgraduate year for gifted minorities. On the other hand, one suspects asking a bright eighteen-year-old to stay another year in his or her high school would not meet with much success.

It is not a surprise that, given all the problems facing public schools, finding funding for gifted minorities is not a high priority. A good case can be made that it is too bad that we continue to ignore or waste some of our best and brightest students. The cost is across-the-board: from the individual who does not get the education he or she deserves, to society that misses the contributions he or she might have made as an adult. To deny education to special students—special in any way—does not reflect well on our society.

There is one last question that needs to be considered, and it is certainly as important as any we have asked so far in this chapter. The question is about inclusion, and what the best ways are to think about and teach students in special education.

INCLUSION

We have traced the way in which humanity has thought about and dealt with people with disabilities as well as the gifted and talented. Only recently has there been a sustained effort to recognize and teach these students. It is amazing to realize that many of your parents were still in school when those with disabilities were given the full rights of other citizens. Their experiences were not the same as yours.

There are genuinely difficult questions about how best to educate special students. We noted that the law calls for as much inclusion as possible for those with disabilities, while advocates for the gifted and talented believe that special classes are best for them. It is important to understand more carefully the costs and benefits of inclusion.

There is an interesting catch (a genuine catch-22, if you will) that helps us see just how complicated these issues can be. Two of the fundamental dynamics about special education students are that 1) they should not be labeled, and 2) there should be full (or, as full as possible) inclusion.

It is argued that labeling is to simply focus on the disability or impairment of a child. The label has a way of staying with the individual, and can cause psychological problems. Peers may use these labels as a way to ridicule their fellow student. Adults might react to the label and hold low expectations for these students. The labels are a way of holding students with disabilities out of general classes, and simply increasing the difficulties these students have in adjusting to the culture of the school.

But here is the catch: If a student is not labeled, then he or she cannot receive special services. Without a label, there can be no individualized program, no special intervention, no teachers who know best how to teach that person. It is built into the law that each person who receives special services must be categorized—must be labeled.

So much for psychological trauma. But there are reasons, other than legal, for labeling students.[47] For example, we know that certain disorders are genetic. The argument is that if we can isolate the genetic problem, then it is much easier to find the best method of teaching or training the student. As we come closer to developing a full, chemical map of the human gene (the Human Genome Project), then it seems reasonable that we will have a much better understanding of the genetic causes of certain disabilities. There can be easy scientific tests to discover what is wrong, and once that is done there should be agreed-upon teaching solutions.

Currently, there are about 750 genetic disorders connected with mental retardation. It seems reasonable, if we know the problem, to concentrate on the type of retardation and not simply the degree of retardation. For example, it is much more helpful to know if a student has Williams syndrome than to know only that there is a student with an IQ between 50 and 60. If we know that the person has Williams syndrome, we would expect him or her to speak articulately and fluently, with a good vocabulary and grammatical precision. We would also know the person would have difficulty with tasks involving visual–spatial recall. But if the child had Down's syndrome, we would expect better performance on visual versus auditory tasks.

What the scientists tell us is that the more accurately we can label the cause of the problem, then the better chance we have of understanding the disabilities and then developing teaching strategies.

So, it is a genuine trap. It seems clear that labels can be destructive in several different ways. The effects of labeling can be both short- and long-term. We can all agree to that. Yet, it makes perfect sense that in order to provide the most effective education and training it is important to know exactly what the disabilities are. The effects of labeling, seen this way, are simply an extension of good science: In order to deal with a problem it is necessary to understand exactly what the problem is.

The response, of course, is that to label a student with a number of disabilities is of no great help to the teacher (which problems do you pay attention to first?), and potentially of great harm to the student. As a teacher, you will not only need to know more about disabilities than you thought you would, but also you will need to decide how you will label—or not label—the student with disabilities.

Inclusion

The reason to focus on those who teach in general classrooms is that we are committed to a policy of the fullest inclusion possible. Inclusion is the policy that is most difficult to realize, and is the focus of a great deal of tension in special education. To best

---

[47] This comes from Robert Hodapp and Deborah Fidler, "Special Education and Genetics: Connections for the 21st Century, *The Journal of Special Education*, Vol. 33, no. 3, 1999, pgs. 130–7.

understand the current state of special education, it is necessary to know the debate about full inclusion.

By the mid-1990s, more than 5 million students (about 10 percent of school-age children) were in special education. The cost was about $30 billion per year. One of the genuine problems was that the outcomes of people in those programs were disappointing.[48] Students with disabilities often had double the dropout rate of other students. Their graduation rate was only 45 percent, and their success in postsecondary education was limited. The rate of special education graduates who go on with their schooling is about half of that of other students. The highest rate of unemployment for any subgroup is those with disabilities, and they have a lack of success in community living. Too many parents report that their adult children with disabilities continue to live at home.

Those who favor full inclusion argue that these statistics would improve if students in special education were not isolated. Their arguments generally begin with a belief that the laws that we reviewed earlier need to be carried out. "The newer laws assume that equal access means full access to regular resources—regular classes and schools, but with special support, to help students 'more alike than different from people without disabilities.'"[49]

The argument is that separate but equal is never equal, and that equal access, in this case, is not equal education. These people argue that mainstreaming is not enough. Not only should special education students have full inclusion, but they will also need help in that environment. For both social and psychological reasons, special education students need to be included in regular school activities and regular school classrooms. The argument is that the more inclusion there is, the better the chance that these students will live a more full and integrated life when they are adults. Given the figures on the poor educational outcomes of students with disabilities, it is clear that something different, and better, needs to be done.

There are several reasons why schools are slow to provide the most inclusion possible for their special education students.[50] Often, the preparation of teachers in general classrooms is inadequate. Because full inclusion is a relatively new policy, too many teachers do not have the training to teach students with disabilities.

Schools often do not have appropriate policies and structures to best help students with disabilities. For example, there might be a lockstep curriculum that works well for regular classrooms but not for inclusive classrooms. Does a teacher, in addition to handling an already overloaded workday, need to shape a different curriculum for each student? There may also be a lack of attention to the cultural aspects of schooling. The point is that the mainstream culture of the school must be one that accepts students with

---

[48] See Dorothy Lipsky and Alan Gartner, "Equity Requires Inclusion: The Future for All Students with Disabilities," in Carol Christensen and Fazal Rizvi, editors, *Disability and the Dilemmas of Education and Justice* (Philadelphia: Open University Press, 1996), p. 148.

[49] Jack Nelson, Stuart Palonsky and Kenneth Carlson, *Critical Issues in Education: Dialogues and Dialectics*, 4th ed. (Boston: McGraw-Hill, 2000), p. 417.

[50] Ibid., p. 425.

disabilities. If it is not, then the chance of genuine inclusion disappears. Finally, often school leadership practices benign neglect towards special education students. For full inclusion to take place, there needs to be strong leadership at all levels of the school for genuine change to take place. Business as usual is certainly the easiest way to run a school, but in too many cases it is neither in the best interest of students with disabilities, nor is it legal.

Problems with Inclusion

Few dispute the idea that the policy of inclusion is a just and good one. However, it is also a very complex policy that we still do not fully understand. We do not have the studies that show us exactly how effective the greatest possible inclusion is, nor do we have the studies that show us the possible negative effects of inclusion. Inclusion is an evolving idea that we need to put into context and both think and speculate about.

The context of inclusion is the public school system.[51] As we know, for the past 150 years that system has been geared to the socialization of students and teaching them to be good citizens and workers. Its focus has not been on individual differences, but on how to school the largest number of children who will produce the best instructional outcomes. Put differently, dealing with individual differences has never been an aim of our schools.

Around the turn of the last century, as the new progressive education philosophy was taking hold, Elizabeth Farrell, a New York City schoolteacher, had the idea of special day-classes for "over-age children, so-called naughty children, and the dull and stupid children."[52] Given the political context that dictated the teaching of "normal" students who would become productive citizens, creating special classes was the obvious thing to do. The idea of inclusion developed very slowly, and as we saw did not become policy until federal law made it so.

The tensions surrounding inclusion are clear. There is an unavoidable truth that human differences come "in conflict with the ambition to build systems of universal mass education."[53] The moral strength of special education's concern for individual differences turns out to be a difficult political problem. What must a school system do to take care of those differences when its goal is to provide the best mass education possible?

Certainly there are benefits for everyone if those with disabilities are included in general classes. But there are also other factors to consider: "it is difficult to dispute the fact of 'disabled' students' lower achievement compared to that of non-disabled peers. There is also little dispute that available remedies will cost more on a *per capita* basis than the public typically expends for students not considered disabled."[54] Do we know the psychological effect on disabled students who do not do as well as their

---

[51] Michael Gerber, "Reforming Special Education: Beyond 'Inclusion'," in Christensen and Rizvi, op. cit., p. 165.

[52] Ibid., p. 161.

[53] Ibid., p. 157.

[54] Ibid., p. 165.

peers? Do we know if it is a wise policy to structure a situation in which a student will always be at a comparative disadvantage?

There is no doubt that if the curriculum remains the same, then access to the general classroom is not good for the special student. If the values of independence and productivity are to be furthered, then most existing instructional arrangements need to be changed. We also know that there seem to be a minority of schools with the leadership, funding, and imagination to make full inclusion work. The point is that we have a policy of inclusion but so far have neither the funds nor the will to implement it in a sensible and sensitive way.

There are two additional legal points that need to be made in order to get a better understanding of the pressures felt by school administrators. In *Honig v. Doe*, the court decided that, once identified, students with disabilities were "explicitly entitled to appropriate educational interventions that cannot be limited or interrupted by unilateral decisions by school administrators."[55] School officials cannot suspend or expel any student who might be "disruptive, aggressive or violent regardless of whether such behavior is related to disability." Naturally, officials are not pleased with the policy. The power of these officials was not only diminished, but the potential for behavioral problems increased.

The second legal point is equally troubling to school officials. It has to do with funding. In *Timothy W. v. Rochester*, the school sought relief from the courts. They believed it was inappropriate to be forced to provide education to a student who was "a completely unresponsive profoundly retarded child." An appeals court overturned the lower court and ruled that the federal law mandating special education "required no test of educability as a precondition for the provision of special education and related services. . . . Simply stated, children do not have to prove they can learn before schools must commit themselves to an exploratory effort to teach them."

It is time to sit back and think about these issues. There are both moral and good pedagogical reasons for students with disabilities to be included in as much general education as possible. The advocates point to the psychological, social, and educational benefits of inclusion. The argument is that inclusion is not only the right thing to do, but also the policy of the nation.

On the other hand, there seems to be a number of serious practical matters that need to be considered. It is legitimate to consider the psychological cost of being in an environment in which you will never achieve as much as your peers. And even in the best kind of inclusive classroom, one in which students with special needs have tutors, how will they feel with that kind of attention? Certainly the financial aspect of first-rate special education has to be considered. It is very possible that school officials will adopt a policy of inclusion in order to move special education funding to general classroom use. While that would be both a corruption of the intent of the policy and a misuse of funds, it would not be a surprise if that is what happens.

We live in a time of increasing academic accountability. There are evolving basic standards that more and more states are adopting. If legislatures are going to increase

---

[55] This and the following quotes come from ibid., p. 167.

the funding for pubic schools, then they will certainly anticipate and insist on higher test scores. How does this square with the public policy that mandates all students be given a chance of an education, even if there is little or no chance for them to learn? Will the legislatures believe this is a waste of funds? Will school officials consciously adopt policies to somehow use special education funds for regular classes in order to achieve more acceptable educational outcomes?

As with so many educational issues, there are few easy answers. To see the situation in the most optimistic way, we have done more in the last quarter of a century for students with disabilities than the combined efforts of humanity going back to the beginnings of civilization. But we now seem stuck as a result of the mix of morality, reality, and competing political ideology. While it may well be that, someday, we will know the best way to handle inclusion, we currently lack the data and imagination to say, without hesitation, what the most effective policy will be.

And, to be realistic, when we do understand what is best, there will be questions about adequate school funding, as well as finding and educating teachers.

The only thing we know for certain is that much work needs to be done so that we can fulfill our commitment to provide a good education to all of our children.

SUMMARY

The history of how people with disabilities have been treated is shameful. From the early Greeks to three-quarters of the way through the twentieth century, those with disabilities were treated as less than human. While there were efforts to make things better, on the whole progress was sickeningly slow.

In 1975, federal law finally recognized the humanity and the rights of those with disabilities. The law called for the best and most inclusive education for special students. We reviewed the laws that related to the handicapped and some of the issues surrounding the funding needed for special education.

We discussed different types of disabilities (both physical and psychological) and who (which populations) were most affected. The data showed there was a relationship between disabilities and socioeconomic status. It is clear that poverty leads to an increased number of disabilities. We discussed the idea that special students may also be gifted students.

Finally, we took up the popular idea of inclusion and tried to figure out if it was the best educational policy for everyone. As with many issues in education, there was no clear answer.

THINK ABOUT

This is less a question than an exercise. It is merely a suggestion of the number of disabilities that people have.

Think about a normal day in your life. Think about your specific living situation, class location, major, social life, and future plans. Now, think about what you did yesterday and spend a few minutes writing it down. After you have done that, think about what that day would have been like if you had one of the following disabilities.

You were run over and paralyzed from the neck down. You have an electric wheelchair that has been adapted so you can steer it with your mouth.

As a result of diabetes, you had to have your legs amputated above the knee. You are a paraplegic. You have recently been fitted with artificial legs and are learning to use them. Your balance on them is poor and you are using a cane.

You slipped on some stairs and suffered a head injury that has brought complete blindness. Doctors don't know if your sight will ever improve.

You were born blind.

You have been completely deaf since birth. The first language you learned was American Sign Language, in which you are very fluent. You can read English acceptably, but you do not lip-read very well. Your speech is difficult for others to understand.

Due to a throat tumor, you have lost your voice completely. Eventually, you may be able to be fitted with an appliance that lets you produce synthetic speech, but for now you are mute.

You have a learning disability. It is a type of dyslexia that makes it just about impossible for you to understand or remember what you read, although you have no trouble understanding and remembering what you hear.

You have a learning disability that manifests itself as problems with spatial organization. You have trouble distinguishing left from right, north from south, up from down, ahead from behind. You can't visualize things in three dimensions. You can't read a map.

You have contracted AIDS as a result of having unprotected sex. You are currently fairly healthy, but must take medications eight times per day. The medications are very expensive and have uncomfortable but not life-threatening side effects. You do not know how long the medications will continue to work.

You are diagnosed with multiple sclerosis. You know it will progress, but you do not know how quickly. You are having more and more trouble walking and you are tired a great deal. The symptoms are episodic and there are occasionally days when you cannot make it across campus to class. Your ability to think and study is unimpaired. At this point you need to use a cane most of the time and getting around campus is really difficult—impossible where there are great distances to cross, stairs, or icy or uneven pavement.

You are an alcoholic. Although you have tried to stop drinking, have gone to treatment and AA and even into an in-patient clinic for a while, you have been unable to stop. When you start drinking, you may binge for days, missing work and classes and not always remember much when you finally sober up. One of your parents says this is a "disease" to which you are prone, while the other says you could quit if you really tried.

CHAPTER NINE

BUREAUCRATS AND POLITICIANS
Who Controls the Classroom?

So long as myths of hierarchy function as the most basic premises of the social sciences they must remain apologetics, teaching every man, in Montesquieu's words, ". . . new reasons . . . to love his prince, his country, his laws"; thus restricting the range of human adaptation, and rationalizing the mad schemes of rulers.

Larry Spence

The stuff of politics properly understood is the continual debate and struggle over the connection between person troubles and collective or constitutional facts and issues.

Michael Leiserson

When you walk into the classroom and close the door, you are in control. That, of course, is only marginally related to reality—sort of the myth of autonomy of the closed door. While you are certainly responsible for many things—what your students learn, how they behave, and the like—the truth is, there are a remarkable number of things over which you have no control.

In this chapter we will review many of the forces that help dictate the conditions in which you teach, what you will teach, and why you will teach it. Public schools seem to be at the will of everything from the federal government to state and local governments, local tax rates, national research institutes that cater to the desires of business, and the familiar belief that business techniques are appropriate for educational institutions.

In the following chapters we will discuss other influences—like popular culture, technology, and the publishing industry—but for now we will focus mainly on the political and business realms. During the election of 2000, education was a major topic. As we have seen, we as a people have always relied on schools to help the United States achieve important goals. A hundred and fifty years ago schooling sought to make us a nation, and then an industrialized nation. Schools helped Americanize new citizens, integrate the population, and provide opportunities for those with disabilities.

From the president of the United States to local school boards to district super-intendents to school principals, from local tax collection to those who believe in the principles of business, people with money and power have tried to dictate the role of schooling and—of course—what each teacher should be doing.

We will begin with the federal government (which pays the least but has great symbolic power) and work our way down. We will see how much truth there is to the idea that when a teacher walks into class and closes the door, he or she is in control.

NATIONAL POLITICS

Education is the largest enterprise of American governments. It employs 20 percent of the labor force in the United States (almost 7 million people), and amounts to about 7.8 percent of the gross domestic product[1]. In terms of numbers, in 1993 there were approximately 14,700 school districts and 110,000 schools in the United States. The majority of the money for these schools comes from local taxes and state aid. The federal government provides less than 10% to public schools. The frequently cited reason is clear enough: Education is not mentioned in the Constitution. It has always been up to state and local districts to formulate and fund educational policy.

But, like most absolutes in American government, it is foolish to believe that the federal government has left schooling alone. The federal government has been involved with public education for about a century and a half. Public lands were set aside in each state by the federal government to help fund state colleges.[2] Almost a hundred years later the government passed the GI Bill, providing money for a college education to soldiers returning from World War II.

Since the 1950s, the federal government has been increasingly involved in pub-lic schools. And, as we will see, both political parties are part of the change. Although Ronald Reagan cut funding to schools, both Presidents Bush and President Clinton were educational activists.

There were two major events that brought the national government into school-ing during the '50s. The first, as we have seen, was civil rights. While funding would follow in later decades, certainly there was a federal presence in the effort to desegre-gate the schools. We need only think about President Eisenhower sending troops to Little Rock to remember what was happening. The second event was when Russia sent a satellite into space.

That satellite caused the public to panic about schooling. There was a great fear that Russian schools (communist, if you will) were much better than schools in the United States. In an effort to produce students who could compete with the international threat, the National Defense Education Act was passed in 1958. It pro-vided money for more and better math, science, and foreign language programs.

---

[1]These are 1992–93 numbers found in Paul Bauman, *Governing Education: Public Sector Reform or Privatiza-tion*, (Boston: Allyn & Bacon, 1996), p. 55.

[2]There were two Morrill Acts that provided public lands.

The federal government had become more active in the business of education. Research universities competed for an increasing amount of research money that was tied to national security.

During the '60s the focus was on poverty and how schools could somehow provide additional help for the disadvantaged. In the mid-'60s the government passed two major pieces of educational legislation. One, the Elementary and Secondary Educational Act of 1965, provided $1.3 billion to schools; the second piece of legislation, the Higher Education Act of 1965, established the National Teacher Corps and a first year allocation of $84 billion for federal scholarships.

By the time Ronald Reagan became president the government had expanded into the areas of women's rights and aid for the disabled. When he came into office, the economy of the United States had been in bad shape for years. There was high unemployment and the national debt was growing. Reagan was ideologically opposed to many governmental programs. For example, he was for increased military spending and for less spending on social services. He was disappointed that he could not get Congress to abolish the Department of Education. However, early in his presidency his huge tax cut was enacted. For some of the population, the economy got much better. During the Reagan presidency the income of richest 1 percent of the population, after taxes, was about equal to the income of the lowest 40 percent.[3] And the national debt was the biggest ever.

During the '60s and '70s the federal government gave money for specific things; it was called *categorical aid*. Money was available, but it was money with strings attached. Put in a more accurate way, with the money went government regulations. The belief by the federal government was that state and local officials failed to get the funding to the people for whom it was intended: minorities, women, the poor, and those with disabilities. Reagan set out to change things.

Of concern for this topic is what Reagan called the "New Federalism." He believed that the federal government should do less while state and local governments did more. He was against the idea of categorical aid. The theory behind the new federalism was that those closest to the problems would be best able to solve them. With his policy of a smaller, less intrusive federal government, funds for social programs were cut. For example, federal aid to elementary and secondary schools fell 21 percent from 1980 to 1984. With his policy of less control, the funds that were appropriated went to states as outright grants. The states could use the money as they wished.

The "New Federalism" gutted many programs for the most needy children. There was less money, not as many regulations, and many fewer students in those programs designed to help students in need. In constant dollars, the federal government continued to spend about 20 percent below the 1980 level on schooling during Reagan's second term. The rich got richer, and poor children paid for it.[4]

---

[3] S. Alexander Rippa, *Education in a Free Society: An American History*, 8th ed. (New York: Longman, 1997), p. 355.

[4] The reality is that the "New Federalism" cut many social programs. In addition, Reagan's economic policies helped make the rich richer, and resulted in the greatest budget deficits we have ever had.

About the time that federal funding was drying up for schools, there was an assault on the quality of education in the United States. There was a conservative attack on schools that was profound and lasting. In ways, we continue to deal with the questions and solutions that came out of the early '80s. In 1983 a key document was produced by the National Commission on Excellence in Education and was titled *A Nation at Risk*. It was the first of many studies and reports that were critical of schooling.

In most political conflicts, the side that controls the agenda generally wins the debate. Any good politician knows that it is totally important to discuss things in your own terms. *A Nation at Risk* captured the terms of the debate. It was a conservative document that set the stage for much of our educational debate for the last twenty years to revolve around conservative ideas. It invaded our classrooms in serious ways.

The basic Reagan/conservative agenda turned away from the major themes that came out of the '60s and '70s.[5] The ideas of equity and access seemed to lose their importance, as did spending much time on those who needed the most help. Given the economic conditions of the early '80s, as well as the perception that the United States was falling more and more behind in global competition, as well as Reagan's brand of capitalism, it was no surprise that the focus of schooling was to produce better workers. The *Risk* part of the title of the report had everything to do with economic risk.

Schooling, in the Reagan vision, was to produce better warriors in the fight for international economic supremacy. The plan was to return to the old virtues of prayer, discipline, and hard work. Nancy Reagan contributed by suggesting a new drug policy: "Just say no." (To give you a sense of the times, the LSD advocate Timothy Leary scolded Ms. Reagan. He said that the policy should be: "Just say no, thank you." Leary, always the gentleman.)

In terms of school policy, the turn to economic primacy meant several things. It meant that the emphases would be on excellence, on ability, and on developing high standards of performance. The administration believed that there should be school choice for everyone—and the choices could be either public or private schools.

As the federal government cut back on its aid to education, it was up to the states to try and pick up the pieces. By the mid-'80s, state funding for education was up. An effort was made to increase the pay of teachers and to modernize schools. The states followed the lead of the Department of Education and began trying schemes that would improve the performance of their students.

Let's circle back to the introduction of the chapter and think about the idea that when you walk into the classroom and close the door, you are in control. If you went into teaching in order to help the dispossessed in society, if you were interested in the poor or disabled, or interested in racial equality or some kind of multicultural fairness, then there were ways in which you would be out of luck. The political culture of the time demanded that the emphasis be on outcomes. The list of people who fell in line was significant: the president, the executive branch, and much of the Congress; state

---

[5]The following comes, in part, from Joseph Newman, *American's Teachers: An Introduction to Education*, 3d ed. (New York: Longman, 1998), pgs. 309–11.

governments and boards of education; local governments and boards of education; superintendents, bureaucrats, principals, and parents began to see the capitalism/ competition light.

I do not mean to imply that the changes were made all at once. With the exception of the money that was taken away pretty quickly, people have been fighting about the other changes since they were suggested. We will get into the details of some of the issues later in this chapter and in the rest of the book, but for now the point is simply this: The conservative ideological invasion of the classroom began with Ronald Reagan, was set in motion with *A Nation at Risk*, and was presented in a strong and often belligerent way by the then–Secretary of Education William Bennett.[5a]

It should be clear that I am not at all neutral about the conservative revolution of the last twenty years.[6] It is simply a bias that I have no desire to hide. But with the bias is this: What Reagan, Bennett, and that crowd did was impressive politics. More than most politicians in the last thirty years, those conservatives stamped their will on a debate that continues to this day. Because the battles are fought on the terms set by *A Nation at Risk*, that means there are ways in which the fundamental issues of every argument have been settled. The question becomes, will the conservatives get less or more of what they want? And the thing we need to remember is that, in the end, we are simply talking about amounts, and not matters of policy.

In 1988 George Bush promised he would be the "education president." During his presidency he did not do much about education. Much of his attention was on the Gulf War. In the "too little too late" category, Bush and his Secretary of Education Lamar Alexander produced a document titled *America 2000: An Educational Strategy* in 1991. It contained proposals for education for the rest of the '90s.

Their proposals have a familiar ring. In part, Bush and Alexander wanted a voluntary national test of core academic subjects; greater flexibility for teachers—along with greater teacher accountability; innovative schools that would be financed by business; and tax-supported educational choice that would apply to both public and private schools. The magic in the proposal was that Bush argued the reforms would need no additional funding: "The answer does not lie in spending more money on old ways—but to redirect our resources and our energies to new approaches."[7]

Congress debated the Bush proposals. They approved modest spending increases, but few programs were fully funded. As they debated educational policy, Operation Desert Storm was fought and won; but Bush could not translate his sudden popularity into a legislative program that would change schooling. The Democratic Congress essentially killed the president's plan. Not long after, the voters killed his attempt to spend a second term in office.

[5a]Bennett has been a strong conservative voice not only in education, but also in advocating a return to "traditional values." It came as a great surprise to everyone (including his wife) that over the last ten years, he lost $8 million gambling.

[6]To be fair, the reaction of political correctness all too often seemed to go way beyond the realm of good sense. In many ways, political correctness shared the divisive biases of the conservatism it tried to correct.

[7]Newman, p. 312.

The periodically liberal Bill Clinton continued many of the policies that the conservative Reagan had begun. He did not reject *America 2000* but decided to add to it. Clinton called for teachers to have more access to programs that would help increase their skills, and advocated more parental involvement in their children's education. These are certainly goals that most would support.

At his core, Clinton was in favor of going back to the basics. He pushed for national standards and assessments. In an interesting turn, conservatives decided that it would be best to have state standards and assessments, so they opposed Clinton's plan. Later, when we discuss a national curriculum and national standards we will see the genuine problems of such schemes. There are two parts of the conservative wish to concentrate on state and local control. First, they are ideologically in favor of a small (or nonexistent) presence of the federal government in education. And second, they rightly believe that they may have more power in setting the rules and the standards at the state and local level.

There are two points that need to be repeated. Because we are debating a conservative agenda, the discussion is about degree and not of basic principle. The question is not about *if* there should be assessments and standards, but who should set them and what they should be. And, second, if you are a classroom teacher, power is being taken away from you. What real difference does it make if your students need to pass a state exam or a national exam? As a teacher, if there is an exam, then you will need to be certain that your students pass it. As a teacher, you will learn to teach to the exam.

There was more to Clinton's educational policy than simply advancing the ongoing conservative agenda. One of the achievements of the Clinton administration was an attitude of inclusion and acceptance. This was the case in education as in other areas. Unlike Reagan and Bush, Clinton was willing to allocate more funds for schooling. It could be argued that the most significant achievement of the Clinton presidency was the sense of inclusion that he fostered. While it is the kind of contribution that really cannot be quantified, there is little doubt that the mainstream mood of the country was simply more accepting under Clinton.[8]

The 2000 Election and "W"

Education was a central issue during the 2000 presidential campaign. Both Al Gore and George W. Bush seemed to agree that schools were in need of help. The agreed-upon critique was this: Schools needed money, students needed to improve their scores on standardized tests, there were questions about the quality of teaching, buildings needed repairs, and families needed more options.

Because Bush is president[9] it is his ideas we will review. They are the ones that set the agenda for at least four years. In his campaign, Bush called for more testing of

[8]If one were to guess, there will be a closing down under Bush. His cabinet appointments were not noted for their openness.

[9]While there is some question that he actually won the election, this is not the place for that discussion.

both students and teachers. He wanted every state to annually test students in grades 3–8 in both reading and math. He promised to provide $3 billion for loan guarantees for new charter schools, and spend another $5 billion to improve students' reading skills. But the most spending would go for testing.

If you are a classroom teacher, the Bush agenda is interesting. For a conservative president who does not believe in an active federal government, Bush wants to broaden its role in education. While the traditional wisdom is that because the Constitution does not mention education, it is something best left to local and state government, what we are seeing is that there is an increasing federal stake in what is going on.

President Bush pointed to the success of education in his home state of Texas as he campaigned. In particular, he pushed testing and, while he was governor he was proud that test scores went up. It is instructive to get a sense of how that success came about.[10] What we can begin to see are some of the issues involved in figuring out success. In a later chapter, we will return to these issues.

While Bush is perfectly accurate in saying that scores went up, three things were going on that make the claim less compelling than one would hope. First, the Center for Study of Testing at Boston College reported that the overall dropout rate in Texas is at least 20 percent, and that the rate is as high as 50 percent for minorities. We read: "Texas has gotten a huge amount of press, but in my view, it is largely a scam. The test scores have been going up because they have been pushing large numbers of kids out."[11] In other words, if the poorest students drop out, then you can expect that scores will improve.

The tests themselves have come into question. A Harvard researcher analyzed the Texas tests and found that the reading tests that were given from 1995 to 1998 had been lowered on a regular basis. For example, a former member of the Dallas School Board "noted that the governor . . . won passage of legislation that would require an 11th-grade test be based on 10th-grade knowledge." While that does not go into effect until 2004, it is acknowledged that the test a student must pass in the tenth grade is based on a minimum skill level of an eighth-grader.

The final part of Texas school improvement has to do with money. Indeed, it is a policy that Governor Bush is firmly against, but is credited with doing a great deal of good. In 1994 the Texas Supreme Court approved something call "Chapter 41." It came to be known as Robin Hood. What the law did was take property tax money from rich districts and give it to poor districts. Before Robin Hood, rich school districts in Texas spent about $6,000 per student, while poor districts spent about $3,500 per student. Robin Hood equalized spending at about $5,400.

The increased funding helped poorer schools. The reason why Bush did not mention this during his campaign is that he opposed a "court-ordered system I tried to change."

The point of all this is not to attack the campaign run by George Bush, or diminish the changes that have occurred in Texas. The point is that it seems presi-

---

[10]We will look at this in more detail in following chapters. This information comes from *The Boston Globe*, written by Michael Kranish, April 23, 2000.

[11] Ibid., p. 3. The quote is from Walter Haney, the author of the Boston College study.

dential elections will play an increasingly important role in how we think about and do schooling. For teachers, the federal government is becoming another player who might control what goes on in the classroom.

Legislation passed during the early Presidency of George Bush may well influence what goes on in your classroom. The key legislation is the No Child Left Behind Act of 2001. The heart of the act requires every state to annually test each student in math and English. In related legislation, the Office of Education, Research, and Improvement was replaced by the new Institute of Education Services. In the new institute, the What Works Clearinghouse was formed. It is the Clearinghouse that is of particular interest.

The Clearinghouse will collect all research data on the most effective ways of teaching. Effective, in this case, means what works best in producing good test results. Remember, the key legislation called for yearly testing—so effective teaching means getting students to do well on tests. It marks, in significant ways, a huge change in the way education is viewed. We have seen how complex teaching and learning is; we have seen the variety of moral and practical aims education can have; we have seen how complex and multifaceted any single school can be. Those things, if we are to take the new Clearinghouse seriously, are just so much clutter.

Continual testing added to the notion that there are scientific ways of obtaining good test results. It will also have dramatic effects of how much control you have in your classroom. In the next chapter we will deconstruct the idea of testing, but for now it is only necessary to say that any science of teaching is rooted deeply in myth and fantasy.

But we know that the federal government is only one of the major players in influencing the direction of schools. We turn our attention to the business community, which is the second strong influence at the national level.

BUSINESS

Earlier, in our overview of the history of education in the United States, there was a discussion of the role of business. To recall some of that discussion, at the turn of the twentieth century, political progressives began turning to professionals in order to make school systems more efficient.[12] By 1915 the work of Frederick Taylor had become a powerful force in American thinking.

What Taylor invented was scientific management. He believed that it was possible to analyze, plan, and control every detail of a manufacturing process. What is important for us is the underlying idea that through standardization and planning there would be increased efficiency. The basic dynamic was simple: If management understood the process well enough, and if workers simply followed directions, then work could be done quickly and efficiently. The rational application of the laws of science, according to Taylor and his followers, would make any (and every) organization better.

---

[12]For a brief description of this, see Kathleen Bennett deMarrais and Margaret LeCompte, *The Way Schools Work*, 3d ed. (New York: Longman, 1999), pgs. 74–9.

This kind of mental revolution was perfect for a population that had begun to distrust political machines. It was an obvious decision to bring the principles of business into the service of public schools. As we will see, there are some serious problems when schools are thought of as factories and teachers as workers in an assembly line, but the principles of business have been a central core of American thought for some time.

Schools, for example, were not exempt from the problems of the Great Depression of the 1930s. In one month, 770 schools closed for lack of funding. There was no provision for 175,000 students.[13] In such times it makes all the sense in the world to try and be as efficient as possible. The lack of money took its toll on schooling in the United States. The argument over how much money schools should get, and how it should be spent, is still with us. In times of economic downturns (and the early twenty-first century is a good example), education and social services are the first to be cut. The idea that the money should be spent in the most efficient manner remains a value with which few will argue.

A second part of the role of business in schooling has to do with a more recognizable political ideology. We can see this most easily in times of tension. For example, during the '30s and '50s there was a big push to introduce programs and materials into the school systems that taught and supported capitalism. The Depression, then the Cold War in which communism was the enemy, mobilized the business community. Capitalism was the American way, and any threat to capitalism was clearly understood as a threat to the United States. Schools were not only expected to produce people with the correct economic preference, but produce good workers. From the beginnings of the industrialization of the United States to right this very minute, one of the major goals of schooling has been to educate the best workforce in the world.

In no small way, business was fully involved with *A Nation at Risk*, the report that dominates our current educational debates. We read:[14]

> The linkage of education to the global economic competition motivated a cross section of American leaders from government and the private sector to reach a consensus on the need for school reform. With the business community's involvement came added pressure and support for the excellence movement; the participation of leading corporate CEO's helped overcome the resistance of fiscal conservatives to increase funding for schools.

Interestingly, the concerns of business were critical in forcing Reagan to not only stop his campaign to dismantle federal aid to education, but to actually reinstate some of the cuts. The monies going to education were to help insure the quality of the future workforce. Other goals, such as equity issues, were put aside.

What is important to understand is that the idea of producing good workers who believed in capitalism is only the tip of the business iceberg. There is a business mindset that is so powerful, and so accepted as part of how our everyday reality

---

[13]This is found in Rippa, op. cit. p. 236.

[14]Robert Carlson, *Reframing and Reform: Perspectives on Organization, Leadership, and School Change* (New York: Longman, 1996), p. 201.

should operate, that we often simply ignore it. It seems appropriate to review at least some of these principles in order to better understand the forces that intrude on a teacher's autonomy.

Much of what follows is from one book.[15] It is most instructive, in no small part, because of the men who wrote it. The main author is Louis Gerstner Jr. At the time, Gerstner was chairman and CEO of IBM. The other authors are: Roger Semerad, a former senior vice president of RJR Nabisco and president of RJR Nabisco Foundation; Denis Doyle, a senior fellow at the Hudson Institute and a former director at the American Enterprise Institute; and finally, William Johnston, who was executive vice president of Burson-Marsteller, a senior fellow at the Hudson Institute, and a member of the RJR Nabisco Foundation.

While *Reinventing Education* is neither the only nor probably the best book about how to change education, for our purposes it may be the most instructive. The authors are powerful men. Their professional accomplishments fill pages, and I have offered only their most recent affiliations. They are very successful, very conservative businessmen. What they have written gives us a very good view of the business mindset that underlies so much of how we think.

The bottom line (and how "business" is that?) is this: "Society pays the bills and wants results."[16] How much more clear could that be? In this vision, we find that "outputs are what markets are about [and] outputs are what schooling is about. Outputs—the difference going to school makes."[17] To make that real, we are told, schools need to state their goals clearly and then measure the progress of their students.

In order to make that happen, money needs to be spent in a different way. More money needs to go to "various technologies of communication and instruction, training, management, record-keeping, diagnostics and testing."[18] Although this is clearly a full takeover of the class from the teacher, remember that these are capitalists who are doing the writing. In order to make their plan acceptable, they suggest something that makes total economic sense: that the teachers who produce the best results should be given the most rewards. And, for these businessmen, the "best" results can be measured.

In order to be productive, schools need to use time more effectively. Four things must change: there needs to be more uninterrupted study sessions, more homework, longer school days, and longer school years.[19] The authors argue that there is simply too much to learn in only 180 days a year. They point to Japan as the model for what needs to happen; in Japan a student attends school 243 days a year. The word *more*, it seems, is an important educational concept.

---

[15]Louis Gerstner, et.al., *Reinventing Education: Entrepreneurship in America's Public Schools* (USA: A Plume Book, 1995).

[16] Ibid., p. 239.

[17] Ibid., p. 51.

[18] Ibid., p. 75.

[19] Ibid., pgs. 77–9.

Currently, we read, there are two inappropriate concepts at work in most schools. The idea of a "student-centered" school is as wrong as the idea of a "school-centered" approach. What we have learned is that "in business and in other high-performance organizations [there needs to be] a science of management."[20] What effective schools need to do is learn how to manage people, not to manipulate them. School leaders need to read the works of Peter Drucker in order to understand that there are no such things as bad workers, just workers who are out of place.

The argument is that neither the teachers nor the students are "bad." The problem is the system. We learn that we need to reconceptualize schools, and understand that students are the workers and teachers are the managers of instruction. Teachers orchestrate the work effort. And technology must be used the way it is used in business. Not only should it take care of tedious tasks (scheduling, record keeping, bus routing, inventory control, etc.) but we read that computers "increase the rate at which students learn and the depth of coverage they are able to achieve."[21] [In Ch.11 we will see that the data does not support this contention.] The good news, we read, is that "schools are so low-tech and labor intensive that they have no place to go but up."

Thank goodness.

We will take up the last part of this business equation in the last chapter, but it is fair to mention it here. At the macro level, solutions can begin to be found by relying on markets. In other words, it is important that schools begin to compete for students. The capitalist model suggests that products are better if there is a free market in which people have choices.

There are, I assume, many of you who have a great deal of sympathy (and possibly even faith) in all or most of what Gerstner and his friends advocate. The ideas have a certain logic, and it may well be that we are on the cusp of serious changes in schooling. This chapter is not about change, but about those forces that intrude on classroom teachers.

There are some basic questions about the business model that need to be taken up. Remember, the values of business revolve around profits. These are the people who gave us things like sweatshops and child labor in the last century, and who are very willing to put plants in other countries and pay young workers very low wages to produce expensive products. Being greedy and selfish are time-honored ways to act in a market economy that is measured by economic results. At the far end of that scale are the leaders of Arthur Andersen, Enron, and WorldCom. What is important to remember is that business skills are not the same as the ability to think.

Two observations by Paul Bauman help us understand in a different way: "When administration is defined as a science, the vocabulary is muted and limited to rational and mechanistic arguments . . . The 'school as a factory' metaphor

[20] Ibid., p. 237.

[21] Ibid., p. 248.

implies that governance should reflect the values of hierarchy, specialization, and control . . . [to use the] metaphor of 'schools as hospitals' signifies the concern that schools should respond to the pain and suffering of children in urban industrial environments."[22]

Here is an earlier critique of business:

> . . . What about market business, and the private contracts which they make with one another in the market place; add, if you wish, cases of insulting behavior, ill treatment, the bringing of lawsuits, the establishment of juries, the payment and assessment of dues that may be necessary in markets or harbour, and all the regulations in the market, the city, or the harbour, and all other such . . .[23]

The critique was made by Plato, speaking through Socrates. As you recall from chapter one, Socrates created his city based on education. I suppose it should come as no surprise that he was no great advocate of the ways of business.

While there is little doubt that there are business techniques that are able to help the administration of schools, there is also little doubt that schooling is infinitely more complicated than business. Schools are not factories, goals are not easily agreed upon, students are never merely workers, and teachers (at least the good ones) are more than and different than simply managers of learning. Abraham Maslow wrote that if you were a hammer, then everything you saw looked like a nail. One fears that these remarkably successful capitalists see everything in capitalistic terms. When it comes to schooling, one size does not fit all—just as one dominating ideology will never satisfy the needs of schooling in a complex and multifaceted and multicultural society.

Administrative Work

The focus of the last part of the business section has to do with more practical concerns for the classroom teacher. The focus is on the nature of administrative work. We know that most schools are part of a larger administrative structure. From the turn of last century, part of the dynamic of schooling has been the bureaucratization of public schools. It began as a way to take control away from political bosses and to help school systems become more efficient. Graduate schools of education began educating men (yes, remember that men were to be bosses, and women were to be teachers) to run the organizations of education.

This is simply a fact of modern life in the United States: In order to understand how things work, it is necessary to understand how organizations work. While this is certainly not the place for even a brief history of how these ideas developed, a good course in organizational theory can give you wonderful insight

---

[22]Paul Bauman, *Governing Education: Public Sector Reform or Privatization* (Boston: Allyn & Bacon, 1996), p. 24.

[23]G. M. A Grube, translator, *Plato's Republic* (Indianapolis, Ind.: Hackett, 1974) p. 91.

into the history of the last hundred years.[24] From the time–motion studies of scientific management, to relatively sophisticated temporary organizations, to the ideas of organizational psychologists, to understand organizations is to understand the past and the present.

There is a traditional tension between a centralized school administration and individual classrooms. Supervisors want control, and teachers want autonomy. The closed classroom door on the long, motel-like school hall, at least temporarily shuts out "superiors." What we have seen is that autonomy is, increasingly, an illusion. While it is certainly true that good administrative practices can save money, it is equally true that there are political tensions that are an everyday part of administrative life.

The built-in tensions between administers and teachers begin with the simple fact that school administrators (those "above" the school principal on the organization chart) are not in the same place as teachers.[25] As managing school systems has become more complex and jobs more specialized, it is no surprise that these organizations have become increasingly bureaucratic. In the school hierarchy, those with the most power are located at a central office, and those at the bottom of the chain of command (teachers and principals) are in different buildings.

Distrust of the central administrators is one of the possible results of this physical distance. Also, decisions made in schools are often delayed or postponed until the central office gives its approval. On a routine basis, those in schools try to guess what the central office might say or might want before making decisions. This constant second-guessing is a natural outcome of bureaucratic structure and physical location. One dynamic of bureaucratic structures is that bureaucrats work hard to keep and expand their power.[26] It is in the best interest of the central administrative office to keep each school dependent. That principals and teachers are kept guessing what their superiors might rule is a way for those at the top to keep their power.

The central staff generally has the first look at those who apply for positions in schools. Those who hire teachers in each school are given a list of applicants that has already been screened. And for a principal to fire a teacher is extraordinarily difficult. With strong unions and much support, it is rare that a teacher is fired. Often, the best a principal can do is have the teacher transferred to another school.

While much of what goes on can be understood in bureaucratic terms, school administration is more and different than that. There are many things over which the administration has no control. For example, it is an organization that does not control its own funding. Part of the work of the central administration is to deal with the politics of the state and federal offices of education, as well as the local politics of taxes

---

[24]On the other hand, a bad course can be deadly boring. Take the course less as a how-to-do-it and more as a way to understand the way our organizations have evolved. Never forget this bottom line: When there is a conflict between an individual and an organization, always bet on the organization. While you might lose a couple of times, mostly organizations win.

[25]Much of this is found in deMarrais and LeCompte, op. cit., pgs. 185–8.

[26]For a description of this dynamic, see Joel Spring, *Conflict of Interests: The Politics of American Education* (New York: Longman, 1988), pgs. 38–41.

and money. The superintendent is at the mercy of a school board. The board is generally an elected body that has the power to fire and hire the chief administrator.

Finally, the central office cannot fully control any single classroom. Given the distance between buildings and the multiple tasks of the administration, there is a certain amount of freedom that each teacher has. To be clearer, it is not unusual that teachers will break rules if they believe they can get away with it. But as we have seen, if the idea of standardized tests becomes a reality, and teachers are judged on how well their students do on those tests, then the freedom of each teacher will be markedly diminished.

THE POWER OF STATES

While the federal government and the mind-set of business are increasingly intrusive in schooling, state governments continue to have more power. Governors, legislators, and state boards of education and state superintendents each have the capacity to make substantial changes in schooling in their state. To recall, because education is not mentioned in the Constitution, it has traditionally been in the realm of state and local officials to control schools.

As the chief administrative official in the state and the person who generally initiates the budget process, each state governor at least has the power to define the terms of educational debates. While they need the approval of their legislative bodies, the governor is in a position to pick the issues he or she believes are most important.

Tied to the issues, of course, are budget recommendations. Those budgets may be modified, and certain recommendations may be turned down altogether, but the key is that the governor presents a whole package. It is rare that a legislature does more than simply react, and sometimes modify, the governor's recommendations. Because education is so expensive (generally between one-third and one-half of what the state spends) legislators spend a great deal of time on educational issues. Those in the legislature who deal with funding and educational issues are often powerful players in the politics of public schools.

The governor may select state officials who are in charge of the schools, while some states elect top officials. State departments of education are under the direction, ultimately, of the governor's office. With the exception of Wisconsin, every state has a state board of education. These boards carry out three very powerful functions:[27] 1) setting the standards for elementary and secondary schools; 2) setting the standards for teacher education and licensing, and 3) distributing both state and federal funds to local school systems. As we saw, the state gained power under Reagan when he decided that federal funding should be given to the states with few strings attached.

During the past twenty years, especially since the publication of *A Nation at Risk*, states have become strong advocates of change. Education has become a popular topic for politicians, and there has been an almost constant call for reform at the

[27]See Newman, op. cit., pgs. 296–8.

state level. We know that change has often taken the form of competency tests for students and in some cases for teachers. We will take up the subject of testing in a later chapter, but here it is important to note that each state is able to decide if there should be a test (or tests), just how difficult the test may be, and what—if anything—the results of the test mean.

In this sense, schools are genuinely at the will of each state. The kind of tests, the difficulty of the tests, and the meaning of the tests are remarkably different from state to state. For example, we saw that the tests in Texas are very easy. But the tests in Massachusetts are very difficult for both students and teachers. In Massachusetts, as the law is written at this time, many students will not be given high school diplomas, and many teachers who failed their tests have gone to other states to teach. Each state is able to dictate what students need to know—and what the cost of not knowing those things will be.

It is impossible to fully understand the particulars of schooling in the United States simply because of the amount of power held by each state. There are significant variations from state to state based on a number of variables from the culture and history of the region, to the diversity of the population, to the amount of money that is available for schooling, to the traditions of each government. And that is only a part of the story. As we turn to the topic of local power, we will see that it is difficult to know the details of schooling in any one state.

LOCAL POWER

The history of schooling in the United States has been the history of each school district. Although there has been an increasing centralization of power and decision making, in order to have an in-depth understanding of how schools work, it is necessary to focus on one school at a time.

Of course this does not mean that if you interviewed people at the local level—the superintendent or the local principals or teachers or staff—that anyone would make it seem they had power. Each would talk about the demands of the state and the federal government, as well as pressure from parents and directives from school boards. Each could (and probably would) offer convincing arguments about the limited range of things they actually controlled.

(To follow the thought a little further, people in positions of power in the state and federal government would counter that they have little power over what goes on in any single district and even less power in what goes on in any single classroom. The interesting part is that all of these opinions would be accurate. All those blindfolded people are touching a different part of that huge elephant.)

Local control begins with local elections.[28] School boards are elected. That means, among other things, that from time to time different kinds of decisions might be made. It is not unusual for local power structures to dictate who will be elected.

---

[28]The exception is Hawaii, which has one school board for the entire state.

They have the money, connections, and interest to run attractive, bright, and electable people for each campaign. There are districts in which the power of the local board is divided between different groups (this is the pluralist version of politics), and in other places the politics are so contentious that it is difficult to know who will win from one election to the next.

School boards vary in size, but generally they average five to seven members. The average member is a college educated, professional, at least middle-class, a white male with a child or children in school. There is little or no monetary compensation for serving on the board. It can be a stepping-stone for higher political office. It is a way for an individual to become a public figure by doing "good" community service.

The central job of the school board is to make policy for the district. Boards have genuine power. They can decide on class size, teachers' salaries, curriculum, textbooks, new construction, the budget, hiring, attendance policies, and more. What they do not do—or, what they really should not do—is get involved in the implementation of those policies. Those boards that try to micro-manage their districts are simply asking for trouble. The superintendent they hire is responsible for implementation.

We know, of course, that the power of the boards of education must be understood in context. The context is this: States really control schooling, there are a great number of laws that must be obeyed, and the federal government has a say in certain areas. In other words, while the school board is responsible for many policy decisions, those decisions must be in agreement with state, federal, and judicial guidelines.

No matter what the makeup of the school board, it generally wants its values reflected by the superintendent. In those districts that are politically homogeneous (or, are at least ruled by an elite), it is not uncommon for a good superintendent to stay for many years. The more contentious the politics, the more difficult it is for the superintendent to satisfy the board.

Local school boards are a natural place for groups to fight. Business leaders believe that the job of public schools is, in large part, to produce a highly skilled workforce. The religious right is much more interested in the souls of those students, while ethnic and racial groups have still other agendas. Finally, in many communities there are taxpayer groups who are focused on reducing taxes.

School boards are more than simply a symbolic center of politics. Those who serve on school boards do have a say about what the next generation might be like. While we know their power is anything but absolute, they are elected representatives of the community who are in a position to at least try to influence the direction of schooling in their district. It is no accident that in stable, middle-class, pluralist communities, the ties between the board and the superintendent are often close and ongoing.

The Superintendent

The superintendent is the educational professional who advises the board on issues of importance. Superintendents are generally white, middle-class males. They are over forty years old, are well paid, and have multiple and important responsibilities. In

1990 only about 3 percent of superintendents were women.[29] The average length of term for a superintendent is five years.

The superintendent oversees the operation of the district. He or she is the main advisor to the board, prepares budgets, keeps current with state and federal regulations, advises on policy, makes personnel recommendations, is involved with the state board of education and state legislature, and is a key spokesperson to the community—among other things. But what is central for any superintendent is a good relationship with his or her board of education. Without the support of the board, the tenure of the superintendent will be short.

Over the years, the superintendent has become more and more isolated from classroom teaching. It is not unusual for the superintendent to hire "a thick layer of administrative assistants, assistant superintendents, and supervisors" who further insulate the superintendent from the business of the schools.[30] This physical distance has made communication between teachers and administrators less and less likely. To recall a past theme, administration is male, and teaching is female.

When a superintendent has meaningful relationships with teachers it is a reflection of the effort of the individual superintendent. Those kinds of relationships are in spite of the system. It takes a conscious and continuing effort on the part of the superintendent to overcome the bureaucratic structure of schooling.[31] The solution is not that more women should be superintendents (although they should be), but that how power is organized needs to be reconceptualized.[32] We will return to this theme later.

Back to school boards. In those stable, middle-class, pluralist communities life is pretty good for the superintendent. It is a context in which the superintendent and the board can readily agree on policy.

There are other kinds of communities. Where there is no local, political consensus, the superintendent is in a no-win position. Any suggestion will be rejected by at least some of the board—and by that part of the community the board member represents. At the other end of the spectrum are those communities that have no interest in local politics. The role of the superintendent is very different in these cases. The power of the superintendent is unopposed in politically disinterested districts, and whatever suggestions are made are generally accepted.

There are endless variations of the politics of school boards and superintendents. Each is meaningful in any particular case, but there are so many differences that it is impossible to generalize about schooling in the United States. Regional cultures, state governments, local politics/school districts/school boards, local cultures, superintendent styles, principal styles, individual school cultures, and each teacher influence education in any one place and for any one student. Any generalization that would fit all schooling in the United States would be so broad and vague, it would be meaningless.

---

[29]Jackie Blount, *Destined to Rule the Schools: Women and the Superintendency, 1873–1995* (Albany: State of New York Press, 1998), p. 4.

[30]Ibid., p. 167.

[31]Ibid., p. 163.

[32]Ibid., p. 165.

On the other hand, there are some things that influence education that do make a difference. The most obvious thing is funding.

FUNDING

While local governments do the majority of funding in about a third of the states, most of schooling is paid for by state governments. It is common that each contribute between 40 and 50 percent of school funding. The federal government pays for less than 10 percent of school funding. We know that money and power are closely connected, so it is not surprising that states have the final say in most school policy.

But when it comes to the quality of public schools, most often the key variable is local funding. Local districts raise money through property taxes. Those districts with a good tax base (with high property values) are able to raise more money more easily than poor districts. The bigger the budget for a school district almost always means the better the schools. States get money from general sales taxes, personal income taxes, corporate taxes, and sometimes lottery money to help fund schools.

It is important to acknowledge that money is not the only variable. What seems to be the case is that the important variables are tied together. For example, a higher level of education for the parents generally translates into parents being more involved and helpful for their children's education—which is an important key to success. What we know is that the higher the level of education, the higher the average income. So, the kids who live in those districts with high property values not only have schools that are very well-funded, but have parents who are well-educated and interested in their children being well-educated. While the dynamic certainly does not fit every single case, it is generally a very accurate way to understand what happens. Schools in affluent communities are, on the whole, much better than schools in poor communities.

Clearly, one of the major problems for each state is to somehow try to provide quality schooling in each district. The goal, ideally, would be for across-the-board excellence in all districts. But the reality of the situation is that because so much of funding depends on local property values, it has been almost impossible for states to figure out the best way to equalize funding across districts. In fact, by 1998, state supreme courts had found that eighteen states were using unconstitutional methods of financing for their public schools.[33] Because education is, constitutionally, a state power, the United States Supreme Court rarely gets involved in these cases. Case law about public school funding is almost always done at the state level.

Changes in how school funding was understood began in California during the late 1960s. Until then, funding was local and the disparity in funding between districts was both huge and tolerated. A man named John Serrano, the parent of a student in a Los Angeles area school, was unhappy at the poor quality of schooling in his district.

---

[33]Peter Hlebowitsh, *Foundations of American Education: Purpose and Promise*, 2d ed. (Belmont, Calif.: Wadsworth, 2001), p. 349. The following discussion comes from Hlebowitsh.

He was advised by the superintendent of schools that the best thing to do was simply move to a more wealthy district. Serrano could not afford the move. Instead, he sued. The case was *Serrano v Priest*, and it got to the California Supreme Court.

The court ruled that it was unconstitutional for the funding of schools to be related to the property values of the district. They set a new standard—fiscal neutrality—that meant funding should depend not on the wealth of any single district, but on the collective wealth of the state. The result was that the state government became very involved in schooling and its funding. Not surprisingly, things changed dramatically.

The initial attempt to solve the problem of unequal funding were flat-grant programs. Basically, many states decided what the minimal needs were to guarantee an adequate education, and provided each district with that minimal funding. The thinking was that if a district wanted to do more than the minimum, it was free to do so. While a seemingly reasonable approach, it takes little imagination to understand the problems that developed with flat-grant programs. First, "adequate education" and "minimal funding" are wholly arbitrary concepts. Each new governor and each new legislature might have a different definition. Standards, as we know, are ever-changing and always in doubt. Second, the wealthy districts continued to provide much more public school funding for their local schools than did poor districts. Serious funding inequalities continued with flat-grant programs.

The next solution to uneven funding was the foundation program. While the basic concept still revolves around minimal needs for each district, these programs work in a different way. The state sets a minimum level of funding for each school district. In order to fund that level, the state requires a standard tax rate in each district. For those districts that meet the minimum requirements with their local taxes, the state provides no additional funding. For those poor districts that cannot meet the minimum requirements, the state funds the difference.

Some form of the foundation program has been adopted by almost 80 percent of the states. The feeling is that the state is able to provide more funding to poor districts through this plan. While that is the case, the bigger reality is that rich districts continue to provide much more funding to their schools than the combination of local and state funding does for poor districts.

One way to insure more equal funding is to have the state fully fund all schools. Hawaii is the one state that funds the entire system, and the state of Washington is doing it in a modified way. But the generalization that holds up pretty well about American schooling is this: Schools in wealthy districts get more money than schools in poor districts. Examples might be helpful.[34] In Vermont, poor school districts spend about $4,550 per student, while wealthy districts spend almost $9,735 per student. In Montana, the difference is $3,193 to $8,150, while in Kansas it is $4,090 to $7,096.

Although it is a little misleading (because of the difference in the wealth of each state), it is still instructive to know that there are big differences in how much each state spends for education. The lowest spending per student in Mississippi is $2,752

---

[34]These figures come from the National Center for Education Statistics (1998), *Inequities in Public School District Revenues* (Washington, D.C.: U.S. Department of Education).

per year, while the highest in the state of New York is $9,112 per student per year. Some districts in Connecticut spend a little over $8,000 per student, while there are districts in Utah that spend only $2,600 per student. The point, crudely made, is this: There are huge spending differences between school districts in each state, and between one state and another. While money is not the only variable in education, it is an important one, and we in the United States have yet to make the decision to ensure either equal funding or equal education for all of our children.

That does not mean that there have been no attempts to equalize funding. It is important to remember that schooling has always been deeply involved with politics. Certainly issues of taxation and spending are the eternal focus of much political decision making. We can use the state of New Jersey to see just how the debate about equal funding of schools is, in the end, the stuff of politics.[35]

In 1990 the Supreme Court of New Jersey ruled that the way schools were funded was "unconstitutional as applied to poorer school districts." The legislature was instructed to devise a plan in which the poorer urban districts had funding "substantially equivalent" to the richer suburban districts. Later that year, Governor Florio submitted a bill that the legislature passed and that Florio signed into law. It called for the state to help the poor school districts with $2.8 billion in new and increased taxes. The plan called for a reduction in aid to wealthier districts by phasing out subsidies for personnel pensions. Teachers unions and school boards opposed the reduction.

The state concentrated its increased aid to "special-needs" urban districts. It was a way to get money to the poorest districts. As this was taking place, the political context was changing. The democratic Senator Bill Bradley barely won reelection. It was a clear sign that the state was becoming more conservative. Governor Florio's popularity was declining. The new taxes were very unpopular, so he decided to reconsider his plan. With the support of the legislature, a much smaller level of financial redistribution was adopted.

Regrettably for Florio, the compromise did not help him get reelected. He was defeated by Christine Todd Whitman, who campaigned on a platform calling for a reduction of state income tax of 30 percent over three years. In 1994, the state Supreme Court again ruled that the state funding of schools was unconstitutional. The Court said the state had to develop a plan to reduce the disparity of funding between the rich and poor school districts by 1996. In the fall of 1997 a bill was passed and signed into law that would allocate an additional $140 million in state aid to the twenty-eight poorest districts. Interestingly, that sum was substantially less than what a lower court had called for earlier.

One can assume that the problems in New Jersey are not over. It is easy to anticipate court rulings in favor of more equitable funding, legislative responses that somehow do not fully respond to the problems, and much of the electorate actively resisting increased taxes.

We know that societies try to replicate themselves by teaching cultural values to their young. What we need to understand is that there is a hidden curriculum that also

---

[35]The following example is taken from Kenneth Wong, *Funding Public Schools: Politics and Policies* (Lawrence, Kansas: University Press of Kansas, 1999), pgs. 88–9.

gets transmitted.[36] While our students learn how to be good citizens and good employees, there are also messages given in schools that have to do with socioeconomic class. Earlier we saw how teaching differed from school to school according to the wealth of the district. The messages of those different teaching styles are part of the hidden curriculum.

To put this in the theme of the chapter, one of the important things that a teacher, a principal, a superintendent, and the school board cannot control is the level of funding in the district. The range of variables that influence local school funding reaches from taxpayer rebellion to international recession. That OPEC might decide to raise the price of oil, and that decision might mean fewer dollars for public schooling in the United States seems wholly unfair, but that is the nature of politics, money, and public education.

SUMMARY

In many important ways no one controls schooling in the United States. That, most agree, is the good news. We are too individualistic, too tied to our regional and local cultures, too afraid of centralized power to accept the notion that others—that "outsiders"—should have power over what our children learn. There are times when even the state legislature seems like an "outsider" to local school committees.

There are, of course, downsides to local control. For generations, local control was code for segregation and bigotry. It meant that blacks were second-class citizens in some areas of the country, immigrants were treated badly in other areas, and those with different religious backgrounds were not accepted in many places. Although those prejudices are now illegal, and the more outrageous acts of intolerance have either disappeared or are prosecuted, we know that local control can still mean intolerance.

The federal government, along with the business community, continues to have an influence on public schools. Many of their attempts to influence policy are made by providing money with strings attached. In communities across the country businesses hook up with local school districts and try to develop and implement a curriculum that will help ensure students will be trained to be good workers. As we have seen, the federal government is increasingly interested in creating an internationally competitive workforce.

Because the states and local districts are responsible for most of the funding, they generally have the greatest amount of power over schooling. The states have the most control over policy, while the local districts (school boards and superintendents) have the final say in day-to-day operations. Put into the day-to-day decision-making is the school bureaucracy, and there are ongoing tensions between the central office and each school. School principals and school bureaucrats are constantly renegotiating decisions and daily operating policies. Funding is further complicated by the huge

[36]For a full discussion see Tomasz Szkudlarek, *The Problem of Freedom in Postmodern Education* (Westport, Conn.: Greenwood, 1993).

disparity from school district to school district, and the seeming right of wealthy communities to spend all they want on their schools. Whatever principle of equal opportunity we have, is tested by our inability to provide equal schooling for the poor.

Schooling is beyond the control of any person or set of people. The individual who feels that most is the teacher, who enters the classroom responsible for the education of each student, but with less and less real power over a remarkable number of important things. As we enter an era of standardized testing, teachers must increasingly be policy implementers instead of creative educators. In the next chapter, we will take up the idea of standardized tests and texts, and the effect they are having on schooling.

THINK ABOUT

1. Do you believe it is a good thing that power is so diffuse in our educational system?

2. What would you be willing to give up in order to move to a wealthy school district so your children could have a first-rate public education?

3. Can the aims of education be managed by the practices of business?

CHAPTER TEN

THE TYRANNY OF NUMBER TWO PENCILS
Testing

To the Standardistos who don't know kids but know products, I commend a Kurt Vonnegut story where a young man admiring the centerfold of a girlie magazine, says, "Look at that woman!" The older man replies, "Son, that's not a woman, that's a photograph." I'd say the same to Standardistos who rely on skills charts and standardized test scores for their notion of children. I want to tell them, "People, those aren't children, those are numbers."

Susan Ohanian

The more you're concerned with what's "realistic," the more critical you should be of standardized tests. How many jobs demand that employees come up with the right answer on the spot, from memory, while the clock is ticking? . . . And when someone is going to judge the quality of your work . . . how common is it for you to be given a secret pencil-and-paper exam?

Alfie Kohn

. . . if we are not careful, human personality in all its fullness [will be] taken captive into some autistic paradise of methodology.

Gordon Allport

When you walk into the classroom for this chapter, it's not what you see in front of you that is important. When you walk into the classroom, you have been preceded by a remarkable history and possibly a curriculum that makes you seem almost irrelevant. The focus of this chapter is standardized testing, and in many ways it brings together much of what we have already thought about.

The range of the discussion goes from our obsession about testing to our place in the international economy. As a nation we seem to stand alone in our belief in the importance of standardized tests. We believe they can tell each of us the level of our mental abilities, how well or poorly we might do in life, how much we have learned and know, and how well we are taught.

While other nations test, and those tests often determine the future educational life of the student, somehow we in the United States are able to make tests even more important than that. There are those among us who begin testing their children at three in order to get them into the "best" preschools. By the time kids are in grade school, standardized testing is simply a way of life. It is estimated that 143 million students take from 400 to 600 million tests a year.[1]

As we saw, *A Nation at Risk* began the latest round of testing. *Risk* was a report claiming that our schools were bad, that our students were not learning, and that one of the results was that we could not compete in the emerging international economy. The call was for higher standards and more tests. Since then the tests have become more and more "high stakes." In some states, high school students get diplomas only if they pass the tests. There are states and school districts in which school funding depends on how well students do on standardized tests. The stakes are high for everyone. At the national level, we know that George W. has legislated that every student be tested every year.

It all seems pretty reasonable. Opposing high standards sounds silly, and how bad can it be to take a test to see how much you know? There is an undeniable logic to the argument.

What we will see is that the argument about standards and standardized tests is complicated. It is reasonable to ask whose standards get tested; it is reasonable to ask if tests can really tell us either how smart we are or how much we know; it is reasonable to ask if we should expect everyone to have the same set of skills and advance at the same rate.

We also need to think about what standardized tests do to the curriculum—and more importantly, what do those tests mean to those who teach that curriculum? Let's look at that a little differently. Many of us had one or two wonderful teachers. They were able to somehow make the context of the classroom so special that we wanted to learn. That is the unstated goal of the very best teachers.

With high-stakes testing, those tests that carry huge benefits and penalties, it is exactly that kind of teaching that is unacceptable. In this chapter we will get a better understanding of what it means to teach to the test.

Finally, when (if and when) we get our high school diploma, our testing days are not over. As juniors—well, sometime as sophomores—we begin taking practice SATs. As seniors, we take the real thing either once or twice in order to make certain we get a good enough score to at least be considered by most of the better colleges.

Of course, if your parents can afford it, you take a course that helps teach you how to take the test. The courses work.

After college there are standardized tests for graduate school . . . or to be a plumber or even a barber in some states . . . and on and on. What is interesting is that the ability to do well on standardized tests generally has nothing to do with life after school. I can think of no profession that requires workers to sit alone and be

[1] Peter Sacks, *Standardized Minds: The High Price of America's Testing Culture and What We Can Do to Change It* (New York: Perseus Books, 1999), p. 221.

given a very limited time to answer a set of multiple-choice questions. In fact, we will see that there might be a negative correlation between test-taking skills and what it takes to do a good job at work.

I believe in high standards. I believe that there are often right answers to questions and good solutions to problems. Things like reading and writing and being able to think in a reasonable way and speak clearly are very important. I also believe that, much more often than not, standardized tests not only fail to help us judge those things, but they actually hinder effective teaching and good learning.

Tests, in the end, generally fail us.

We will begin the chapter with a history of testing. Earlier in the book there was a brief history; here we will take a more serious look at how our testing culture began.

THE HISTORY OF TESTING

Charles Darwin's cousin, a man named Francis Galton, believed that every person had a measurable general mental ability. He believed that these abilities were inherited and could be passed along from generation to generation. A kind of Darwinian natural selection of the mind. He made up the word *eugenics* to name the field he invented.

In his theory, Galton hypothesized that there was a strong correlation between eugenics and meritocracy, and that it was the role of society to help make certain that the best and the brightest filled the most important roles.[2]

It took a fellow member of the British upper class, Charles Spearman, to quantify Gelton's theory. In 1904, in a paper in the *American Journal of Psychology*, Spearman reported that he had discovered the "general factor" of intelligence. Later, in 1927, Spearman claimed that he could measure human intelligence with "precise accuracy."[3] Although his was a belief that has been enthusiastically accepted in the United States, it is important to keep two serious problems in mind. First, his methodology was very flawed. Second, and probably more importantly, there are real doubts that there is the kind of general factor of intelligence that Spearman believed he had found.

There is little reason to repeat in detail the ideas of Alfred Binet. For our purposes, it is interesting to note that Binet believed that intelligence could be improved. It was not, in other words, fixed at birth and decided only by heredity. People could get smarter and, I suppose, less intelligent. We have seen how the Stanford professor Lewis Terman modified the Binet tests, and most of us, at one time or another, have taken some version of the Stanford-Binet test.

Terman understood that the test he had developed could be an important tool for social change and control. In 1916 he wrote:

---

[2] Ibid., p. 19.

[3] Charles Spearman, *The Abilities of Man* (New York: Macmillan, 1927), p. 411, quoted by Sacks, page 21.

It is safe to predict that in the near future intelligence tests will bring tens of thousands of . . . high grade defectives under the surveillance and protection of society. This will ultimately result in curtailing the reproduction of feeble-mindedness and in the elimination of an enormous amount of crime, pauperism, and industrial inefficiency.

The suggestion that IQ be the basis of social policy is a subtheme that remains with us. There continue to be periodic studies that claim to prove that whole races of people are genetically inferior. The claims are not only racist and wrong, in one way they are also the legitimate legacy of our early testing.

In 1923, Carl Brigham published *A Study of American Intelligence*. It was remarkable for many reasons. The book was based on the tests he had given to army recruits for World War I. It was a big study that included 81,000 "native-born" Americans, 12,000 immigrants, and 23,000 black Americans.[4] He found that foreigners were "intellectually inferior" to native born. (The tests, as you might guess, were remarkably culture and class bound.) Indeed, Brigham was able to color-code intelligence. The calculation was this: Lighter skin is better.

Brigham decided that there were four distinct racial strains in the United States. "At the pinnacle were the Nordics, the blue-eyed original settlers and the group [this is a surprise] to which Brigham naturally assigned himself."[5] The further one got from blond and blue-eyed, the lower one's intelligence. Throughout the book Brigham had separate charts for blacks and Jews because he did not consider them "Americans."

Brigham was a bigot who campaigned against "interbreeding." He was always afraid that the mixing of blood would lead to the end of civilization as he wanted it. He never lost that attitude.

But Brigham was not just another bigot. He is an important person not only in our intellectual history, he has also had an influence on almost every one of us. As a young professor at Princeton University, he developed a test that the school began to require for admission in 1925. In that same year Brigham was appointed to develop an intelligence test that could be used for all college admission. For all practical purposes the SATs are his invention.

The only book that Brigham wrote was, essentially, a racist tract. That the members of the College Board either did not know that, or chose to ignore it, seems remarkable today. It is also interesting to note that blacks, even now, continue to score lower than whites. Later we will discuss how different groups do on these tests, but for now it is enough to say that testing in the United States is deeply rooted in all kinds of bigotry.

World War II provided a huge windfall for testing. In particular the College Board offered its services for the war effort. They developed tests for military personnel, for admission to the Naval and Coast Guard academies, and scholarship programs. A biographer of the Board wrote: "Under a single contract the Board handled for the

---

[4] The numbers are from Sacks, p. 29.

[5] David Owen, with Marilyn Doerr, *None of the Above: The Truth Behind the SATs, Revised and Updated* (New York: Rowman & Littlefield, 1999), p. 177.

Bureau of Naval Personnel approximately one hundred service jobs, including printing or reprinting 133 tests, answer sheets, and bulletins—a total of 36,000,000 pages."[6]

From being in financial trouble during the 1930s, the nonprofit Board had a surplus of $300,000 in 1943. More importantly, testing was becoming more ingrained in our culture.

To jump in time, we periodically revisit those studies of how intelligence is inherited and how some races are just superior to others. In 1994, Herrnstein and Murray made the argument in *The Bell Curve*.[7] They argued, basically, that there were inequalities in the United States because of genetic inequalities. Their belief was that people inherited different cognitive abilities. It is, at its core, the warmed-over Darwinism of Francis Galton. Distressingly, their book found an audience among many conservative groups.

Before the discussion about just what these tests can and cannot do, we need to get a sense of why as a culture we seem so test oriented. The reasons are many and varied.

WHY STANDARDIZED TESTS?

There is no one, strong, underlying reason why we are so fascinated with testing. A place to begin is with two notions that tap into some of our basic prejudices. First, there is the promise that we will be able to know something scientifically. The very earliest claims were that, finally, there could be scientific tests that would show a person's intelligence. One of the tenants of our liberalism is a belief in the products of science.

The second liberal principle testing promotes is competition. Standardized tests are nothing if not competitive. In most of the tests we take, it is a race to complete. Number two pencils sharpened and ready, go to your seats, get ready, fill in the blanks. But the competition is beyond personal. As we will see, more and more policies are aimed at making schools compete for rewards—and the measure used is test results. There are even cases in which individual teachers are rewarded for how well their classes do on standardized tests.

So, somewhere near the heart of our obsession with testing are the twin principles of science and competition.

As we saw in the preceding section, testing can be put to a cultural use. Under the cover of science and fairness, it has been used to sort the population on the basis of race and income. Also, to put a little different twist on it, testing gives a culture without a hereditary aristocracy at least a standardized test aristocracy. This standardized test aristocracy, as we know, has the best chance to get into the best colleges and graduate schools. Interestingly, this aristocracy is much like the hereditary one in that it is often passed on from generation to generation.

Another broad reason for testing falls under the heading of standards. Since the mid-1800s in Massachusetts, people involved with schooling have believed that standardized tests would not only help make certain that students would learn the

[6] Ibid., p. 183.

[7] R. J. Herrnstein and C. Murray, op. cit.

right things, but could be held to high standards. We have revisited the theme often in our history.

About fifty years ago, during the 1950s, there was great concern that education was in trouble. SAT scores were falling and a back-to-basics movement was born.[8] Things got more complicated with the Russians beating the United States into space. There was much complaining about schooling and a call for at least minimum competency testing. The reform did little good.

During that time, outcomes-based education (OBE) came into being. Generally, it was the idea of setting goals by which student performance could be measured. The first set of outcomes seemed to be more about attitudes than measurable data, and there was little support for OBE.

By the mid-1960s the cultural and educational changes were far from standard-setting and outcome testing. In a context in which everything was being questioned, and education was under greater attack from the left than from the right, ideas like back-to-basics would never get a hearing. (It should be noted that, even then, students dutifully took college boards and colleges made important decisions based on them. In some cases, they were literally life and death decisions, because going to college meant not going to Vietnam.)

As a kind of an aside, let me give you a sense of what standards people think of progressive educators. In a discussion about what method of reading is the "best"—the best here is from a person committed to "competitive" education—there is this description of one progressive thinker: "the still famous John Dewey."[9] The point of the aside is that a discussion of standards is also a discussion of teaching methods and curriculum. If a system is committed to certain testable standards, it is safe to assume it is not committed to anything resembling progressive education.[10] If the question is, Where you are going?, then the matter of how you get there becomes very important.

For many, things just got worse. Beginning in the 1980s there was serious concern that schooling has had a negative effect on the economy. *A Nation at Risk* focused on how we were losing out internationally because our schools were so bad. Better students would make better workers, and better workers would mean a stronger economy. The latest incarnation of the standards-based reform movement grew out of that line of thinking.[11]

The standards-based argument continues with a vengeance. Presidents Reagan, Bush, Clinton, and Bush are all advocates of standards and testing of one kind or another. There was even another *Nation at Risk—A Nation Still at Risk: An Educational Manifesto*—written by William Bennett. Written in the mid-'90s, Bennett was still

---

[8] Andrew Coulson, *Market Education: The Unknown History* (New Brunswick N.J.: Transaction Publishers, 1999), p. 117.

[9] Ibid., p. 162.

[10] I do not mean to imply that *all* progressive educators are against testing. There are all kinds of progressives and all kinds of testing.

[11] Deborah Meier, *Will Standards Save Public Education?* (Boston: Beacon Press, 2000), p. 11.

convinced that schooling in the United States had gone to hell, and only standards, accountability, and testing could save it.[12] In the preceding chapter we saw that the No Child Left Behind Act is based, in part, on yearly testing.

There is seeming agreement that there are problems in our educational system. The very first line of the introduction to a book about testing reads: "Most people seem to agree that America's schools are in need of repair." And on the next page the authors ask a rhetorical question: ". . . who could possibly be against 'high standards'?"[13] Milton Friedman argues that for the first time in our history, this generation is "worse educated than the preceding generation."[14]

There are arguments that students' tests are lower now then they were in the 1950s, and that, if we are to believe SAT scores, students know less now than they ever have.[15] Finally, when compared with students internationally, students in the United States do not score well. (It should be noted that in 1900 about 3 percent of the population of the United States graduated from high school. Today, up to 91 percent graduate. In Japan, the number is only about 67 percent.)[16]

For some, the answer to all these problems is higher standards, an obsession with results so that our students will achieve international benchmarked levels, incentives for teachers, and more competition between schools.[17] There is an insistence on accountability in the belief that it will surely lead to achievement.

Is It True?

The question is simple enough: How much of this is true? We will begin with the easier points and progress to the more complicated ones.[18]

During the Reagan years, the economy was awful. There was high inflation and unemployment. The rich were getting richer, the poor were getting poorer, and the Japanese and German economies seemed as if they were going to swallow the United States. In retrospect it is now clear that Reagan's own economic policies helped get us into that huge mess. What happened, and this is certainly a recurring theme, is that many of our economic problems were blamed on schooling. Bad students were bad workers, and bad workers led to a bad economy. The genuine problem with this reasoning is that while critics continue to argue that schools have not gotten any better,

---

[12] Sacks, op. cit., p. 164.

[13] National Research Council, *High Stakes: Testing for Tracking, Promotion, and Graduation* (Washington D.C.: National Academy Press, 1999), pgs. 11–12.

[14] Susan Ohanian, *One Size Fits Few: The Folly of Educational Standards* (Portsmouth, N.H.: Heinemann, 1999), p. 25. Ohanian goes on to mention that "we didn't even try to educate everybody in preceding generations."

[15] Coulson, op. cit., pgs. 117 and 187.

[16] Ohanian, op. cit. pgs. 139–40.

[17] Marc Tucker and Judy Codding, *Standards for Our Schools: How to Set Them, Measure Them, and Reach Them* (San Francisco: Jossey-Bass, 1998), pgs. 18, 20, 21, 23, 127.

[18] The discussion comes from many sources. Particularly see Sacks, op. cit.

during the '90s the United States had an unprecedented economic boom. We had low unemployment and low inflation and remarkable prosperity, and we had those things with people who made the same kind of test scores that students made in the 1980s. What changed, in part, were the economic policies.

Realistically, our educational system can take neither the blame nor the credit for bad or good economic conditions. If nothing else, the last twenty years have made that very clear.

Third International Math and Science Study

Is it true that our students do poorly when compared with students from other countries? The test that caused the most concerns was the Third International Math and Science Study (TIMSS). The United States ranked "significantly worse" than sixteen developed countries in math, and "Americans scored worse than any other nation except for the developing nations like Cyprus and South Africa."[19]

Those results are not encouraging. Critics believe that TIMSS are flawed and inappropriate, "a useless comparison of apples to oranges owing to highly various cultural differences." And there were a remarkable number of reasons offered about why students from the United States did so poorly. Some of the reasons, for example, were that students in the United States watch more TV, they hate math and science, and they are younger than most students in other countries. Interestingly, the "statistical czar" of the National Center for Educational Statistics (NCES) wrote "What is remarkable is that . . . so few of the factors examined one-by-one could account for our relatively poor performance."[20]

It is possible that we can get an insight about test scores by considering the entire TIMSS. There were two parts of the TIMSS studies. For our purposes, we need to consider the pedagogical part of the test. Over three years, classes in eighth-grades were videotaped in Japan, Germany, and the United States. The tapes were analyzed. Those findings were widely ignored in the United States.

It turns out that in both Japan and Germany, the emphasis was on the teaching of thinking instead of skills. "The learning goal of 73 percent of the Japanese teachers was to develop thinking skills and the understanding of mathematical ideas; that was the goal of just 22 percent of the American teachers."[21] In the United States, teachers focused on procedures and steps for finding answers while the Japanese were much more likely to encourage students to present their own solutions to problems.

American classrooms generally tried to deal with two topics per class, while the Japanese barely got through one lesson. Put differently, classes in the United States were more likely to do a great deal and not be terribly concerned with understanding, while the Japanese tried to do in-depth teaching. It is possible that the main reason

[19] Sacks, op. cit., p. 131. The following comes from Sacks.

[20] Ibid., pgs. 132–3.

[21] Ibid., p. 133.

why students from the United States did not do well compared to students from other countries is because of how they were taught.

What this suggests, at least in part, is that the goal for students in the United States differs from the goals of students in other countries. In order to get a better understanding of why we teach the way we do, it is necessary to focus on what standardized tests can tell us, and the cost of our current involvement with testing, standards, accountability, and achievement.

To anticipate the discussion, it may well be that our students do poorly on standardized tests because we focus on them so much.

STANDARDIZED TESTS

There is a centralizing trend for schooling at the state level. Governors, state legislators, and state schooling bureaucracies have assumed more and more power that once belonged to local districts. States are using high-stakes testing in order to make certain students have learned what they are mandated to learn. The results of those tests affect not only individual students but their teachers and their schools. States reward or punish schools according to how well their students do on statewide tests.

Students might not pass from one grade to the next (or even graduate in some states) because of their test scores, and schools might lose money, or worse, if standardized grades are bad. In some states teachers get good raises—or no raises at all—depending on how their students do on tests.

The argument of the state is easy to understand. There is a belief that each student must know certain things. Language, math, science, and social studies are often tested. The belief is that if a student cannot reach an acceptable level of knowledge (say, a 70 on a standardized test), then that student should not be promoted to the next grade. We know that what is "acceptable" is a purely arbitrary judgment, and may change from year to year.

In the high-stakes states, the reasoning is that to ensure people will work hard and do well on tests, there must be high expectations, incentives, and accountability. A high school diploma is high incentive, and each student is held accountable for his or her own work. So too are the teachers and the school. It is in the best interest of everyone in the school to make certain that students are prepared to take the state tests. In terms of accountability and incentives, both school and individual funding might rest on student test scores.

It all seems so reasonable. Tests, many believe, are a scientific way to assess what a student knows. It is a way to compare students with each other, and to see how effective individual schools are. In a competitive way, students, teachers, and schools become responsible for results, and the state can use different incentives for the outcomes they want.

The stance of these states might be more political than educational. In order to understand standardized testing, it is necessary to think through the process and the outcomes.

Who Supports Testing?

Who supports this kind of testing? Generally, more conservative Republicans than liberal Democrats support high-stakes testing. The word "generally" is a tip-off that nothing in human affairs is 100 percent. Here is another way to think of it: *The further from the classroom you get, the more likely there is support for high-stakes testing.* So, teachers and students (and most likely their parents) are most opposed to these tests; then school administrators and district administrators. By the time you get to the state and national level, expect to find people who support these tests.

The truth is that testing cuts into the real teaching that should go on. Later, we will see the effects of teaching to the test. For now, William Bennett explains why it is easy for those not in the classroom to support high stakes testing. A school board member once asked Bennett how new standards (and with them, new testing) would work. Bennett answered: "I deal in wholesale; you're going to have to work out retail for yourselves."[22] While it was a clever, and heartless, response, Bennett nailed the reality. It is much easier to set high standards and deal out rewards and punishment than to actually have to teach students.

The further away from the classroom a person is, the more reasonable standardized tests seem. There is something intuitively right in assuming that students need to know something, and the way to assure they know it is through a test that everyone is required to take. But if you teach, you understand that each student is different, often requires something special, and proceeds at his or her own speed. To believe that everyone the same age should know the same thing and that thing can be tested is totally *counterintuitive*. The passion stems, in part, from the fact that what is intuitively right to one side is counterintuitive to the other.

It is as if each side is saying to the other: But don't you understand?

A second thing to understand about tests is that *those who know most about testing—those professionals who study testing—are constantly warning us about the limitations of the tests.* In a book edited by members of the National Research Council, we are told early in the book that tests are not perfect, that they must be understood in the context in which they are given, and that test scores alone cannot justify bad decisions about students.[23] While they argue that "blanket criticisms" of tests are not justified, they tell us that many of our policies exceed the technical capacity of testing.[24]

These are interesting warnings: 1) Tests should not be used alone to make decisions, and 2) we are unable to technically produce tests that our policies need. In a word, we have high-stakes tests that are unable to measure what we want, and we are making decisions with too little information.

There is another warning that we need to keep in mind.[25] Tests cannot be wholly objective. Those who construct the tests constantly make judgments about

[22] Ohanian, op. cit., p. 34.

[23] *High Stakes*, op. cit., p. 3.

[24] Ibid., pgs. 30–1.

[25] This discussion and following quote is found in Alfie Kohn, *The Case Against Standardized Testing: Raising the Scores, Ruining the Schools* (Portsmouth, N.H.: Heinemann, 2000), pgs. 4–5.

what is important, about what the test taker needs to know. To further complicate test construction, the most superficial things are the ones most easily objectified. Alfie Kohn writes: "The quest for objectivity may lead us to measure students on the basis of criteria that are a lot less important. . . . *The critical point is that standardized tests do not provide objectivity.*"

Intelligence and Achievement Tests

The chapter began with how testing developed. The initial effort was to find the unchanging mental ability of an individual. By the 1920s people were assured there were scientific tests able to do just that. While the tests were both technically flawed and remarkably bigoted, we continue to believe that there is an IQ that each of us is born with and is basically unchangeable. Currently forty-nine states use "some form of standardized IQ scores and achievement test results in their identification process" for gifted programs.[26]

One of the interesting things about using both IQ and achievement tests is that, at least in the popular mind, they measure different things. We were brought up to believe that achievement is one thing, and basic intelligence is another. But the truth is something different.

Possibly the most basic problem is that there has never been an agreed-upon definition of intelligence. We read: "Numerous attempts have been made to define intelligence, yet educators and psychologists have never been able to come to complete agreement on the term or on the concepts it involves. Substantial progress has been made in the measurement of intelligence, however . . . our definition of intelligence is circular, since we are in effect saying that intelligence is what intelligence tests measure . . ."[27]

We find support for this idea in interesting places. For example, Henry Chauncey, the first president of the Educational Testing Service, believed that the SAT was an IQ test. In 1963 he wrote: "Intelligence tests and scholastic aptitude tests have the same purpose: to estimate the capacity of the student for school learning. . . . For all practical purposes, and in all of their school uses, they are the same kind of test."[28]

Academics are in agreement. Stephen Ceci, a human development expert at Cornell, writes: "[both IQ and achievement tests are] highly similar and inseparable both theoretically and statistically."[29] If that is true, and there is good evidence that aptitude and achievement scores are highly associated, then there are real problems in testing.

It may well be that the people who developed IQ tests in order to prove the relationship of heredity and fixed intelligence were simply wrong. A current problem is

[26] Sacks, op. cit., p. 49.

[27] Owen, op. cit., p. 5.

[28] Ibid., p. 193.

[29] Sacks, op. cit., p. 49.

this: What explains the fact that people are getting smarter? Or, to be more accurate, that people are scoring higher on IQ tests? Since 1918 IQs have risen 24 points in the United States. It is agreed that genetically a population cannot change that quickly. And 24 points is a huge change. Individually, it could be the difference between "normal" and "superior."[30]

Tests would have us believe that we are smarter than ever. But why? If there is a fixed IQ, then getting that much smarter that fast is simply biologically impossible.

The data indicates that heredity is 75 percent of intelligence, but that doesn't leave enough room for the environment to have an effect. A man named James Flynn has proposed that "IQs are affected by both environment and genes, but . . . their environments are matched to their IQs." Put differently, genes cause people to seek certain environments. (He calls this the Flynn Effect.) For example, people with high IQs will just naturally seek certain environments that will enhance that genetic advantage. The smart get smarter.

It is a clever twist on the nature/nurture debate. While it strikes at the heart of a fixed intelligence, there seems to be no acknowledgement of the idea that the tests themselves are so culture-bound that the debate itself might be bogus.

We are left with a serious question: What, exactly, do tests tell us? If we do not know if they are really intelligence or achievement, then how can we hold schools responsible for scores? Or, possibly, there is no such thing as basic intelligence. We know that there are ways people can improve their achievement scores—and that means there are ways in which they can improve their scores on basic intelligence tests.

The tests we are talking about are generally timed, are multiple choice, begin when students are young, and are given frequently. There are some tests that are open-ended, and are read by "impartial" readers. These traits converge to give us a good sense of what these tests might measure and mean.

TESTING YOUNG CHILDREN

We begin testing our children when they are young. And, remarkably, these first tests can be high stakes. Peter Sacks believes that "testocracy's epicenter" is New York City.[31] He writes that many schools require three- and four-year-olds to take either the *Weschler Preschool and Primary Scale of Intelligence Test-Revised* (WPPSI-R), or the latest version of the Stanford-Binet test.

These "baby boards" are timed and rely heavily on verbal skills and knowledge. Test performance is heavily weighted on time of completion. Put differently, it is best that these three- and four-year-olds come from a well-educated family and not get bogged down in getting all of the answers right. A young child who gets involved in the details is a young child who will not do well on the tests.

Hunter College Elementary School is possibly the most elite school in New York City. It is an excellent school and is free. The school requires each student to take

[30] Sharon Begly, "Are We Getting Smarter?" *Newsweek*, April 23, 2001, pgs. 50–1.

[31] Ibid., pgs. 35–43.

the *Stanford-Binet Intelligence Scale.* A couple of years ago, 1,200 children applied. The first cut Hunter made was from the test scores. If the prospective student did not score in top one or two percent, he or she was automatically rejected.

Hunter took forty-eight of the 1,200 applicants. That is 4 percent. In 1998, Harvard accepted 13 percent of its applicants, and Yale took 18 percent. Hunter, then, was at the top of the exclusive list, and they used standardized tests to eliminate most of those who tried to get in. High stakes, indeed.

While other private schools in Manhattan say that they do not weight the tests as heavily as Hunter, there are serious questions about the validity of the tests.

I talked with a highly respected pediatrician from New Orleans. Like New York City, the best private schools in his city want their applicants to be tested. He told me this story.

A mother came to see him about her five-year-old son. Both she and her husband were very successful professionals with many years of graduate education. They wanted their son, who the pediatrician said was a very bright child, to go to one of the best private schools in the city. The boy took the IQ test and was immediately rejected.

The person giving the test said that the boy had an IQ of 65, and listed the traits that showed how below average he was. Not surprisingly, the mother was an emotional mess. The pediatrician asked if she saw those traits in the boy and she said she did not. The doctor then called the school. He knew the person giving the test and knew she was a moody and sometimes erratic woman. Her opinion of the child always weighed heavily in the test results.

The doctor spoke to the head of the school and questioned the use of tests for children that young. The head of the school replied that "they have always served us well." Maybe not, the doctor said. He asked if the school would accept new results if the boy in question was tested by someone else. The head said all right.

The new test showed the boy's IQ was 165, not 65. If we believe tests, he was a genius and not an idiot. Everyone agreed it was a remarkable jump in "native ability" in two months. The school accepted him and fired the person who gave him the first test.

While the story has a happy ending for one child (and his parents) in one city, the problem of testing remains. James Popham writes: "The use of standardized achievement tests with children, at least until the end of the third grade, is a definite no-no. The validity of score-based inferences that such testing will yield is likely to be inadequate."[32]

An advisory group of the National Educational Goals Panel believes that standardized achievement tests should not be given to young children. "Before age 8, standardized achievement measures are not sufficiently accurate to be used for high-stakes decisions about individual children and schools."[33] Studies show that the high stress levels experienced by young children during these tests affect their scores. Often, under conditions of less stress they are able to answer questions correctly.

[32] James Popham, *Testing, Testing!: What Every Parent Should Know About School Tests* (Boston: Allyn & Bacon, 2000), p. 145.

[33] *High Stakes*, op. cit., p. 119.

The tests are inaccurate and biased. "Readiness tests are either thinly disguised IQ tests (called developmental screening measures) or academic skills tests. . . . Both types of tests tend to identify disproportionate numbers of poor and minority students as unready for school."[34] While there are few good things to be said about standardized tests, there are no good things to be said for giving them to young children. To make important decisions based on tests for young children is simply wrong.

MULTIPLE-CHOICE TESTS

The first and most obvious thing about multiple-choice tests is that they encourage shallow thinking. Multiple-choice exams, at best, are a rough measure of a persons' short-term memory. Thoughtful answers, answers that are generated by the test taker, have no place in these tests. We read: ". . . researchers found that the group that scored highest on the SAT actually tended to use more superficial thinking strategies, relying on surface and achieving approaches more often than those who scored in the low and moderate range."[35]

It may not be surprising that the bias of shallow thinking favors males. We read that: "Boys outscored girls on the multiple-choice achievement test, and girls outperformed boys on the free-response exams."[36] This is also true of most ethnic groups. "Multiple-choice tests favor men and Asians, while essays favor women, blacks, Latinos, Native Americans and even those for whom English was a second language."[37]

Roger Farr, a professor at Indiana University, writes: "I don't think there's any way to build a multiple-choice question that allows students to show what they can do with what they know."[38] There is no way these tests can measure cognitive skills. To make matters worse, we know that any multiple-question exam is a reflection of the prejudice of those who have created it.

We can take the SAT as an example. The instructions on the exam call for the "best" answer. The best answer is not necessarily a good answer, or even a correct one. David Owen sent several questions from the verbal section of the SAT to high-powered people who think and write for a living. The responses are instructive:[39]

Nicholas von Hoffman: "How can there possibly be one right answer?"

William F. Buckley Jr.: ". . . authors of the test questions are not equipped to ascertain exactly what they insist they are ascertaining."

Elizabeth Hardwick: "By way of certain thought patterns and a close examination, any of the alternatives could be described as reasonable, with the exception of

---

[34] L. A. Shepard quoted in High Stakes, p. 119.

[35] Sacks, op. cit., p. 209.

[36] Ibid., p. 205.

[37] Ibid., p. 206. These are the results of the SATs.

[38] Quoted in Kohn, op. cit., p. 11.

[39] Owen, op. cit., pgs. 61–3.

perhaps C. Everything considered, I think I would have answered D." (SAT would not have given her credit for D.)

Andrew Hacker: "Like Burden's Ass, who starved to death when faced with two piles of oats, I would have wasted so much time on this question, that my final score would have been dismal."

And, of course, any multiple-question exam can test only a small fraction of what a student knows. Even if a student knows what is being asked, there is always a chance he or she will answer in a different way than those who make up the test.

There have also been problems with math tests. In the most famous case, a high school student named Daniel Lowen proved that there were at least two correct answers to a math problem in the SATs. The testers admitted their mistake and raised the scores of 240,000 people who took the test. For the sake of accuracy and fairness (or, the lack of either) it is estimated that few of those got the "wrong" answer for the "right" reason.

For our purposes, it is important to understand that scoring is imprecise at best. Not only is there no assurance that there is only one correct answer, but any score is better understood as being in a range of scores. For example, in a standardized math test given to sixth-graders, the minimum passing score in Texas is 71. But, given measurement error for individual scores, a 71 might actually be as high as 77 or as low as 64.[40] The then-governor of Texas, George W. Bush, wanted to flunk all sixth-graders who made lower than a 71. In New York City, 8,600 students were forced to go to summer school based on a scoring error of the test they took.

A researcher found that a student whose "real" achievement was at the fiftieth percentile will actually score within five points of that percentile about 30 percent of the time on the SAT-9 math exam and 42 percent of the time on the reading exam.[41] In sum, multiple-choice tests may do more harm than good. They certainly do not give reliable enough data to make high-stakes decisions; indeed, they may not provide much of the data that those who favor the tests are looking for.

Regrettably, open-response items might not be any better.[42] Part of the problem has to do with the quality and construction of the test. In order to help standardize the answers, the texts are often "a dull chunk of text" that calls for a "bland" assessment of the topic. "Preparing kids to turn out high-scoring essays can *inhibit* the quality of their writing." Often, the tests are read by "low-paid temp workers" who "spend no more than two or three minutes on each one."

One former essay reader said: "I know that this sounds bizarre, but you could put a number on those things without actually reading the paper." The bottom line was this: After reading eight thousand papers, the reader was given a $200 bonus.

This is how Alfie Kohn sums it up: "In short, we can't assume that an essay test is a valid measure of important things. But we can be reasonably certain that a multiple-choice test *isn't*."[43]

[40] Sacks, op. cit., p. 114.

[41] Kohn, op. cit., p. 21.

[42] The following is found in ibid., pgs. 12–13.

[43] Ibid., p. 13.

TIMED TESTS

When discussing the president's proposed national exams in both math and science, Tucker and Codding argue the problem is not that the exams will be timed, but that the standards are not what they want.[44] There are genuine problems with timed tests.

If an entire test is timed we can easily infer that speed is the premium value.[45] Thoughtfulness and thoroughness become traits that will help guarantee a low score. We can see this in several different ways.[46]

For the youngest children (ages 3 to 7), the Wippsie R test is built for speed. Given certain problems with statistical reliability, the Psychological Corporation that makes the test needed to add "bonus points for speed on the object assembly subtest." One of the results is that a child could get every "object assembly" puzzle right but still score in the ninth percentile on that subtest if no bonus points were awarded for speed.

According to one source, on the *Weschler Intelligence Scale for Children* (WISC-III), 40 percent of the total points on four of the subtests came from bonus points awarded to quick responses. Sixty percent of the points were for presenting the correct solution. When identifying the IQ of the children taking the test, speed was an important variable. The difference between a "gifted" child and a "bright" child might be the difference of only a few seconds.

We read: "The possibility of overemphasis on speeded performance on the WISC-III subtests may preclude adequate identification of some children who are abstract, reflective thinkers but are not as highly able in speed because of their visual motor abilities."[47]

The emphasis on speed continues through school. David Owen writes: "One of the first tasks the creator of a multiple-choice test facts is how to make people miss questions whose subject matter they actually understand. This sounds silly, but it's important. One way it's done is by limiting the amount of time allowed for answering questions. Veteran test-takers know, for instance, that the key to doing well on ETS math items lies in finding *quick* solutions; if you have to perform a complex or lengthy calculation, you've missed the trick."[48]

GIRLS AND BOYS

Speed seems to be a built-in advantage for males. "One research study notes, 'substantial evidence exists that from birth females are conditioned by society to more closely follow rules than males, to be neater, and to be more careful in their approach

---

[44] Tucker and Codding, op. cit., p. 60.

[45] Kohn, op. cit., p. 13.

[46] The following comes from Sacks, pgs. 213–15.

[47] Ann Fishkin and John Kampsnider, "WISC-III Subtest Scatter Patterns for Rural Superior and High-Ability Children," March 1996, ERIC Document ED 394 783, pgs. 154–8. Quoted in Sacks, ibid.

[48] Owen, op. cit., p. 44.

to problems than males. . . . It is sad to think that these problem solving characteristics, which are desirable traits in many respects, would become a liability when attempting to take college entrance examinations to qualify for admissions and scholarship.'"[49]

In 1998 the combined scores for the average female on the SATs were 42 points below the average score for boys. "Many scholars believe certain tendencies in thinking styles and behavioral traits of girls and women don't add up to a particularly efficient match for the speeded, pressurized nature of the multiple-choice format found on most achievement and aptitude tests. Girls and women may tend to be more focused on the process of learning rather than scoring points in the gamey context of most tests."[50] As we have seen, girls do better than males on tests that are not timed.

Some schools (MIT and the University of California, Berkeley, to take two high-profile, high-powered examples) make allowances for differences in male and female test scores. Timed, multi-choice tests underestimate the skills of women, and schools are beginning to simply add points to females' test scores. Women routinely do better in college than males, even though they do not score as well on the very tests that are supposed to predict success in college.

In recent years the Educational Testing Service has tried to narrow the difference in male and female test scores. The reason for the effort is because a civil rights complaint was filed against them and the College Board. FairTest of Cambridge, Massachusetts, filed the complaint in 1994, and after two-and-a-half years of negotiation, the ETS revised the PSAT for 1997. Scores for the new PSAT have started to narrow. The question is whether similar efforts will be made to change the SATs.

It is important to know that these tests favor white males. Women and minorities (with the exception of some Asians) do not score as well. What has been said about women holds true for minorities. These tests are simply biased. For cynics, it is easy to say that the tests are a very good reflection of those who began to develop them during the first quarter of the twentieth century. While it would be unfair to claim that today's tests are racist and sexist by the design of those who have developed them, if one only looked at test results, the claim of racism and sexism would be valid.

THE EFFECTS OF STANDARDIZED TESTS

Students

The effects of standardized testing can begin when you are three years old and continue through the time you apply for graduate school. In some cases, there are standardized tests that you will need to pass in order to get a license to practice your profession—or to do something as important as being able to take third party payments.

For most of us, after the getting into college, our standardized testing days are over. (Unless you count going to a new state and taking a written driving test.) While we

---

[49] Ibid., p. 224.

[50] Sacks, op. cit., p. 206.

know that there is practically no job in which one's ability to do well depends on the skills needed to take tests with a #2 pencil, these exams continue to dominate our early years.

As we saw in the preceding section, the SATs are poor predictors for how well one will do in college. They underestimate the skills of women and minorities. Earlier, we saw that these tests can systematically exclude bright and thoughtful kids from the "best" elementary schools. While being excluded from the elite elementary schools does not doom a child to failure, one would feel better if all kids had an equal chance to go to these outstanding schools.

The widest range of effects from standardized testing are felt in public schools. To understand this better, we will first discuss retention, followed by what it means to teach to the test.

Testing is used in the sorting-out process for students. It should be no surprise that money is an important variable in how well kids do in school, and the lack of money is probably even more important.[51]

- Eight out of ten eighth graders from the wealthiest 25 percent of the families are in "academic" tracks that will lead them to the best colleges. Well *under* half of the eighth graders from the poorest quarter of the families are in those same tracks.

- About seven out of ten eighth graders who score in the bottom quartile on achievement tests come from poor and middle-class families.

- One-third of the wealthy high school seniors score at least 1,100 on the SAT. That is the cut-off for many of the elite colleges. That is twice the rate of students from moderate backgrounds and four times the rate of the poorest high school students.

- For students from families that earn at least $75,000 a year, nearly nine out of ten meet the qualifications for acceptance to four-year colleges and universities. Less than half of the students in families earning less than $25,000 meet the qualifications.

It is easy to see how this pattern emerges early and is seemingly a natural byproduct of testing. In his 1998 state of the union message, President Clinton called for an end of social promotion. He argued that retention should be the policy for those children who did not meet certain standards. One assumes that the best way to know if a student was ready for the next class level would be by passing a standardized test.

There are serious problems with this seemingly sensible plan. To repeat what we know, test scores are very unreliable for children under the age of eight. We read about younger students who are judged by standardized tests:

> In many cases, the instruments developed for one purpose or even one age group of children have been misapplied to other groups. As a result, schools have often identified as "not yet ready" for kindergarten, or "too immature" for group settings, large proportions of youngsters (often boys and non-English speakers) who would benefit enormously from the learning opportunities provided in these settings. In particular,

---

[51] Ibid., pgs. 263–4.

because the alternative treatment is often inadequate, screening out has fostered inequities.[52]

We know that low test scores for students of all ages may be the result of many things that have little to do with ability. "Influences associated with socioeconomic status, ethnicity, language, age, gender or specific disabilities"[53] are often relevant variables when considering test scores. As an extreme example of how test scores are misapplied, it was found that comparable Asian and Hispanic test scores were treated differently. The Asians were routinely placed in a higher academic track.

The National Research Council found that retention was a worse problem than social promotion. While the social promotion versus retention dichotomy might be false (those who need help should get it in order to be promoted), the facts seem pretty clear: ". . . most research on retention shows that retained students are generally worse off than their promoted counterparts on both personal adjustment and academic outcomes."[54] More specifically, a "review of 16 controlled studies found 'no difference academically between unready children who spent an extra year before first grade and at-risk controls who went directly on to first grade.'" However, there was evidence that most of the children were traumatized as a result of being retained. Further, "matched schools that do not practice kindergarten retention have just as high average achievement as those that do but tend to provide more individualized instruction within normal grade placements."[55]

In lower grades, boys are more likely than girls to be held back. They tend to fall further behind as they move through school. In higher grades, there is a bigger difference between minorities and whites than boys and girls. Blacks and Hispanics are more and more likely to be held back: ". . . at ages 15 to 17, rates of age-grade retardation range from 40 to 50 percent among blacks and Hispanics, and they have gradually drifted up from 25 percent to 35 percent among whites."[56]

There seem to be two undeniable results of retention.[57] First, "On the average retained children are worse off than their promoted counterparts on both personal adjustment and academic outcomes." Retention does not lead to improved academic achievement. And second, in a study that followed 5,000 students for eight years, it was found that "students who were currently repeating a grade were 70% more likely to drop out of high school than those not currently repeating a grade."

The costs of testing, then, seem to be remarkably high.

To tie up one last thread of the argument. Earlier we saw that testing was used for tracking, and that tracking seemed to favor whites. It was found that low-track

[52] L. Shepard, S. Kagan, and E. Wurtz, eds., *Principles and Recommendation for Early Childhood Assessments* (Washington, D.C.: National Education Goals Panel). Quoted in *High Stakes*, p. 95.

[53] Ibid., p. 98.

[54] Ibid., p. 42.

[55] Ibid., p. 120.

[56] Ibid., p. 122.

[57] The following information comes from ibid, pgs. 129–30.

classes had such poor curriculum and instruction and expectations that the National Research Council recommended that "low-track placements be eliminated, whether based on test scores or other information."[58]

Teachers

Testing, and especially high-stakes testing, is as hard on teachers as it is their students. High-stakes testing affects not only what can be taught, but how to teach it. These tests change life in the classroom, and the changes are neither welcomed nor positive.

Earlier the idea of high standards was mentioned. To look a little more closely at what this means will help us begin to understand what these high, international standards might mean in the classroom. One of the things it means is that the students are "frequently assessed." Frequent indeed; we read: "A high achievement is expected of all students, which means that students take weekly tests developed by CMSP."[59]

Weekly tests have an impact on education. "These are a new kind of teacher's guide, one that lays out a program or course of study for a year that will enable students to reach the standards for that year in a particular subject."[60] If you are teacher, this is not a neutral statement. What the standards people are saying is that in order for you to make certain that your students will be able to pass a test at the end of the school year, you will be given a complete course of study for that year.

In many ways, the standards people and the high-stakes testing people are on the same page. Both believe that goals can be met by a combination of incentives and accountability. While incentives and accountability are not exactly the same, in reality it is not unusual for a state to have a formula that rewards schools for improvement of test scores. (This can lead to strange results. For example, schools where students always score high are not rewarded because there is a lack of improvement, while schools with very low test scores get rewarded for having only low test scores.)

Rewards differ. Schools may be provided money that will mean modest pay raises to the teachers, while "bad" schools are at risk of closing.

High-stakes testing can lead to competition between teachers if money is the issue.[61] It can lead to bitter teacher/student relationships. Consider how a teacher might feel when a student is unwilling or unable to do well on the test. The teacher knows that this student is going to hurt both the individual class and possibly the entire school. It is not uncommon for the teacher to put pressure on the student to go into another class. Bad teacher/student relationships then become bad teacher/teacher relationships.

In order to help make certain test scores rise, a teacher might do either or both of the following. The first is to overspecialize. It is not uncommon for the teacher to constrict what is taught. Test scores will rise if the student has done little else than study what might be on the test. And, second, the teacher will narrow his or her goals.

---

[58] Ibid., p. 103.

[59] Tucker, op. cit., p. 69. CMPS is the Comprehensive Math and Science Program.

[60] Ibid., p. 88.

[61] The following comes from Kohn, op. cit., p. 27–8.

For example, abstract thinking is not a virtue for most standardized testing. A teacher might decide to pay little or no attention to deeper, more abstract thought in favor of shallow, risk-taking thought that is rewarded by testing.

A less obvious point concerns responsibility and authority. "Standards" and high-stakes testing shifts authority from the teachers and parents to outside bodies. It undermines the capacity of schools to demonstrate independent qualities of mind—the kind demanded in a democratic society.[62] Teachers are no longer responsible for teaching their own ideas. People at the local level are simply instruments for judgments imposed by others. There is no longer an environment in which students grow up "in the midst of adults who are making hard decisions and exercising mature judgment in the face of disagreements."

The role of teaching is diminished when faced with a curriculum that is aimed at making certain their students score well on high-stakes tests. There are new terms for what is going on. We are told that there should be "teacher-proof curriculum." Put differently, schools may try to make certain that the teacher has virtually no say in what is taught, or even how it is taught. It is a way to "de-skill" the teacher.

It is safe to say that one of the results of high-stakes testing is that the best teachers will leave. Why would they want to stay? If you have become a teacher because you enjoy children and think schooling is important to society and to every student, then teaching to the test fulfills neither of those requirements. Why be part of a process that aims to take away your skills?

The Rhythm of Test Results

In countless examples, we know that scores on tests can be improved. We also know the rhythm of the improvement. Tests are given and the results are disappointing. A great effort is made to make certain that it does not happen again. Teachers spend more and more time teaching those things they believe will be on the test. The students practice and learn and take more practice tests. And the scores improve.

The scores continue to improve until the basic test is changed. At that point the scores fall, the teachers begin teaching to the new test, and as before, the scores slowly improve. High test scores too often simply reflect better test-taking skills by the students. This kind of focus on improved test scores might produce better results, but there is nothing to suggest that it helps learning in any way.

Another consequence of high-stakes testing is this: Nine of the ten states with the highest dropout rate have high-stakes testing.[63] One can speculate that is not an accident. The results are predictable: If those who do not test well drop out, then the average scores of those who stay will probably go up. Certainly high test scores do not indicate high levels of thinking.

Interestingly, high-stakes testing may not be the best way to improve test scores. We read: "Meeting these [new] standards is both more important *and more problematic* when a test is used for high-stakes purposes, particularly if it involves consequences for

---

[62] Meier, op. cit., pgs. 4–5.

[63] *High Stakes*, op. cit., p. 175.

individuals rather than institutions."[64] In the mid-1990s, a study found that "states *without* high-stakes exit exams actually showed more improvement on . . . the eighth-grade National Assessment of Educational Progress test (NAEP), than states with such graduation exams. Evidence from other countries is similarly discouraging."[65]

In other words, test scores seem to rise faster if there are not high-stakes consequences for students. To add the obvious, while high standard, high-stakes testing might seem perfectly reasonable to a state legislator or the president of the United States, the data indicates that kind of thinking leads to self-defeating policies.

High-Stakes Testing for Students and Teachers

While everyone will be affected by the new high-stakes testing in my home state of Massachusetts, for one population the effects will be particularly negative. As I write, the policy is that no one will be given a high school diploma if he or she does not pass the test. The assumption is that all students should know the same material by the end of their senior year. Given what we know, that does not make much sense for "regular" high school students. Regrettably, it makes even less sense for the students in vocational high schools.

Why would a person interested in becoming a plumber stay in school after the age of sixteen? To stay in school would mean taking many courses that would have little or nothing to do with plumbing. I have a great love for liberal arts, and think life is much better if a person has an understanding of philosophy, art, literature, and on and on. As it stands now, vocational students do get some of that in school. They are at least introduced to the liberal arts.

But if they are forced to take the same curriculum as those in the regular high school, then they will simply drop out. They can apprentice, take the plumbing test, and live a wholly satisfactory life without a high school degree from the state of Massachusetts. What the high-stakes tests will do is *not* force them to know more but almost guarantee that they know less. The research people call that an unintended consequence. The people who teach in vocational high schools call it criminal.

Teachers not only must remake the classroom in order to help their students develop the skills it will take to pass a standardized test, but they are being required to take tests in order to teach. There have been teachers' tests forever, but some states have decided to make the tests more difficult. Under the banner of high standards, the testing of teachers has become an important issue.

Let me summarize the key line that reappears in the literature about teachers and the tests they must take. The quote is attributed to either the Massachusetts Speaker of the House, Thomas Finneran, or the former Massachusetts Board of Education Chairman John Silber. The subject is the new test to certify teachers: "I can tell you who won't be a great teacher, the idiots who took that test and flunked so miserably."

Massachusetts decided to develop a new test for teachers. The reasoning is familiar: In order to ensure the competency of teachers, it is reasonable to have them

---

[64] Ibid., p. 39. Emphasis added.

[65] The studies are cited by Kohn, op. cit., p. 26.

pass a rigorous test. (Something, it is necessary to add, that neither Finneran nor Silber had to do in order to qualify for their positions.) The state announced that the new test would be given as practice. In other words, it was being offered as a no-stakes way to see if the test was well constructed.

It was a wide-ranging test—some multiple choice, some grammar, a little of this, a little of that. It was not a particularly good test. For example, it was possible to know too much.[66] One woman who was a history major, with a master's degree in history and who had spent another year studying at Queen's University in Belfast, where she won an award for her teaching and writing in a competition with her two hundred classmates, failed the test. She was one of those idiots.

She found the test confusing: It would skip from one historical period to the next, from topic to topic, randomly. It was multiple choice, so the goal was to make quick adjustments, have shallow thoughts, make a fast/best guess and go on. But this woman knew too much. She was thoughtful. In a reasonable world, several of the answers could be defended. She failed the test. She was officially an idiot. If she chose, she could cross the border to Connecticut, take their much easier test, pass it, and be paid more money to teach in their public schools.

Another woman, who had recently earned her doctorate from the Massachusetts Institute of Technology in physics, failed the reading comprehension section of the new teacher test. She had graduated magna cum laude from college and was fluent in three languages. Her native language was English. She even had a job translating science, engineering, and business documents for people around the world. The very essence of her work was to find the essential meaning of what was being said. She failed the reading comprehension part of the teachers' exam. Wow.

That the test seemed to be terribly flawed is only one problem. It is possible that the decisions made by the Commonwealth of Massachusetts were even more flawed. After promising people that the test was simply a pilot, they decided that it should "count." Those who passed were certified by the state, those who didn't were in trouble.

This is the example that stands out in the literature. It seems to represent the far end of what bad teachers' tests and bad policy decisions look like. The bottom line is this: Are these tests valid? Here is one answer: "National Evaluation Systems [the folks who produced the Massachusetts test] has offered no proof whatsoever that its teacher test measures what is supposed to be measured. . . . It appears that this teacher test may not be doing what is it supposed to do: namely, tell us which candidates do and do not meet minimal standards for literacy and content knowledge."[67]

I do not mean to suggest that the Massachusetts test is the only bad one. In 1990 a study was done on the predictive power of two tests that are widely used: the *California Basic Educational Skills Test* (CBEST) and the *National Teacher's Examination* (NTE). The result was that "Except for the writing part of the CBEST, which showed just a

---

[66] Sacks, op. cit., pgs. 185–90.

[67] Ibid., p. 194.

modest relationship with grades in the teacher training program, *none* of the standardized test scores showed *any* association with a teaching student's success. On the other hand, undergraduate grades and a teaching student's performance in one prerequisite reading methods course were highly predictive of success in the program."[68]

Angelo John Lewis writes "As far as I know, there is no such thing as a test of teacher aptitude or potential, and I know of no test, including the NTE, that proports [*sic*] to measure teacher effectiveness. One problem in judging is that there is no general agreement about what an effective teacher is. The number of definitions is about equal to the number of professional educators."[69]

The high-stakes testing of teachers seems as sensible as high-stakes testing of students—only possibly worse. If teaching is in part an art and attributes of that art cannot be tested, then high-stakes testing-of-teacher states like Massachusetts seem to be guaranteeing failure. They are using tests that cannot produce wanted results, and by making prospective teachers take those tests three things can happen—and two of them are bad. 1) People will chose not to teach in those states.[70] It is a reasonable response to stupidity. 2) Many who take the test and pass it will not be good teachers. The only thing one can be certain of is that they are good at taking bad tests. 3) A good teacher might take the test and pass it. Still, by requiring the exam the state is putting itself in a losing situation.

WHAT WE KNOW ABOUT STANDARDIZED TESTS

We know many things about standardized tests. Here is a sample list:

1. "Before age 8, standardized achievement tests are not sufficiently accurate to be used for high-stakes decisions about individual children and schools."[71]

2. "The main thing that they [standardized tests] tell us is how big the students' houses are . . . (Indeed, one educator suggested that we could save everyone a lot of time and money by eliminating standardized tests and just asking a single question: 'How much money does your Mother make?'"[72]

3. "SAT scores have risen with family income. For families making $30,000 to $40,000 a year in 1994, the average SAT verbal-plus-math score was 885; for families with

---

[68] Cited in ibid., p. 195.

[69] Angelo John Lewis, *Making the Public Schools Work*, Focus 9 (Princeton, N.J.: ETS, 1982), pgs. 11–12. Cited by Owen, op. cit., p. 250.

[70] School will begin in Massachusetts in about three weeks. As I write, the state is short 1,000 teachers. Low salaries/high standards/high-risk testing seem to be a very powerful combination—in the most negative way.

[71] *High Stakes*, op. cit., p. 119.

[72] Kohn, op. cit., p. 7.

incomes of $50,00 to $60,000 a year, the combined score jumped to 929. Those students whose family income was greater than $70,000 could expect an average total of 1,000."[73]

4. "Recent data show that someone taking the SAT can expect to score an extra thirty test points for every $10,000 in his parents yearly income . . . for highly selective colleges, fully one-third of these high scorers came from the upper-income brackets; that's compared to well under a tenth of high SATs scores who emerge from the lower economic rungs."[74]

5. On the 1997 SATs, "the mean scores for the verbal test were 434 for blacks, 526 for whites. The mean scores for math were 423 for blacks, 468 for whites."[75] In 1998 "the College Board says that females scored an average of 998 on the combined verbal and math portions of the SAT . . . which was forty-two points below the average score for male test takers.[76]

6. "Although women typically fared consistently worse on college entrance exams than men, females have invariably outdone men in terms of their actual performance in college."[77]

7. Tests show that there is "a 17.7-point gap in the average IQ score of white and black children." "'What our analyses do show is that age-five I.Q. differences between black and white children are almost completely eliminated by adjusting for differences in neighborhood economic conditions, family poverty, maternal education, and learning experiences.'"[78]

8. "When it comes to standardized mental tests, whether it's an IQ test, the school's ordinary achievement test, or college admissions tests, *class rules*, trumping all other factors."[79]

9. "When accounting for economics, the Biddle team estimated that math scores in 'advantaged' American schools (those with high funding and low poverty rates) would beat *all* European counterparts and come in second only to Japan."[80]

10. "In 1997, Dr. Linda Wightman of the Law School Admissions Council [LSAC] conducted a study on law school students admitted in 1990 and found that LSAT scores were poor predictors of graduation and bar exam passage for both white and minority students."[81]

---

[73] Owen, op. cit., p. 227.

[74] Sacks, op. cit., p. 8.

[75] Owen, op. cit., pgs. 207–8.

[76] Sacks, op. cit., p. 204.

[77] Ibid., p. 204.

[78] Ibid., p. 56.

[79] Ibid., p. 60.

[80] Ibid., p. 161.

[81] Cited in Owen., op. cit., p. 200.

11. "Take physician training. Standardized entrance tests that emphasize knowledge in basic sciences, it turns out, are decidedly poor predictors of medical students' success in their clinical training during the final two years of medical school, which is the stuff of real doctoring . . . the further one gets down the path of professional experience and all the expertise that entails, the worse tests become as predictors of anything worthwhile."[82]

12. Not only do GREs fail to predict success, "in some instances, the correlations of GRE scores and graduate performance were actually negative. This was particularly true of women's performance at Yale's graduate psychology program."[83]

The list is long enough. Years ago there were popular books of lists. The above dozen items are simply a sample. It would be fairly easy to write a book of lists about standardized tests. Let me end this section with two summary paragraphs. The first is by the educator Bill Ayers.

"Standardized tests can't measure initiative, creativity, imagination, conceptual thinking, curiosity, effort, irony, judgment, commitment, nuance, good will, ethical reflection, or a host of other valuable dispositions and attributes. What they can measure and count are isolated skills, specific facts and functions, the least interesting and the least significant aspects of learning."[84]

The second summary paragraph (and it is a long one) will lead us into the next topic. That topic is about what it takes to do well on standardized tests. We read this about the SATs:

"I can think of many subgroups for whom the SAT is unfair: the subgroup that believes coaching doesn't work; the subgroup that thinks guessing is wrong; the subgroup that takes the test under the supervision of incompetent proctors; the subgroup that takes the test under the supervision of incompetent observers from 'Princeton'; the subgroup that doesn't cheat; the subgroup that believes the SAT measures what the College Board once called 'the future worth of candidates'; the subgroup that attends schools where ETS tests are not a way of life; the subgroup that doesn't understand the way the test is constructed; the subgroup that uses the Arco strategy for answering analogy items; the subgroup that applies to colleges with uninformed admissions officers."[85]

We know a great deal about standardized tests, and what we know is not encouraging. The tests are not only to produce the anticipated results (they fail to predict what they are supposed to), but they are unreliable, biased, and hurtful. High-stakes tests have the ability to change what is taught to our children. Because doing well has become increasingly important, it is in our interest to know what is involved with improving test scores.

---

[82] Sacks, op. cit., p. 197.

[83] Ibid., p. 279.

[84] William Ayers, *To Teach: The Journey of a Teacher* (New York: Teachers College Press, 1993), p. 116. Cited by Kohn, op. cit., p. 17.

[85] Owen, op. cit., p. 214.

DOING WELL ON STANDARDIZED TESTS

To say the obvious, the proven route to doing well on tests is to be a male who lives in a big house, in a good neighborhood, with well-to-do and well-educated parents. While this might not work for every person who fits that description, we know statistically this group has the highest chance of success.

Students can be taught to improve their test scores. There are examples of entire school systems that have devoted themselves to higher standards as reflected by higher test scores. One example is the city of Chicago. With great pride, an author of the efforts to improve Chicago's public schools relates how school accountability for student performance has led to "gains, some of them quite large."[86] The central idea is to set high standards and make certain there are costs if those standards are not met.

Another analyses is this: "Chicago is the home of get-tough reform, and all these changes have been made in terms in the name of upgrading 'standards.' The results? Test scores over the past three years have risen, we are told, by 3.4 percent in Chicago. That's a few more right answers on a standardized test, maybe."[87]

An instructive example of how to raise test scores was Tacoma, Washington.[88] They hired a man named Randy Crew to be their new superintendent of schools. The Tacoma test scores were low, so in 1994 Crew convinced the school board to spend $2,000,000 to train teachers in efficacy techniques. The motto was: "Think You Can. Work Hard. Get Smart." The training for each teacher was a four-day workshop.

The results of the *Comprehensive Test of Basic Skills* (CTBS) in the fall of 1994 were disappointing. So, in an unusual move, Crew arranged a special retest of the fourth and eighth graders for the following spring. The spring results were surprising. The fourth grade average score jumped twenty-one points, and the eighth grade score went up an average of thirteen points. Of interest to us is how this remarkable improvement took place.

The Tacoma example is nothing more than teaching-to-the-test on steroids. It began with district-wide training workshops that helped teachers and principals understand how to "practice test-taking skills with students." The district created "lesson plans on 'various test-taking skills' as well as a 'test-taking handbook' of 'reminders' . . . about how to prepare the students for tests."[89] At the school level, principals organized test-taking teams of a testing coordinator, parents, teachers, and the principal.

A fourth-grade teacher explained part of the process: "We took a look at that kind of test and said [to pupils], 'When you are asked questions on a test, this is what you need to do; read through the questions first, then read the passage, and then read the questions again.' . . . The staff got together and decided to write questions similar to the questions that were on the test, the same kind of style, so the kids were pretty familiar with the kinds of questions, the style of questioning they would be asked. It really helped the kids."

[86] Tucker, op. cit., p. 215.

[87] Meier, op. cit., p. 3.

[88] All of the following is taken from Sacks, op. cit., pgs. 143–51.

[89] Ibid., p. 144.

In some of the schools, the curriculum was changed "in order to suit 'the same style of questions that the kids would be tested on.'"

This is the most generous analysis of what was going on. While this kind of massive effort to ensure better test scores might be somewhere between immoral and amoral, it was not considered *cheating*. Nor, of course, could it ever be considered good education.

But, at the time, those in Tacoma were truly excited about the remarkable improvement shown by their children. The school board renewed Crew's contract and gave him a $10,000 a year raise. What wasn't there to like? Crew, the author of improvement, was now a national star. He was exactly the person many others school districts wanted to lead them to the test-score promised land. He denied he was moving. Well, he denied he was moving until the day before he accepted the $195,000-a-year job as chancellor of New York City Schools. He was to be the leader of 1.1 million students with an $8 billion budget. A princely payoff for improved test scores.

More interesting was what happened to the students of Tacoma. Without the completely focused effort on testing, their test scores returned to the "disappointing" category. The scores returned to the pre-Crew levels.[90] Put simply, the good scores were a one-test spike that would not be repeated unless there was a return to teaching-to-the-test. As I write, Crew has been replaced as chancellor in New York City.

There are some teachers who do cheat on the tests. They try to find what will be on the test, they help their students during the exams, they change answers. There is no real reason to dwell on cheating. It is undeniably wrong. It is undeniably one very bad response to high-stakes testing. But illegal is illegal, and it is my sense that this kind of cheating does not impact large numbers of students.

Teaching to the test is another matter. It is technically legal and, as we saw with Tacoma, effectively raises scores. Teaching to the test is one of the great unintended consequences of those who mandate standardized, high-stakes testing. In an effort to ensure that students are held to a high standard, and that they are competitive on an international level, and they can "prove" they know what "important" things are, in-depth teaching is replaced with shallow drilling.

In a world that demands high-test scores, it is not surprising that it becomes more and more necessary for students to understand the techniques of test taking. It may be necessary to be familiar with the tests that are being given. *If we put aside the idea that we are talking about education*, then it is totally reasonable for people to teach to the test. It makes personal sense for each student and economic sense for the teachers, schools, and school districts.

Of course, if you have decided to become a teacher for other reasons; if you decide not to put the idea of education aside; if shallow techniques and practice test-taking are not your idea of time well spent in the classroom, then teaching-to-the-test is an invitation to leave the profession.

At the end of public schooling, for many who want to go to college, there are the SATs. There are people who have figured out how to score well on the SAT, and

---

[90] In the same time period, 1993–97, scores in middle-class and upper-middle-class school systems in Washington state did not change. Without that one spring, the tests in Washington state simply reaffirm what we know: tests reflect class.

for hundreds of dollars you can improve your score. It is worth our time to see some of the ways these people figured out how to "beat" the SATs, and make a lot of money in the process.

Beating the SATs

For many years the Educational Testing Service was proud to call attention to the "A" in SAT. They wanted the world to know that these were Aptitude tests. What they implied—certainly what ETS wanted everyone to believe—was that the tests were an accurate measure of aptitude, and coaching could not significantly improve a person's score.

We know that scores can be significantly improved with coaching, and ETS has dropped all references to aptitude. It is possible to learn about the SATs by understanding a little about how to "beat" them.

In 1981 a man named John Katzman graduated from Princeton. He went to work on Wall Street but didn't like it.[91] When he was in high school he had worked at a coaching school, so to kill time between jobs he started his own course. His first class was nineteen students and they met in his parents' apartment. His second was forty-three, and not long after, his mother kicked the course out of the apartment.

At that point, SAT said that if a student took the test twice—once as a junior and once as a senior—the average improvement was about 10 points on math and 15 points on verbal. For 40 percent of the students who repeated the test, scores actually declined. The people who took Katzman's course improved an average of 140 points on the math and verbal combined.

In the mid-'80s Katzman got together with Bob Scheller, the man who had run the course Katzman worked in during high school. Scheller and Katzman were getting the same results using different, but complementary approaches. They decided to combine their techniques. Katzman said: "When we combined our approaches, both of our results went up, to about 185 points. That's our average. With kids who are serious, our average is closer to 250 points. Roughly 30 percent of our students this past spring went up over 250."[92]

What Katzman and Scheller had done was find weaknesses in the test. They used statistical analyses of the tests that were possible because the ETS's "obsession with consistency" made their tests "extremely predictable." In essence, they tried to understand the mind-set of the people who created the tests, and teach that mind-set. They did not teach material that would not be on the test. We can see this more clearly from the 1994–97 Princeton Review Course Manual:

"The people in charge of producing the SAT are Jim Braswell and Pamela Cruise. Jim is in charge of producing the math SAT. Pam is in charge of the verbal. Picture typical high school teachers and you'll have a pretty good idea of what they're

[91] The following comes from Sacks, op. cit. See the chapter "Beating the Test."

[92] It is interesting to note that the Princeton people believe it is *easier* to prep for the graduate exams than the regular college boards. Because fewer people take them, less effort goes into changing them. To find patterns and teach them is simply easier to do.

like. . . . The instructions of the SAT tell you to select the *best* answer to each question. What does 'best' mean? The best answer is not what *you* think is best, not what *we* think is best, nor what your high school teacher may think is best. The best answer to a math question is the choice that Jim thinks is right. The best answer to a verbal question is the choice that Pam thinks is right."

(A note of irony. As we saw earlier, the greatest mind of our time, Stephen Hawkings, believes the goal of science is to discover what is in the mind of God. On a more practical note, in our market economy, the trick is to understand what is in the minds of Jim and Pam.)

While the details of what Katzman and Scheller figured out are interesting, this is not the place to explore them.[93] One example will be instructive.

For a question to be included on the SAT, one of the qualities it must have is this: High-scoring students tend to get it right, and low-scoring students tend to get it wrong. In a multiple-questions test, the right answer is always there. The right answer has to look wrong to the low-scoring students. If not—if the right answer looks like the right answer to the wrong people—it never makes it to the regular SAT. The people who write the answers try to anticipate errors that will be made by different sets of students. An "effective" item is one that will trick the low-scoring student away from the right answer.

For those who coach people on how to improve their scores, that is the opening they need. Adam Robinson was the man who first figured it out. He invented an average test-taker and named him Joe Bloggs. His average Joe scores 450 on the SAT. The people from ETS lay traps for Joe, and the Princeton Review people teach students to avoid those traps.

When they get to hard questions, the students are coached to ask themselves: "What would Joe do here?" Then they are coached to do something else. In one of the examples offered by Sacks, a student could easily eliminate two of the four answers because they are the two that Joe would have liked. There were two left, and it was easy to figure out which one was right.

Of course, Joe is not always wrong. When a question is easy, then the obvious or apparent answer is the one the student should choose.

We can put this in a different way. The hundreds of dollars spent on the Princeton Review course is money well spent. While the student might learn things that will never be helpful again in his or her life, in a culture of testing, then knowing how to take any particular test is important. And, to end with the obvious, this legal test-taking advantage is a socioeconomic class advantage.

THE ECONOMICS OF TESTING

Money and testing are related in different ways. The business of testing is big business. While the exact numbers are impossible to know, it is estimated that in 1998 a student entering a school in the California state system could expect to take at

---

[93] Sacks does a good job. He gives test examples and how Katzman and Scheller coach people to find the "best" answer.

least ten standardized tests before graduating from high school. In Chicago, a student can expect to take two dozen tests from the middle of the third grade to the end of the fourth.

For education alone, it is estimated that anywhere from 143 million to nearly 400 million standardized tests are given yearly.[94] As many as 200 million are given for business, industry, government, and the military. If we take the highest estimates, that means 600 million standardized tests are given in the United States every year—or, a little more than two for every person. It takes exactly no imagination to understand that there is money to be made in testing.

It is estimated that in 1999 the corporations that manufacture and score standardized tests took in revenues of $250,000,000.[95] For more than a decade, revenues have been growing rapidly and there seems to be no slowdown in sight. In terms of irony, the money has been sensational for the nonprofit Educational Testing Service. In 1983 this private, tax-exempt organization had revenues that exceeded $130 million. It pays no income tax and does not have to report any financial information to the U.S. Securities and Exchange Commission. By 1996 revenues were over $413 million. Even better. That year they had a cash position of $41 million.[96] The next year they had a $46 million cash reserve.

In 1998, their fiftieth anniversary, they had a budget of $460 million and employed 2,400 people with offices across the country. A sense of how testing has increased: From 1980 to 1995 their sales increased 256 percent. One example: The revenues for standardized tests for teachers and others in the academy increased 300 percent during that time.

ETS does much more than the SAT. Indeed, they have over a hundred testing programs. Among other things, they do the graduate record exams, the national teacher exam, the national assessment of education process exam. In addition, they do dozens of occupational certification and licensing exams.[97] They are not part of the government. They are an independent, nonprofit organization that makes a great deal of money.

At some point it might be interesting to visit their 360-acre campus. To see the swimming pool, the hotel, the tennis courts, and the offices, it becomes clear that they spend much of that money on themselves. In August 2000, Kurt Landgraf became the president of ETS. In his first ten months on the job, he was paid $800,000.[98] That year, fifteen ETS officers received bonuses totaling $2 million. The ETS is a remarkably powerful organization that answers to no one and does not pay taxes.

(As a kind of trickle-down from ETS, the income of the Princeton Review was about $60 million a year in the mid-'90s. There are no dollar figures for the Stanley

[94] Ibid., p. 221.

[95] Kohl, op. cit., p. 3.

[96] Owen, op. cit., p. 8.

[97] Ibid.

[98] "Nonprofit test company pays 6-figure bonuses," *The Boston Globe*, November 24, 2002, p. A25.

Kaplan Company—they are owned by the Washington Post Company—but in 1997 they had 125,000 customers. One can calculate they did a little better than Princeton.)

Much of the rest of the money is divided by only a few major corporations. General Cinema Corporation, formally a chain of movie theaters, bought the publisher Harcourt Brace. Now called Harcourt General, it signed a four-year deal with the state of California to provide its *Stanford 9* achievement tests to more than four million students. In 1998 alone, the deal was worth $30 million.[99] In 1995, they also bought a company that provides electronically delivered employment tests. By 1998 those revenues had doubled to $50 million.

Houghton Mifflin owns the Riverside Publishing Company that publishes the *Iowa Test of Basic Skills*, the *Stanford-Binet Intelligence Scale*, as well as about 240 other tests. In 1998 they bought an electronic testing company (Computer Adaptive Technologies) in an effort to get into that $1.6 billion market. Given the interest in standardized testing, the Riverside company reported a 17 percent sales increase in 1997. Houghton Mifflin did $800 million in sales in 1997, but did not break down how much it made with each test.

National Computer Systems is now a $400 million company that is in the business of "managing massive amounts of data that comes with standardized testing of schoolchildren on a large scale." In the late 1990s, the company estimated that the "test administration" part of the testing business was worth about one billion dollars. In 1997 its sales grew 23 percent, and from 1994 to 1997 its revenues increased nearly 60 percent. By 1997 NCS was processing more than 50 million tests a year.

CTB/McGraw-Hill is another big player. It does the biggest business in the norm-referenced tests. These are the tests that indicate a score in its relationship to the national average. The comparison to national average is becoming more popular. They publish the *California Achievement Tests*, the *Comprehensive Test of Basic Skills*, and the *National Educational Development Test.* They make, sell, process, and administer the tests. While sales are not broken down, the educational and professional division contributed half of the $3.5 billion sales in 1997.

There are other money matters that need only be mentioned. For example, at one point recently, the state of Texas spent most of its education budget on testing. The more high-stakes the testing, the more each state spends money that was intended for education on testing. And, of course, there are the everyday numbers that we just accept. Nationwide we spend about $5,000 a year on each student and $22,000 a year on each prisoner.[100] From that point, it is an easy path to think about gross injustice.

Someone did this math. Michael Ovitz was fired from his job at Disney. His work was inadequate. Ovitz worked for sixty weeks, and his bonus for being fired was between $70 and $100 million. If you take the "low" figure, then Ovitz got a bonus of $29,166.67 for each hour of his unsatisfactory work.[101] For some perspective, in 1995 one-third of all children lived in homes with incomes less than $25,000. Or, to the

[99] These and the following numbers come from Sacks, op. cit., pgs. 223–9.

[100] Ohanian, op. cit., p. 118.

[101] Ibid., pgs. 114–5.

point, their yearly income was less than Ovitz bonus for one hour of work that was judged failing.

This is simply more data that money is important, and the lack of money is even more important.

SUMMARY

In an earlier chapter, the professions of education and medicine were compared. Interestingly, the medical profession came up again, at least metaphorically, in the reading I did for this chapter. The medicine/education relationship is an appropriate way to begin our summary.

The first example, not surprisingly, has to do with familiar material. Susan Ohanian (who, by the way, is a wonderful writer), reminds us that "25 to 45 percent of the 190 million doses of antibiotics administered even in hospitals are unnecessary, never mind those administered out of the physicians' offices. . . . In 1995, methicillin-resistant staph infections killed 1,409 people in New York City. That is 200 more people than were murdered in the city during the same year.

"Although I believe that schools induce bugs as pernicious in their own way as those in hospitals, I don't want to carry this metaphor too far. But I do insist that we should not look at children as a disease that we need to cure."[102]

The second is a hospital analogy that is concerned with teaching to the test. It is from Linda Darling-Hammond.[103] "Suppose it has been decided that hospital standards must be raised, so all patients must now have their temperatures taken on a regular basis. Shortly before the thermometers are inserted, doctors administer huge doses of aspirin and cold drinks. Remarkably, then, it turns out that no one is running a fever! The quality of hospital care is at an all-time high! What is really going on, of course, is completely different from providing good health care and assessing it accurately—just as teaching to the test is completely different from providing good instruction and assessing it accurately."

Finally, there is simply the matter of fairness.[104] "Where is the thunderous denunciation of the American Medical Association because the U.S. ranks twenty-eighth in the incidence of low-birth-weight infants? Japanese children outscore Americans on math tests. They also have half the risk of infant mortality. . . . Yammering about standards . . . shifts responsibility . . . [from]looking at issues of poverty, teen pregnancy, drug use, violence, and the safeguarding of children . . . [to] 'Let's prove we have standards by giving a national test.'"

There is a continual tug about what the real issue should be, who is at fault, and how to cure the problem. It is all remarkably political. If the discussion is about "standards" and high-stakes testing, then the idea of education seems to get lost almost at

[102] Ibid., p. 62.

[103] Found in Kohl, op. cit., p. 32.

[104] Ohanian, op. cit., p. 115.

once. The conservatives who have insisted the debate should be about high-stakes testing have already won. The political rule is simple: If you control the topic you have won the argument. High-stakes testing is not about education, nor does it focus on any problem that is remotely important. But it has been in the spotlight for almost two decades. We know that schooling has always followed the rules set for it by its society. No one should be surprised that schools are obsessed with testing.

Tests, of course, are not all bad. We know that one of their weaknesses is also one of their strengths. That they are standardized and everyone takes the same test means that it is possible for anyone to do well. There are many examples of students from low-income neighborhoods and go to rundown, inner-city schools who score brilliantly well on exams. Because of that, they are recruited by the elite and educated and trained to succeed. Without standardized tests those people would have almost no chance.

And we know that other kinds of testing help identify the needs of different students. The tests identify weaknesses and strengths that are necessary for educators to know. If used carefully, this kind of testing is very useful.

Data indicates that it is not that simple. Standardized testing is something like Mother Justice. There she stands, blindfolded, with the scales of justice in one hand, a sword in the other. The image is wonderful. Justice is blind. It is equal justice for all. (In pre-revolution France they talked about equal justice, and no one believed the ironic line that it was the same for the pauper living under the bridge as it was for the aristocrat.) In reality, standardized tests and justice in the United States are strikingly similar. Lower class and minorities have about the same chance in courts as they do taking standardized tests.

What we know is that prisons are full of minorities and the poor—not the white middle-upper-middle and upper classes. In standardized tests that offer the same kind of equal chance for everyone, we get exactly the same kind of skewed results.

Not surprisingly, testing has been challenged in the courts. The most well-known case is *Debra P. v Turlington* (1981). It was a case in which Florida's minimum competency test was found illegal. The U.S. court of appeals found that if a high school graduation test covered material that had not been taught, then the test violated the Fourteenth Amendment to the U.S. Constitution. While there are scores of other cases, it is important for us simply to note that testing, like so many other things in our society, generally ends up in litigation. We can expect more and more court action as testing becomes increasingly high-stakes.

To understand testing and the tests more clearly, we turn to psychometricians. These are the people who design the tests. It is part of their business to know what tests are capable of doing and under what conditions. In the next two sections we will see what an appropriate test might look like, and a list of suggestions about what we need to consider about future testing.

Not all tests are bad and not all testing is harmful. The National Assessment of Educational Progress (NAEP) may be as good as any large-scale test. It is part multiple-choice, part performance-oriented, and part open-ended. It tests reading, math, science, and other subjects, and is given to fourth-, eighth-, and twelfth-graders. While the test is not given to all students every year, they have gotten reliable results for states using samples from different parts of the country.

It is called "the nation's report card" and gives us a sense of the proficiency of our students. There are several very important things we need to know about the test.

1. It is well constructed. The data it provides are valid and the information is useful.

2. It is low-risk. Indeed, it is a no-stakes test. The competitive pressure is off. The fear of not being promoted to the next grade, or not getting a diploma is not there. The test, then, has a chance of getting a more accurate picture of what the students know.

3. "NAEP is forbidden by law to report the results at an individual or school level."

These three characteristics are overwhelmingly important when we think about testing. They give us an important sense about what good and appropriate testing is all about. The NAEP tests conform to the standards suggested by psychometricians. They are more than multiple-choice. Good tests allow the person who takes the test to provide answers as well as select them. We have seen that low-risk or no-risk testing is more reliable than high-risk testing. The data we reviewed showed that those states with high-risk testing had the lowest rates of improvement on standardized tests.

These tests are appropriate. Psychometricians tell us that there must be measurement validity; that it must be the right test for the particular purpose of the test. There must be appropriate attribution of cause. In other words, a student's performance on the test must reflect his or her knowledge or skills. Other influences such as poor instruction, language barriers or disabilities that are irrelevant to the material being measured must be eliminated. And finally, the results of the test must lead to educationally beneficial decisions for the person being tested.[105]

Good testing seems as easy as one, two, three: 1) the test must be well constructed; 2) the test should be low-risk; 3) the results must be used in appropriate ways. To fail at any of these means that the tests might do more harm than good. The problem is that the psychometricians cannot (and probably will never be able to) construct tests that will satisfy the demands of the policy makers. In terms of outcomes, a well-constructed test, used in an inappropriate way, is simply a bad test.

The Congress of the United States asked the National Academy of Sciences to "conduct a study and make written recommendations on appropriate methods, practices, and safeguards to ensure that" tests adequately assess student reading and mathematics comprehension and achievement and do so in a nondiscriminatory manner. Let me list some of the recommendations.

1. "In general, large-scale assessments should not be used to make high-stakes decisions about students who are less than 8 years old or enrolled below grade 3."

---

[105] Roughly, these have been the criteria of the National Research Council for two decades.

2. "Accountability for educational outcomes should be a shared responsibility of states, school districts, public officials, educators, parents and students. High standards cannot be established and maintained merely by imposing them on students."

3. "A test may appropriately be used to lead curricular reform, but it should not also be used to make high-stakes decisions about individual students until test users can show that the test measures what they have been taught."

4. "Policy-makers should monitor both the intended and unintended consequences of high-stakes assessments on all students and on significant subgroups of students, including minorities, English-language learners, and students with disabilities."

5. "All students are entitled to sufficient test preparation so their performance will not be adversely affected by unfamiliarity with item format or by ignorance of appropriate test-taking strategies. Test users should balance efforts to prepare students for a particular test format against the possibility that excessively narrow preparation will invalidate test outcomes."

6. As tracking is currently practiced, low-track classes are typically characterized by an exclusive focus on basic skills, low expectations, and the least-qualified teachers. Students assigned to low-track classes are worse off than they would be in other placements. This form of tracking should be eliminated. Neither test scores nor other information should be used to place students in such classes."

7. "If a cutscore is to be employed on a test used in making a tracking or placement decision, the quality of the standard-making process should be documented and evaluated."

8. "Scores from large-scale assessments should never be the only sources of information used to make a promotion or retention decision. No single source of information—whether test scores, course grades, or teacher judgments—should stand alone in making promotion decisions. Test scores should always be used in combination with other sources of information about student achievement."

There are dozens of recommendations. They range from test construction, to students with disabilities, to the appropriate use of test scores. These are serious recommendations offered by people who know testing from the inside out.

Will policy makers take these recommendations as seriously as they were offered? A good guess would be no. Rarely does data get in the way of ideology. Standards and high-stakes testing are with us for the foreseeable future.

If the policy makers are unmoved by the reality of testing and test results, then maybe it is time that the people who make the tests become involved. The psychometricians have the best understanding about what tests can and cannot do. Their focus, understandably, is on test construction. It is their job to construct valid tests.

But what we have seen is that a well-constructed, valid test may have harmful outcomes. We are at a point in schooling that the "how a test is used is not my business" defense of the psychometricians simply does not hold up. To ignore the context of your work, in the end, is not viable. To shrug off the uses of tests by policy makers is to assume that schooling is not a public issue.

The quickest way for testing to be used in an appropriate way would be for psychometricians to insist on it. It would be interesting if psychometricians had the same passion for the appropriate use of tests as they do for a well-constructed test. It seems a necessary ethical position. Public schools await the political emergence of those who construct their tests.

THINK ABOUT

1. If education is all about excellence, then what is so bad about testing for it?

2. True or false: We each have an innate intelligence that is ours forever. What we need are better ways to measure that intelligence. Explain why you think the way you do.

3. Do you agree that it is the right of any society to reward certain skills and not others?

CHAPTER 11

THE SKY IS FALLING
Who Are These Kids?

Contemporary culture is rushing like a hungry Rottweiler down the hill at our kids.
Walt Mueller

There is no terror in the bang, only in the anticipation of it.
Alfred Hitchcock

Man thinks and God laughs.
Yiddish saying

You walk into the classroom and see a generation that is, in ways, different than your generation. The events of the world in which they are growing up are not what yours were. In this chapter we are not going to dwell on the differences of the students sitting in your class; we are going to concentrate on what they have in common. What they have in common is culture.

The culture in the United States is overwhelmingly strong. It dictates much of what we do. Even if you hate it, you are forced to spend a great deal of time thinking about it in order to fight it. In other words, like it or not, the culture of the United States is remarkably powerful. (And this is not simply a national fact. The terrorist war against the United States is as much about what is seen as our moral/cultural corruption as our foreign policy choices. American culture is understood by many in the international community as nothing less than an imperialism of Western capitalist decay.)

The students sitting in your classroom are ground zero when it comes to our culture. As we will see, youth control a huge amount of spending, and the predictable result is that much of advertising, media, and music are aimed at that money. For the last few decades there has been a heightened sense that youth is more highly valued than age. Since the rebellions of the '60s, young has been better than old. From the time that you couldn't trust anyone over thirty, the idea of aging has been a bad idea in the United States. As we saw earlier, a huge industry has developed that is devoted to help us at least look younger.

The result of being the target of so much attention means something. In this chapter we will see how people understand the effects of culture on our youth. The chapter will be divided into three sections. The first section will deal with broad themes. We will review ideas about how youth is affected by what it sees and hears in the popular culture.

In the second section, our attention will be on computers. As you know, there has been a huge push to make certain that every student in every school should have access to computers. We will see that many families believe it is important for their preschool children to become computer literate. What we do not know is the effect (if any) computers might have on them. It is also important to think about how computers help, or hurt, education.

Finally, there will be a short discussion about law. As a teacher it has become increasingly important to be familiar with legal issues. As we have seen, litigation is one of the driving forces in education. It ended segregation and opened schooling for the disabled, to remember two positive examples. But litigation is woven into the core of our culture. It was simply a matter of time before it entered the classroom. In this section, we will discuss what that means to the teacher.

We begin with the effects of culture on our students.

"Where are you going, my fine feathered friend?" asked Foxy Woxy. He spoke in a polite manner, so as not to frighten them.
"The sky is falling!" cried Chicken Little. "We must tell the King."
"I know a shortcut to the palace," said Foxy Woxy sweetly. "Come and follow me."

THE SKY IS FALLING

There seems to be a general sense that the sky has fallen. Much of the literature about the current generation of students is that it has fallen under the evil cloud of culture, and things are bleak beyond belief. Of course there are those who believe everything is either all right (or even better than ever), but generally culture—and its children—take a beating by older folks.

What we will see is a surprising amount of agreement by the conservatives and liberals. Although they disagree on solutions, they seem to agree on the problems caused by popular culture. It is clear that the people we will study are passionately committed to what they understand to be higher goals. What is less certain is the accuracy of their critiques and the validity of their pessimism. In truth, I do not believe we know what we're talking about when we make pronouncements about the effects of culture on our society.

It is certainly possible, and even admirable, to discuss what you like and what you dislike. That seems to be at the root of our politics as well as our capitalism. But I'm not convinced that we can actually sort out causes and effects of cultural dynamics. Most of the studies are inconclusive. We will see the old truth that there are lies, damned lies, and statistics.

This is not a new dynamic. The first generation Puritans did not trust their children. That seems to be the first case of a generation gap in the New World. As we saw earlier, during the 1980s *A Nation at Risk* tried to document the horrible state of our schooling—and our students. Now that we have gotten to the twenty-first century, nothing much has changed. The only difference is that the satan of the Puritans is now clothed in popular culture. Like those early white people who landed in Massachusetts, we continue to believe that the next generation is damned to a kind of secular hell.

What follows is a sampling of what a variety of authors think about the current generation of students. The book *Greater Expectations: Overcoming the Culture of Indulgence in our Homes and Schools*[1] won the Parent's Choice Book Award. On the cover of the book we read that it "exploded many of the misconceptions about children. . . ." The author, William Damon, is a professor at Brown University.

Basically, this is Damon's view of our young people. "All the commonly accepted standards for young people's skills and behaviors have fallen drastically. Less is expected of the young, and in turn less is received. . . . Too many children . . . are drifting through their childhood years without finding the skills, virtues, or sense of purpose that they will need to sustain a fruitful life . . . [there is] a loss of moral standards and a debilitating lack of spirit."[2]

In his studies and travels, Damon writes that he came to appreciate the "full seriousness of the youth crises that has been building for at least the past few decades." It is important to note that the crises are widespread. For him, class, color, and culture cannot protect a child from the crises.

Walt Mueller has his master's in Divinity from the Gordon-Conwell Theological Seminary. His is a book with a Christian focus. On the back cover is this: "CAUTION: Because of the nature of today's world of music and media, chapters 4 and 5 contain unusually graphic material."[3] His book won the Gold Medallion Book Award.

Mueller writes that "It is a big mistake to think of our children as liabilities; they are a reward from God, given as a sign of God's favor."[4] He then quotes a report from the National Association of State Boards of Education:

> For the first time in the history of this country, young people are *less* healthy and *less* prepared to take their places in society than were their parents. And this is happening at the time when our society is more complex, more challenging, and more competitive than ever."[5]

Morris Berman is equally pessimistic. His critique is more inclusive, although later we see that he has a special problem with our youth. Berman believes that "hype and life have merged in the United States." That when we consider "the collapse of American

---

[1] William Damon, *Greater Expectations: Overcoming the Culture of Indulgence in Our Homes and Schools*, (New York: Free Press Paperbacks, 1995).

[2] Ibid., pgs. xii–xiv.

[3] Walt Mueller, *Understanding Today's Youth Culture, Revised & Expanded* (Wheaton, Ill.: Tyndale House 1999).

[4] Ibid., p. 6.

[5] Ibid., p. 38

intelligence, we find a picture that is unambiguously bleak." And he quotes, with appreciation, from the novel *White Noise:* "Were we this dumb before television?" [6]

Berman believes that civilization, as we know it, is about over. It is his belief that we will enter a new version of the Dark Ages, and the chosen few need to be prepared. (We should note the irony that this is the same vision that the 9/11 terrorists see as positive. Their vision of the good life seems to be close to that of the Dark Ages.)[7]

The final example of how we understand our students comes from Henry Giroux. Giroux argues that "childhood is being reinvented, in part through the interests of corporate capital." [8] He believes the "ongoing demonization" of young people is a result of corporate capital, and is leading to diminishing public space and freedom to grow. Put differently, our culture has used youth in a way that has been destructive.

If we are to believe what these writers say, and they are a good cross-section of the current thinking, then when you walk into the classroom, your students will not be a happy bunch. Nor will they be bright, well-motivated, well-prepared, or well-mannered. The question is simple: What happened?

THE SINS OF CULTURE

There seems to be much wrong with our culture and we are told that its effects are everywhere. Walt Mueller gives us a list:

1. The changing family. Mueller means there is too much divorce. There are 1.2 million divorces finalized a year, and it is estimated that as many as 60 percent of the children born in the '90s lived in a single-parent home. Over 27 million children under the age of eighteen live apart from their biological father. He writes: "It is no surprise to learn that 60 percent of America's rapists, 72 percent of adolescent murderers, and 70 percent of long-term prison inmates grew up without a dad."[9] We will return to this point, and question why Mueller seems to fault single mothers.

There is an increase in family violence. One of four girls and one of seven boys have been sexually abused.

2. Music and other media give the wrong messages to our children. It has led to too much sex, materialism, substance abuse, depression, and suicide.

3. Finally, modern philosophy is dangerous. Postmodernism, with the message that there is no objective truth has led to a terrible moral relativism. It is a "way of thinking and living that allows people to discover and invent truth for themselves."[10]

---

[6]Morris Berman, *The Twilight of American Culture* (New York: W. W. Norton, 2000), pgs. 3, 33, 42.

[7]The idea of the Dark Ages being anything like the "good life" is, for most Westerners, a foolish notion. For example, not many believe in the absolute subjection of women or doing away with most of our modern technology.

[8] Henry Giroux, *Stealing Innocence: Corporate Culture's War on Children* (New York: Palgrave, 2000), p. 14.

[9] Mueller, op. cit. p. 40.

[10] Ibid., p. 46.

For many, postmodernism is an empty and corrupt philosophy that, it is claimed, has led to a meaningless life for those who accept it.

To take this last point for a moment. It seems reasonable that a minister would have trouble with postmodernism. The idea of god, after all, is merely one of many competing ideas in this philosophy. But Morris Berman is certainly no minister. He is a self-described elitist who believes our society needs to be saved from our corporate, consumer culture. Berman also dislikes postmodernism and the deconstructionists.

While the students in your class have probably not studied these contemporary ideas, the ideas are part of the cultural context in which they live. Berman writes that current philosophy "promotes a valueless universe." That "one value is as good as another, that there is no difference between knowledge and opinion, and that any text or set of ideas is merely a mask for someone's political agenda."[11]

We read that "postmodernism brought to the table not merely the denial of truth but also the denial of the *ideal* of truth. Facts are regarded as 'fetish,' all methodology is 'problematic,' and sometimes even the highest forms of culture are despised . . . . This is not merely intellectual failure; it is moral failure as well."[12]

A philosophy of despair leads, it seems, to a life of despair. Drugs, violence, and suicide are seen as signs that life is meaningless to our youth. In this view, the moral corruption of our philosophers has led to the general corruption of society. I suppose we can really date this back to the 1800s when existentialists began to write. As the great-great-great-grandchildren of Nietzsche, should we be surprised that we have a generation of students unwilling to accept more traditional values?

It is interesting that both liberals and conservatives do not like postmodern thought. There is, of course, absolutely no way to show that postmodernist thought is responsible for any action of any student—much less the "character" of an entire generation. Indeed, it is almost charming to believe that philosophy has such an immediate effect on everyday life.

MOVIES AND THE CORPORATE MEDIA

There seems to be much to criticize about movies and television. Media, controlled by huge corporations, produces too much violence, sex, drugs, and general mindlessness. The specific evils are in the eyes of the beholders, so in order to get a sense of how movies and television corrupt our youth it is necessary to review what different people find objectionable.

Morris Berman begins his objection of movies with their very location. He quotes David Denby:[13] "The mass audiences view these Hollywood-formula products

[11] Berman, op. cit., p. 50.

[12] Berman is discussing the thought of Alvin Kernan from *In Plato's Cave*. Ibid., p. 51.

[13] David Denby, "The Moviegoers," *The New Yorker*, 6, April 1998, pgs. 94–101. Ibid., p. 60.

not at individual theaters, 'but at malls and twelveplexes, among video games and roller rinks, where they absorb the quick turnover attitude toward merchandise which mall life imposes on everyone.'"

Movies, to follow this reasoning, are merely fluff used to entice kids to go to the mall. (He points out in horror that 4 billion square feet of land is devoted to malls in the United States.)[14] The underlying assumption seems to be that movies would be better if they were in individual theaters, if only because of the lack of video games in individual theaters. Berman believes that the mall moviegoers are "totally uninterested in artistic quality." That the United States has become a "culture-free zone" and the actual location of movies is visible proof.

To show that we are becoming increasingly thoughtless, Berman writes:[15] "The celebration of ignorance that characterizes America today can be seen in the enormous success of a film like *Forrest Gump*, in which a good-natured idiot is made into a hero." To enjoy *Forrest Gump* in a theater located in a mall is, for Berman, a combination of mass culture and artistic corruption that condemns both adults and children to a bleak future.

Henry Giroux is equally passionate about the sins of our corporate culture. Here is his list of bad movies:[16] "Films such as *Jawbreakers, Varsity Blues, Ten Things I Hate About You*, and *Cruel Intentions* relentlessly celebrate mindless, testosterone-driven, infantilitized males at the top of a repressive school pecking order or equally vacuous, but also ruthless, arrogant, sexually manipulative girls, who come dangerously close to being cold-blooded psychopaths . . . . *Election* . . . views, . . . white suburban kids as inane, neurotically self-centered, or sexually deviant." And heroin looks chic in the movies *Another Day in Paradise* and *Pulp Fiction.*[17]

For Giroux, these films reinforce the negative assumptions that adults have about kids. The films help adults come to the conclusion that "kids are in need of medical treatment, strict controls, or disciplinary supervision." In his terms, the "media machine" helps legitimate the "cultural face of corporate power." It provides an excuse to impose corporate values on the young.

At a more concrete level, Walt Mueller is able to find serious problems with a wide range of movies. He begins with statistics:[18] "nearly one quarter of all PG and PG-13 films include the 'f-word'; 61 percent take the Lord's name in vain; 71 percent contain vulgar references to excretion, intercourse, or the genitals; 50 percent imply sexual intercourse while 13 percent show intercourse; 30 percent feature explicit nudity; 75 percent display moderate or severe violence; and 74 percent depict alcohol and/or other drug use." Mueller gives us examples of the movies that are harmful to our children.

---

[14] Ibid., p. 119.

[15] Ibid., p. 41.

[16] Giroux, op. cit., p. 20.

[17] Ibid., pgs. 70–1.

[18] Mueller, op. cit., p. 154.

The Basketball Diaries has a fantasy sequence in which a young man goes into his classroom in a Catholic high school and kills his classmates. All of the *Die Hard* series were too violent, as was *Total Recall*. In *Interview with the Vampire*, 1,114 people were killed. Then there are the horror movies—the *Nightmare on Elm Street* series, the *Scream* series, *Pet Cemetery*, and *Dancing in the Dark* that are not suited for children.

There is also too much sex. *Showgirls*, or worse yet, *Boogie Nights*, which was about a young man with a big penis who became a porn star. *Basic Instinct* and *Love Crimes* linked love with death and abuse. There is incest: *Sleepwalkers* had mother–son intercourse, and *Oliver* was about brother and sister sexual relationships.

According to Mueller, "a growing number of films promote, glorify, or at the very least open the door on the closet of homosexuality. . . . Films like *The Birdcage* and *In & Out* humorize homosexuality, making it cuddly and snuggly."[19] Movies can also "honor the dishonorable." In *The Bridges of Madison County*, "moviegoers drawn into the story raved, and in effect, glorified an adulterous couple."[20]

Finally, we read that a "frightening message" of *Home Alone* and *Home Alone 2* was that "parents are stupid and incompetent idiots . . . while children are competent to survive on their own, even in the midst of life-threatening danger. The bottom line: Who needs parents?"[21]

In the preceding chapter we saw how some "experts" responded to what they understand as a crisis in education by demanding certain standards be met in test scores. While it seemed clear that test scores were most closely related to socioeconomic status and sex, we now must consider a broader critique. We can use movies not only as a metaphor for what is wrong with our culture, but critics tell us they are a genuinely bad influence on our youth.

Most telling about the above list of movies is that almost nothing seems suitable for either children or adults. Without much trouble, we could find something disagreeable with every movie. Did the *Basketball Diaries* lead to the slaughter of students in Catholic high schools? Was that the point of the movie? Did people who saw *The Bridges of Madison County* suddenly decide that adultery was glamorous? Was Robin Williams, who starred in *The Birdcage*, so "cuddly and snuggly" that young men decided to be gay? Or, did it make homosexuality seem OK which, apparently to Mueller, is a bad thing?

In truth it is difficult to know what to make of these particular cultural critiques. While each may be accurate, taken as a whole they are pretty foolish. The list is, at once, characterized by both moral self-righteousness and a lack of reality. They have deconstructed and analyzed movies in a way that reflects their biases. They have taken a "text" and shown us what they wanted us to see. Is it possible to laugh at *The Birdcage* and not want to be gay, cry at *The Bridges of Madison County* and not want to commit adultery, or watch *Forrest Gump* and still be able to read books, think and talk in an intelligent way?

[19] Ibid., p. 158.

[20] Ibid., p. 159.

[21] Ibid., p. 160.

Not to labor the point, but we are told that the students in your classes are surrounded by a corrupt culture and, it follows, they are being corrupted.

The critics would have us believe that the sky is falling.

Sex

The most troubling thing about the commercializing of sex, for most critics, is the emphasis on youth. They argue there is little difference between the marketing of adolescence and pornography. Sexy young people in ads are meant to appeal to the youth market as well as the prurient interest of the adult market. It destroys innocence and demeans adults. But, in our society, making money is the heart of prosperity, and selling to the young is good business. The youth market is a powerful economic force. It is estimated that teens spend almost $100 billion a year and influence how more than $300 billion is spent.[22]

Calvin Klein seems to have set the standard for being offensive. We read:[23] " . . . in his most recent jean ads, innocence becomes a fractured sign and is used unapologetically to present children as the objects of desire and adults as voyeurs. . . . Sexualizing children may be the final frontier in the fashion world, exemplified by the rise of models such as Kate Moss, who represent the ideal woman as a waif—sticklike, expressionless, and blank-eyed."

Again, about Calvin Klein:[24] "Klein's most controversial ad campaign featured wide-eyed teenagers in various states of dress and undress, all exposing their underwear. Getting lost in what was rightfully labeled child pornography was the fact that the ads were for jeans."

We see the ads, and Calvin Klein is not the only person to produce them. Beautiful people, both young and very young, are in our advertising consciousness. While we might not buy the cars, deodorant, beer, perfume, sheets, ovens, or whatever they are selling, we certainly see a remarkable number of attractive people everywhere we look.

What most of us do not see, but what Henry Giroux believes is symbolic of what we are doing to our children, are the beauty pageants.[25] It is estimated that, for children under twelve years old, there are 3,000 beauty pageants a year. More than 100,000 girls compete. Entry fees are between $250 and $800 for the national pageants, and the costs of preparing for a pageant (lessons, coaches, and costumes) are much more than that. At the low end, some pageants charge contestants only a dollar a pound.

In terms of the economy, that means there is money to be made on these young beauties. The promoters can make as much as $100,000 per event. There are the

---

[22] The first figure comes from D. Leonhardt and K. Kerwin, "Hey, Kid, Buy This!" *Business Week*, June 30, 1997, p. 62; the second comes from P. Zollo, "Talking to Teens," *American Demographics*, November 1995, in Mueller, op. cit., pgs. 162–3.

[23] Giroux, op. cit. p. 60.

[24] Mueller, op. cit. p. 164.

[25] What follows comes from Giroux, pgs. 51–8.

countless coaches and consultants, costume designers, and photographers. *Pageant Life*, a trade magazine, has a circulation of 60,000, and it is one of several.

Pageants, we are told, are good for many reasons. For parents, they are "a route to get their kids into lucrative careers such as modeling or to win college scholarships, financial rewards, and other prizes." For kids, they not only help build self-esteem, but are fun: "many young girls look at pageants as a protracted game of dress-up, something most young girls love."

The nature of pageants has changed over the years. During the '70s, the contestants wore little-girl dresses with ribbons in their hair, and did little-girl talents like tap dancing and baton twirling. Current contestants are "coquettish young women whose talents were reduced to an ability to move suggestively across the stage."

In the end, Giroux argues that these pageants have become a "degrading spectacle." They teach the young contestants that the culture will reward them for "their looks, submissiveness and sex appeal." He believes that "self-esteem often becomes a euphemism for self-hatred, rigid gender roles, and powerlessness."

The pageants are an expression of what goes on in the rest of American culture. Popular culture can be a realm of fantasy that includes "the promise of escape, possibility, and personal triumph."[26] That they center on children and sexuality makes them symbolically important. The argument is that it is bad enough that adult culture is one, big, corrupt beauty pageant, but it is shameless and destructive that our children are now involved in the same dynamic.

To walk into a class at almost any grade is to walk into an environment where there is competitive dressing and overt sexuality. For Giroux, this trend simply "suggests how vulnerable children are to learning the worst social dimensions of our society: misogyny, sexism, racism, and violence."[27]

Music is at the cutting edge of where the culture is sexual—and music has everything to do with our youth. There is little reason to recite the details. Love and sex has always been a major theme and subtheme of music. While "I Want to Hold Your Hand" isn't quite the same as "Me so Horny," the idea that kids and their music is about sex has been with us for decades.

From the Sex Pistols, who were seemingly out of control, to the '90s gangsta' rap, parents have been horrified with what their children listen to. (To be fair, parents have been unhappy with music since the '60s. To be accurate, country music has always been violent and sexist. Listen to the music of Hank Williams Jr., or Johnny Cash or even Tennessee Ernie Ford. Cash, for example, sings about shooting someone "just to see him die.")

Back to parents. They are horrified by the language, the message, and the messengers of their children's music. Raping women and killing police, not wholly unknown musical themes, are just not acceptable to many people. And with MTV, we get to see beautiful people make less than noble ideas seem attractive—or so it seems

[26] Ibid., p. 58.

[27] Ibid., p. 61.

to many adults. It is as if everything a kid both sees and hears is about sex. What is a teacher to do? The sky is falling.

Television

For years one of the ongoing critiques of our culture, and how it affects our children, has been about television. In 1946 there were about 10,000 television sets in the United States and about 54 million in 1960. By 1996, 99 percent of the households had at least one television, two-thirds had three or more sets, and about half of the households with children under eighteen had at least three sets.[28] We own more television sets than telephones, and the only thing more of us do than watch TV is brush our teeth (91 percent vs. 95 percent).[29]

An average child in the United States watches between four and five hours of television a day, and up to nine hours a day on weekends and vacations.[30] By the time the average student graduates from high school, he or she has watched about twenty-three thousand hours of television. That same student was in school about eleven thousand hours. By the end of elementary school, the student will have seen about eight thousand murders on television and a hundred thousand acts of violence. By the end of high school, a teenager would have seen Kenny die in every South Park show. Mercifully Kenny has finally stayed dead.

A study done in 1998 found that:

1. Perpetrators are unpunished in 73 percent of all violent scenes.
2. Almost half of the violent interactions show no harm to victims.
3. A little over half of violent interactions show no pain.
4. Twenty–five percent of the violence involves guns.
5. A little over half of all programming is violent.[31]

In 1960, 875 third-grade boys and girls were studied to see if there was a relation between the violence they saw on television and how they acted at school. When they were thirty years old they were studied again, and it was found that "those who had watched significant amounts of violent television were more likely to have been convicted of more serious crimes, to be more aggressive when drinking, and to inflict harsher punishment on their children."[32]

---

[28] "Facts about Media Violence," *American Medical Association Page*, 1997 (March 24, 1998); Steve Sherman, "A Set of One's Own: TV Sets in Children's Bedrooms," *Journal of Advertising Research* (November/December 1996), in Mueller, op. cit., p. 137.

[29] The teeth statistic comes from Mary Hapburn, "Medium's Effects under Scrutiny," *Social Education*, September 1997, p. 246. Ibid., p. 138.

[30] Damon, op. cit., p. 30.

[31] "National Television Violence Study," *Media Awareness Network Homepage* (March 24, 1998). In Mueller, op. cit. p. 142.

[32] "Sons of Violence," *Psychology Today*, July/August 1992. In Ibid., pgs. 143–4.

The general level of programming, violent or not, was criticized: "the content of most programming assumes an audience of morons. It also has something to do with a medium that creates an attention span in its viewers of about ten seconds, and assumes that real things can take place via images."[33] The author of the quote, Morris Berman, is offended by the lowbrow humor of *Cheers*, as well as the fact that Oprah Winfrey was asked to deliver the commencement address at Wellesley.

The angry Berman writes: "We live in a collective adrenaline rush, a world of endless promotional/commercial bullshit that masks a deep systemic emptiness, the spiritual equivalent of asthma."[34]

What are schools and teachers to do about it? For Neil Postman, the last thing in the world they should be doing is putting television sets in the classroom. But we know that is what is happening. There are now about 10,000 schools that accepted an offer of free, expensive television equipment, with a satellite dish. The school gets the equipment and their students get a ten-minute version of news every day.

The students also see two minutes of commercials with the news. Postman writes: "[It is]the first time, to my knowledge, that an advertiser has employed the power of the state to force anyone to watch commercials."[35]

If the sensitivity and sensibility of students are different because of television—if their attention span is shorter, their behavior worse, and they are used to being treated like morons—then what should a teacher do? Is it smart to reenact the rhythm of television? Should the classroom become live entertainment so the students, who have been weaned on the ever-changing violent and sexy electronic images of television, will enjoy coming to school?

Put differently, if these critiques of the media—and our children who watch it—are true, then is it the job of the teacher to re-create education so that these new (and very flawed) students are able to learn?

Before we try to answer that question, it is necessary to question the critiques. It is my sense that much of what we read has only tenuous ties to what we experience. Before getting to more serious questions, we need to consider the whole "the sky is falling" attitude about our culture.

FEAR ITSELF

The above version of reality—that corporate capitalism is everywhere, that the media portrays a life many of us do not endorse, and that sex and violence appear to be in everything we see and hear—is difficult to deny. There seems to be too much violence, too many drugs, too many lost children, and too much power that is centralized in a few huge corporations. The general sense of our youth is that

[33] Berman, op. cit., p. 42.

[34] Ibid., p. 54.

[35] Neil Postman, *The End of Education: Redefining the Value of School* (New York: Vintage Books, 1995), p. 34.

they are angry, lazy, unfocused, uninformed, sexually active too young, too indulged, too violent, and take too many illegal drugs. I say illegal drugs because some say they need more legal drugs, while others believe that they are given too many legal drugs.

We come to this question: Is the sky falling? Have we created a culture of fear that affects the way we understand and then treat our youth? Is ours a cultural wasteland? Is the next generation doomed? Do the kids you know fit the profile offered by the critics?

The basic assumption that children cannot tell the difference between reality and fantasy is deeply rooted in Western culture. As we saw in chapter one, Plato believed that there needed to be censorship of myths and poetry because "children cannot distinguish between what is allegory and what isn't." He believed that the myths children grow up with are the ones that stay with them for life. In the United States, before television, the critics believed that radio was going to be bad for youth for the very same reason: the inability to know the difference between fantasy and reality.

We need, then, to question the premise that there is a direct effect from what we see and hear on how we act. We need to look more carefully at the difference between the facts and our fears.

Violence

In the mid-1990s, two-thirds of Americans believed that crime rates were soaring. The truth is the crime rate had fallen every year from 1991 to 1997.[36] What we know for certain is that youth crime seems to be a cultural theme in the United States. Columbine is the metaphor for how many think about our young people and our schools.[37] From inner-city poverty to overindulged suburbs, it seems that no place is safe from violence.

In 1850 New York City recorded more than 200 gang wars. The gangs were made up mostly of adolescent boys. In 1946 a juvenile court judge wrote:[38] "A new army of six million men are being mobilized against us, an army of delinquents. Juvenile delinquency has increased at an alarming rate and is eating at the heart of America." Since the first-generation Puritans mistrusted their children, we have worried that the next generation is out of control.

In the past decade, there has been the perception that schools are unsafe. Inner-city schools have metal detectors and police, while suburban and rural schools are places where students massacre anyone in sight. In truth, three times as many people are killed by lightning every year than in schools. Studies show that "public schools are safer . . . than other locations where kids hang out, such as cars and

---

[36] Barry Glassner, *The Culture of Fear: Why Americans are Afraid of the Wrong Things* (New York: Basic Books, 1999), p. xi. Much of the section comes from this book.

[37] See Windy Murry Zoba, *Days of Reconning: Columbine and the Search for America's Soul* (Grand Rapids, Mich.: Brazos Press, 2000).

[38] Glassner, op. cit, p. 75.

homes. Attacks of all types against kids occur far more often away from schools than inside them."[39]

In 1996 teachers were asked about the biggest problems in their schools. Their list is revealing: parent apathy, lack of financial support, absenteeism, fighting, and too few textbooks. Almost 50 percent said that textbook shortages prevented them from assigning homework and that about 20 percent of the classroom disruptions were the result of students being forced to share textbooks.[40] It is hard to imagine, given the focus of the media, that teachers are most concerned with the lack of textbooks. School critics would have us believe that what most teachers wanted was permission to carry a weapon into their classroom in order to protect themselves.

If the perception of violence in schools is more than the reality of violence, then where do we get our fears? Missing children have been in our consciousness for decades. Every year more than 800,000 children disappear. A national survey found that 75 percent of parents feared that their child would be kidnapped by a stranger. The headlines and feature stories about abducted children regularly appear in our newspapers and on television. We see the faces of missing children on milk cartons, billboards, and posters. We teach our children to be afraid.

It is hard to think of anything worse than having your child taken by a stranger. "Don't talk to strangers" has always been good advice. One cannot be too careful.

To put the numbers in perspective is helpful. The "majority of missing children are runaways fleeing from physically or emotionally abusive parents. Most of the remaining number of missing children are 'throw aways' rejected by their parents, or abducted by estranged parents . . . . [A] total of 200 or 300 children a year are abducted by non-family members and kept for a long period of time or murdered. Another 4,600 of America's 64 million children (.001 percent) are seized by non-family members and later released."[41]

The bottom line seems to be that, while it is important that children be careful, there is no reason to create an environment of fear. Drs. Spock and Brazelton believe that kind of environment is unhealthy. Brazelton said:[42] "I don't think it's really appropriate to make them [kids] afraid of everybody."

The relationship of television to violence and despair has been a concern for some time. In the above section, we read the statistics about the remarkable amount of violence our kids see every day on television. The media add to this. Between 1990 and 1998, the nation's murder rate declined by 20 percent. At the same time, the number of murder stories on network news increased 600 percent—and that's not counting the O.J. coverage.[43] The statistics are frightening, but they are, after all, statistics. We need to revisit the world our kids watch everyday.

---

[39] Ibid., p. 76.

[40] Tamara Henry, "Textbooks Too Few, Too Old, Say Teachers," *USA Today*, February 29, 1996, quoted in ibid., p. 76.

[41] Ibid., p. 61.

[42] Ibid., p. 63.

[43] Ibid., p. xxi.

The Center for Communication Policy at UCLA studied 3,000 hours of programming on the major networks in the mid-1990s.[44] The study found that "a large proportion of the most sinister and decontextualized acts of violence on TV appear in cartoon shows . . . and on goofy prime-time programs such as 'America's Funniest Home Video's,' neither of which is likely to be confused with real life. By contrast, some of the most homicidal shows . . . portrayed violence as horribly painful and destructive and not to be treated lightly."[45]

If we are a violent country, and compared with others we certainly are, the variable might not be television. In a study of comparative violence, researchers found that the murder rate was 31 times greater in Detroit, Michigan, than it was in Windsor, Canada.[46] What makes the study interesting for our purposes is that the two cities are across the river from each other and see the same television shows.

There is another way to understand television. Patrick Cooke believes that there are more acts of kindness on television than acts of violence. "On sitcoms, romantic comedies, movies of the week, soaps, medical dramas, and even on police shows, people are constantly falling in love and helping each other out." Cook writes:[47] "[TV characters] share so much peace, tolerance and understanding that you might even call it gratuitous harmony." He asks if it isn't reasonable to conclude that "TV encourages niceness at least as much as it encourages violence?"

Tied to violence is the suicide rate of children. Between 1952 and 1992 teen and young adult suicides nearly tripled. In '92 the number of suicides was 1,847, or one in ten thousand. More of our young people are killed in automobile accidents. Or, more pressing, one out of nine goes hungry for a part of each month.

Since 1992 the suicide rate has fallen.

It is important to have some perspective on the environment in which our children live. There are more serious problems than the possible effects of television on our children. While we focus on media, we ignore the genuine effects of poverty. While we count the number of times Kenny is killed, we choose to forget that violent crimes are connected to guns. There are more guns *stolen* in the United States each year than some countries have guns.

Possibly, we are focusing on the wrong things.

Drugs and Sex

I will not make a case that drugs are good. We all know people who have had their lives destroyed by illegal drugs. What I would like to do is put drug use into perspective.

---

[44] The study, released in September 1995, was directed by Jeffrey Cole.

[45] Glassner, op. cit., p. 42.

[46] David Horowitz, "V Is for Vacuous Censorship," *Los Angeles Times*, February 8, 1996, p. B9.

[47] Patrick Cook, "TV Causes Violence," *New York Times*, August 14, 1993, cited by Glassner, op. cit., p. 43.

Perceptions first: in the late 1990s the majority of adults ranked drug abuse as the "greatest danger to America's youth."[48] While eight out of ten adults said that drugs had caused no problems with their families, they still believed that drug abuse was a major problem. In fact, the number of drug users had decreased by half since the late 1980s, and almost two-thirds of high school seniors had never used any illegal drugs, and that includes marijuana.

More Americans use legal drugs for nonmedical reasons than use cocaine or heroin, and more than half the people who die from drug-related medical problems or seek treatment for those problems are abusing prescription drugs. The American Medical Association estimates that "at least 15,000 doctors sell prescriptions to addicts and pushers."[49] Yet, our great fear is illegal drugs and in order to stop them we declared war on them years ago. We spend billions of dollars a year on the war on drugs, and only 1 percent of that budget is spent trying to stop the misuse of legal drugs.

About ten to fifteen kids out of a thousand report they use hard drugs as frequently as one time a month. Half of the college graduates get through without even a puff of marijuana, and a little over one in ten has tried cocaine in any form. Fears about the "date rape" drug seem exaggerated. Between 1996 and 1998 rape victims who believed they had been given the date rape drug were tested. Only 6 of 1,033 of the tests showed signs of the drug. About a third showed no drugs at all, and the rest had contained a variety of legal and illegal substances. The most common drug, far and away, was alcohol.[50]

Finally, the vast majority of teens who use drugs give them up in their early thirties. A study of more than 33,000 young Americans over an eighteen-year period, found that when people marry, drug use decreases dramatically. The habit that was most difficult to kick was cigarettes. Seven out of ten students who were smoking half a pack or more a day when they were seniors in high school were still smoking at the age of thirty-two.[51]

What's going on? The things we seem to fear the most—the drugs and sex (more about that later) and violence and television—may not be the most pressing problems. We really have little idea what effect television has on our children. While they may not be positive (the average weight of our children may be some combination of bad diet and sedentary life), there is no reason to believe they are as bad as the critics would have us believe.

What we find is that it isn't the illegal things as much as the legal things that we should fear. Guns, alcohol, legal drugs, and cigarettes are the cause of immediate and long-lasting harm and trauma. One problem with putting the normal critique in perspective is that it seems to diminish the horror that is violence, drug abuse, and child abduction. These are horrible things. Heart-breaking things. They destroy children and their families.

[48] Ibid., p. xi.

[49] Ibid., pgs. 131–2.

[50] Ibid., p. 148.

[51] Ibid., p. 143.

The problem is that we focus on the wrong things.

For some, the problem is that our culture is not like the culture they grew up in. In a general way, we can see this in the work of William Damon. He believes that we are raising our children with "mistaken beliefs." That a "diminution of standards and expectations for young people has occurred in every corner of the modern world."[52] What he implies is that there was a better time, a time when parenting assumed better beliefs.

Damon goes back to the Great Depression for a good example. Children were asked to help their families during that time. We read:[53] "These data show no overall ill effect of asking children to provide daily household help and other family services. On the contrary, all indications from the data are that children adapted to such demands as a matter of course. . . . In an old-fashioned phrase, they were character-building experiences." While giving children things to do around the house continues to be a good idea, Damon would have us believe that we have all lost those "old-fashioned" experiences.

Walt Mueller is more to the point. This is how he remembers TV violence growing up:[54] ". . . three little boys got in big trouble . . . their behavior was out of control. . . . It wasn't long before they [their parents] discovered that the boys were only imitating antics they had seen during the daily TV doses of *The Three Stooges*. My brothers and I still maintain our innocence, but that didn't stop our parents from removing Moe, Larry, and Curley from our TV diet for a few weeks." Now, he writes, he believes his parents were right: that life imitates art.

His connection with materialism has the same, sweet ring:[55] "My brothers and I used to fight over the Sears Christmas catalog. Each of us would spend hours paging through the toy section in the back, dreaming about the toys and games we wanted for Christmas." But he learned that even if he got those toys, they would not bring the satisfaction he had hoped for. That scale of consumerism could teach an important lesson. It was a far better way to learn it than the remarkable amount of things available and desired today.

Finally, Morris Berman offers examples of the good old days. He tells of visiting creative writing classes at a college in the Midwest "only to discover that not a single student in any of these classes had ever heard of Robert Browning, whereas I was memorizing 'My Last Duchess' when I was in high school."[56] A few pages later we read: "When I graduated from high school in 1962, littering the halls was considered a serious offense. Within ten years, at the very same high school, a girl was raped in broad daylight, and the situation has only escalated as the years have gone by. . . . [and one last shot at the "ignorant youth" of today] . . . if I memorized Robert Browning at age sixteen, most of today's college graduates have never heard of Robert Browning. . . ."[57]

---

[52] Damon, op. cit., p. 15.

[53] Ibid., pgs. 84–5.

[54] Mueller, op. cit., p. 135.

[55] Ibid., p. 280.

[56] Berman, op. cit., p. 38.

[57] Ibid., p. 43.

What I am suggesting is that at least part of the underlying critique of today's youth rests on the idea that the last good time to grow up was when the person doing the critique grew up. As if the Sears Christmas catalogue, high-energy kids playing out the Three Stooges (then getting that taken away), doing chores around the house during the Great Depression, and memorizing Robert Browning at sixteen were some kind of high-water marks for our culture.

Where is the talk about the repression of the '30s and the '50s? The racism and the sexism and the idea that kids should sit in straight rows, memorize lessons, and generally be seen and not heard? While the critiques have a certain ring of truth, citing the good old days does not do much to strengthen their cases.

That was then—enjoy your memories but get over it. It seems unreasonable to believe that the current generation wants to (or should) reenact your childhood.

The values these critics suggest are ones we need to consider, but they need to be put into the context of the twenty-first century. There are too many good kids doing extraordinarily good things to think we need to go back to repressive times in order to find virtue.

COMPUTERS: PRO AND CON

Pro

Reading the literature, it seems that television is really old news; it has been replaced with computers. We need to turn our attention to what this generation is doing. The voices for and against computers are strong, but it is important to remember this: We really do not know exactly what computers might be doing to the development of our children, or what a computerized world might be like. We don't know because computers are too new. There can be no long-term studies because computers haven't been around long enough.

We do know certain things. First, most of our children are much more comfortable and capable with computers than most adults. To butcher and misuse metaphors, computers are the sea our kids swim in, and when it comes to computers, adults are fish out of water. As we will see, power might be an issue around computers. Second, while there are many advocates of computers in the classroom, the benefits of this technology are vague. While there is some evidence that computers might have a serious downside, all we know for certain is that the financial costs are high.

In the above section we reviewed some of the critiques of television. What we read is that the Boomers, not this generation, grew up on television:[58] ". . . to today's media-literate kids, television's current methods are old-fashioned and clumsy . . . Today's kids watch less television than five years ago and much less than their parents did at the same age. . . . The digital media is swallowing TV. . . ." The new generation is between the ages of three and twenty-five in 2002. Two of the names for this generation are the *net generation* or *screenagers.*

---

[58] Don Tapscott, *Growing Up Digital: The Rise of the Net Generation* (New York: McGrew-Hill, 1998), pgs. 2–3.

The critique of television is that it is passive. While computers are interactive, television allows you to just sit back and veg out. TV robbed kids of time to play, but computers restored it. The argument is that the action of the computer is more appealing than the passiveness of television. The average American Online (AOL) home watches 15 percent less television than the U.S. average.[59] It works out to about an hour less of television a day.

It is possible that television may affect the conditions necessary for "creative imagination" and a "reflexive style of thinking." It is a time-consuming, passive media that impairs the ability to sustain thoughtfulness.[60] Proponents of computers say that those days are over. We are told that the net generation "represent[s] an evolutionary leap in human consciousness because they aren't bound by old-fashioned ideas of order but rather thrive in the state of chaos found on the Internet."[61]

Don Tapscott suggests ten important themes that explain the net generation.[62]

1. This generation has a strong sense of "independence and autonomy." It comes, in part, from the freedom found on the Web.

2. This generation has an emotional and intellectual openness. In an unfortunate choice of words, Tapscott tells us that when they go online they "expose themselves." He believes that this kind of self-expression leads to a genuine openness.

3. Because of the Web, this generation is very inclusive. Anyone can participate in chat rooms and the like. Where you are from or how you appear is of no concern.

4. The net "exposes" users to a wide range of ideas and opinions. Free expression naturally leads to strong and diverse views.

5. The net generation is "constantly looking for ways of doing things better." It is a generation of innovation.

6. There is a preoccupation with maturity. When on the computer, those of the net generation believe they are taken more seriously by adults. They appear as responsible and grown-up as they like.

7. After being on the Web awhile, the net generation wants to understand how things work. They learn to investigate. They understand the underlying assumptions of the software in order to feel empowered.

8. Computers offer an immediacy. If they are curious about something, they go on-line and find out. If they want to contact someone, E-mail is immediate while regular mail now seems to take forever.

---

[59] Ibid., p. 30.

[60] Ibid., p. 100.

[61] Douglas Rushkoff, *Playing the Future: How Kids' Culture Can Teach Us to Thrive in the Age of Chaos* (New York: Harper Collins, 1996).

[62] Ibid., pgs. 68–75.

9. This generation has a "sensitivity to corporate interest." It is suspicious of "corporate media outlets," and wants to have freedom from corporate interests.

10. "Because of the anonymity, accessibility, diversity and ubiquity of the Net, children must continually authenticate what they see or hear on the Web. Many sites provide inaccurate, invalid, or even deceptive information."

There are other important benefits of computer use. The use of computers help children develop social skills.[63] A positive step can be seen in video games. In early days, they were solitary, and now they are games with multiple users. In terms of power, this is the first generation to "control . . . critical elements of a communications revolution."[64] Parents now ask their children how to enter the new world of media.

The digital media has clear implications for education. To oversimplify, education needs to begin to impersonate computer reality. For example, linear learning needs to be replaced with "more interactive and nonsequential" ways of accessing information. Teachers should lead their students to "construction and discovery," and not "instruct" them. Computers, of course, can be programmed to do this task.

The classroom moves from being teacher-centered to learner-centered. As part of that, school is less about absorbing material and more about "how to navigate and how to learn." Learning how to navigate is exactly a skill that can be best learned at a computer. Schools must progress from "learning as torture to learning as fun." The idea is that computer learning is fun, so schools need to catch-up. Finally, the teacher should become less a transmitter and more a facilitator; a technical consultant in the web of discovery.

Because there is such a faith in what computers can do, it seems reasonable that this new reality serve as the basis of a new way to understand education. One of the problems is this: In a 1997 survey of teachers and others who work with computers, 87 percent "believe that Internet usage by students in grades 3 to 12 does not help improve classroom performance."[65] Tapscott explains: "This is an amazing number, perhaps explained by the sad reality that most of these teachers have not attempted to use the Internet to change the way learning is imparted."

This sampling gives us a good sense of how some understand the benefits of computers. If these theorists are right, then just about everything is different. How we learn, how we think, how we are, will change for the better. Reality as we know it, with its linear thinking and slow, single-minded rhythm will be a thing of the past. We will be more open, nonsequential, multitasked, diverse, opinionated, curious, and free.

And it's about time parents and teachers picked up on this new reality.

Transitional Note: This is a kind of reality check in this discussion of competing data and ideas. I love E-mail and the Internet. Most of all, I love writing on the computer. And I love TV. I watch sports and a few shows and a bad movie now and then. Sometimes I even watch

---

[63] Ibid., p. 107.

[64] Ibid., p. 26.

[65] Ibid., p. 138.

good and serious stuff. And I buy things on-line, and search out meaningless and even meaningful things on the computer.

But this is the bottom line: I'd really rather live in a sunny and warm climate and play games outside and worry about putting enough sunscreen on my bald head.

Con

We just read that 87 percent of the teachers did not think computers helped classroom performance. One writer believed the "sad reality" was that these teachers had not tried computers and, essentially, didn't know what they were talking about. The imperfect human in the electronic age. There is literature that suggests other reasons for the opinion of the teachers.

It is necessary to back up and get some sense of the context. For example, not everyone from three to twenty-five is a screenager. Fifty percent of the 1.2 billion children in the world between the ages of six and eleven have never even placed a phone call.[66] When we talk about a computer culture, we are talking about something that is primarily happening in developed countries. In the United States, in 1997, 60 percent of the homes with children had a computer. The calculation is simple: There is a direct relationship between income and access to computers and the Internet. That holds for higher and lower income schools.

The context of the new age of computers is that those with money will have a decided advantage.

Computers cost school districts a huge amount of money. In 1996–97, schools spent $4.34 billion dollars on technology. The Department of Education suggested that there be one computer for every five students. It would require an annual investment of something between $10 and $20 billion a year, for an unspecified number of years, to meet that recommendation.[67] There are costs beyond simply buying the hardware and software and, of course, constantly upgrading it.

There is theft. In one California school district $150,000 worth of equipment was stolen. It cost $2,000 to install an alarm system. There are constant glitches that require time to fix. Schools need technical support. In one demonstration project in New York City, there was one teacher for every twelve students—as well as one full-time technical support person in the class at all times. Educating teachers in the new technology is expensive. The workshops cost money, as does the time teachers need to take off to learn.

And, old buildings need to be upgraded in order to handle the demands of the new technology.

The money, the billions of dollars spent, come at the expense of everything else. To take the obvious example, teacher salaries in the United States are smaller than that of twenty-two other major nations.[68] The best research we have continues to show that good teachers make the biggest difference in learning.

---

[66] Nicolas Negroponte, "2B1," *Wired*, June, 1997, p. 184.

[67] Jane Healy, *Failure to Connect: How Computers Affect Our Children's Minds—and What We Can Do About It* (New York: Touchstone, 1998), p. 80.

[68] Ibid., p. 92.

There may not be a need for computers in every classroom. In truth, it does not seem to be a disadvantage if a student gets to college and knows nothing about computers. Colleges want students who can read, communicate, and think. Computer literacy is far down on their list. Here are three estimates of how long it takes for someone completely naive about computers to "get up to speed" once on campus:[69] "a) one month; b) one semester; c) one week (in a course required of all freshmen, regardless of past experience)." In other words money, in public schools, might be much better spent hiring more teachers and having smaller classes, than chasing unneeded computer skills.

We were told that television was passive and computers were interactive. Tom Snyder, an educational software designer writes this: "The most interactive experience you ever had with your computer is less interactive than the most meaningless experience you ever had with your cat!" One point he is making is that the interaction of a computer consists of pressing a key and looking at a show. It is not interaction in any kind of living sense.[70]

Another way to understand the difference is that computers give us a kind of sterile reality. Nature, after all, is "raw and untidy." It is anything but the controlled and antiseptic version that we see on our computer screen. It is, in part, the genuine sense of the uncontrolled nature of our environment that leads to creativity. The argument is that the "creativity" discussed by those who support computers is often merely a person who is clever at finding his or her way through different sites on the Web.

There is certainly a kind of creativity and even genius that goes into making both the software and hardware we use. But, for most of us, using a computer is not a creative process. Dean Meyer is a highly trained and sophisticated user of hypertext. He composes these texts. Meyer is very good at what he does, and believes that the use of technology has changed the way he thinks.

There are some downsides to his new way of thinking. He believes that "he would probably score low on the scale of intuitive thinking," that "perhaps my creativity to consider radical departures from my current cognitive structures is lower," and possibly there are some implications for his memory. He says: "Perhaps I don't practice my memory as much."[71]

There are also health problems associated with too much computer use.

Vision is affected by computer use. The picture on the screen must constantly refresh its phosphor coating so the image won't fade. It does this more than sixty times a second in order to avoid a "flicker." While we might not be conscious of this, our eyes do pick up these subtle changes. And it causes strain. Also, kids are more likely to stare without blinking more often than if they read a book or are playing. One specialist said that "The strain is like standing with your knees locked for five to ten minutes."[72]

---

[69] Ibid., p. 27.

[70] Ibid., pgs. 39, 48.

[71] Tapscott, op. cit., p. 104.

[72] Healy, op. cit., p. 113.

There are developmental problems possibly more serious than eyestrain. Part of normal child development depends on "integrating . . . visual systems with body movement in the three-dimensional real world . . . . Balance, literally (feeling left and right, and being able to cross the midline of the body), and body image all take lots of experience." Movement is important to both mental and visual development. Dr. Ann Barber, a developmental optometrist says:[73]

"When the child is born the wiring is all there; the light hits the retina but he makes no sense of it. He needs to learn by touching, putting things in his mouth, moving around, and then he has to integrate all this with vision and the other senses to make an intelligent child that's ready for school. There are eight or ten perceptual processes developing in the preschool years that go beyond the eyeball, and so much . . . is done with the body, manipulating objects, practicing how to catch or kick a ball, hit a target. The child also must focus on what's important and make sense out of the world. How can you understand 'above, below, inside, outside' if you're not crawling into the cardboard box and seeing and feeling it? But today we see so many kids are delayed in these skills—six-, seven-, eight-year-olds who are more at the four-year-old level."

As a note, the government reports that health problems increase if adults use VDTs (video display terminals) for more than half of the workday. The most common problem involves vision (eyestrain, double vision, blurring, etc.). The next most common problems are musculoskeletal (back strain, carpal tunnel syndrome, neck/shoulder/arm strain, etc.).[74] Children are at risk for the same problems. There is something called "video wrist" that resembles carpal tunnel syndrome and includes numbness, pain, and sometimes tendinitis in the wrists and hands.

We can turn the discussion over a little. While there are health problems that may result from too much computer use, there are other health problems that might develop because the child is not doing something else. The something else, of course, is exercising.

Regular exercise increases oxygen and energy to the brain with the increase in blood flow. It helps the brain work better. The chemicals secreted during and after exercise help reduce stress, anxiety, and counter the effects of depression. The best kind of exercise in kids is "unforced." The best kind of exercise, to put it a different way, is the "spontaneous play in which children just naturally engage."[75] In no way does an "interaction" with a computer compare to the normal play of a child.

It is important to remember that the problems with computers have to do with kids who use them when they are too young, or kids who use them too much. One way to understand the problem of too young is to keep in mind that a brain responds to its environment, and becomes "custom-tailored" to it. The anti-computer people warn us that kids who begin using computers early, and too much, are in danger of developing "visual intelligence" at the cost of verbal forms. That the patterns built up

---

[73] Quoted in ibid, p. 114.

[74] Jan Hawkins, "Technology in Education: Transitions." Pre-Summit Briefing Material for the National Education Summit. Palisades, New York: 1996, p. 1. Ibid., p. 111.

[75] Ibid., p. 121.

with computer use might hinder skills needed in school. For example, a brain trained to understand the screen-based culture of icons might have difficulty with a written text, and connections made from reading. (Barry Sanders, in *A Is for Ox*, argues that those who are brought up on electronics and cannot read do not develop the kind of "soul" as those who can read.)

Learning generally develops from very concrete things (touching, feeling, manipulating, putting things in your mouth) to more symbolic representations (letters, pictures, words, stories) and finally to abstract modes of thought (hypothesis-testing, understanding and using rules of grammar, metaphor).[76] Computers do not come into play until relatively late in the learning process. It is simply a mistake to believe that a child's learning will be accelerated by having the early use of a computer. The opposite seems to be true.

Developmentally, if a child uses a computer too much before the age of seven or eight then he or she will probably develop at a slower rate.

Finally, emotional development depends on dealing with people. Stanford professors Bryon Reeves and Clifford Nass believe that the human brain has not evolved to deal with technology.[77] They argue that even the most sophisticated technology users respond to computers in human terms—although they understand how illogical that is. For children, especially under the age of five, it is difficult to distinguish real and make-believe. Computers might be all too "real" for children.

Sherry Turkle has done important work in the area of the interplay between humans and machines. This is one of her summary statements about older children and adults who spend much of the "social" life sitting at a computer:[78]

> The new practice of entering virtual worlds raises fundamental questions about our communities and ourselves. . . . For every step forward in the instrumental use of a technology (what the technology can do for us) there are subjective effects. The technology changes us as people, changes our relationships and sense of ourselves . . . There is no simple good news or bad news.

It seems appropriate to end the section on computers with Neil Postman. Postman's detractors are as strong as those who admire his ideas. What makes him useful for us is his ability to clarify issues. As you will see, he is no friend of computers.

It is Postman's belief that technology is able to arrange the world so that we do not experience it.[79] The reason this is particularly bad is that he believes public schools are about shared experiences and stories. If the heart of teaching is human dialogue, then technology robs education of its most important quality.

---

[76] Ibid., p. 135.

[77] See Healy, op. cit., p. 192.

[78] Sherry Turkle, *Life on the Screen: Identity in the Age of the Internet* (New York: Simon & Schuster, 1995), p. 232.

[79] Neil Postman, *The End of Education: Redefining the Value of School* (New York: Vintage Books, 1996), p. 10.

Schools, in Postman's view, are not about information. He argues that we certainly do not need computers in order to find out things. There are, he tells us: "260,000 billboards, 17,000 newspapers, 12,000 periodicals, 27,000 video outlets for renting tapes, 400 million television sets, and well over 500 million radios, not including those in automobiles. There are 40,000 new book titles published every year, and each day 41 million photographs are taken."[80] The point is made; we are overloaded with sources of information before we even get to computers.

Postman goes further by disputing the idea that kids will use computers for learning. He had a classic exchange with a strong supporter of computers, a person named Diane Ravitch. Ravitch writes: "In this world of pedagogical plenty, children . . . [can] . . . learn whatever they want to know, at their own convenience. If Little Eva cannot sleep, she can learn algebra instead. At her home-learning station, she will tune in to a series of interesting problems that are presented in an interactive medium, much like video games. . . . Young John may decide that he wants to learn the history of modern Japan, which he can do by dialing up the greatest authorities and teachers on the subject, who will not only use dazzling graphs and illustrations, but will narrate a historical video that excites his curiosity and imagination."[81]

Certainly a positive sense of the future. But not so for Postman: "In this vision, there is, it seems to me, a confident and typical sense of unreality. Little Eva can't sleep, so she decides to learn a little algebra? Where did Little Eva come from, Mars? If not, it is more likely she will turn into a good movie. Young John decides that he wants to learn the history of modern Japan? How did young John come to this point? How is it that he never visited a library up to now? Or is it that he, too, couldn't sleep and decided a little modern Japanese history was just what he needed?

"What Ravitch is talking about here is not a new technology but a new species of child, one that, in any case, hasn't been seen very much up to now." Postman, agreeing that technology might produce new kinds of people, asks if we will like the kind of person who is produced.

While more complicated than this, the bottom line is that Postman has a clear sense of what he believes schools are about. He believes that Ravitch leaves out things central to the educational process. Postman refers to *All I Ever Really Needed to Know I Learned in Kindergarten* for a list of lessons all children need to learn in school: "share everything, play fair, don't hit people, put things back where you found them, clean up your own mess, wash your hands before you eat, and, of course, flush."[82]

The debate about computers is intense. We know that the world of our children will, electronically, be almost unimaginably different than the world of our childhood. The central questions should be focused on what we need to keep as our human condition changes. We are forced to ask the most basic questions about how children are affected by technology, and what is gained and lost as changes occur.

---

[80] Ibid., p. 43.

[81] Ibid., p. 39. The following quote is also found on page 39.

[82] Ibid., p. 46.

It is no mistake that the section on computers ends with a reminder to wash your hands before you eat and, of course, flush. It seems the right counterpoint to Little Eva and her inability to sleep.

THE LAW

The context for everything seems to be the law. It is hard to imagine a teacher or an administrator who would be foolish enough to go through a degree program without taking a course in school law.

For our purposes, there is no reason to either critique or endorse the idea that the law seems to be ever-present in our lives. If nothing else, it lingers in the background of every conversation, assignment, activity, and even choice of apparel. Since the Mayflower Compact, we have been surrounded by contracts, laws, and litigation.

Schools traditionally operated under the doctrine of **in loco parentis.** The schools, in other words, acted "in place of the parent." Schools had the power to be (substitute) parents, and the Courts upheld that power for a long time.[83] But the current dynamic is much different.

The substitute parent–child relationship has been changed to one of legal due process. The due process may be procedural (for example, were procedures used to suspend a student fair?[84]) or substantive (was the student deprived of constitutional rights such as privacy or property?), but in either case the dynamic is adversarial. It is difficult to overestimate what a huge difference that has made. As a teacher, you might feel, and often act, like a substitute parent—but the bottom line is you are dealing with people who have legal rights and are always a lawyer away from suing you.

In order to get a sense of this not-so-silent legal context, we can sample the book *Teachers and the Law.*[85] The copy I am looking at is the fifth edition. The book is well-written, thorough, and popular.

In the introduction, the authors tell us they want to "demystify" the law. It is their belief that most legal problems are not intended, but come from a misunderstanding of the law. That being the case, it is necessary for teachers and administrators to understand the law well enough to use it as a "source of guidance and protection." They believe that by understanding school law, those in school will be able to practice "preventative law."

In other words, you need to know enough law to keep you out of trouble.

The premise is sound, and the authors proceed carefully to explain the laws that deal with matters of schooling.

---

[83] J. Johnson, V. Dupuis, D. Musical, G. Hall, D. Gollnick, *Introduction to the Foundations of American Education*, 12th ed. (Boston: Allyn & Bacon, 2002), p. 261.

[84] The case in point is *Goss v Lopez*; see Michael LaMorte, *School Law: Cases and Concepts*, 7th ed. (Boston: Allyn & Bacon, 2002), p. 120.

[85] Louis Fischer, David Schimmel, Cynthia Kelly, *Teachers and the Law*, 5th ed. (New York, Longman, 1999).

In other chapters we have seen some of these laws. Integration and people with disabilities are two areas in which law changed the way we did schooling. They helped change the way our society functions.

We know, too, that there are serious penalties for sexual harassment. Those are laws everyone needs to understand.

It is easy to agree that these issues have had an important impact, but the point I am making is a little different. School law goes way beyond the issues we all know. Let me give a number of examples:

1. Do teachers have a constitutional right to dress the way they wish? The answer is no.
2. A black teacher in Florida refused to cut his goatee and was not rehired. Was that legal? The answer is no.
3. Can girls be prohibited from wearing slacks? No.
4. Must public schools recognize gay student groups? Probably.
5. Does the Equal Access Act apply to elementary schools? No.
6. Can public schools deny the use of their facilities to religious groups? It depends on the circumstances.
7. Can schools prohibit the distribution of material not written by a student or a school employee? Probably not.
8. Are teachers at private schools that receive state funds protected by the First Amendment? Probably not.
9. Can students sue teachers for negative statements made in letters of recommendation? No.
10. Can students sue teachers for giving them low grades? No. Giving low grades is not libelous.

The examples are endless.

What is important to see is that there has been a court case concerning just about everything you can think of. To overstate a little, when you walk into a classroom, you are a lawsuit waiting to happen. If there is one overriding context of schooling, it is the law.

We can see this in another way. The National Education Association (NEA) has a code of ethics for educators. What follows are five of the points under the section Commitment to the Student:[86]

> In fulfillment of the obligation to the student, the educator—
>
> 1. Shall not unreasonably restrain the student from independent action in pursuit of learning.
> 2. Shall not unreasonably deny the student's access to varying points of view.
> 3. Shall not deliberately suppress or distort subject matter relevant to the student's progress.

---

[86] This can be found in Hlebowitsh, op. cit., p. 131.

4. Shall make a reasonable effort to protect the student from conditions harmful to learning or to health and safety.
5. Shall not intentionally expose the student to embarrassment or disparagement.

What we need to understand is that each of these points is tied to a series of court rulings. These are not simple guidelines for those who teach—these are huge road signs about how you should act and what you need to avoid.

What happens when we put this code of ethics in our contemporary context? We have a society that seems to believe our children are hopelessly out of control, and now we put them in your classroom and you are told how they should be treated. Indeed, we are threatened by legal action if we don't treat our students in certain ways.

It is hard to disagree with the above list: What, after all, is so bad about not "intentionally" exposing the student to embarrassment or disparagement? But what happens if we look past the particulars and at the basic dynamic: Does the presence of due process hinder what teachers need to do in the classroom? Even if the teacher would do nothing different, does the underlying threat of legal action interfere with how we teach? Can we be our best selves in the classroom if the nagging of the law is constantly present?

This is not an easy point to make. In no way am I making the argument that administrators and teachers should be tyrants. I am not a "spare the rod and spoil the child" kind of guy. What I am after is a basic dynamic. While legal rights certainly help control those who might abuse their power, what is much less clear is how those same rights affect the dynamics of a classroom. The question is this: Do all those laws, regulations, and guidelines get in the way of good teaching?

The authors of *Teachers and the Law* are right to argue that it is in the best interest of teachers and administrators to understand and be comfortable with school law. But that is only half of the equation. Teachers and administrators need to decide if they want to work in an environment that pays little, has long hours, and is subject to more laws than they will ever know.

The context of schooling—the culture of the United States—seems strong and disruptive. While politicians constantly campaign for better schooling and a well-educated work force, what seems to be missing is funding. At the first sign of an economic downturn, education seems to be the first to get hit. (The poor are a close second.)

The bottom line is this: Schools are simply not well-funded enough to challenge those parts of popular culture that seem disagreeable.

In the last decade the frustration has been so great that a series of experiments have begun. In the last chapter we will explore what has been changing in our schooling. We will see the various responses to lower test scores and what seems a higher level of intolerance for the culture of our young.

SUMMARY

Since there have been Puritans in America, it seems as if the older generation has not trusted the younger generation. That certainly seems to be the case as we enter the twenty-first century.

Critics tell us that the kids in your classroom are lazy, undisciplined, and unprincipled. Baby beauty pageants, movie theaters in malls, the films shown in those theaters are—to some—clear signs that our youth are intellectually and morally lost.

Bad television and even worse music drives our innocent children to sex, drugs, and violence. The commercial society that caters to our youth is driving our culture into a new Dark Ages: books, ideas, and thinking will be things of the past. Ours, if the critics are right, is a future of Columbines and cannabis.

In this chapter, we noted that it is possible that we are looking at the wrong things. To focus on the sensational is to miss the underlying problems of poverty and guns. To ignore the need for textbooks or more, and more well-paid, teachers by demanding billions of dollars for a failed war on drugs is, quite literally, close to criminal negligence.

We also noted that the "good old days" of some of the critics—the Depression of the '30 or the repression of the '50s—were the kind of days that many of us are happy to avoid. That was then, now is now. While childhood memories can certainly be sweet, they are not always the best model for the future.

The pros and cons of computers in schools were explored. There were, we found, some serious cons. The money spent on computers and the attending expenses of experts, rebuilding, insurance, and the like, might be better spent on more teachers and textbooks.

Finally, we found the context of the classroom might have been fundamentally influenced by the introduction of legal due process. It was difficult to sort out the positive and negative influences of the introduction of law in schooling.

THINK ABOUT

1. Can you imagine a time when "your music" is considered "old" and you are considered out of touch? Can you imagine that might happen when you are twenty-five and teaching eleventh graders?

2. Do you believe that a computer can teach as well as you can? Put differently, how necessary are humans in the classroom?

3. Have you ever wanted to sue your school? What do you think it will feel like if one of your students wants to sue you? In the end, what do you think the introduction of due process has meant to schooling?

CHAPTER 12

RESTRUCTURING SCHOOLING
Looking for Answers in All the Wrong Places

When the shameless compete against the spineless, the shameless always win.

Julian Bond

The point should be made by now: There will be a remarkable number of tensions in any classroom you walk into. The tensions are a reflection of the surrounding culture, and you, as a teacher, are asked to resolve them. The divisions you find are deep and long-standing, and the best any of us can do is be as thoughtful about them as possible.

This chapter is not about what happens when you walk into your classroom. It is about what happens before you get there—it is about the current politics of public schooling.

From the beginning, I have tried to argue that the debates about schooling are political debates. To read *The Republic* is to see the close relationship between the shape of education and the state in which it exists. In our own history, we have seen how schooling follows the politics of the times. The "best" "educational thinking" of any era, it turns out, is often simply a statement about the kind of citizens the government wants its schools to produce. Public schools are a product of our political decisions.

For the last decade or so we have been in a period of educational change. The changes reflect the tensions of our political and economic realities. From free-market thinkers to fundamentalist Christians, our schools and what we think about schooling are being reformed.

In this chapter, we will look at the politics of the changes that are taking place. The range will be from deschooling to schools owned by the teachers. In between, there are charter schools, religious schools, and voucher programs. Many of these changes grow naturally from earlier discussions about the state of our public schools, about how they are failing and need to be replaced. There are those who believe that we are a nation at risk because of our public school system, that one good way to solve the problem is to break up that system.

Change is here, and it is important to know what it is and what, exactly, we know about it.

The one thing we do know and should not forget is this: It all revolves around politics.

SAYING NO TO CHOICE

There are a remarkable number of school options.[1] There is **open enrollment** (the student gets his or her choice of schools within a district), **alternative schools** (tries to offer a model different from traditional schooling), **magnet schools** (they tend to specialize in a particular curriculum or approach), **out-sourcing** (a district can hire a private educational company to provide schooling), **site-based management** (the school district decentralizes), **private schools** (religious or nonsectarian), and **charter schools** (generally publicly funded and free from most local and state regulations). There are also **voucher programs** that provide funding for students to choose the school of their choice.

To do some numbers, about 10 percent of the school population goes to private school, 2 percent are educated at home, 11 percent have some sort of public school choice, and about 1 percent attend charter schools.

We will study some of these choices in detail, but we begin with those people who opt out of sending their children to school. These people either **homeschool** or **deschool.** There is a difference and it is deeply political.

The deschoolers believe that the homeschool advocates miss the point of keeping children away from schools. To see why that is the case, we need to understand what deschooling is all about.

John Holt was the spiritual leader of deschooling.[2] Holt strongly believed that schooling was very destructive and could not be changed. Given the great diversity in human learning, he believed that in order for a child to be given the best and most appropriate education, it was up to each family to educate its children.

In a letter he wrote during the late '70s, Holt quoted Paul Goodman: "Suppose you had had the revolution you were talking and dreaming about. Suppose your side had won, and you had the kind of society you wanted. How would you live, *you personally*, in that society. *Start living that way now!*" Holt writes that is "very good advice" and goes on to say: "The trick is to find ways to put your strongest ideals into practice in daily life. . . . You don't have to wait for a million people to agree with you, you can begin right away."[3]

Matt Hern writes that "the abject failure of monopoly, state-controlled, compulsory schooling is evident to anyone who looks. . . . [it] is a system that nurtures

---

[1] For a good list, see Andrew Effrat, "Defining the Terms," *Educational Connection*, Winter 2000, pgs. 2–4.

[2] Among other things, see John Holt, *How Children Learn* (Pitman, 1964) and especially his *Growing Without Schooling;* the first issue was published in 1977.

[3] "Celebrating 100 Issues," *Growing Without Schooling #100*, Vol. 17, No. 3, July/August 1994, quoted in Matt Hern, ed., *Deschooling Our Lives*, (Gabriola Island, BC: New Society Publishers, 1996), pgs. 87–8.

the worst in humanity and simultaneously suppresses individuality and real community." He believes that compulsory schooling fails "morally, educationally, economically, physically, and spiritually." It is a view held by most deschoolers.[4]

Aaron Falbel believes that learning is like breathing, and that genuine learning can be neither "forced, seduced or coerced." He thinks those who refuse formal education have the right idea and that they should not be understood as "delinquents" or "failures" or "dropouts." Falbel writes "let us view them instead as wise *refuseniks*."[5] What Falbel is saying, in part, is that the words we use to describe some of our children are political in nature and have nothing to do with learning. Deciding not to participate in a politically corrupt institution (school) is understood as a brave and wise action.

Finally, a black woman—Donna Nichols-White—gives us her sense of schooling. "Black homeschoolers [she means deschoolers] tend to view institutionalized education as a form of slavery. And they fear the government will enact truancy laws, like the fugitive slave laws, more often upon black families than white families."[6]

The lesson is clear enough: Deschoolers believe that schooling is just plain bad. They believe that it is little more than a political expression of a corrupt culture. Grace Llewellyn writes that "choice is a fundamental essence of life, and in the fullest life, each choice is deliberate and savored. . . . All the time you are in school, you learn through experience how to live in a dictatorship."[7] Given this political view of public schools, it only makes sense to educate your children at home.

The positive side of deschooling is built on a unified vision of child rearing, education, and human development. The fundamental idea is that learning is natural, that each child has a natural rhythm, that learning can happen any time and anywhere, and that education should be tailored to each child.[8] True education begins with the child and his or her interests and, as a practical and political matter, it is impossible for any school to offer that kind of education.

Much of this might remind you of a combination of Dewey and Rousseau. The emphasis on experience and the natural curiosity of the child has been with us for centuries. We should remember that Rousseau wrote in opposition to the culture in which he lived, and Dewey in response to what he thought a new citizen would have to know. Deschoolers fit easily within these traditions.

Deschooling has a drastic effect on families. It depends on adults and children spending huge amounts of time together, and adults giving up much of their traditional control. The parents need to be role models and facilitators, but be willing to give up power. They must be willing to admit what they do not know, and explore things along with their children. When a learning situation arises, the parent must be

[4] Ibid., pgs. 1–3.

[5] Aaron Falbel, "Learning? Yes, of course. Education? No, thanks." In ibid., p. 67.

[6] Donna Nichols-White, "Dinosaur Homeschool," ibid., p. 73.

[7] Grace Llewellyn, "Sweet Land of Liberty," ibid., p. 35.

[8] Mary Griffith, *The Unschooling Handbook: How to use the Whole World as Your Child's Classroom* (Roseville, Calif.: Prima Press, 1998), pgs. 22–3.

ready to guide the child through the lesson. The adults must be fully involved for deschooling to be successful.

The bottom line is this: child care is a political activity.[9] By taking a child out of the system and making certain he or she gets the best (the correct) education, deschoolers are convinced they are practicing the best kind of politics. We read: "Our role as parents and caregivers is not to ensure that our children develop the capacity to survive the rigors of modern life. Our task is to establish ways of childrearing so that children develop in a non-hierarchical relationship with others, and with the natural world. . . ."[10] This is, clearly, not the role of schooling that is advanced by our political leaders. To take the obvious example, standardized testing seems to be one way to get our children ready to "survive the rigors of modern life." Standardized testing is not the way of deschoolers.

Let me back up for a minute and fill in some facts. When we talk about homeschooling and deschooling, we are really talking about maternal education. On a day-to-day basis, with very few exceptions, the mother is the teacher. Just like the good old days on the frontier before there were common schools. I think it's fair to wonder exactly what it means, in terms of equality, that the woman stays home and the man goes to work. Maybe it means the woman gets the best job—I don't know.

The vast majority of families who educate their children at home are white.

Those children who have been educated at home and took the SATs in the year 2000 did better than the national average: 1100 compared to the national average of 1019. There are several reasons that we should treat these statistics with caution.[11] Nonetheless, it is clear that many of the parents who keep their children home are more concerned with education than most.

Finally, about 80 percent of those who keep their children home make an explicit link between education and Christianity. The other 20 percent make no explicit link with religion. I would guess that most of the deschoolers fall into the latter category.

We can now get a better sense of the difference between deschooling and homeschooling. Deschoolers believe that homeschoolers simply replicate the hierarchical structure of society and government. The homeschool parents stay in control and go through lesson plans the way it is done in school. For those who deschool, the family may act as a "powerfully subversive force, challenging those institutions organized along lines of command and obedience. . . ."[12]

Either kind of schooling changes the family. It is not easy to imagine how hard it is to be responsible for the education of your children. The amount of time and energy and thought that needs to go into planning and carrying out a complete edu-

---

[9] Geraldine Lyn-Piluso, Gus Lyn-Piluso, and Duncan Clarke, "Challenging the Popular Wisdom: What Can Families Do?" in Hern, op. cit., p. 55.

[10] Ibid., p. 57.

[11] Gardner, op. cit., p. 53. For example, we need to look at how many homeschoolers don't take the exams, and for what reasons.

[12] Hern, op. cit., p. 54.

cation is beyond my imagination. To read the literature is to read about people who genuinely love and are committed to what they are doing.

Everyone agrees that these families need support. Whether it is neighbors or support groups or nationwide organizations, it is clear that no single family can do everything. The homeschoolers are more well-organized in part because many of them teach a fairly standard curriculum. There are books like *Home Learning Year by Year: How to Design a Homeschool Curriculum from Preschool Through High School* that can be a thirteen-year educational guide.[13] It lists what is age-appropriate to learn and ways to teach the lessons. We know that this is exactly the kind of help scorned by deschoolers.

There are a huge number of details associated with this kind of schooling. Many have to do with the fact that each state has a different set of regulations. Some states are much less rigid than others in terms of how the children are evaluated.

The broader point is this: There are parents who do not want the state educating their children. While the focus has been on deschooling, it's important to remember that most of the children who stay home are there, in part, because of religious reasons. They believe that the secular state will not provide a moral education.

One educational choice, then, is to keep your kids out of school.

CHARTER SCHOOLS

One of the revolutions in our history of education was when it became public policy to educate everyone. The traditional model was the neighborhood school, and in our collective minds little girls and boys walked to school carrying their lunch pails. After *Brown v Board of Education of Topeka*, we took a closer look at those neighborhood schools and found they were segregated.

When the Supreme Court ruled that the schools needed to integrate, the argument against integration that held enormous emotional appeal was that the decision would do away with neighborhood schools. While the most contentious plans to desegregate centered on busing students outside of their neighborhoods, it seemed that magnet schools were a more acceptable option.

During the 1970s a great many communities created magnet schools. These schools provided high quality education for a diverse population. Students chose to attend magnet schools. Many were specialized, and focused on things like fine arts or science. They were created to provide quality education to an integrated population. They have been very successful. In 1996 a study of 24,000 eighth- and-tenth grade students in magnet schools outperformed their counterparts in public schools, private schools, and Catholic schools.[14]

Magnet schools helped with desegregating segregated systems, produced high quality educational results, and showed that there were things other than the

---

[13] Rebecca Rupp, *Home Learning Year by Year* (New York: Three Rivers Press, 2000).

[14] R. A. Gamoran, "Student Achievement in Public and Magnet, Public Comprehensive, and Private City High Schools," *Educational Evaluation and Policy Analysis*, 18(1), 1996, pgs. 1–18.

neighborhood that people should consider. There were parents who were more than willing to bus their children to a viable and attractive alternative school.

By the 1980s we got *A Nation at Risk* and the idea that a free market economy was capable of solving all of our problems. The value of neighborhood schools became less important than the principle of freedom of choice. By the early 1990s states and school districts began experimenting with charter schools—a kind of second-generation magnet school.

The reasoning behind charter schools is familiar. Given what people believed was the sad state of public schools, and the importance of choice for each child, there needed to be a way to institute democracy in schooling. There has always been choice for some (those with money have always been able to send their children to private schools, or move to the suburbs and better school districts), and now the argument was that charter schools would provide the luxury of choice for everyone.

The critics believe that because public schools have become so rule-bound and institutionalized that it is impossible for them to make the needed changes. The idea was that the charter schools would be able to be created without the problems of the institutionalized public schools. Individuals could apply to begin a school,[15] and many of the regulations that applied to regular schools would not apply to them. They would be exempt from most of the laws that govern public schools. The theory was that the absence of regulations would allow all charter schools to be more creative and cost-efficient. They could, in other words, be better able to provide a superior education.

The list of benefits offered by its advocates is impressive. Schools can be smaller, and there could be better teacher/student ratios. Teachers can be involved in creating the curriculum, and the school could have a shared vision. The students would choose to go to the school and, with their parents, be emotionally invested in their choice. These schools could provide a community atmosphere in which specialized education would be provided.

Charter schools blur the line between public and private. The funding is public, but the feeling is private. While there could be no admissions tests (unless it was a specialized school—like, for example, fine arts), the school would be exempt from most regulations. Teachers would not have to be certified, and budgets would be given as a lump sum and not as line-items.[16] Charter schools are autonomous and encourage competition and change. Indeed, charter schools may even be run by large education companies. Edison Schools are charter schools in many communities. They have schools all over the country and are a for-profit organization. It is worth our time to look more closely at Edison Schools.

The Edison Project is a corporation created to do the business of schooling.[17] With a high-tech approach, a new curriculum, longer school days, longer school year

---

[15] For a good description of these schools, see Robert Barr and William Parrett, *How to Create Alternative, Magnet, and Charter Schools That Work* (Bloomington, Ind.: National Educational Service, 1997). Much of the following comes from this book.

[16] Put differently, instead of having to spend x number of dollars on teachers and another x number of dollars on textbooks, each school could decide to spend the money any way they wanted.

[17] Much of the following comes from Gerald Bracey, *What You Should Know about the War Against America's Public Schools* (Boston: Allyn & Bacon, 2003).

approach, its founder Chris Whittle believed that his corporation could do a better job of schooling than public schools. He also believed he could do it at the same cost as public schools.

The company was formed in 1991, with plans for a thousand Edison Schools by the year 2000. The plan was to have school districts pay Edison to run their schools. Edison promised good results. Good results meant improving test scores. By the year 2000–2001, Edison Schools were in ninety buildings (by its own count, Edison ran 113 schools).[18] By 2002, the company had lost $300 million.[19]

To read about Edison Schools is to read about two bottom lines. One is economic. While losing all that money, and seemingly always on the verge of bankruptcy, the company continues to survive. Not only that, the top management continues to be well-paid. Some executives earn $300,000 a year.

The second bottom line has to do with how well the schools are performing. While their self-evaluations seem generous, other evaluations show that Edison Schools are, at best, uneven. There are more bad results than good results. The Edison Schools have lost contracts because they have failed to live up to their contractual arrangements, and have had problems finding new clients. Later in the chapter we will take a closer look at how well charter schools are doing.

We might speculate that one curricular model simply does not fit all schools. In many places, Edison Schools have had trouble keeping teachers. Many teachers resist being told the one best way to do things. In San Francisco, for example, 70 percent of the teachers quit after the first year of Edison taking over the schools. It seems very naïve to believe that one pedagogy fits all schools, teachers, and students.

Back to the general point: Advocates believe that charter schools are good for everyone. They bring democracy to schooling; there are no captive audiences; the teachers love the added power and smaller classes; there is no more tracking; and power is finally returned to the local level. Barr writes that they 1) help failing students, 2) give entrepreneurs a chance, 3) expand the range of schools, and 4) encourage schools to change.[20]

It is difficult to discuss details of charter schools. Each state has different regulations, as does each district. These schools are set up to educate very different populations in many different ways. Some are very strict, back-to-the-basics schools that target students who have fallen behind. Others focus on arts or sciences or dropouts or parents who want their children to be educated in a Montessori system.

Some clearly help those at the lower end of the socioeconomic scale, while others are created for the well-off.

Charter schools have a great appeal to those who believe in the "free market." The dynamic is clear enough: Because people have a choice, if schools are not working, they will simply not get students and go out of business. Of course, these "free markets" are exactly as "free" as a "free lunch." Taxpayers foot the bill. Still, the idea

[18] Ibid., p. 105.

[19] Peg Tyre and Barbara Kantrowitz, "Philly's Tough Lessons," *Newsweek*, October 21, 2002, p. 63.

[20] Barr, op. cit., pgs. 145–6.

of choice is increasingly appealing in our liberal/capitalist atmosphere, so it is not surprising that charter schools have become increasingly popular.

There are critics of charter schools.[21] They say charter schools take money from local schools. In Massachusetts, for example, they receive money first, off the top of a community's education funding. Because of the flexibility of charter schools to control enrollment, they often will not take students with learning disabilities or special needs. It is left to the public schools to educate these students—and their education is the most expensive. Charter schools hesitate to provide bilingual education—again, an expensive proposition that is left to the public schools. Put differently, if a virtue of public schools is inclusiveness, then as schools using public funding, charter schools fail. Not only that, they take money away from those schools that must accept everyone.

There is a lack of public control over charter schools. The rules that apply to other schools are purposely put aside for the sake of innovation. The problem is the lack of objective measures to assess student achievement. The result is that public monies are spent with almost no public oversight. Charter schools do not have to hire certified teachers. Nationally, in an average charter school, 48% of the teachers lack certification. In traditional public schools, about 9% of the teachers are not certified.[22] While it is clear that not all certified teachers are good, one has no idea what a teacher without certification knows. Finally, there are states that allow charter schools to charge "fees" and solicit "donations" from the families of their students. Instead of charging tuition, these charter schools get money other ways, and charter schools use public funds to become private schools for the well-to-do.

There seems no question that charter schools are the wave of the present and at least the near future. They are appealing for many reasons, and to many segments of the population. Later, after we have discussed vouchers, we will return to charter schools and ask the bottom line question: do they work?

VOUCHERS

The argument for vouchers is not new. In 1955, Milton Friedman suggested that we have a universal voucher system. He thought that every school-aged person should be given a voucher and go to the school of his or her choice. The program would be unregulated. The student could go to any public or private school.[23] The Friedman proposal is where the logic of the free market leads. Each consumer is given *x* amount of dollars to choose the most appropriate school—the simple-minded, free-market answer to just about everything.

---

[21] See Paul Dunphy, "Does Privatization Undermine Educational Reform?," *Education Connection*, Winter, 2000, pgs. 20–3, and Barr, ibid., pgs. 146–7.

[22] Anand Vaishmar, "Flaws Cited in Charter Schools," *Boston Globe*, April 13, 2003, p. C21.

[23] Milton Friedman, 1955, "The Role of Government in Education," in Robert Solo, ed., *Economics and the Public Interest* (Piscataway, N.J.: Rutgers University Press). Also, see Friedman's *Capital and Freedom*.

In 1970, Christopher Jencks suggested a modification of the Friedman system. Jencks proposed that the voucher system be highly regulated so that it favored low-income families. Given that the public school system favored rich school districts, Jencks and his colleagues believed that poor students could be given a better chance if they were given vouchers. Vouchers were understood as a way to help students escape bad public schools. They would be a way to give the most needy students a more equal opportunity.

John Coons and Stephen Sugarman came to the same conclusion. As legal scholars, they argued that vouchers could be understood as a matter of justice for the poor. That was a way for the poor to have school choice—a choice that the middle and upper classes have always had.

Like charter schools, voucher plans vary from state to state and school district to school district. Basically, they are programs that allow students to apply their public school dollars toward tuition at the school of their choice. That choice might be either a public or private school. As of 2002, the choice might include parochial schools.

Vouchers, then, provide a wider choice for students. Depending on the system, families can use vouchers to send their children to fine private schools. In some places, that means the schools that take tax dollars are allowed to have selective admissions. (To get a sense of this, in Milwaukee, of the eighty-six schools that accept vouchers, only seven said they offered special education.)[24]

Some of the voucher plans allow tax deductions for school tuition. This is part of the federal plan proposed by President Bush. Clearly, this kind of plan favors those wealthy enough to afford to send their children to private schools. To be fair, other plans are limited to families who are on the low end of the socioeconomic scale. Indeed, most voucher plans are structured to help poor families.

It may help to give some examples of the range of voucher programs. In Milwaukee, the Milwaukee Parental Choice Program (MPCP) offered scholarships of $5,300 to low-income students. The families who were eligible could not have an income of over $25,000. The schools that took the vouchers were not allowed to charge additional tuition and were required to admit all applicants if there was available space.

Most voucher programs are more modest. In 1997, New York City offered scholarships worth up to $1,700. In Dayton, Ohio, Washington D.C., and Charlotte, North Carolina, vouchers ranged from $1,200 to $2,500, and the recipients were picked by lottery. In New York, the average income of the families was $10,000, and in Cleveland it was $18,000.

In California, Proposition 38 was a ballot issue that dealt with vouchers. The ACLU and two teachers unions agreed that, if passed, it would favor families with higher incomes. In some states, it is all right for private schools to both take vouchers and charge tuition. This kind of system is little value to low-income families.

---

[24] Wisconsin Legislative Audit Bureau, 2000, cited in Brian Gill, P. Michael Timpane, Karen Ross, and Dominic Brewer, *Rhetoric versus Reality: What We Know and What We Need to Know about Vouchers and Charter Schools* (Santa Monica, Calif.: Rand, 2001), p. 150.

To generalize, vouchers are most frequently used for those who need financial help. On the other hand, it is foolish to think that $2,000 is going to buy a student a place in a top private school. Two thousand dollars will not buy even a modest education.

As we saw, the voucher system has its roots in free-market politics. On the whole, it is an effort to give the greatest amount of choice to those who have traditionally had the least amount of choice. Proponents of vouchers argue that the competition from all other schools will force public schools to improve. Florida, for example, grades its schools. If a school has a failing grade two years out of four, all of the children in that school are offered vouchers so they can transfer. Vouchers, in this case, are used to help ensure that all public schools will feel the heat of educational competition.

Opponents believe that vouchers are even worse than charter schools. The idea that public money can go to private—even parochial—schools is particularly upsetting. With vouchers, there is not even the pretense of the openness of public schools. Private schools choose their students, and parochial schools are centered on a particular religion. They do not have to accept those students who might not meet their academic standards, or who might need special services during the course of the school day. Vouchers can be used to skim the best students from the public system.

Amy Gutmann argues a more democratic point.[25] Instead of beginning with family or even state choice, she believes that the focal point of decision making needs to be a "democratic state of education." That means, in part, the public interest is best served when the diverse interests of the society make collective decisions about which democratic values to teach. She argues that only through continued public debate from plural interests and perspectives can we expect to have schools reflect our collective judgment.

One of the serious critiques of both charter schools and voucher systems is that our schooling will be "balkanized." It will, in other words, become fragmented into specialized parts, and cater to its particular clientele. It will be, in a sense, a return to a segregated system—only now we will segregate according to class, culture, skill, and taste, as well as color.

Both charter schools and vouchers are at the cutting edge of our political debate about education. Politics aside, we need to know what, if any, difference they make.

DO THEY WORK?

If you read just about anything Paul Peterson has written about vouchers and charter schools, you would be convinced that school choice is not only a very good thing, but that it works.[26] Given his starting point, "public education in the United States seems incapable of self-improvement,"[27] and that inner-city schools are the worst, Peterson

---

[25] *Democratic Education*. This discussion comes from Gill, ibid., p. 190.

[26] See, for example, Paul Peterson and Bryan Hassel, eds., *Learning from School Choice* (Washington, D.C.: Brookings, 1998).

[27] Ibid., p. 3.

believes that "choice" should begin there. While he sometimes suggests that the data are still limited, there is no question that he believes the future of good education lies in charter schools and voucher programs. Peterson is an advocate.

The problem is that the evidence about the value of charter schools and voucher programs does not support the idea that they are superior to public schools. An example might be helpful.[28] In 2000, Peterson and his group published a study of the voucher programs in Milwaukee, New York City, and Dayton, Ohio. The study argued that, at least for black students, the voucher program (used in private schools) produced better results than public schools. As soon as the results were presented, a member of the research team said that Peterson was wrong about New York City.

Martin Carnoy writes: " . . . the three-city study is not nearly as reliable as its authors claim . . . the question to ask is not *whether* these Peterson-group reports overestimate private school effects, *but by how much*." Peterson and his fellow researchers seemed more intent on getting the right results than they were at making sure the results they got were accurate. There are, as we will see, a number of serious methodological problems when trying to understand the effectiveness of charter schools and voucher programs. What we know for certain is that the meaning of the data is often in the eyes of the beholder, and when it comes to studies about schooling, the eyes of the beholder are heavily influenced by political belief.

There have been many studies of the Milwaukee voucher program. But one of the serious problems with these studies is that voucher schools in Milwaukee are not required to take the state tests. It seems impossible to compare, when schools are not doing comparable things. How different would public and private schools be if they were not required to have every student take the state exams? Would they be better—or worse? It depends on what you think about standardized testing. But it is clear that you can't make firm comparative statements when the institutions you study don't do the same things.

In another study, the Peterson group argued that those students who used vouchers did better in their third and fourth years in private schools than those who stayed in public schools. That was true, but what one needs to know is that the gains were not large, and "only a fraction of the voucher students stayed in private schools."[29] It is very difficult to make any meaningful statements from that kind of data. We would need to know, for example, why those other students left, and what effect the private school experience had on them.

In Cleveland, voucher students who went to religious schools made greater gains in science than did nonvoucher students. But that was the only area in which their achievement was higher. The voucher students who went to commercial schools (privately owned schools) did significantly worse than either nonvoucher students or voucher students who attended religious schools. In Cleveland, like Milwaukee, the attrition rates of voucher students who went to private schools was high over the first

---

[28] Martin Carnoy, *School Vouchers: Examining the Evidence* (Washington D.C.: Economic Policy Institute, 2001), pgs. 5–6.

[29] Ibid., p. 32.

two years. What can that data tell us? Can we make any reasoned argument about the voucher program in Cleveland with that information?

Everyone that I read seems to agree with this statement: "Small-scale, experimental, privately funded voucher programs targeted to low-income students suggest a possible (but as yet uncertain) modest achievement benefit for African-American students after one to two years in voucher schools (as compared with local public schools.) . . . For children of other racial/ethnic groups, attendance at voucher schools has not provided consistent evidence of either benefit or harm in academic achievement."[30] This is, at best, a very tentative and almost insignificant finding. We could play it out and reach this conclusion: Vouchers might possibly help, in a marginal way, a small segment of the population.

If that statement is true, and widely agreed upon, how much popular support do you think vouchers would get?

The achievement results for charter schools are mixed. They do not support the notion that charter school results are dramatically better than those of public schools.

When we look at academic outcomes, then, we can speculate that some small-scale programs might help poor, urban blacks. There is even a catch to this very guarded result. If the voucher programs were to become large-scale, it is altogether possible that they would lose what little chance they have of being successful.

Another clear outcome of these schools is that the parents who keep their children in these choice programs like them a great deal. The approval rate is very high. As an interesting aside, mothers of low-income students who choose voucher programs have more education than mothers of low-income students who stay in the public schools. It may well be that those who apply for voucher programs are a skewed sample of the population. To recall, one key to how well lower-income black students test is the education of their mother and grandmother. It is possible that the voucher programs aimed at the poor are really aimed at those women with the most education.

The last problem of evaluation we should look at has to do with success. As mentioned, there are some successes with both charter schools and voucher programs. While isolated and generally statistically meaningless, it would be foolish to overlook the good programs. The question is central: Why do the good programs work? There is, regrettably, almost nothing written about what goes on in those schools that have gotten good results.

Is it because classes are small; or because there is strict discipline; or because there is little discipline; or because of the positive atmosphere; or that teachers are sometimes active in creating the curriculum; or because the schools are new and experiencing the Hawthorne effect; or because they are old (Catholic schools) and have figured something out? In other words, if we knew what worked in the good schools, why couldn't we do the same thing in public schools?

Reason and evidence suggest that there is no one reason why good schools work. There are just too many variables involved. We know that human differences are so great, that one kind of education will never be appropriate for everyone. There is,

---

[30] Gill, op. cit., p. 203.

then, no way to hook on to an idea (like the Edison schools) and believe they will be successful in any particular district in any particular state.

In the summer of 2002 the American Federation of Teachers (AFT) released a study of charter schools. "On the average, charters (especially the for-profits) spend more on administration and less on instruction than local public schools. Student performance is usually no better, and often worse. Charters are more homogeneous in race and class than their comparative school district . . . [and] few charters are doing anything truly innovative and too many are permitted to opt out of public comparisons of their students' results."[31]

While one might wonder about the neutrality of the AFT, it seems their assessment of charter schools simply reinforces what we already know.

There is one last point that voucher advocates make that needs to be discussed. They argue that the very existence of vouchers will help improve public schools. Florida is in the forefront of using vouchers as a way to force schools to do better. The Florida example is especially useful as a way to understand the nature of how people use research.

The state of Florida decided to grade its schools. In 1999 any school that received an *F* two years out of four was eligible for corrective action. The grades were based on the average score students made on the Florida Comprehensive Assessment Test (FCAT). One of the corrective measures was to offer vouchers to all the students in the failing school. The vouchers could be used for the student to go to another school, either public or private. Jay Greene studied the results of this kind of threat (Greene, by the way, is a member of the Peterson group) and found that it was very effective. He found that the "performance of students on academic tests improves when public schools are faced with the prospect of their students receiving vouchers."[32] Greene found that the gains made by the *F* schools were higher than those made by the *A–D* schools. The *F* schools even improved more than the *D* schools.

If we stop here, then Greene has made his case. We would accept the idea that the poorest schools, when threatened by vouchers, will show dramatic improvement on standardized tests.

Of course, it would be foolish to stop here. What we know is that individuals, or groups of individuals, who do something either extraordinarily poorly or well one year cannot be expected to replicate that the next year. Martin Carnoy offers the example of baseball players and batting averages.[33] Over the years, a player might have some very good years and even some very bad years. Generally, a good year will follow a very bad year not because of the threat of being sent to the minor leagues, but because of the normal variations associated with batting. The normal rhythm of things makes it unlikely that a major league batter will have two bad years in a row. It is also normal, after a remarkably good year, for a batter not to do quite as well the next year.

---

[31] "The Report Card on Charter Schools, Newsweek, July 22, 2002, p. 7.

[32] Jay Greene, "An Evaluation of the Florida A-Plus Accountability and School Choice Program" (New York: Manhattan Institute for Policy Research, Center for Civic Innovation, 2002).

[33] Carnoy, op. cit., p. 22.

The same holds true with testing. Those schools at the very top have a difficult time improving their scores. Often, they slip a little and then do well again. The same is true with those schools that test very poorly. It is normal for them to improve the most after a particularly bad year.

The study Greene made in Florida was replicated in Texas. Those schools that did poorest on the state test were studied the following year. The study is interesting for our purposes because there was no threat of vouchers in Texas. The result was just what you would expect: "failing schools in Texas made relative gains as large or larger than the gains Greene attributes to Florida's voucher plan."[34]

A study of low scoring schools in North Carolina, a system without the threat of vouchers, showed the same thing: Low-performing schools made significantly larger achievement gains than schools in other categories.[35]

The Greene study got favorable press. Commentators saw it as a sure sign that vouchers were a way to improve public schools. The logic is somehow appealing: Under the threat of losing students, certainly teachers and administrators will work harder. The logic, regrettably, is both wrong and demeaning in this case. The fact of the matter is, low-performing schools improve—threat or no threat. The logic makes demeaning assumptions about why people are educators. It is as if teachers and administrators are children and can only be made to do well in order to avoid punishment.[36]

From everything we know, a better assumption is that teachers and administrators do their best with what they are given. Certainly those who work in low socio-economic districts are keenly sensitive to the range of problems they face—and that their students face. They understand how difficult it is to get students to the point of doing well on standardized tests. When the students do poorly, they understand it is more a reflection of the conditions in which they live than on the quality of their instruction. To believe that the threat of a voucher program is going to do anything but demoralize them is a misunderstanding of reality.

Are there bad teachers? Yes. Should there be changes in some of the ways in which inner-city kids are schooled? Probably. Is it wise to believe that "choice" will solve the problems of our most vulnerable school? Not according to the facts as we know them.

Before trying to sum up "choice" there are two more areas that need to be reviewed. The first has to do vouchers and parochial schools and the second has to do with teachers owning their own schools.

Parochial Schools

Until June of 2002 it was illegal to have public money go to parochial schools. The long-standing separation of church and state had been the Constitutional gold standard respected by the Supreme Court. But the 2002 court decided there was some-

---

[34] Ibid., p. 28.

[35] Ibid., p. 30.

[36] In the last few years, an odd dynamic has occurred in business. CEOs who have done poorly are given huge amounts of money to leave. If I understand correctly, that is not the way capitalism is supposed to work.

thing more important: choice. By a 5–4 vote, the Supreme Court ruled that vouchers could be cashed in for a parochial school education *if* parents had more than one choice of where to send their children. The reasoning was that because the state was not forcing a religion on anyone, then there was no church/state conflict.

President George Bush, a great believer in vouchers, said: "The Supreme Court has offered the hope of an excellent education to parents and children throughout our country. This decision clears the way for other innovative school-choice programs so that no child in America will be left behind."

To review a little of what we know: There is about a thimbleful of evidence that show vouchers might make only a little difference to a very small number of students; it is estimated that more than 50 percent of the parochial schools that will take vouchers will be Catholic; the breakdown of the separation between church and state has just about nothing to do with "other innovative school-choice programs." A conservative Supreme Court made a ruling that furthered the conservative agenda. That is certainly fair. The ruling is simply politics-as-usual in the United States.

For our purposes, it is necessary to better understand what might go on in religious schools. They have been around for a long time, and we know that some are very good—just as we know that many public schools are very good. While no great fan of parochial schools, it is clear to me that they serve a purpose for many well-meaning and well-educated people. But in the following section our question is this: What difference does a parochial point of view make to education?

Parochial schools (and many private schools) discriminate in the admission of students and in the hiring of teachers. They want a particular kind of student and a teacher who shares the beliefs of the school. They can discriminate in almost any area (in a careful, out-of-the-public-eye kind of way) and generally get away with it. And, of course, there is no public debate about the curriculum. Amy Gutmann's idea of a democratic state of education is not an option. Parochial education dances to God's music.

There is no sense in picking out one denomination to demonstrate the role of religion in parochial education. Alan Peshkin writes about a Baptist Academy: it is a "total institution . . . a school based on absolute truth."[37] The school's mission is to "inform children about the Word of God; to keep children immersed in God; to keep children separate from the world; to encourage children to proselytize the unsaved; to lead children into service as preachers, teachers, evangelists; and to have children become fully committed Christians, living their lives first and foremost for the glory of God."[38]

In *The Amish School*, we read that "religion is taught all day long in lessons and on the playground. The goal of Amish schools is to prepare children for usefulness by preparing them for eternity. . . . An Amish child has an enormous sense of security

---

[37] Alan Peshkin, *God's Choice: The Total World of a Fundamentalist Christian School* (Chicago: The University of Chicago Press, 1986), quoted in Edd Doerr, Albert Menendez, and John Swomley, *The Case Against Vouchers* (Amherst, New York: Prometheus Books, in cooperation with Americans for Religious Liberty, 1996).

[38] Ibid., p. 52.

in community. Leaving that security for the fleeting pleasure of higher education is not only risky but fearsome for most."[39] Since 1948 a company (the Old Order Book Society) has been reprinting textbooks that have been discontinued by public schools. The books are used by the Amish because they are considered "wholesome."

Canon 803 of the Catholic Church reads: "It is necessary that the formation and education given in a Catholic school be based upon the principles of Catholic doctrine; teachers are to be outstanding for their correct doctrine and integrity of life. . . . Even if it really be Catholic, no school may bear the title of Catholic school without the consent of the competent ecclesiastical authority." The Reverend Neil McCluskey writes: "The function of the Catholic school is not merely to teach the formulas of the Catholic religion but . . . to impart in a thousand ways, which defy formularization, the Catholic attitude toward life as a whole."[40]

Orthodox Jewish schools fit the mode: " . . . there was no acknowledgment that anyone but us, sitting there poring over the Talmud, had any religious validity. Christianity was unmentionable. . . . We were also taught to shun those in the more liberal Reformed and Conservative branches of Judaism. Just as one was not permitted to enter a church (even if only to escape the rain), one could not walk into a Reform or Conservative Temple."[41]

Two commonly used textbooks in fundamentalist schools give us a sense of what goes on in some parochial schools. In *The American Republic for Christian Schools*, Rachel Larson and Pamela Creason write that religious liberalism has "hardened Americans in their sin," while Raymond St. John, in *American Literature for Christian Schools*, says that "Religious liberalism is only a modern form of the paganism of Christ's day."[42]

In *World History for Christian Schools*, by David Fisher, we read: "The Jewish religious leaders whose blindness and hypocrisy Jesus had denounced, sought to put him to death. . . . Although Pilate found no fault in Jesus, he desired to maintain the peace. Giving in to the Jewish demands, he sentenced Jesus to death by crucifixion."[43] Later, he writes that Catholicism is "a perversion of biblical Christianity." In *United States History for Christian Schools*, Glen Chambers and Gene Fisher tell us that: "Catholicism enslaves man. From this corrupted system emerged the Roman Catholic Church."[44]

For biology, we get this: God "demands sexual purity" and sexual sins are "a transgression of God's commandment and defile the body and mind." It follows that

---

[39] Sara Fisher and Rachael Stahl, *The Amish School* (Intercourse, Pa.: Good Books, 1986), in Doerr, op. cit., pgs. 55–6.

[40] Ibid., p. 61.

[41] Ari Goldman, *The Search for God at Harvard* (New York: Random House, 1991), in ibid., p. 63.

[42] Rachel Larson with Pamela Creason, *The American Republic for Christian Schools* (Greenville, S.C.: Bob Jones University Press, 1988) and Raymond St. John, *American Literature for Christian Schools, Book 1* (Early American Literature and American Romanticism), Teacher's Edition (Greenville, S.C.: Bob Jones University Press, 1991), in ibid, p. 68.

[43] Quoted in ibid., p. 69.

[44] Quoted in ibid., p. 71.

"The diseases that may result are a reminder that God punishes sinners."[45] There is, of course, the rejection of the theory of evolution.

One last example. According to one book, one factor in the Civil War was the South's desire to retain its "Protestant identity," and we are reminded that "the Bible does not specifically condemn slavery."[46]

That should be enough to offend most people's common sense. There is no reason to produce the long and exhaustive list of prejudices we could find in those texts. I picked these examples because they struck me as particularly outrageous. The not-so-subtle point I want to make is that religious belief can be a very serious business.

At this moment in history, we are in an awkward position. We are under attack by a group of people who have what many consider to be a perverted religious belief. They are attempting to live out a set of religious principles that are rooted firmly in the seventh century, and are counter to most of our liberal freedoms. On the other hand, we often fail to acknowledge that some of the religious beliefs in the United States are extreme. They are intolerant and bigoted.

There might be serious problems when belief and education are mixed. For the true believers, that mix is a beautiful thing. Religious parents are assured that their children are given the proper training to live in a secular and, in their view, immoral world. I am not making the argument that all religions are extreme or intolerant or bigoted. All of us know that is not true. We know that some of the great sweetness of humanity is expressed in our religious beliefs. What I want to talk about is the mix of religion and education.

For those who do not believe, or who have different beliefs, the church/state, religion/education mixes are frightening. Simply because the above examples do not represent mainstream parochial schools does not mean we should ignore them. They do represent the way some schools teach their students. They also remind us why, until now, the policy has been to separate church and state. The Supreme Court ruled that, because voucher programs permit the student a choice of schools, the state is not forcing anyone to go to a parochial school.

What got lost in the ruling is that tax dollars will be going to schools that advocate particular religious beliefs. Do any of us want our money going to schools that teach what we think is wrong and quite possibly dangerous? Or, in a less defiant voice, do any of us want our money to go to a god we don't believe in?

Was the finding by the court surprising? Not really. This was the court that, many argue, made George Bush President. Four days after the voucher ruling, Bush made a speech praising the decision. He said that "Our government should not fear faith in our society." What he meant, in part, was that the decision will allow the federal government to give money to church-based social programs. The line between church and state will blur even further.

---

[45] William Pinkston Jr., *Biology for Christian Schools, Book 2*, Teacher's Edition, (Greenville, S.C.: Bob Jones University Press, 1991), in ibid., p. 73.

[46] Ibid., pgs. 71, 75.

In a book about vouchers and charter schools, the authors write this: "Fortunately for us, however, Americans in general are not especially ideological."[47] That is a surprisingly wrong statement. We are, of course, deeply ideological. We are liberals. The reason we are at war with terrorists is because of our liberal ideology. We believe in individualism and at least a representative democracy, and some form of capitalism as well as a series of different freedoms. To give money to parochial schools is a political decision. The question is this: How much will that decision clash with our liberal ideology?

Put differently, we know that schooling in the United States has always been a reflection of the political will. If our political will has changed, and it is now acceptable for the government to cross the church/state boundary, does that signal other, deeper changes in our society? If it does, then the nature of schooling will certainly be affected in ways that we cannot imagine.

This book—indeed, most books about education—will be out of step and out of date.

It is time to look at one last suggested change in our schooling. It is, like the fundamentalist religious schools, at the far end of change. It is about capitalism, and teachers owning their own schools.

Selling Our Schools

In *Can Teachers Own Their Own Schools?* Richard Vedder takes us to one of the logical conclusions of the choice/capitalist train of thought.[48] What follows is Vedder's vision.

As most educational critics, Vedder begins with the notions that piecemeal changes will not work, and that the best idea is for school districts to privatize and outsource their school systems. He argues that the private realm is simply better than the public realm. Federal Express and United Parcel Service have taken a "large amount of business" from the United States Postal Service, and "more people visit tourists attractions of the Disney Co. in Florida and California than National Park Service sites with great beauty such as the Grand Canyon."[49]

While this is not the time to speculate about how it is possible to compare Disneyland and the Grand Canyon, it is fair to say that it is logic only a certain kind of economist can appreciate.

Vedder's plan is for teachers to own their schools. Literally own them. The first step is for each teacher to get stock that would reflect how many years he or she had taught. The same would go for administrators, with the only difference being that administrators would get more stock for years in service. For additional start-up cash, a limited amount of stock would be sold to the general public.

---

[47] Gill, op. cit., p. 28.

[48] Richard Vedder, *Can Teachers Own Their Own Schools? New Strategies for Educational Excellence*, (Oakland, Calif.: The Independent Institute, 2000).

[49] Ibid., p. 11.

The school districts would give the real estate to the new corporations, as well as the existing supplies. To ease the transition, no taxes would be paid for the first five years. The schools would be obligated to honor all voucher students who applied to their schools. Also, at least at first, the new schools would not be allowed to charge additional tuition.

For their part, the schools would not be bound by state school regulations and would not have to honor collective bargaining agreements. The stage would be set, according to Vedder, for a genuinely free and competitive school system.

Each school would vie for students. One advantage, for example, might be smaller classes. But that would be an economic disadvantage for the teachers who owned the school, so a couple of things might happen. First, teachers would be paid less. Vedder believes because teachers had gotten some stock, and because they would enjoy their jobs much more because they owned the school, that lower pay would be all right. And, they could always hire aides. These low-paid assistants would help the teacher. Teachers would need help because, economically, it makes sense to have larger classes.

If a school became popular, it would begin charging tuition. After all, that would be the economic reward for winning over consumers. If a school began losing students, it would be forced to change or go out of business. I suppose that some other group could come in and take over. Or, maybe the school that was doing really well could buy it out and become, after some time, a monopoly. That is, if we have learned anything from history, the logic of the free market. Capitalism leads to monopoly capitalism. Why couldn't a strong, teacher-owned school drive other schools out of business? With the right management, we could count on it.

Back to the vision. The school district is out of business, which, for Vedder, is a good thing. The students, now given real choices, are much better off. And, if we are to believe Vedder, teachers are now happy owners.

This is the deal teachers get: some stocks. One has no idea what they might be worth. A real voice in the curriculum. Ownership. The downside is that their salaries will decrease, they will lose tenure, benefits, and retirement. The price of happiness, to put it differently, is less money, no security and a diminished life when they retire.

It is the free market at its best. The underlying ideas go something like this: If we could only get those foolish educators to understand that everyone would do better with competition and the promise of money. That every job can be boiled down to debits and credits and the profit motive. That to acknowledge the only reason we work is to own more and have more and consume more would be the right first step in making our educational system second to none. We have remarkably sophisticated economic models that prove the point. Why go to the Grand Canyon when you can see Goofy?

I have probably gone past the stopping point for an issues in education book. The far ends of the free market and fundamentalist religion are interesting because they help point out bottom-line prejudices in some of the directions our politics are taking us. Our centrist liberal values make us shy away from these extreme positions, and not take them seriously. But it would be a mistake to ignore them. People believe in these positions in passionate ways. They exist, they are real, and they may be a big part of our future.

UNDERSTANDING CHOICE: POLITICS AND ECONOMICS

As we have seen, it is easy to find "issues" in education. People seem to choose what they believe is most pressing (testing or the role of sex or special education, or race or . . .) and do their best to convince us that if we solve that problem then things will be much better. The loudest current debate is about school choice. The most simple form of the argument is this: If we can somehow just deconstruct public education, then the free market will certainly solve all of our problems. There are economic and political ideas we need to look at.

We can begin with the economic point. As we saw in chapter two, the magic of a free market is not rational decision making. The free market, according to Adam Smith, worked because of the "passions and appetites" of the individual, and the magical "invisible hand" would guide the entire process. The system depended on each citizen acting in his or her self-interest. Reason was just a way to understand the most efficient way of getting to the goal set up by passions.

The underlying argument is that rational choice will be the result of free markets. It may well be that the opposite is true. We cannot assume that self-interest is the same thing as reason. Equally importantly, we cannot assume that any kind of reasonable general interest will be the collective product of every person's self-interest. One needs to wonder what the effect of "passions and appetites" will be on schooling.

If that is the underlying dynamic of choice in schooling, then it is clear that the nature of schooling in the United States will change. And change dramatically.

It is easy to speculate about what might happen. For example, in chapter eleven we saw how advertising targeted the youth population. In a genuine free market for education, it is reasonable to expect that powerful for-profit interests will do what they can to enroll the greatest number of students. As a teenager, I would be interested in attending a school where the students looked like Calvin Klein or Abercrombie & Fitch models—models who would, of course, all be wearing glasses (if nothing else) to show they were studious.

The point is that if people have a problem with popular culture, and then put schooling in the middle of that culture, the results should not be surprising. The winning school corporation will be the one with the biggest advertising budget; the one that can produce the most appealing ads.

The second point about free markets is that it is easy to think of better ways of making money. One of the current buzzwords is "outsourcing." Let some company like Edison run schools. Edison, while not yet profit making, is the strongest of the for-profit companies.

Here's a plan: Why not hire well-educated people with green cards? No one says teachers have to be citizens. Hire them part-time so they don't get benefits. Pay them as little as possible. Have a few master teachers to direct them. Certainly it would be possible to make a profit.

The free-market people could easily argue that if the students do well on the standardized tests, who cares if the English was taught by someone from India, or the math taught by someone from Mexico or Albania? The capitalist point is that there is no reason why people with green cards cannot teach kids how to do well on tests. The bonus is that the corporation would make money from a staff of well-educated but poorly paid teachers.

As I write, big corporations are "outsourcing" business to India. They hire college-educated Indians to answer your calls about health insurance or credit card or Internet problems. They are paid $3,000 a year. Why couldn't we do that for schools?

Enough of the economic point. There have always been serious problems with free markets, and there is no evidence that they would work in education.

The more serious point is political. From the beginning I have made the argument that schools produce the kinds of citizens that are wanted and needed by the culture. The interplay between the state and education was made first, and best, by Plato. The *Republic* is a journey through the ties that bind learning and governing.

In the history of education in the United States, we have seen schooling go through different phases. From nation building to producing factory workers; from Americanizing immigrants to producing scientists; from integrating the population to providing an equal opportunity to all children, our schools have systematically tried to solve our social problems.

In the previous section we asked the question, Does choice work? We went through all the empirical studies to see if we could find evidence that charter schools or voucher programs somehow helped kids read better or learn more or stay in school longer. It seemed surprising that there wasn't more positive evidence that "choice" produced better outcomes.

It could well be that those studies are looking at the wrong things. The underlying messages of choice are this: Government regulation is bad; free markets are good. Charter schools and voucher programs are teaching exactly those messages that conservatives want taught. The structure of how schooling is now presented is the lesson being taught. This is the Reagan/Bush/Bush agenda.

At the turn of the twentieth century schools taught children how to become factory workers. They did that, in part, by sitting students in rows, having bells ring so they could go from class (task) to class (task), making sure students always show up on time—and on and on. The subjects being taught were not really the point: The structure of schooling was the point. The form and rhythm of schools took children out of a rural, natural mind-set and socialized them into an industrial reality.

Apply that same thinking to the political agenda of many of the strongest advocates of choice. The basic critique is that public schools are so corrupt that they cannot be saved. While there is a small minority that says all schooling is corrupt, the vast majority of critics tell us that *public* schools are corrupt. By implication, all other schools are all right. The most highly structured parochial schools, or all the for-profit schools are somehow better than public schools because . . . well . . . because they are not public.

The first lesson to be learned is simple: Mistrust government.[50]

---

[50] The irony, of course, is that the government has assumed a great deal of power to look into our private lives in the name of Homeland Security. It seems we are forced to trust the government with a surprisingly large amount of information about our very own selves.

The second lesson is, choice will produce the best results. It seems part of our collective intuition that a free market will produce the best possible schooling. We believe in choice. We like the idea that there are five brands of peanut butter and dozens of cars to choose from. We think, and we're probably right, that somehow that kind of competition will give us both better peanut butter and better cars.

The problem is that schools might be different than consumer products. The fact is we have had a wide variety of schools before we decided that choice would be a public policy. Different schools have had different structures and "personalities" for decades. More importantly, we actually lose something with the coming of choice. The value of neighborhood schools has somehow disappeared. Once the foundation of the community, we have moved past the values that are associated with our kids walking to school with their friends. Also lost is the idea of any kind of civic culture that is taught to everyone. Collective decisions and public control are lost. The higher good is now the free market and competition. Everything else will, somehow, be taken care of by—who knows—maybe an invisible hand.

A good argument can be made that it is wrong to judge choice at the immediate level of testing and achievement. The results, unless they are just awful, don't really matter. It has never been *that* kind of political question. The political question has been about structure. If we measure success this way, then choice is highly successful. That students don't learn more, or differently, just isn't the point. That they get a taste of free enterprise, free-markets and choice means they have learned the lesson. They are on their way to becoming the kinds of citizens many in our culture want to produce.

SUMMARY

Are the critics right? Are public schools hopeless? Is the system so awful that the best possible thing we could do is eliminate it in favor of some scheme that takes control out of the hands of the public?

I am unconvinced that the critics are right. We need to sort out what the problems are, and what seem to be the causes.

There are remarkably good public schools in the United States. By all measures, the graduates of these schools are well-educated students and responsible citizens. And because they are public schools, they are under the control of what many argue are suffocating, irrational, massive bureaucratic structures.

We also know that there are horrible public schools in the United States. By the same measures, these schools fail. They are public schools, and the critics blame those massive, irrational, suffocating bureaucratic structures for what has gone wrong.

What if the variables that affect what is good and bad education have little or nothing to do with either the structure of schools or their teachers? What if the important variables center around a different set of issues?

We need to know what we want out of our schools, and then be willing to pay for it. Decades ago we decided that all children in the United States should have an equal educational opportunity. Over those decades we have done our best to make certain that when we talked about all children we really meant all children.

We have been committed to an equal education regardless of color, sex, class, language, learning ability. That is a remarkable commitment. It is one that makes teaching an attractive profession for many people.

What I want to argue is this: The problem is neither our school system nor our teachers. The problems are more deeply rooted in our culture. First, we need to figure out how to help get children out of poverty. We know there are good public schools and bad public schools and they operate under the same state systems. Instead of good and bad schools, it would have been just as easy to say that there are schools in rich neighborhoods and poor neighborhoods. Schools in higher socioeconomic districts are generally good. Money and the quality of education correlate. More, in this case, is better.

As a society we ask poorly paid teachers in poorly supported ghetto schools to somehow make their students competitive with those in the privileged suburbs. To believe that a $2,500 voucher will somehow buy a first-rate education is simply wrong. Yes, there are some positive results in voucher programs and in charter schools, but those programs do not address the basic issue of poverty.

While there is an argument to be made that schools might be less institutionalized, that there should be less state regulation, and that experimentation should be encouraged in our public schools, it seems dead wrong to blame all teachers when things go bad. It seems equally wrong to believe that a free-market model has anything to do with how effective teachers are.

Just to make the obvious point, there has never been anything like a free market in the United States. (OK, maybe illegal drugs represent a free market.) The markets in the United States have always been a creation of the government, and have needed the regulation of the government. When there is no regulation, we get things like Enron. To make another obvious point, teaching is not a capitalist activity. While teachers deserve more pay, they clearly do not enter the profession to amass their fortunes.

Why a capitalist cannot understand there are reasons, other than money, to work is a real flaw. To believe we can continue to pay our teachers very low salaries because they are doing meaningful, enjoyable work, is equally flawed thinking.

But, if schooling is as important as all of the critics in government believe it is, shouldn't teachers be paid more, buildings be updated, and teaching materials be available to everyone? If education is the key to upward mobility, then to literally shortchange it is unthinkable.

The public school system, and its teachers, have done a remarkable job in the United States. Over the last one hundred and fifty years, society has asked much of its schools and, to a surprising degree, schools have done their job. I am not convinced that this generation of high school and college graduates is somehow inferior. I am not convinced that teachers don't know what they are doing. I am convinced of this: Many of the critics don't know what they are talking about.

What I believe is that there are systemic social problems that schools cannot deal with. Until we focus on the real problems, no amount of tinkering with school schemes will help. In the meantime, to dismantle our public schools in search of a free-market solution is an ideological ploy that ignores deeper issues. It also ignores the hardworking, good-hearted, talented educators who are doing their best in the worst of conditions. Change can be a very good thing. Mindless change can sometimes do more harm than good.

Schools are constantly sorting out individual needs and societal goals; they are forever trying to come to terms with how to best juggle personal differences in a society that believes in equality. Every school board in every school district in the United States needs to decide its version of what policies best represent the public good. The process is ongoing.

These broad themes are some of the important underlying tensions of education in the United States. In chapter after chapter, we have seen how these social tensions have been played out in our public schools.

In the end, I genuinely believe that all the schemes and techniques and technologies might help in incremental ways, but they will not make a bad teacher a good one. The things that made teachers good a thousand years ago are the same qualities that make teachers good today. I am not saying there is one model of a good teacher. As students, it is always surprising that some of our friends like (and learn) from teachers we can't stand.

What I am saying is, there is a fundamental caring that seems to be a trait of those teachers we admire. What's interesting is that it does not seem to matter a great deal exactly what the caring is for: it might be for students, for the environment, for history, or for two-year-olds. The good teacher somehow is able to convey that care to his or her students. Being articulate and good-looking and well-organized and really smart are all helpful, but none are really necessary.

There is a love of the task, a great caring for a subject that can overcome a sloppy lesson plan or a bad-hair day.

So, you are walking towards your classroom. It will be you and your students, and every strength and weakness as well as every potential and problem of what the United States was, is, and will be. Before you open the door, there are a surprising number of very hard questions you should have already started to answer.

Some of the questions are best discussed with others. Some of the questions only you can answer.

Ability grouping, 174
Academic work, and gender, 135–138
Achievement tests, 270–271
"Acting white," 180–182
Adams, John Quincy, 48
Addams, Jane, 192–193
ADHD (attention deficit hyperactivity disorder), 127, 221–223
Administrative work, 249–251
Administrators, professional, 190–191
Adolescence, 62, 66
Aesthetic sense, 14, 18
Affirmative action, 167, 176, 183–184
AFL. *See* Chicago Federation of Labor
AFL-CIO, 116
African Americans
   black education, 160–167
   distinct black race, 155
   early attempts to educate, 53
   Ebonics, 208
   infant mortality rates, 167–168
   as irrational beings, 39
   migration to North, 188
   white-black test gap, 175–178
AFT. *See* American Federation of Teachers
Agrarian America, 33–34, 57
Alcohol, 311
Alexander, Lamar, 242
Alienation, 120
Allport, Gordon, 260
Alternative schools, 326
Amalgamation, 196
American Association of Mental Retardation, 223
American Association of University Professors, 74
American Federation of Teachers (AFT), 113–116
American Indians, 157–158
   Americanizing, 189
   as irrational beings, 39
American Philosophical Society, 48
Americanizing, 67, 193, 206
American Indians, 189
Americans with Disabilities Act (1990), 218
Amherst, Jeffery, 157
Ancient Greeks, 3–6
Anglican Church, 28
Anthony, Susan B., 112–113
Anti-school movements, 83
Apprenticeships, 27–28, 31
Armendariz, Gloria, 203
Armstrong, Henry, 90
Articles of Confederation, 40, 48, 49
Asian Americans, 158–159
Assimilation, 193–194, 196, 206
Athletics, and boys, 139–140
Attention deficit hyperactivity disorder. *See* ADHD

Balkanization, 334
Barber, Ann, 318
Bauman, Paul, 248–249
Beauty pageants, 304–305
Behavioral disorders, 221–223
Bell, Andrew, 52

Bennett, William, 242, 265
Berlin, Isaiah, 41
Berliner, David, 99
Berman, Morris, 299–302, 307, 312
Bethune, Mary McLeod, 68
Bethune-Cookman College, 68
Biases, 16–17
   and liberalism, 35
   and test scores, 177–178
Bilingual education, 203–208
   court rulings and legislation, 204–207
   dual language program, 203–204
   maintenance/developmental programs, 203–204
   pullout program, 203
   structured immersion, 203–204
   transitional program, 203–204
Bill of Rights, 49
Binet, Alfred, 262
Biology, girls and boys and, 126–128
Black language, 208
Blank slate (*tabula rasa*), 37
Body image, 140–142
Bond, Julian, 325
Boston Public Latin School, 26
Bourgeoisie, origin of word, 34
Boys. *See* Girls and boys
Bradley, Bill, 257
Braswell, Jim, 288–289
Brigham, Carl, 263
Brown University, 58, 299
Brown v. the Board of Education of Topeka, 68, 81, 172, 194
Bruno, Giordano, 34–35
Buckley, Jr., William F., 273
Bullying, 141
Bureaucracies and education, 238–259
   See also Federal government; Local government; State government
Bush, George H.W., 239, 241–242, 265
Bush, George H.W. and Alexander, Lamar, *America 2000: An Educational Strategy*, 241–242
Business, and education, 67, 245–251
Busing, 172

California Achievement Tests, 291
California Basic Educational Skill Test, 282–283
Calvinism, 43, 58
Capitalism, 2, 18, 42, 50
   Adam Smith's contribution, 35–36
   teen spending, 62
   See also Smith, Adam
Cardinal Principles of Secondary Education (1918), 70–72, 78, 191–192
Carnegie Forum on Education and the Economy, 103–104
Carnegie Foundation, 168
Carnoy, Martin, 335, 337
Cash, Johnny, 305
Categorical aid, 240
Catholic Church, parochial schools, 339–340

Catholic curriculum, 16
Catholicism, 188
Ceci, Stephen, 270
Censorship, 5–6
Center for Communication Policy (UCLA), 310
Centralized school administration vs. individual classrooms, 250–251
Certification, 105–112
Chambers, Glen, 340
Charter schools, 31, 326, 329–332
   criticism of, 332
   Edison Schools, 330–331
   effectiveness of, 334–338
   lack of public control and certification, 332
   See also Voucher programs
Chauncey, Henry, 270
Chicago Federation of Labor (AFL), 11
Child development, 66
Child-centered schools, 77–78
Childbirth rates, in agrarian America, 34
Children
   sexualizing, 304–306
   testing young, 271–273
   See also Girls and boys
Children's Defense Fund, 88
Chinese Exclusion Act (1882), 189
Chipman, Alice, 74
Chodorow, Nancy, 125–126
Choice, politics and economics, 344–346
Christian schools, 339–341
Church and state separation, 338–342
Citizens, schooling to become good, 2
Civil freedom, 41
Civil Rights Act, Title VI, 204–205
Civil Rights movement, 83–84, 171, 176, 194, 239
Clark University, 66
Class, and tests, 283–285
Class size, 184
Classical cultural pluralism, 196
Clinical sites, 103
Clinton, Bill, 170, 239, 243, 265
Clitoridectomy, 201
College Board, 263
College Entrance Examination Board, 79
College of William and Mary, 29
Colonial education. *See* Schooling history
Colonial theater, 197
Columbia University, 74, 92
Committee of Nine on the Articulation of High School and College (1911), 70
Committee of Ten (1894), 69–70
Common reality, 195
Common schools, 57–64
Communication disabilities, 221
Community, 18
Comprehensive Test of Basic Skills, 286, 291
Computer Adaptive Technologies, 291
Computers, pro and con, 313–321

Conant, James, 83
Confidence, in girls, 139–141
Conflict theory, 16
Conservative reaction to sixties, 84–85, 103
Constitution, 48, 49
   spiritual father of (John Locke), 37
Constitutional Convention, 48
Content bias, 178
Context, 2, 15
Cook, Philip, 181–182
Coons, John, 333
Copernicus, Nicolaus, 34
Cornell, 270
Corporate media, 301–307
Coser, Lewis, 16
Counts, George, 186
Cowboy culture, 7, 18
Cremin, Lawrence, 79
Crew, Randy, 286–287
Crime, moral problem, 63
Critical theory, 16
Cruise, Pamela, 288–289
CTB/McGraw-Hill, 291
Cultural diversity, defining, 196–197
Cultural tradition, 14
Culture, 297–324
   changing family, 300
   computers, 313–321
   drugs, 310–313
   the law, 321–323
   media, 300
   modern philosophy, 300–301
   movies and corporate media, 301–304
   music, 300
   sex, 304–306, 310–313
   television, 306–307
   violence, 308–310
Culture of poverty, 205
Curriculum of liberation, 16
Curti, Merle, 165
Cutri, Ramona, 203

Damon, William, 299, 312
Dark Ages (new), 300
Darwin, Charles, 66, 74
Daytona Beach Normal and Industrial School for Negro Girls, 68
Debra P. v. Turlington, 293
Decentralization, 58
Deism, 38
DeMarris and LeCompte, 100
Democrats, and testing, 269
Department of Education, 181, 207, 240
Deschooling, 326–329
   See also Homeschooling
Desegregation, 80–82, 172, 239
   See also Segregation
Deutsch, Helen, 124
Dewey, John, 60, 73–78, 88, 92, 190, 192–193, 327
Dewey School (experimental elementary school), 74–75
Disabilities, 220–225
   behavioral disorders, 221–223
   learning disabilities, 225
   mental retardation, 223–224
   physical, 220–221
Disney, 291

Distribution of wealth, 41–42
Diversity, and values, 195
Dock, Christopher,
　Schul-Ordnung, 30
Doctorates in teaching, 103, 111
Dominant classes, 16
Dominant values, 197
Doty, Duane, 64
Drugs, 310–311
Dual language bilingual education,
　203–204
DuBois, W.E.B., 160–164
Durkheim, Emile, 1
Dyslexia, 127

Eastman, George, 165
Eating disorders, 140–141
Ebonics, 208
Economic freedom, 41
Economic tasks, 99
Economics, Adam Smith, 35–36
Ed.D., 92
Edison Schools, 330–331
　See also Charter schools
Education
　and business, 67, 245–251
　career choice, 19
　common schools, 57–64
　defined, 14
　and federal government,
　　239–245
　federal, state, and local debate
　　about, 48–52
　as a field, 104
　funding, 255–258
　and the individual, 17–19
　and John Locke, 37
　and liberalism, 41, 44–45
　and local government, 252–255
　origin of word, 14n.17
　personal nature of, 18–19
　progressive era, 74–78
　promoting the values of
　　society, 2
　Southern with Northern money,
　　164–167
　and states, 251–252
　statistics, 239
　world, 21
Educational methods, 103
Educational Policies
　Commission, 78
Educational Testing Service (ETS),
　270, 276, 288–289, 290
Effective schools, 173–175
Effrat, Andrew, 109, 326
Eighties, education, 240–242
Eisenhower, Dwight, 81–83,
　172, 239
Elementary and Secondary
　Educational Act (1965), 240
Eliot, Charles, 70
Elites, 161
Emile (Rousseau), 6–10
Emotional development, 319
Empowerment, 198–199
Encyclopedia Africana, 161
English as a second language,
　funding, 18
Enlightenment, 47, 53, 54
Entrepreneurs, 18
Environment, 12–13
　socialization and, 131–132
Equal access, 2
Equal opportunity, 5
Equitable society, 12
Ethnicity, vs. race, 152
European culture, 199
"Eve" (single common ancestor), 154
Evolution, 153–155
Exercise, 318
Exodus, 210

Experience, 8–9, 76
Experimental psychology, 69

Faculty theory of the mind, 72–73
FairTest, 276
Faith in reason, 38–39
Falbel, Aaron, 327
Families
　changing, 300
　changing number of
　　children, 189
Family income, by race, 167
Farr, Roger, 273
Faubus, Orval, 81
Federal government, and
　education, 239–245
Feminist movement, 194
Feminist theories, 16
Ferguson, Ronald, 177
Ferrin, Scott, 203
Feudalism, 32–33
Fifties, 82, 194
Finneran, Thomas, 281
Fischer, Louis, 321, 323
Fisher, Sara, 339–340
Fisk University, 160
Florida Comprehensive
　Assessment Test, 3
Ford Foundation, 92
Fordham, Signithia, 180
Foreign languages, 14
Franklin, Benjamin, 28
Free school movements, 83
Free School Societies, 52–53
Free-market system, and schools,
　331–332, 344–347
　See also Charter schools; Voucher
　　programs
Freedom, 51–52
　types of, 41
Freedoms, 5–6
Freire, Paulo, 16
Freud, Anna, 124
Freud, Sigmund, 123–125
Friedman, Milton, 266, 332
Funding
　equal funding, 256–257
　school systems, 255–258
　spending per student by various
　　states, 256–257

Galton, Francis, 229, 262
Gangs, 308
Gardner, Howard, 110–111,
　146–147, 229
Gender, and academic work,
　135–138
Gender socialization, 132–135
General Cinema Corporation, 291
General Education Board
　(GEB), 165
General will of a state, 7
Genetic variability, 152
Germans, 62
Gerstner, Louis, et.al., 247
GI Bill, 239
Gifted children, 227–231
Gilligan, Carol, 125–126
Girls and boys, 122–150
　biology, 126–128
　differences, 144–145
　early human learning, 129–131
　environment and socialization,
　　131–132
　gender and academic work,
　　135–138
　gender socialization, 132–135
　kindergarten and grade school,
　　134–135
　middle and high schools,
　　138–143
　multiple intelligences, 146–147

psychology, 123–126
　retention, 278
　sex-role stereotypes, 143–144
　in special education, 225
　testing, 275–276
　thinking styles, 147–149
Giroux, Henry, 300, 302, 304–305
Goodman, Paul, 326
Gopnik, Alison, 129
Gordon-Conwell Theological
　Seminary, 299
Gore, Al, 170, 243
Government, and John Locke, 37
Governmental intervention, 41
Governors, 251
Grade school, 134–135
Grant, Roberta, 74
Great Depression, and schools, 246
Greene, Jay, 337–338
GREs, 285
Gross domestic product,
　education's share of, 239
Gutmann, Amy, 198, 334, 339

Hacker, Andrew, 274
Hall, G. Stanley, 66, 74
Hampton Institute, 162, 165
Hanus, Paul Henry, 91–92
Harcourt General, 291
Hardwick, Elizabeth, 273–274
Harris, William, 64
Harvard University, 161
　educating teachers, 91–92
Hawking, Stephen, 38
Hearing impairment, 220–221
Henry, Patrick, 40
Herbst, Jurgen, And Sadly Teach, 91
Hern, Matt, 326–327
Herrnstein, R.J., 264
High schools, 138–143
　standardization, 64–66
High-stakes testing, 268–269,
　279–283
Higher Education Act (1965), 240
Hirsch, Jr., E.D., 100
Hispanics, 156–158, 195
　in California, 206
　demographics, 156–157
　school achievement, 157
Hobbes, Thomas, 18, 42
Hofstadter, Richard, 69
Holmes Group (Holmes
　Partnership), 103–104
Holt, John, 326
Homeschooling, 9, 30–31,
　326–329
　See also Deschooling
Homo sapiens, 153
Homogeneous communities, 57
Honig, Bonnie, 201
Honig v. Doe, 235
Hornbook, 25
Horney, Karen, 124
Houghton Mifflin, 291
Human Genome Diversity
　project, 153
Hunter College Elementary
　School, 271–272

IDEA. See Individuals with
　Disabilities Education Act
Ideal citizen, 4, 8
IEP. See Individualized education
　program
Immigrants, 187–194
Immigration, 61–62, 90
　new, 194–195
In loco parentis, 321
Inclusion
　problems with, 234–236
　special needs students, 231–236
Indiana University, 273

Individual, and education, 17–19
Individual classrooms vs.
　centralized school
　administration, 250–251
Individual vs. state needs. See State
　vs. individual needs
Individualism, 2, 7, 18, 39
　See also Emile (Rousseau);
　　Liberalism
Individualized education program
　(IEP), 216–219
Individuals with Disabilities
　Education Act (IDEA),
　215–218
Industrial arts, 166
Industrial education, 162
Industrialization, 60–64
Infant mortality rates, 167–168
Institute of Educational
　Research, 74
Institutionalization, 60–64
Integration, 167
　See also Desegregation;
　　Segregation
Intellectual freedom, 41
Intellectual tasks, 99
Intelligence, defined, 146
Intelligence tests, 191
Intelligences, multiple, 110–111,
　146–147
Interest groups, 43
Interpretive theories, 16
Invisible hand, 36, 42
IQs
　gifted students, 228
　Howard Gardner's challenge
　　to, 229
　mental retardation and, 224
　testing, 270–273, 275
　whites vs. blacks, 284
Irish, 62
Ivins, Molly, 122

Jackson, Jesse, 199–200, 208
James, William, 71, 72–73, 74
Jay, John, 48
Jeanes, Anna, 165
Jeanes Teachers, 165–166
Jefferson, Thomas, 7, 29, 40, 48,
　49–52
Jencks, Christopher, 333
Jewish schools, 340
Jews, 188
Job preparation, 2
Johns Hopkins University, 66, 74

Kaestle, Carl, 61
Katzman, John, 288–289
Keniston, Kenneth, 21
Kesey, Ken, 21
Kindergarten, 134–135
King, Jr., Martin Luther, 161, 208
Klein, Melanie, 124
Knox, Samuel, 48–49
Kohn, Alfie, 260, 274
Korean War, 194
Krupnick, Catherine, 138
Kuhl, Patricia, 129

Labeling, and special needs
　students, 231–232
Labeling bias, 177
Labor, 36
Lancaster, Joseph, 52
Larson, Rachel, 340
Lau v. Nichols, 205
Law, 321–323
Law School Admissions
　Council, 284
Learning, 18
　early human, 129–131
Learning disabilities, 127, 223, 225

Leiserson, Michael, 238
Leviticus, 210
Liberal arts, 102
Liberal heritage, 7
Liberal ideology, 2
Liberal/capitalist thought, 35
Liberalism
  Adam Smith, 34–37
  critiquing, 41–45
  faith in reason, 38–39
  freedom, 41
  John Locke, 37–39
  nationalism, 40
  natural law, 39
  progress, 40
  rationality, 35–36
  reason, 35–36
  republican virtue, 39–40
Liberty, 7
Life adjustment education, 78–80
Linguistic diversity, 203
  See also Bilingual education
Little Rock, Arkansas, and
  desegregation, 81–82, 172, 239
Local government, and education,
  57–58, 252–255
Localism, 40
Locke, John, 2, 18, 37, 41–43
Lowen, Daniel, 274
Lower class, 62
LSAT, 284
Ludwig, Jens, 181–182

McCluskey, Neil, 340
Machado, Kit, 196–197
McIntyre, Alice, 178
McLaren, Peter, 180, 197, 202
McLaurin, George, 100, 80–81
Macro view, 16
Madison, James, 48
Magnet schools, 173, 326
Mainstreaming, 210
Maintenance model of bilingual
  education, 207
Mann, Horace, 58–60, 90
Mann, Stephen, 58
Marshall, John, 29
Martin, Jane Roland, 144–145
Marx, Karl, 16
Massachusetts colony, 23–26
Masters, 27–28
Master's in teaching, 103
M.A.T. program, 92
Media, 300
Medicine, as standard for teachers,
  94–99
Melting pot, 193, 196
Meltzoff, Andrew, 129
Mennonites, 30
Mental retardation, 223–224
Merit pay, for teachers, 108
Micro view, 16
Middle Atlantic colonies,
  education history, 29–31
Middle school, 138–143
Milwaukee Parental Choice
  Program, 333
Mitochondrial DNA, 154
Monitorial schools, 52
Monroe, James, 29
Montessori schools, 331
Moral education, 2
Moral lessons, 57
Moral questions, 44
Morality, 12, 39
Mormons, 201
Morris, George, 74
Movies, 301–304
MTV, 305
Mueller, Walt, 297, 299,
  302–303, 312
Multicultural education, 194–202

Multiculturalism, 156
  critics of, 199–200
  liberal principles and, 202
  theories of pluralism, 196–199
  and whites, 179
  women's rights and, 200–201
Multiple intelligences, 110–111,
  146–147
Multiple-choice tests, 273–274
Music, 300, 305

NAACP, 68, 81, 161
Nass, Clifford, 319
Nation at Risk, A (National
  Commission on Excellence in
  Education), 56, 84, 94, 103,
  241–242, 246, 261, 299, 330
Nation Prepared, A (Carnegie
  Forum on Education and the
  Economy), 103
National Assessment of
  Educational Progress, 293
National Association of
  Manufacturers (NAM), 67
National Association for Gifted
  Children, 230
National Association of State
  Boards of Education, 299
National Board Certified
  Teacher, 109
National Board for Professional
  Teaching Standards, 108
National Center for Educational
  Statistics (NCES), 267
National Commission on
  Excellence in Education, 56,
  84, 94, 103, 241–242, 246,
  261, 299, 330
National Computer Systems, 291
National Defense Education Act
  (1958), 115–116, 239
National Education Association
  (NEA), 113–116, 191–192
  Commitment to the Student,
  322–323
National Education Longitudinal
  Study, 181–182
National Educational Development
  Test, 291
National Educational Goals
  Panel, 272
National Institute of Child
  Health and Human
  Development, 130
National politics, and education,
  239–245
National Research Council, 269
National system of education,
  48–49
National Teacher's Examination, 282
National testing, 79
National university, 48
Nationalism, 40
Natural aristocracy, 49–52
Natural law, 39
Natural life, 7
Natural rights, 40
Nature, and society, 7–9
NEA. See National Education
  Association
Negative freedom, 41
Net generation, 313–315
New England colonial education,
  23–28
New England Primer, 25–26
"New Federalism," 240–241
New York City, urban
  education, 188
Philosophiae Naturalis Principia
  Mathematica, 35
Nichols-White, Donna, 327
Nieto, Sonia, 197–198

Nineteenth century setting, 57–60
No Child Left Behind legislation,
  94, 245, 266
Normal Schools, 99
Normalcy, 194

Ogbu, John, 180
Ogden, Robert, 165
Ohanian, Susan, 260, 292
Okin, Susan, 200
"Old Deluder Satan Law," 24
One-parent families, 176, 226
Open enrollment, 326
Oppressive education, 16
Ordinance of 1785 (Northwest
  Ordinance), 49
Orthodox Jewish schools, 340
Out-sourcing, 326
Outcomes-based education, 265
Ovitz, Michael, 291
Owen, David, 273

Paine, Thomas, 38
Parallel evolution theory, 154
Parenting, 176
Parochial schools, 338–342
Patriarchal patterns in teaching,
  90–91
Patriarchy, 40
Patriotism, 67
Pay, and teachers, 107–108
Peabody, George, 165
Peirce, Charles, 71, 74
Personal empowerment, 198–199
Personal theories, 16
Peterson, Paul, 334–335
Philosophy, modern, 300–301
Philosopher-kings, 5
Physical differences, 152
Physical disabilities, 220–221
Physical world, 14
Pillow, Carolyn, 122
Pinkney, Charles, 48
Pioneers, 18
Plato, Republic, 1, 3–6, 52, 79
Plessy v. Ferguson, 80
Pluralism theories, 196–199
Police, 63
Political freedom, 41
Political tasks, 99
Polybius, 1
Polygamy, 201
Polygenes, 153
Pope, Harrison, 142
Popham, James, 272
Postman, Neil, 307, 319–320
Postmodernism, 300–301
Poverty
  and education in the 60s, 240
  moral problem, 63
  and schooling, 168–169
  and special education, 225–227
  and test gap, 176
Powell, Arthur, 92
Pragmatism, 71
Prep schools, 170
Preschool experience of minority
  students, 184
Princeton Review Course Manual,
  288–289, 290–291
Princeton University, 263
Private educational company, 326
Private schools, 105–106,
  169–170, 326
Prodigy, 227
Professional, defined, 93
Progress, 40
Progressive Era, 69, 74–78
  See also Dewey, John
Progressives, 190–194
Proposition 38 (California), 333
Prosser, Charles, 79
Protestant Reformation, 39

Protestantism, 43
Protestants, 188
Prussian system, 59
PSAT, 276
Psychology, girls and boys and,
  123–126
Public schools, 12, 99
Pullout bilingual education, 203
Punishment, 8
Puritans, 18, 23–26

Quakers, 30

Race, 151–185
  American Indians, 157–158
  Asian Americans, 158–159
  black education, 160–167
  and class, 167–172
  defining, 152–155
  desegregation, 80–81
  "Eve" (single common
    ancestor), 154
  family income by, 167
  genetic variability, 152–153
  gifted students and, 230
  Hispanics, 156–158
  parallel evolution theory, 154
  physical differences, 152
  as political concept, 155
  second-generation segregation,
    172–175
  separate but equal, 80
  skin color, 152–153
  socioeconomic class, 156
  Southern education and
    Northern money, 164–167
  statistics on children in special
    education, 225
  teachers by, 89
  vs. ethnicity, 152
Racism, 171
  eliminating, 172–175
  whites avoiding topic, 178–179
Raikes, Robert, 52
Rape victims, marrying rapist, 201
Rationality, 35–36
Ravitch, Diane, 199, 320
Reading, 18
Reagan, Ronald, 84, 170, 173, 239,
  240–241, 265, 266
Reason, 35–36, 38–39, 43, 45–48
Redistributing funds for public
  schools, 11
Reeves, Bryon, 319
Regionalism, 40
Rehabilitation Act (1973), 218
Religion, 5–6
  and feudalism, 32
  and homeschooling, 328
  and liberalism, 39
  and schooling, 16
  See also Parochial schools
Rensberger, Bruce, 155
Repressive schooling, 83
Republican virtue, 39–40
Republicans, and testing, 269
Research approaches, 15–17
Retention, 278
Revolutionary War, 40
  and schooling, 31–32
Ritalin, 222–223
Riverside Publishing
  Company, 291
Robin Hood (Chapter 41–
  Texas), 244
Robinson, Adam, 289
Rockefeller Brothers Fund, 83
Rockefeller, John, 165
Rockfish Gap Report, 51
Rod and frame test, 127–128
Roosevelt, Franklin, 68, 170
Rote memorization, 25–26, 27, 192

351

Rousseau, Jean-Jacques, 3, 145, 327
Rupp, Rebecca, 329
Rush, Benjamin, 48–49

Sacks, Peter, 271, 289
St. John, Raymond, 340
Sanders, Barry, 319
SAT. See Scholastic Aptitude Test
Schaar, John, 21
Scheller, Bob, 288–289
Schlesinger, Jr., Arthur, 199
Scholastic Aptitude Test (SAT), 79,
    265, 285
  class and race, 284
  declining scores, 266
  doing well on, 286–289
  and family income, 283–284
  female/male result
      differences, 276
  homeschooling results, 328
  multiple-choice, 273–274
  origin of, 263
School administration, 92
School boards, 252–254
School districts, 50, 255
  decentralization, 326
  origin, 25–26, 30
School law, 321–323
Schooling
  defined, 13
  and racism, 29
Schooling history, 21–55
  colonial, 23–31
  transformation, 31–54
"Schoolmaster to America" (Noah
    Webster), 53
Schools, teacher owning,
    342–343
Scientific ideas, 34–35
Scientific method, 69
Screenagers, 313
Searle, John, 14, 18
Second-generation segregation,
    172–175
Secondary schools, first, 26–28
Segregation, 167, 172
  second-generation, 172–175
  See also Desegregation
Self-rule, 50–52
Separate but equal, 80
September 11 terrorist attacks,
    71–72
Serotonin, 127
Serrano, John, 255–256
Serrano v. Priest, 256
Settlement Houses, 192
Seventies, 194–195
Sex, and corporate media,
    304–306
Sex-role stereotypes, 143–144
Shanker, Albert, 114
Shinner Box, 47
Silber, John, 281
Single-parent families, 176, 226
Site-based management, 326
Sixties, 84–85, 194–195
  education, 240
Skin color, 152–153
Skinner, B.F., 47
Slavery, 28–29, 160
  and Jefferson, 50
  in New England, 24
Smith, Adam, 35–37, 42
Smith, Samuel, 48
Social norms, 195
Social tasks, 99
Social theories, 16
Socialization
  and environment, 131–132
  gender, 132–135
  and women, 46
Society, and nature, 7–9

Socioeconomic class, 156, 167–172
  and student outcomes, 101
Socrates, 3
Soul and the state, 4–5
South
  education history, 28–29, 67–69
  education with Northern money,
      164–167
Spatial perception, 127–128
Spearman, Charles, 262
Special education, 174, 210–237
  gifted students, 227–231
  historical background, 211–214
  inclusion, 231–236
  individualized education
      program (IEP), 216–219
  Individuals with Disabilities
      Education Act (IDEA),
      215–218
  labeling, 231–236
  least restrictive environment
      (LRE), 217
  number in, 233
  and poverty, 225–227
  recent history and legislation,
      215–220
  statistics on those in, 225
  See also Disabilities
"Special-needs" urban districts, 257
Specialization, 3
Speech disabilities, 221
Spence, Larry, 238
Spock, Benjamin, 82
Spring, Joel, 186, 194
Sputnik, 82–83, 239
Standardization of high schools,
    64–66
Standardization of teaching, 94–99
Standardized intelligence test, 147
Standardized testing, 104,
    264–296
  doing well on, 286–289
  economics of testing, 289–292
  effects of, 276–283
  girls and boys, 275–276
  high-stakes, 268–269, 279–283
  intelligence and achievement
      tests, 270–271
  known things about, 283–285
  multiple-choice, 273–274
  reason for, 264–268
  recommendations for, 294–295
  supporters of, 269–270
  Third International Math and
      Science Study (TIMSS),
      267–268
  timed tests, 275
  young children, 271–273
  See also Testing
Stanford 9, 291
Stanford-Binet Intelligence Scale,
    262, 271–272, 291
Stanley Kaplan Company, 290–291
State
  church and state separation,
      338–342
  general will of, 7
  limits on, 20
  and soul, 4–5
State government, and education,
    251–252
State vs. individual needs, 1–20
Stereotypes, sex-role, 143–144
Sternberg, Robert, 147
Steroids, 141–142
Stream of consciousness, 72–73
Structured immersion bilingual
    education, 203–204
Student outcomes, 100–101
Substitute teachers, 106
Sugarman, Stephen, 333
Suicide, 142–143, 310

Sun Chief, 56
Sunday School Society
    (Philadelphia), 52
Sunday Schools, 52
Superintendents, 253–255
Supreme Court segregation and
    desegregation cases, 80–81
Sweatt, Herman, 80–81

Tabula rasa (blank slate), 37
Talmud, 340
Tapscott, Don, 314–315
Tartt, Donna, 56
Tax deductions, for school
    tuition, 333
Taylor, Frederick, 245
Teachers, 88–121
  certification, 105–112
  demographics, 89–90
  educating, 99
  engaging and motivating, 102
  expectations of public
      schools, 99
  judging, 107–109
  judging and evaluating
      students, 102
  knowing students, 102
  knowing stuff, 102–103
  leaving teaching, 120
  medicine as standard for,
      94–99
  owning schools, 342–343
  patriarchal pattern, 90–91
  pay, 107–108
  reason to teach, 117
  results, 99–101
  as role models, 102
  standards for good, 108
  teaching as profession, 91–105
  teaching teachers, 102–103
  unions, 112–117
  working conditions, 118–119
Teachers associations, 112
Teacher's College, 91–92
Teaching areas, 103
Teaching methods, 101
Television, 306–307
Terman, Lewis, 228–229, 262
Test scores, 3, 100–101
  standardized, 147
  white-black test gap, 175–178
  See also Standardized testing
Testing
  history of, 262–264
  national, 79
  See also Standardized testing
Testosterone, 127–128, 142
Theories, 15–17
  conflict, 16
  critical, 16
  feminist, 16
  interpretive, 16
  personal, 16
  social, 16
Thinking styles, 147–149
Third International Math and
    Science Study (TIMSS),
    267–268
Thomas, Clarence, 199–200
Thorndike, Edward, 73, 74
Timed tests, 275
Timothy W. v. Rochester, 235
Toleration, 197–198
Toys, 134–135
Tracking, 174
Trade, 34
Traditional schooling, 77–78
Training, 13–14
Transitional bilingual education,
    203–204
Tuskegee Institute, 165
Twain, Mark, 1

Undergraduate education major, 102
Unions, and teachers, 112–117
Unitarians, 58
University of California,
    Berkeley, 159
University of Chicago, 74
  educating teachers, 91–92
University of Henrico, 29
University of Michigan, 74
University of Oklahoma, 80
University of Texas Law School, 80
University of Vermont, 74
University of Virginia, 51
Urban education, 187–194
Urbanization, 60–64
USSR, 82–83

Validation, 198
Valium, 82, 194
Values, 12
Valverde, Leonard, 203
Vedder, Richard, Can Teachers Own
    Their Own Schools?, 342–343
Vietnam War, 194
Violence, 308–310
Virtue, 6
  republican, 39–40
Visual disabilities, 220
Vocational schools, 56
Vocational training, 3, 11–12
Volkschule, 59
von Hoffman, Nicholas, 273
Vonnegut, Kurt, Hocus Pocus, 153
Voucher programs, 326, 332–334
  criticism of, 334
  effectiveness of, 334–338
  financial aid, 333–334
  parochial schools, 339–342
  selected, 333

War on Poverty, 176, 205
Ward, Lester, 90
Warren, Earl, 172
Washington, Booker T., 160,
    162–164
  Atlantic Compromise, 163
Washington, George, 48
Washington Post Company, 291
Web, 314–315
Weber, Max, 16, 93
Webster, Noah, 48, 53
Weschler Preschool and Primary
    Scale of Intelligence Test–Revised,
    271, 275
Western civilization, 199
Western thought
  Emile (Rousseau), 6–10
  Republic (Plato), 3–6
What Works Clearinghouse, 94
White-black test gap, 175–178
Whiteness, 178–180
Whitman, Christine Todd, 257
Whittle, Chris, 331
Wife/mother role, 45–47
Wigglesworth, Michael, 26
Wightman, Linda, 284
Winner, Ellen, 227
Wippsie R test, 275
Wollstonecraft, Mary, 45–48
Women
  challenges to Freud's view,
      125–126
  early teachers, 59, 63
  as irrational beings, 39–40
  Jefferson's view of, 50
  and reason, 45–48
  and Rousseau, 9–10
  teachers, 90
  and tranquilizers, 82
  wife/mother role, 45–47
Women's rights, 200–202
Work ethic, 39